The Plays of Ben JONSON

a reference guide

A Reference Guide to Literature

Everett Emerson
Editor

The Plays of Ben JONSON

a reference guide

WALTER D. LEHRMAN

DOLORES J. SARAFINSKI

ELIZABETH SAVAGE, SSJ

G.K.HALL &CO.

70 LINCOLN STREET, BOSTON, MASS.

Library of Congress Cataloging in Publication Data

Sarafinski, Dolores.
The plays of Ben Jonson.

(A Reference guide to literature)
Includes indexes.
1. Jonson, Ben, 1573?-1637—Bibliography.
I. Lehrman, Walter D., joint author. II. Savage,
Elizabeth, S.S.J., joint author. III. Title.
IV. Series: Reference guides to literature.
Z8456.6.S27 [PR2631] 016.822'3 80-22686
ISBN 0-8161-8112-8

This publication is printed on permanent/durable acid-free paper
MANUFACTURED IN THE UNITED STATES OF AMERICA

Contents

Introduction

Although often uneven in quality, criticism and commentary on Ben Jonson's plays have substantially increased in quantity over the sixty-four years from 1911 (the year of the first scholarly book in English) to 1975. Like the canon itself, they offer God's plenty.

Study of the vast amount of scholarship reveals significant trends and changes. Beginning under the general editorships, respectively, of Albert S. Cook and W. Bang, _Yale Studies in English_ and _Materialen zur Kunde des älteren englischen Dramas_[1] provided between them, in the years 1903 to 1917, at least one scholarly edition of each of Jonson's plays except _Eastward Ho_, which was edited as part of the Chapman canon in 1914 by T. M. Parrott. In 1925 C. H. Herford and Percy Simpson published the first two volumes of the Oxford _Ben Jonson_; by 1952 all of Jonson's plays, as well as commentary and textual notes, had been published as part of this uniform edition of Jonson's complete works.[2]

Jonson's plays provided topics for a handful of doctoral dissertations published in Germany in the late nineteenth and early twentieth centuries: most of these were either source studies or explorations in cultural history. The earliest full-length scholarly study of Jonson written in English was Charles Read Baskervill's _English Elements in Jonson's Early Comedy_ (1911). Aside from this work, and Mina Kerr's _Influence of Ben Jonson on English Comedy, 1598-1642_ (1912), the early period of book-length studies (1911-1931) reflected an interest in rather general concerns: Jonson's life, his popularity, and his overall relationship to his era.

After the initial period a greater proportion of full-length studies explored specific aspects of Jonson's dramatic art. Satire, comic theory and practice, morality, rhetoric, dramatic structure and

1. Cited in this bibliography by its English title: _Materials for the Study of the Old English Drama_.

2. Herford died in 1931. Evelyn M. Simpson became a co-editor beginning with Vol. VI (1938).

devices, and the relationship of Jonson's plays to the classical and native traditions have received increasingly detailed attention. Few of the texts have focused on a single play. New editions of individual plays, many with fully developed critical introductions, continue to appear.

As might be expected, the larger volume of criticism and commentary has come in shorter studies. These, too, have moved towards the specific. Subjects traditionally associated with the study of Renaissance dramatists continue to be treated: theme, characterization, plot structure, sources, stage history, and so on. Modern critical trends are shown in several studies that approach the playwright from the psychoanalytical, myth-ritual, and structuralist points of view. The shorter works have also examined the reciprocal influences between Jonson and other writers, his moral vision, social attitudes, and artistic theories. Textual and linguistic questions still occupy scholars' attention, and many continue to investigate his uses of symbolism, allegory, psychology, history, and philosophy.

Volpone, *The Alchemist*, and *Bartholomew Fair* have consistently drawn the greatest amount of scholarly inquiry; *The Case is Altered*, *The Magnetic Lady* and *The Sad Shepherd* have attracted very little. Interest in the two tragedies, *Catiline* and *Sejanus*, has risen considerably in the past thirty years. Contemporary scholars, investigating and reflecting upon the last plays, have come to see more in them than did Dryden, who dismissed them as "dotages."

Jonsonian drama has become an increasingly popular topic for doctoral dissertations. Since 1960, more than 150 Ph.D. candidates in England and the United States have written on a variety of topics, including rhetoric, dramatic techniques, sources, and relations to works by other authors.

Understandably, in view of their difficulty for today's theatregoers, Jonson's plays are more likely to be written about than staged. Modern directors have occasionally attempted *Bartholomew Fair*, *Epicoene*, and *Every Man in his Humour*, but the more accessible *Volpone* and *The Alchemist* are the only plays produced with any frequency. These two are also the plays for which the greatest number of foreign-language translations and adaptations are to be found. Indeed, though little seen today, in the 1930s the Zweig-Romains version of *Volpone* virtually extinguished the Jonsonian original, both in Europe and America.

A survey of criticism quickly reveals a major shift in the estimation of Jonson over the years. Although early scholarship often dealt with him, much of it did so chiefly to illustrate a point about Shakespeare, usually in an effort to enhance his reputation even further. Jonsonian drama emerged as among the best of "the other," that is, the inferior drama of the period.

Introduction

Jonson's plays increasingly have been studied on their own terms and for themselves, by modern scholars and critics. They have become recognized as carefully designed pieces of theatrical art based on clearly defined theories and aimed at specific goals. The best make some of the best theatre we have.

Like the criticism his plays have generated, Jonson's life shows distinct periods and characteristics. Born near London in 1572, Jonson attended a private school in St. Martin's Church and Westminster School, where he enjoyed the friendship and tutelage of William Camden, then second master. Forced to leave school in 1588 and assume his stepfather's occupation of brick-laying, Jonson continued to cultivate the intellectual stimulus aroused by Camden. Greek and Roman authors, especially the historians and poets, remained among his major interests, and helped shape his intellectual and creative life.

Balancing an intense interest in and appreciation for the past and for the scholarly was a brilliant comic talent and a full awareness of the present. Jonson possessed the successful caricaturist's ability to discover and portray the "different" in both persons and circumstances. His sharp, critical wit understandably led him to assume a satirical stance toward many topics. Given an innate dramatic sense, his movement toward the theatre was natural.

Jonson began his association with the theatre the same way many of his contemporaries did: working for Philip Henslowe. He took the part of Hieronimo in Thomas Kyd's _The Spanish Tragedy_ and played minor parts in other works. After a short period of acting he moved to writing, completing _A Tale of a Tub_ in 1596 and finishing Thomas Nashe's _The Isle of Dogs_ by 1597. He had become sufficiently known as a dramatist by 1598 to be mentioned as such in Francis Meres's _Palladis Tamia: Wit's Treasury_.

Real prominence did not come, however, until the performance of _Every Man in his Humour_ at the Curtain Theatre by the Lord Chamberlain's Men in 1598. In the years following, Jonson continued to write for this troupe as well as for the Admiral's Men and The Children of the Chapel Royal.

The theatre was seldom a calm place for Jonson. Involvement in Nashe's satiric comedy brought him a short stay in the Marshalsea Prison almost at the beginning of his career. On September 22, 1598, he killed the actor Gabriel Spencer in a duel; he escaped hanging only by pleading benefit of clergy.

The War of the Theatres provided him an opportunity to joust with fellow dramatists Thomas Dekker and John Marston. The latter had satirized Jonson in his revision of the anonymous _Histriomastix_ and then recognized himself as Clove in Jonson's subsequent _Every Man out of his Humour_. The battle continued for several years (1599-1601),

Jonson answering Jack Drum's Entertainment with Cynthia's Revels, in which he took aim at Dekker also. Marston's What You Will followed; Jonson again attacked both playwrights in Poetaster. Dekker's Satiromastix concluded the war, a phenomenon many critics consider a highly over-played portion of English literary history.

Periodically incensed by London audiences' condemnations of his plays, Jonson occasionally stormed away from "the loathed stage." He never travelled so far, however, that he could not return with yet another play. His occasional failure in the theatre stemmed from the way he implemented some of his views on the function of drama. Traditional criticism had taught, and Renaissance playwrights and audiences generally seemed to believe, that a play should instruct as well as delight. But Jonson went to extremes in applying this principle, and set about in all seriousness to improve his stage and his audience. Both Sejanus and Catiline exhibited great "truth of argument" (i.e., historical fidelity) and moral instruction, but contained such a profusion of classical material, handled so didactically, that even Renaissance audiences found the plays dull, complex history lectures rather than exciting theatre. They expressed their opinions directly, hissing Sejanus off the stage. This only reinforced Jonson's negative opinion of audiences and made him even more direct in subsequent efforts to improve the stage.

The late comedies, the so-called dotages, reflect the growing alienation between Jonson and his audience. Concomitantly, they show on the whole a diminishing of Jonson's comic touch. But the "great" comedies, Every Man in his Humour, Volpone, Epicoene, The Alchemist, and Bartholomew Fair, performed between 1598 and 1616, established Jonson as one of the leading dramatists of his age. He rivalled Shakespeare in popularity throughout the seventeenth century.

Confident of the importance of his plays, Jonson took the logical but then revolutionary step of printing them in a collected edition: The Workes of Beniamin Jonson. William Stansby, printer, published the folio volume in 1616. Jonson himself designed the frontispiece, an emblematic title page showing the various types of drama. In addition to masques and poetry, the folio contained nine plays: Every Man in his Humour (revised version), Every Man out of his Humour, Cynthia's Revels, Poetaster, Sejanus His Fall, Volpone, or The Fox, Epicoene, or The Silent Woman, The Alchemist, and Catiline His Conspiracy. Not included were The Case is Altered (Jonson did not acknowledge this early play), Eastward Ho, and Bartholomew Fair. Jonson took an active, ongoing interest in the printing, regularly stopping at Stansby's shop to proofread and make press corrections in his Workes.

In 1631, copies of Batholomew Fair, The Devil is an Ass, and The Staple of News were bound and published in an "unofficial" folio intended for non-commercial distribution to friends and patrons of

Jonson. The "official" Second Folio appeared in two volumes in 1640. The first volume reprinted the 1616 Folio; the second reprinted the plays from the 1631 edition and added The Magnetic Lady, A Tale of a Tub, and The Sad Shepherd.

Eleven of Jonson's plays appeared first in Quarto editions: Every Man out of his Humour (1600), Every Man in his Humour (1601), Cynthia's Revels (1601), Poetaster (1602), Sejanus His Fall (1605), Eastward Ho (1605), Volpone, or The Fox (1607), The Case is Altered (1609), Catiline His Conspiracy (1611), The Alchemist (1612), Epicoene, or The Silent Woman (1612? 1620).[3] The New Inn was published in octavo in 1631.

Although clearly a master of the drama, Jonson did not confine himself to that genre. Supported first by King James I and Queen Anne, and later by Charles I and Henrietta Maria, he wrote twenty-seven court masques between 1605 and 1631. Many were created in collaboration with Inigo Jones, the designer and architect. Their relationship dissolved in 1631 because of disagreements about the relative prominence of spectacle. Jonson had also established himself in the world of poetry, publishing Epigrams and The Forest in 1616 and Underwoods in 1640. Also in 1640 appeared Timber, or Discoveries, a miscellaneous collection of observations based on Latin sources.

Jonson's health declined steadily during his last years. He remained, however, a major literary force. Upon his death on August 6, 1637, he was buried in Westminster Abbey. His epitaph remains apt: "O rare Ben Jonson!"

The audience for this bibliography is seen as consisting of Jonson students and scholars. Their potential needs, as well as the standards of the G. K. Hall Reference Guides Series, have been the touchstones for the compilers. The most important question we asked in sifting through the many thousands of items that came to our attention was whether a given item would really benefit a student or scholar desiring or needing information about Jonson's plays. Many pieces, though interesting in themselves, do not meet this test; the bibliography, therefore, does not contain a citation to every work mentioning Jonson. Items that merely acknowledge his existence, summarize his life or his plays, refer to him as a general part of literary history, or discuss some personal characteristic (his drinking habits and places were popular topics for a time) have, for the most part, been omitted, though several difficult-to-acquire items of little value have been deliberately included merely to save the scholar the trouble of searching them out needlessly. Standard histories of English literature have also been excluded, on the assumption that the student or scholar would be familiar with them and would consult them as needed.

3. That there was a 1612 Quarto of Epicoene is still in doubt. If there was not, then the 1616 Folio contains the earliest printing.

The same test was applied in deciding about information on reprints of the plays. The major dramas appear in countless anthologies. Most, however, lack any introduction and offer no information about the text they present or are based on. These many items, therefore, have not been included.

The bibliography officially covers the years 1911-1975. In attempting to include all the relevant scholarship of those years, we have tried to keep closely attuned to Renaissance bibliographies published in 1976 and 1977. We have included some of the rather easily accessible scholarship of those years in order to give the user a little bonus. Their "plenty" has certainly not been exhausted!

Readers familiar with earlier volumes in the G. K. Hall Reference Series will note a difference in the organization of this bibliography. The compilers judged that a student or scholar using a bibliography about a large dramatic canon would find a chronological arrangement of scholarly literature less useful than one which led him directly to discussions of specific plays and major topics.

The bibliography, therefore, has been divided into four major sections:

I. Book-length Studies and Essay Collections. When available, bibliographical information about reviews is included at the end of an annotation.

II. Editions and Studies of Specific Plays. Within their categories, comedy, tragedy, and pastoral, the plays are listed alphabetically. Editions are given first, listed by date of publication. The annotations are based on the editions' introductory material. The remainder of criticism and commentary is arranged alphabetically by author. Since Catiline and Sejanus are often discussed together, a section encompassing both plays has been included, as well as separate sections for each.

III. Special Topics. These include: Humours Theory, Influence and Allusions, Jonson and Shakespeare, Language and Usage, Literary Relations and Sources, Textual Studies, Theatrical History, and War of the Theatres.

IV. General Topics. This group includes topics not covered in other sections.

A detailed Subject Index is provided. In addition, after each major topic heading (e.g., Language and Usage) a "see also" section refers the user to items in other sections of the bibliography (e.g., an article on a specific play) that deal substantively with the same topic. Specific item-to-item cross references are also provided.

Introduction

Almost 1500 citations appear in the bibliography. They are non-evaluative. The length of any citation is not intended as a subtle evaluation. In "associative" studies (for example, Jonson and Shakespeare, Jonson and Dickens) emphasis has been placed on the Jonsonian elements, with the other author presented chiefly in a relational manner.

Much significant Jonson scholarship has been reprinted and anthologized. The most recent and accessible reprints of books, monographs, and articles have been noted as far as possible. The user should be cautioned, however, that not every reprint has been seen by the compilers, and that in some cases reliable bibliographical data regarding reprints is not available. Where only a reprint, and not the original, has been seen, the citation gives the reprint information first; information about the original publication follows in brackets. Items that have been noted in reliable bibliographies, but not actually seen in any form by the compilers, have been marked with an asterisk.

Dissertations have been listed, alphabetically by author, in Appendix I. No annotation has been provided. Published dissertations are included in the bibliography proper.

Reviews of modern performances of Jonson's plays have been included in two ways, for two reasons: each helps to establish the record of Jonson's continued popularity as a playwright; some offer critical insights into the plays staged. Reviews of the latter type have been abstracted and placed in the alphabetical list of works on specific plays. The others, which focus on the particular performance, are listed in chronological order, without an abstract, at the end of the material on the play.

Throughout the bibliography, names of authors are given as they appear in the specific work cited. Thus, some authors' names appear in variant forms. The single preferred form of an author's name, as far as it can be determined, appears in the Author Index. For the sake of editorial consistency, titles of plays are standardized by underlining, regardless of how they appear in the work cited. Abbreviations of journal and series titles, keyed to the Master List and Abbreviations, are those of the MLA International Bibliography.

The annotations employ modern spelling and punctuation except in cases where older forms are standard, or where an older form occurs in the title of an entry or in quoted material. The same rule applies in the Subject Index. Should entries differ in their spelling, the modern spelling prevails in the Index. Since there is no consistency in modern spellings for the names of some of the characters in the plays, the compilers have in each case made what is felt to be a reasonable arbitrary choice among currently used variants. The standard forms of Jonson's titles (Volpone for Volpone, or The Fox) are used in the annotations. When total page numbers are given for books, they represent the sum of roman and arabic pagination. Act, scene, and line references are to the Oxford edition.

The successful study of any significant topic may well depend on its bibliography. In turn, a successful bibliography certainly depends on the help of many dedicated people. For their help in the preparation of this Jonson bibliography, the compilers offer their individual and collective thanks to Rev. Casimir Lubiak (Director, Nash Learning Resource Center, Gannon University), Katherine M. Brewer and Kathleen Sweeney (Research Assistants, Gannon University), Grace A. Davies (Acquisitions Librarian, Gannon University), Rita Ann Nies (Reference Librarian, Gannon University), John Thomas (Assistant Head, Reader Service Section, Library of Congress), the Gannon University Faculty Research Grant Fund; to the Sisters of St. Joseph of Buffalo, New York; Medaille College; to Claibourne E. Griffin (Dean, Buchtel College of Arts and Sciences, The University of Akron), Frederik N. Smith (Head, Department of English, The University of Akron), the Research (Faculty Projects) Committee of The University of Akron, Ruth E. Clinefelter, Nancy A. Knight, Judith K. Mowery (Research Librarians), Marjorie Louise Forsch (Head, General Information), and Valerie M. Johnson (Inter-library Loan Assistant), all of Bierce Library, The University of Akron; and Antoinette M. Bukovitz, Alexander Fleming, Theresa Smeiles, and Becky Tompkins.

Master List and Abbreviations

AN&Q	American Notes and Queries
Archiv	Archiv für das Studium der Neueren Sprachen und Literaturen
ArielE	Ariel: A Review of International English Literature
AUB-LG	Analele Universității, București, Limbi Germanice
AUMLA	Journal of the Australasian Universities Language and Literature Association
BJRL	Bulletin of the John Rylands Library of Manchester
BNYPL	Bulletin of the New York Public Library
BRMMLA	Rocky Mountain Review of Language and Literature [Formerly Bulletin of the Rocky Mountain Modern Language Association]
BuR	Bucknell Review
CE	College English
CJ	Classical Journal
CL	Comparative Literature (Eugene, Oregon)
CLAJ	College Language Association Journal
CompD	Comparative Drama
ContempR	Contemporary Review (London)
CR	The Critical Review (Canberra, Australia)
DR	Dalhousie Review
DUJ	Durham University Journal
DVLG	Deutsche Vierteljahrsschrift für Literaturwissenschaft und Geistesgeschichte
EA	Etudes Anglaises
E&S	Essays and Studies (London)
EDH	Essays by Divers Hands
EIC	Essays in Criticism (Oxford)
EIE	English Institute Essays
EigoS	Eigo Seinen [The Rising Generation] (Tokyo)
ELH	[Formerly Journal of English Literary History]
ElizS	Elizabethan & Renaissance Studies (University of Salzburg, Austria)
ELN	English Language Notes
ELR	English Literary Renaissance
ELWIU	Essays in Literature (Macomb, Illinois)
EM	English Miscellany

EngR	English Record
ES	English Studies
ESA	English Studies in Africa (Johannesburg)
ESRS	Emporia State Research Studies
ETJ	Educational Theatre Journal
FLe	Fiera Letteraria
FMod	Filología Moderna (Madrid)
FP	Filološki Pregled (Belgrade)
Gids	De Gids
GW	Germanica Wratislaviensia (Wroclaw, Poland)
HAB	The Humanities Association Review/La Revue de l'Association des Humanités (Formerly Humanities Association Bulletin)
HLB	Harvard Library Bulletin
HLQ	Huntington Library Quarterly
HudR	The Hudson Review
ISLL	Illinois Studies in Language and Literature
JAF	Journal of American Folklore
JDS	Jacobean Drama Studies (University of Salzburg, Austria)
JEGP	Journal of English and Germanic Philology
JHI	Journal of the History of Ideas
JMSUB	Journal of the Maharaja Sayajirao University of Baroda
KN	Kwartalnik Neofilologiczny (Warsaw)
L&P	Literature and Psychology (Teaneck, New Jersey)
LeedsSE	Leeds Studies in English
Library	The Library
LJ	Library Journal
LMonog	Literary Monographs
LR	Les Lettres Romanes
M&L	Music and Letters
MLN	[Formerly Modern Language Notes]
MLQ	Modern Language Quarterly
MLR	Modern Language Review
MP	Modern Philology
MQR	Michigan Quarterly Review
NA	Nuova Antologia
N&Q	Notes and Queries
NCarF	North Carolina Folklore Journal
NDQ	North Dakota Quarterly
Neophil	Neophilologus (Groningen, Netherlands)
NEQ	New England Quarterly
NM	Neuphilologische Mitteilungen: Bulletin de la Société Néophilologique/Bulletin of the Modern Language Society
NY	New Yorker
PBA	Proceedings of the British Academy
PBSA	Papers of the Bibliographical Society of America
PLL	Papers on Language and Literature
PQ	Philological Quarterly
PR	Partisan Review
PTRSC	Proceedings & Transactions Royal Society of Canada
PUASAL	Proceedings of the Utah Academy of Sciences, Arts, & Letters

QJS	*Quarterly Journal of Speech*
QQ	*Queen's Quarterly*
RANAM	*Recherches Anglaises et Américaines*
RECTR	*Restoration and 18th Century Theatre Research*
Ren&R	*Renaissance and Reformation/Renaissance et Réforme*
RenD	*Renaissance Drama*
RenP	*Renaissance Papers*
RenQ	*Renaissance Quarterly*
RES	*Review of English Studies*
RLC	*Revue de Littérature Comparée*
RLV	*Revue des Langues Vivantes*
RMS	*Renaissance & Modern Studies*
RORD	*Research Opportunities in Renaissance Drama*
RS	*Research Studies* (Pullman, Washington)
SAB	*South Atlantic Bulletin*
SAQ	*South Atlantic Quarterly*
SatR	*Saturday Review*
SB	*Studies in Bibliography*
SCB	*South Central Bulletin*
ScholS	*Scholia Satyrica*
SCN	*Seventeenth-Century News*
SCr	*Strumenti Critici*
SEL	*Studies in English Literature, 1500-1900*
SELit	*Studies in English Literature* (Tokyo)
ShakS	*Shakespeare Studies* (Knoxville, Tennessee)
Shavian	*The Shavian*
SHR	*Southern Humanities Review*
ShS	*Shakespeare Survey*
ShStud	*Shakespeare Studies* (Tokyo)
SJW	*Shakespeare-Jahrbuch* (Weimar)
SLitI	*Studies in the Literary Imagination*
SLM	*Southern Literary Messenger*
SMR	*Studier i Modern Språkvetenskap*
SN	*Studia Neophilologica*
SoR	*Southern Review* (Baton Rouge, Louisiana)
SoRA	*Southern Review: An Australian Journal of Literary Studies* (Adelaide, Australia)
SovL	*Soviet Literature*
SP	*Studies in Philology*
SQ	*Shakespeare Quarterly*
SR	*Sewanee Review*
SRen	*Studies in the Renaissance*
SUS	*Susquehanna University Studies*
TA	*Theatre Annual*
TLS	[London] *Times Literary Supplement*
TN	*Theatre Notebook*
TSL	*Tennessee Studies in Literature*
TSLL	*Texas Studies in Literature and Language*
TvL	*Tydskrif vir Letterkunde*
UCTSE	*University of Cape Town Studies in English*
UES	*Unisa English Studies*

UFMH	University of Florida Monographs, Humanities Series
UMCMP	University of Michigan Contributions in Modern Philology
UMSE	University of Mississippi Studies in English
UTQ	University of Toronto Quarterly
WascanaR	Wascana Review (Regina, Saskatchewan)
WHR	Western Humanities Review
YES	Yearbook of English Studies
YR	Yale Review
YWES	Year's Work in English Studies

Ben Jonson's Plays

	Date of Publication
The Alchemist	1612
Bartholomew Fair	1631
The Case is Altered	1609
Catiline His Conspiracy	1611
Cynthia's Revels, or The Fountain of Self-Love	1601
The Devil is an Ass, or The Cheater Cheated	1631
Eastward Ho (with George Chapman and John Marston)	1605
Epicoene, or The Silent Woman	1612? 1620
Every Man in his Humour (two versions)	1601, 1616
Every Man out of his Humour	1600
The Magnetic Lady, or Humours Reconciled	1640
The New Inn, or The Light Heart	1631
Poetaster, or His Arraignment	1602
The Sad Shepherd	1640
Sejanus His Fall	1605
The Staple of News	1631
A Tale of a Tub	1640
Volpone, or The Fox	1607

A Bibliography of Ben Jonson's Plays, 1911-1975

A Bibliography of Ben Jonson's Plays, 1911-1975

BOOK-LENGTH STUDIES AND ESSAY COLLECTIONS

1 ARNOLD, JUDD. A Grace Peculiar: Ben Jonson's Cavalier Heroes. The Pennsylvania State University Studies, 35. University Park: The Pennsylvania State University Press, 1972. 86 pp.

Jonson's "cavalier gallants" rather than his "fuming moralists and malcontents" are the dramatist's spokesmen. "Cavalier heroes," the intellectual aristocrats, triumph over the fools, knaves, and railing reformers.

Reviewed by R. B. Parker in MLR 70 (1975):145-48; C. J. Summers in SCN 31 (1973):12-13.

2 BAMBOROUGH, J. B. Ben Jonson. London: Hutchinson, 1970. 191 pp.

A concise, detailed introduction to Jonson's career as playwright, poet, and critic. Discusses, in order, the early comedies, the tragedies and masques, the "great" plays, the last plays, and Jonson's poetry, prose, and criticism.

Reviewed by B. Harris in YWES 51 (1970):194; F. L. Huntley in RenQ 24 (1971):275-76; R. Southall in EIC 22 (1972):83-91; in TLS, 16 October 1970, p. 1187.

3 BARISH, JONAS A., ed. Ben Jonson: A Collection of Critical Essays. Englewood Cliffs, N.J.: Prentice-Hall, 1963. 180 pp.

Includes an introduction by Barish and the following essays: T. S. Eliot, "Ben Jonson" (see 1102); L. C. Knights, "Tradition and Ben Jonson" (see 935); Harry Levin, "An Introduction to Ben Jonson" (see 1173); Edmund Wilson, "Morose Ben Jonson" (see 1255); Arthur Sale, "Introduction to Every Man in His Humour" (see 304); C. H. Herford, "Introduction to Every Man Out of His Humour" (from Herford and Simpson, Ben Jonson, Vol. 1; see 21); Jonas A. Barish, "The Double Plot in Volpone" (see 487); Paul Goodman, "Comic Plots: The Alchemist" (see 86); Edward B. Partridge,

"Epicene" (from his The Broken Compass, see 13); Ray L. Heffner, Jr., "Unifying Symbols in the Comedy of Ben Jonson" (see 1131); Joseph Allen Bryant, Jr., "Catiline and the Nature of Jonson's Tragic Fable" (see 637).

4 BAUM, HELENA WATTS. The Satiric and the Didactic in Ben Jonson's Comedy. Chapel Hill: University of North Carolina Press, 1947. 198 pp. [Reprint. New York: Russell and Russell, 1971.]

Defends Jonson against commentators who assume "that the motive behind his comedy is conventional morality." Jonson "was not--in any strict sense--either moralist, sociologist, economist, or reformer. . . . He was a comic dramatist, and he used the didactic theory for literary and dramatic purposes. . . . His basis for judging life was intellectual; ignorance and stupidity were the cardinal sins." Provides as background material the Renaissance theories of the function of poetry, Jonson's theory of comic poetry, and a study of five chief topics of dramatic satire--avarice, lust, drunkenness, witchcraft, and Puritanism--in the comedies of Jonson, Middleton, Dekker, and Heywood. Surveys the comedies from The Case is Altered to Volpone to determine Jonson's materials and methods as a satirist, and argues that his change of technique from the early comedies, in which the satire was only incidental, to the compelling satire of the later comedy is evidence of Jonson's serious purpose as a dramatist.

Reviewed by A. Davenport in MLR 44 (1949):402-03; G. B. Evans in JEGP 47 (1948):306-08; F. R. Johnson in MLN 64 (1949):213; A. K. McIlwraith in RES 1 (1950):166-68.

5 BLISSETT, WILLIAM; PATRICK, JULIAN; and VAN FOSSEN, R. W., eds. A Celebration of Ben Jonson. Papers presented at the University of Toronto in October 1972. Toronto and Buffalo: University of Toronto Press, 1973. 207 pp.

Includes Clifford Leech, "The Incredibility of Jonsonian Comedy" (see 1169); Jonas A. Barish, "Jonson and the Loathèd Stage" (see 1062); George Hibbard, "Ben Jonson and Human Nature" (see 1135); and D. F. McKenzie, "The Staple of News and the Late Plays" (see 422).

6 BRYANT, J. A., JR. The Compassionate Satirist: Ben Jonson and His Imperfect World. Athens: University of Georgia Press, 1972. 204 pp.

Explores the thesis that Jonson's plays are best understood when the critic or reader views them as a dramatization of "the public roles that he [Jonson] saw the poet as being obligated to assume from time to time--specifically those of moralist, literary critic, and satirist."

Discusses Jonson's concept of morality, his view of the purpose of poetry, his specific use of various modes of satire, and his method of structuring the plays, bringing into focus the development of Jonson's thought and technical skill.

Reviewed by J. S. Dean in LJ 99 (1974):486; A. C. Dessen in JEGP 74 (1975):123-26; J. K. Gardiner in MP 73 (1975):184-86; R. B. Parker in MLR 70 (1975):145-48.

7 CAPONE, GIOVANNA. Ben Jonson: l'iconologia verbale come strategia di commedia. Bologna: Casa Editrice Pàtron, 1969. 506 pp.

The comedies deal with sets of opposites--e.g., body vs. soul; linguistically immobile, fideist, "sacerdotal" agonist vs. linguistically mobile, faithless, "demonic" antagonist--that are reconciled metaphysically through comic experience, which is not moral, but existential, ritualistic, and "pre-ethical." What is ideologically paradoxical in the comedies is partly owing to Jonson's capacity for a variety of world-views: Platonism, Pythagoreanism, stoicism, occult pantheism, mystic Christianity, and his own scepticism--all reflected in the language of his comedies.

8 CHAMPION, LARRY S. Ben Jonson's "Dotages": A Reconsideration of the Late Plays. Lexington: University of Kentucky Press, 1967. 156 pp.

Attempts to redeem the "dotages" from the critical limbo to which they had been cast by scholars and critics. "Jonson's comic intent, his theory of art, and his manipulation of material for both instruction and entertainment, is precisely that of his acknowledged masterpieces . . . the plays can hardly be branded 'dotages' of a 'washed-out brain.'"

Reviewed by W. R. Davis in SCN 27 (1969):14-15; C. Hoy in SEL 8 (1968):384-85; F. J. Hunter in QJS 54 (1968):298; R. E. Knoll in MLQ 30 (1969):144-45; C. G. Thayer in RenQ 21 (1968):363-65; in TLS, 27 March 1969, p. 318.

9 CRAWFORD, CHARLES, comp. A Complete Concordance to the 1616 Folio of Ben Jonson's Works; also to the Quarto Versions of "Every Man in his Humour," "Every Man out of his Humour," "Cynthia's Revels," "The Poetaster," "Catiline," "The Fox," and "The Alchemist." 5 Vols. Ann Arbor and London: University Microfilms, 1923-1924. [Not printed; holograph ms.]

The concordance is based on an original copy of the 1616 Folio, reliable reprints, and transcription of quarto editions of the plays.

Bibliography

Book-length Studies

10 CHUTE, MARCHETTE. *Ben Jonson of Westminster*. New York: Dutton, 1953; London: Robert Hale, 1954. 380 pp. [Reprinted as an Everyman book, 1960.]

Presents a biography and assessment of Jonson's works. In addition to providing factual biographical information, describes in detail "background information" on such topics as Westminster and the character of Camden. Draws extensively on sound scholarship and her own critical judgment to provide an understanding of Jonson's plays, masques, and poetry.

Reviewed by A. Harbage in *New York Times Book Review*, 18 October 1953, p. 3; J. W. Krutch in *SatR*, 17 October 1953, pp. 13-14; M. Poirier in *EA* 8 (1955):339-40; C. T. Prouty in *YR* 43 (1954):471-73; in *CJ* 49 (1953-54):139.

11 DICK, ALIKI LAFKIDOU. *Paedeia Through Laughter: Jonson's Aristophanic Appeal to Human Intelligence*. The Hague: Mouton, 1974. 141 pp.

Both Aristophanes and Jonson saw people as ignorant self-seekers, but correctable through laughter and study; were concerned for society; employed satire, with its distortion, earthiness, and vivid language. Jonson was particularly influenced by Aristophanes in *Volpone*, *The Alchemist*, and *Every Man out of his Humour*. The playwrights had similar kinds of imagination and attitudes toward language.

Reviewed by R. V. Holdsworth in *RES* 28 (1977):86-93; K. Lever in *RenQ* 29 (1976):452-54; J. M. Nosworthy in *RQ* 19 (1976):452-56.

12 DUNN, ESTHER CLOUDMAN. *Ben Jonson's Art: Elizabethan Life and Literature Reflected Therein*. Smith College Fiftieth Anniversary Publications, No. 3. Northampton, Mass.: Smith College, 1925. 176 pp. [Reprint. New York: Russell and Russell, 1963.]

Attempts to show how Jonson's experience at court, the practice of Renaissance stagecraft, contemporary scholarship, Jonson's theory of non-dramatic poetry, and the life of the times are reflected in his plays.

Reviewed by W. D. Briggs in *MLN* 42 (1927):539-46; E. K. Chambers in *MLR* 25 (1927):244; in *TLS*, 8 April 1926, p. 266.

13 ENCK, JOHN JACOB. *Jonson and the Comic Truth*. Madison: University of Wisconsin Press; Farmingdale, N.Y.: Brown Book Co., 1957. 289 pp.

Presents a theory of the development of Jonson's drama, showing that Jonson's progress was self-conscious and coherent. Demonstrates that Jonson experimented in all his plays. Finds a shifting of emphasis evident among the main elements of plot and characterization, but that Jonson's concern with the problems of society, especially order, authority, and justice, remains constant; his topic is always man's ability, or inability, to distinguish between appearance and reality.

Reviewed by J. B. Bamborough in *RES* 10 (1959):306-08; J. A. Bryant in *SR* 67 (1959):691-703; J. I. Cope in *MLN* 74 (1959):738-41; M. T. Herrick in *JEGP* 57 (1958):547-49; E. Partridge in *MP* 56 (1958):133-35; A. Sackton in *MLQ* 20 (1959):100-01; C. G. Thayer in *Books Abroad* 32 (1958):444; in *N&Q* 203 (1958):494-95.

14 EVANS, WILLA McCLUNG. *Ben Jonson and Elizabethan Music*. Lancaster, Pa.: Lancaster Press, 1929. 137 pp. [Reprinted with a preface added. New York: Da Capo Press, 1965 (*see* 15).]

"Jonson's rise and decline as lyricist and playwright were paralleled by the degree of his intimacy and collaboration with musicians." Traces Jonson's use of songs in the plays, noting his early experience and later successes. The more elaborate songs appear in the plays written for the children's companies, which consisted of trained musicians.

Reviewed by S. G. in *M&L* 12 (1931):206.

15 _____. *Ben Jonson and Elizabethan Music*. New York: Da Capo Press, 1965. 143 pp.

A reprint of the 1929 edition (*see* 14), with an added "Preface to a Second Printing" bringing bibliography up to date.

*16 FERRAT, ALVERT. *Ben Jonsons vier grosse Komödien und die Literaturtheorien seiner Zeit*. Effretikon: Nova Werke, 1973. 149 pp.

17 FRICKER, FRANZ. *Ben Jonson's Plays in Performance and the Jacobean Theatre*. Cooper Monographs of English and American Language and Literature, 17. Theatrical Physiognomy Series. Bern: Francke, 1972. 151 pp.

The methods and terminology of Rudolph Stamm assist in isolating and studying elements of Jonson's theatrical physiognomy. Jonson's numerous stage directions are highly functional and related to the particular theatres he wrote for. Mirror passages and reported scenes relate closely to stage business.

Book-length Studies

17a GAYLEY, CHARLES MILLS, ed. Representative English Comedies, with Introductory Essays and Notes and a Comparative View of the Fellows and Followers of Shakespeare. Vol. 2. The Later Contemporaries of Shakespeare: Ben Jonson and Others. New York: Macmillan, 1932. 645 pp.

Contains four plays by Jonson, each with an introduction by the editor indicated: Every Man in his Humour (C. H. Herford), Epicoene (Charles Mills Gayley), The Alchemist (George Arnold Smithson), Eastward Ho (John W. Cunliffe).

18 GIBBONS, BRIAN. Jacobean City Comedy: A Study of Satiric Plays by Jonson, Marston, and Middleton. Cambridge, Mass.: Harvard University Press; London: Hart-Davis, 1968. 223 pp.

Studies certain plays produced between 1597 and 1624 designated as "City Comedy"--"a distinct dramatic genre with a recognizable form and conventions of theme, setting and characterization." Provides a history of the development of the genre and explores the interacting influences of the three dramatists. Studies the social, political, and economic background of the plays, and shows that the world of the city comedy is similar to that of Machiavelli's The Prince and Hobbes' Leviathan, a world in conflict with the Christian Tudor model.

Reviewed by M. Eccles in SEL 9 (1969):373-74; B. Harris in YWES 49 (1968):173; C. P. Lyons in RenQ 22 (1969):288-89.

19 GOTTWALD, MARIA. Satirical Elements in Ben Jonson's Comedy. Travaux de la Société des Sciences et des Lettres des Wroclaw, Ser. A, No. 137. Wroclaw: Ossolinski, 1969. 164 pp.

Jonson gradually grew from an indignant moralizer to an ironic observer, and shifted his concentration from general to particular vices. A conservative, he aimed his satire chiefly at middle-class cupidity and social aspiration, but he recognized the follies of the gentry as well. He did not despise the common folk. The "plebian sympathies" seen in some of his portraits show that Jonson did not identify with the social élite, as is often claimed. "Jonsonian distinction is . . . based on intellectual rather than class criteria." Though influenced by classical authors, he depended on them less than is commonly thought.

Reviewed by B. Harris in YWES 50 (1969):190-91.

20 GUTMANN, JOSEPH. Die dramatischen Einheiten bei Ben Jonson. Würzburg: Drescher & Reichart, 1913. 101 pp.

Deals with Jonson's theory and practice of the dramatic unities. Although he followed the unity of time in his comedies, in the tragedies his artistic creativity led him to break the rule. In general he observed the unity of place as much as possible within the limits of his concern for naturalism and probability. He did not observe the unity of action, but rather one of idea, of thought. Gutmann concludes that the contrast between Jonson's theory and practice in the matter of unity of action shows that for Jonson the principle reflected a desirable ideal but, like the other unities, was not to be followed when it got in the way of artistic creativity.

Reviwed by Max Förster in Shakespeare-Jahrbuch 50 (1914):239-41.

21 HERFORD, C. H.; SIMPSON, PERCY; and SIMPSON, EVELYN M. Ben Jonson. 11 vols. Oxford: Clarendon Press, 1925-1952.

Volumes 1 and 2 (1925) trace Jonson's life and career, supported by documentation in several appendixes (including the conversations with Drummond) and provide introductions to all of the works. Volumes 3 (1927), 4 (1932), 5 (1937), 6 (1938), and 7 (1941) contain the texts of the plays and the masques and entertainments. Volume 8 (1947) contains the texts of the poems and prose works. Volumes 9 and 10 (1950) examine the text of the Jonson canon and the stage history of the plays, and provide commentaries on the plays and the masques and entertainments. Volume 11 contains: commentary on the non-dramatic works, contemporary commendatory poems, verse and prose criticism, and elegies on Jonson's death, material supplementing earlier volumes, corrections and additions, and an index to the eleven volumes.

Reviews: Vols. 1 & 2: P. Aronstein in Anglia Beibl. 37 (1926):10-14; F. Birrell in Commonwealth and Empire Review, October 1925, pp. 392-96; W. D. Briggs in MLN 42 (1927):404-11; E. K. Chambers in Library, 4th Series, 6 (1925):179-82; S. C. Chew in Nation, 23 September 1925, pp. 33-34; W. W. Greg in MLR 21 (1926):201-10; G. B. Harrison in Reader 1 (October 1925):34-36; R. B. McKerrow in RES 2 (1926):227-30; A. MacMechan in DR 5 (1925):419-20; M. Praz in La Cultura 6 (1925):543-51; G. Saintsbury in Bookman 68 (1925):279-81; J. C. Squire in Observer (London), 19 July 1925, p. 4; L. Woolf in Nation & Athenaeum, 25 July 1925, p. 216; in New Statesman, 28 November 1925, pp. 209-10; in TLS, 30 July, 6 August, and 13 August 1925, pp. 501-02; 521; 533.

Book-length Studies

Vol. 3: P. Aronstein in Anglia Beibl. 39 (1928):194-95; W. W. Greg in MLR 23 (1928):75; G. Saintsbury in Bookman 73 (1927):294-96; L. Woolf in Nation & Athenaeum, 2 July 1927, p. 447; in Nation, 9 November 1927, p. 518; in New Statesman, 2 July 1927, p. 378; in Oxford Mag., 26 January 1928, p. 249; in TLS, 2 July 1927, p. 500.

Vols. 1, 2, and 3: C. R. Baskervill in MP 25 (1928):366-68; W. D. Briggs in MLN 44 (1929):44-47; T. S. Eliot in Dial 85 (1928):65-68; W. P. Frijlinck in English Studies 11 (1929):102-07.

Vol. 4: P. Aronstein in Anglia Beibl. 43 (1933):336-39; O. Elton in MLR 27 (1932):331-33; W. W. Greg in RES 9 (1933):102-04; M. Praz in English Studies 17 (1935):31-34; C. Saltmarshe in Bookman 82 (1932):36; G. W. Whiting in MLN 48 (1933):473-74; in Nation, 13 April 1932, p. 439; in TLS, 25 February 1932, p. 129.

Vol. 5: E. Bowen in New Statesman, 8 May 1937, p. 775; W. Fischer in Anglia Beibl. 49 (1938):124-25; W. W. Greg in RES 14 (1938):216-18; M. Praz in English Studies 19 (1937):226-32; H. Spencer in MLN 53 (1938):450-53; S. Young in New Republic, 16 June 1937, pp. 158-59; in TLS 5 June 1937, pp. 417-18.

Vol. 6: W. W. Greg in RES 14 (1938):344-46; K. M. L. in Oxford Mag., 24 November 1938, pp. 227-28; M. Praz in English Studies 21 (1939):24-46; G. W. Whiting in MLN 53 (1938):625-27; in TLS, 23 April 1938, p. 277.

Vol. 7: A. H. Gilbert in MLN 58 (1943):469-73; C. J. Sisson in MLR 37 (1942):203-05; in TLS, 25 November 1941, pp. 566, 569.

Vol. 8: M. C. Bradbrook in MLR 43 (1948):259-60; W. W. Greg in RES 24 (1948):65-66; in TLS, 17 May and 5 July 1947, pp. 243, 336.

Vols. 9 & 10: M. C. Bradbrook in MLR 47 (1952):63-64; W. W. Greg in RES 2 (1952):275-80; E. H. in New Mexico Quarterly 22 (1952):469-71; in TLS, 12 January 1951, p. 19.

Vol. 11: M. C. Bradbrook in MLR 48 (1953):460; S. C. Chew in New York Herald Tribune Books, 1 February 1953, p. 14; W. W. Greg in RES 4 (1953):285; in TLS, 10 October 1952, p. 661.

Vols, 9, 10, and 11: J. Gerritsen in English Studies 38 (1957):120-26.

22 HIBBARD, G. R., ed. The Elizabethan Theatre IV. Papers given at the Fourth International Conference on Elizabethan Theatre held at the University of Waterloo, Ontario, in July 1972. Toronto: Macmillan; Hamden, Conn.: The Shoe String Press, Archon Books, 1974. 190 pp.

Includes S. Schoenbaum, "The Humorous Jonson" (see 1231); William Blissett, "Your Majesty is Welcome to a Fair" (see

154a); Eugene M. Waith, "Things as They Are and the World of Absolutes in Jonson's Plays and Masques" (see 1249); S. P. Zitner, "The Revenge on Charis" (see 236); and E. B. Partridge, "Jonson's Large and Unique View of Life" (see 1208).

23 HINZE, OTTO. Studien zu Ben Jonsons Namengebung in seinen Dramen. Weida, Thuringia: Thomas & Hubert, 1919. 84 pp.

For the names of his characters, Jonson depends on historical sources only in the Roman plays and Poetaster. In the remaining dramas, the names usually are either invented or used for their common associations, in both cases to reflect the world of the play. In general the names foreshadow the future and illustrate the most important characteristic of the person, perhaps his occupation. Jonson intended the audience to understand his names' associations immediately.

24 HYLAND, PETER. Disguise and Role-Playing in Ben Jonson's Drama. JDS 69, 1977, 225 pp.

Use of disguise usually signals Jonson's movement into the moral dimension of personality, with consideration of the character's capacity for self-knowledge and consistency. Major figures in the great comedies (The Alchemist, Volpone, Bartholomew Fair) assume such total disguises that they do not know themselves and thus defeat themselves. The tragedies employ role-playing, not disguise. In the late plays, disguise becomes a source of illusion but does not exist at the center of the work. Disguise can be "verbal"; cant and jargon cover up non-existence of personalities.

25 JACKSON, GABRIELE BERNHARD. Vision and Judgment in Ben Jonson's Drama. Yale Studies in English, 166. New Haven and London: Yale University Press, 1968. 186 pp.

Describes Jonson's perfect poet (and Jonson) as "simultaneously visionary and judge--super-human seer and public man of action." Studies Jonson's concepts of poets and poetry in Discoveries and the poet-figures in his plays. Shows how in a Jonsonian play the ideal is embedded in the basic structure, and examines the methods and techniques used to pattern Truth.

Reviewed by J. Arnold in SCN 27 (1969):48-49; I. Donaldson in N&Q 214 (1969):383-84; C. J. Gianakaris in JEGP 69 (1970):517-20; B. Harris in YWES 49 (1968):172; R. Levin in MLQ 31 (1970):377-79; L. Tennenhouse in SCN 28 (1970):53-54; J. R. Willingham in LJ 93 (1968):2242; in TLS, 27 March 1969, p. 318.

Book-length Studies

26 JOHANSSON, BERTIL. *Religion and Superstition in the Plays of Ben Jonson and Thomas Middleton*. Essays and Studies on English Language and Literature, 7. Uppsala: Lundequist; Cambridge, Mass.: Harvard University Press, 1950. 339 pp. [Reprint. Nendeln, Liechtenstein: Kraus, 1973.]

Sketches briefly the playwrights' lives and the history of religious strife in England from the Reformation to the execution of Charles I. Examines the organized religions, the Elizabethan conception of the world, and the evidence in the plays of contemporary ideas on astrology, alchemy, magic, and witchcraft.

Reviewed by K. M. Lea in *RES* 4 (1953):171-72; J. Jacquot in *EA* 5 (1952):248; H. C. White in *JEGP* 55 (1956):161-62.

27 JONES-DAVIS, MARIE THÉRÈSE. *Ben Jonson*. Théâtre de tous les temps, No. 22. Paris: Editions Seghers, 1973. 192 pp.

Discusses the plays generally, in terms of their use of poetic language, and various aspects of theme, characterization, structure, dramatic technique, and point of view. Praises Jonson's imaginative realism in depicting life in general, social movements, and economic realities. Examines theory of humours and its relation to comedy; moralistic comedy; comic and tragic satire; animal imagery; the seven deadly sins; and Jonson's primary message regarding the need for order and reason in men's lives. Includes French translations of several passages from the plays reflecting Jonson's dramatic theories, and a list of performances of plays in Great Britain, North America, and France since the mid-18th century.

28 KERNAN, ALVIN, ed. *Two Renaissance Mythmakers: Christopher Marlowe and Ben Jonson*. Selected Papers from the British Institute, 1975-76, NS 1. Baltimore and London: The Johns Hopkins University Press, 1977. 221 pp.

Includes Gabriele Bernhard Jackson, "Structural Interplay in Ben Jonson's Drama" (*see* 1143) and Ian Donaldson, "Jonson and the Moralists" (*see* 1096).

29 No entry.

30 KNIGHTS, L. C. *Drama and Society in the Age of Jonson*. New York: George W. Stewart; London: Chatto and Windus, 1937. 358 pp. [Reprint. New York: Barnes and Noble, 1957; New York: W. W. Norton, 1968.]

Investigates the economic situation of the late 16th and early 17th centuries, the social significance of economic development, and the ideas that influenced social and economic problems, with a view toward commenting on the relationship between these events and Elizabethan or Jacobean comedy. States that "neither critic nor historian has made a study of economic conditions and the drama, in conjunction, in order to throw light on one of the more important problems of our own time: the relation between economic activities and general culture."

Reviewed by E. Bowen in New Statesman and Nation, 8 May 1937, p. 775; R. Davril in EA 16 (1937):182-83; L. Ennis in MP 35 (1937):199-200; L. G. Salingar in Scrutiny 6 (June 1937):118-20; in TLS, 5 June 1937, pp. 417-18.

31 KNOLL, ROBERT E. Ben Jonson's Plays: An Introduction. Lincoln: University of Nebraska Press, 1964. 223 pp.

Provides a critical study of each play, with a summary of the scholarship, observations on structural patterns, survey of literary influences, and a thematic analysis. Finds Jonson to be so completely a Christian humanist that "by the time he had reached maturity his classical learning had been assimilated into his English body, and his sophisticated morality plays preached Christian sermons."

Reviewed by J. Arnold in SCN 24 (1966):10; J. A. Barish in SEL 6 (1966):373-76; R. Davril in EA 18 (1965):415-16; J. J. Enck in MLR 61 (1966):673-74; C. J. Gianakaris in JEGP 64 (1965):727-30; N. N. Holland in Renaissance News 18 (1965):345-46; D. Novarr in CE 28 (1966-67):67; R. W. Van Fossen in SAQ 64 (1965):575.

32 LINKLATER, ERIC. Ben Jonson and King James: A Biography and a Portrait. London: Jonathan Cape; New York: Cape and Smith, 1931. 328 pp. [Reprint. Port Washington, N.Y.: Kennikat Press, 1972.]

A popular biography presenting Jonson's life and times, giving brief summaries of the plays and situating many in the literary life of the Renaissance. Posits reasons for changes within the Jonson canon.

Reviewed by I. Brown in Week-End Review, 17 October 1931, p. 490; E. C. Dunn in SatR, 9 April 1932, p. 647; J. Laver in Spectator (London), 24 October 1931, pp. 535, 537; in TLS, 22 October 1931, p. 816.

33 PALMER, JOHN LESLIE. Ben Jonson. New York: Viking Press; London: Routledge, 1934. 341 pp. [Reprint. Port Washington, N.Y.: Kennikat Press, 1967.]

Presents a biography of the man and a study of his achievements as poet, dramatist, and writer of masques. Presents Jonson as "the greatest of English worthies" representing the Renaissance in England. Sees as the best in Jonson his concentration on permanent and evident aspects of human character and intellectual exploitation of theme. In the "dotages" Jonson's principal weaknesses are

Book-length Studies

his tendency merely to indicate theme rather than to explore it dramatically, and his failure to integrate the best scenes of the plays.

Reviewed by F. S. Boas in YWES 15 (1934):199-201; R. Gilder in Theatre Arts Monthly 18 (1934):801-02; A. H. Gilbert in SAQ 33 (1934):430-32; J. W. Krutch in Nation 138 (1934):623; H. T. E. Perry in YR 34 (1935):641-43; S. Young in New Republic, 6 June 1934, p. 103; in TLS, 3 May 1934, p. 319.

34 PARTRIDGE, EDWARD B. The Broken Compass: A Study of the Major Comedies of Ben Jonson. London: Chatto and Windus; New York: Columbia University Press, 1958. 254 pp. [Reprint. Westport, Conn.: Greenwood Press, 1976.]

Studies Jonson's imagery, specifically his metaphorical language, in his "major" and last comedies in order to show how he used metaphor to determine tone and develop theme. Partridge applies his views to Volpone, The Alchemist, Epicoene, and to a lesser extent The Staple of News and The Magnetic Lady.

Reviewed by R. L. Clubb in CL 12 (1960):89-90; H. Feinstein in QJS 45 (1959):336-37; M. T. Herrick in JEGP 58 (1959):528-30; G. K. Hunter in EIC 9 (1959):406-11; K. Muir in London Magazine 6 (1959):77-78; M. Poirier in EA 12 (1959):350; H. Popkin in Kenyon Review 21 (1959):320-26; A. Sackton in MLQ 20 (1959):100-01; TLS, 20 February 1959, p. 98.

35 PLATZ, NORBERT H. Ethik und Rhetorik in Ben Jonsons Dramen. Heidelberg: Carl Winter, Universitätsverlag, 1976. 288 pp.

Jonson is the rare case of a playwright taking seriously the ethical demand that art be subservient to a moral aim. Emphasizes the correlation between ethics and rhetoric and analyzes the ethics of Jonson's plays against the background of the philosophical propositions of his time. Study of the individual plays and their characters' behavior reveals that Jonson affirms Christian Humanist ideals and refutes those of the Counter-Renaissance.

Reviewed by B. Gibbons and B. Harris in YWES 57 (1976):149.

36 SAVAGE, JAMES E. Ben Jonson's Basic Comic Characters and Other Essays. Hattiesburg: University and College Press of Mississippi, 1973. 208 pp.

The title essay classifies the "basic comic characters" under three major headings: the choric, the broker, and the humourous. These are further subdivided into eight categories. This essay is partially an expansion of 1229. (For the others, see 181, 234, 430, 1228.)

Reviewed by S. Henning in MP 72 (1975):418-19; W. H. Magee in LJ 98 (1973):1822; R. B. Parker in MLR 70 (1975):145-48.

37 SMITH, G. GREGORY. Ben Jonson. London: Macmillan, 1919. 316 pp. [Reprint. Norwood, Pa.: Norwood Editions, 1978.]

Studies Jonson's life, works, and literary aims, concluding with an examination of his influences on his contemporaries and later writers. Jonson's "literary conscience," his didacticism, forces him to fragment his material; e.g., by developing his characters as "humours" he fails to characterize adequately. Unlike Shakespeare's characters, Jonson's end where they begin. Smith claims that further damage results from Jonson's effort to follow the rules in the classical tradition, and his cerebral approach. Jonson's innate critical habit of thought discloses itself most vigorously in the comedies; since it is the nature of comedy to be critical, it is not surprising that his best work is in that genre.

Reviewed by M. Summers in YWES 1 (1919-20):74; in TLS, 13 November 1919, p. 637.

38 STURMBERGER, MARIA. The Comic Elements in Ben Jonson's Drama. 2 vols. JDS 54-55, 1975, 524 pp.

Jonson's satire was often personal; his teaching, negative and ironic. Although he considered nothing too sacred to satirize, pretenders of any kind are aimed at most regularly. A variety of literary techniques--burlesque, parody, grotesquerie, irony--appears throughout the canon and highlights Jonson's intellectual, unemotional comedy.

39 THAYER, C. G. Ben Jonson: Studies in the Plays. Norman: University of Oklahoma Press, 1963. 292 pp.

Offers an extensive exposition of each of Jonson's plays except A Tale of a Tub and The Case is Altered. Finds these common elements: Jonson's commentary on art, a presiding artist figure, and a closer affinity to Old Comedy than to New Comedy.

Reviewed by J. J. Enck in Renaissance News 16 (1963): 345-46; W. F. McNeir in Books Abroad 38 (1964):74 and in CL 15 (1963):183-86; T. A. Stroud in SatR, 15 June 1963, p. 43; E. M. Waith in SEL 4 (1964):327-28; TLS, 2 August 1963, p. 594.

40 THOMAS, MARY OLIVE, ed. Ben Jonson: Quadricentennial Essays. SLitI 6 (April, 1973):1-271.

Includes Alvin B. Kernan, "Alchemy and Acting: The Major Plays of Ben Jonson" (see 1151); George A. E. Parfitt, "Virtue and Pessimism in Three Plays by Ben Jonson" (see

579); Marvin L. Vawter, "The Seeds of Virtue: Political Imperatives in Jonson's *Sejanus*" (*see* 692); L. A. Beaurline, "Volpone and the Power of Gorgeous Speech" (*see* 489); David McPherson, "Rough Beast into Tame Fox: The Adaptations of *Volpone*" (*see* 565); Richard Levin, "'No Laughing Matter': Some New Readings of *The Alchemist*" (*see* 99).

41 TOWNSEND, FREDA L. *Apologie for "Bartholomew Fayre": The Art of Jonson's Comedies*. Modern Language Association Revolving Fund Series, 15. New York: Modern Language Association of America; London: Oxford University Press, 1947. 110 pp. [Reprint. New York: Kraus, 1966.]

Defends Jonson against critics from Dryden to Herford who have measured him by the classical yardstick and shows that he did not limit himself to following Plautine and Terentian models, but created his own type of plot to express the rich complexity of his contemporary matter. Proposes that rather than following the line of classical comedy--the method of the straightforward narrator--Jonson substituted instead the method of the weaver, interlacing with variety the many threads of his plots on his dramatic loom. Surveys the criticism from Dryden to Herford, provides a sketch of what Jonson's contemporaries thought of him, then proceeds to an analysis of the individual comedies in four periods of his art: "The Apprentice," "The Journeyman," "The Master Workman," and "The Aging Craftsman." Speculates about the content of Jonson's lost Apologie for *Bartholomew Fayre* and proposes the new laws on the unities, characterization, and structure that he might have formulated.

Reviewed by D. C. Boughner in *MLN* 64 (1949):135-37; J. Gerritsen in *ES* 31 (1950):183-84; D. J. Gordon in *MLR* 44 (1949):110; M. T. Herrick in *JEGP* 47 (1948):305-06; P. Simpson in *RES* 24 (1948):252-54.

*42 WADA, YUICHI. *Ben Jonson*. Tokyo: Kenkyusha, 1963. 214 pp.

43 WILLIAMS, MARY C. *Unity in Ben Jonson's Early Comedies*. JDS 22, 1972, 230 pp.

Jonson's dramas changed as his critical views changed. Early in his career he moved away from freedom to control by rules. His major methods for achieving unity included: restricted time schemes, substantial five-act structure, assembly scenes, specific types of characters, and concentrated themes.

Reviewed by R. B. Parker in *MLR* 70 (1975):145-48.

44 WITT, ROBERT W. Mirror Within a Mirror: Ben Jonson and the Play-Within. JDS 46, 1975, 154 pp.
Jonson employs the full technique of the "play within a play" in very few dramas, but develops variations of it in many. He uses the device for the same purpose that other playwrights use it: comment, action, and spectacle.

45 WOLF, WILLIAM D. The Reform of the Fallen World: The "Virtuous Prince" in Jonsonian Tragedy and Comedy. JDS 27, 1975, 154 pp.
Considering the world polluted, Jonson turned to the prince as one to offer solutions. In the tragedies, evil people embody what the leader should possess: vigilance, counsel, self-knowledge, action, sense of respect for public good. The major dramas work out the prince-world relationships, with Catiline offering the clearest presentation.
Reviewed by R. B. Parker in MLR 70 (1975):145-48.

EDITIONS AND STUDIES OF SPECIFIC PLAYS

Comedies

The Alchemist: Editions

46 The English Replicas. New York: Payson & Clarke, 1927. n. pag. [Copies of this edition appear with the tipped-in imprint: "This book is now published in the United States by Columbia University Press for the Facsimile Text Society."]
A facsimile reprint of the British Museum copy of the 1612 Quarto.

47 The Noel Douglas Replicas. London: Noel Douglas, 1927. n. pag.
Identical with 46 except for name of series.

48 R. J. L. Kingsford, ed. Cambridge: Cambridge University Press, 1928. 147 pp.
The play offers a good reflection of London life and a strong presentation of the theory and practice of alchemy. It shows Jonson's scholarly and satirical qualities at their best. The text follows Gifford's 1816 edition.

The Alchemist

49 Gerald Eades Bentley, ed. New York: F. S. Crofts, 1947. 127 pp. [Reprint. New York: Appleton-Century-Crofts, n.d.; Northbrook, Ill.: AHM, n.d.]

For Jonson, the function of comedy was to help improve society by leading men to more rational behavior. A realistic depiction of contemporary Londoners, speaking a real language, contributed to this aim, although the realism of the dialogue presents difficulties to the modern reader. The Alchemist best illustrates Jonson's concern with preserving decorum and the unities. His use of the alchemical swindle attacks actual practice, but the satire on the Puritans is the most vicious in the play. The Alchemist displays rapid action and "masculine virility."

50 Henry de Vocht, ed. Materials for the Study of the Old English Drama, Series 2, Vol. 22. Louvain: Uystpruyst, 1950. 307 pp. [Reprint. Vaduz: Kraus, 1963.]

Based on the 1612 Quarto, the edition provides detailed textual information, with variants noted between the Quarto and the second issue of the 1616 Folio, which was based on the Quarto but, unlike it, was printed without Jonson's involvement. Includes an extensive study of Jonson's verse.

51 John I. McCollum, Jr., ed. Woodbury, N.Y.: Barron's Educational Series, 1965. 157 pp.

Evaluation of Jonson's literary career indicates The Alchemist as the high point in his comedy. The play's power rests more in its architecture than in its stiking lines. Classical parallels abound, and characterization is well done. The language of the play is admirable.

52 Douglas Brown, ed. London: Ernest Benn, 1966. 176 pp.

In discussing "the faces of greed" in The Alchemist, points to Jonson's use of the hieroglyphic and the emblem traditions. Claims that in the society of the play "justice is unpredictable and arbitrary, and cleverness is its own virtue." Points out further that Jonson uses clashing jargons to prevent communication and that he develops the central image of the play, transmutation, in the language and in visual terms through a continuous procession of shifts and disguises.

Reviewed by G. Bas in EA 22 (1969):310; G. R. Proudfoot in N&Q 212 (1967):356-60.

53 J. B. Bamborough, ed. London: Macmillan; New York: St. Martin's Press, 1967. 191 pp.

Jonson, a rigorous, self-controlled satirist, belongs to the European tradition, and should be compared with Molière rather than Shakespeare. The brilliant construction of The Alchemist depends on the unities, especially the unity of action. The play is a study in "Greed and Self-deception," both associated historically with alchemy. The play succeeds in being "topically funny without going out of date very quickly." Jonson must have enjoyed himself in writing it.

54 F. H. Mares, ed. Cambridge, Mass.: Harvard University Press, 1967. 287 pp.
Relates the history and chief principles of alchemy employed by Jonson to the cosmology of the time. The principles of the three unities focus discussion of the method of staging, which emphasizes Jonson's symbolism. Absence of choric characters leads the viewer to recognize reflections of his own folly in the acts of major characters. Play's blank verse exhibits great tonal variety. Mares assumes the first performance was at Blackfriars. The text has been prepared from the 1616 Folio with consideration of the Quarto and second Folio editions.
Reviewed by G. Bas in EA 22 (1969):311; B. Harris in YWES 48 (1967):180-81; E. Lehmann in Anglia 89 (1971):391-95; R. B. Parker in YES 6 (1976):244-45; in TLS 11 January 1968, p. 46.

55 J. B. Steane, ed. Cambridge: Cambridge University Press, 1967. 153 pp.
Argues for "the prevailing spirit of fun" in the play; does not see it as didactic or moralizing.
Reviewed by B. Harris in YWES 48 (1967):180; in TLS, 19 October 1967, p. 997.

56 S. Musgrove, ed. Berkeley and Los Angeles: The University of California Press; Edinburgh: Oliver and Boyd, 1968. 163 pp.
Traces Jonson's life and career. Sees "humour" as a single, ruling passion, and thus "the legitimate object of satire." Though less realistic than often claimed, Jonson's plays reflect human experience. In The Alchemist, the visions of wealth and power are "created and sustained by Jonson's poetry." The symbolic and metaphorical aspects of alchemy complicate the play, which is about human transmutations that, like alchemy, do not work. Brief accounts of sources and stage history of the play. Text based on 1616 Folio.
Reviewed by R. Gill in RES 20 (1969):491-94.

The Alchemist

57 Arthur Sale, ed. London: University Tutorial Press, 1969. 255 pp.

The play itself is an alchemical process in which subject matter, conception, and treatment all form one body, a reality in which all is an illusion. Comparison with Thomas Tomkis' *Albumazar* (1615), fragments of which are printed in this edition, shows Jonson's superiority in language, dramatic technique, and compressed force of characterization. The text is based on the 1616 Folio.

Reviewed by B. Harris in *YWES* 50 (1969):185-86; in *TLS*, 6 November 1969, p. 1289.

58 Menston, Yorkshire: Scolar Press, 1970. 94 pp.

Facsimile reprint of 1612 Quarto. Briefly reviews facts of publication; states that Jonson probably supervised the printing.

59 Amsterdam: Theatrum Orbis Terrarum; New York: DaCapo Press, 1971, n. pag.

A facsimile reprint of the 1612 Quarto.

60 F. H. Mares, ed. London: Methuen, 1971. 232 pp.

The plot is "beautifully simple," highly unified, and flows virtually without interruption. Rather than offering a "crude moralism" about punishment and reward, Jonson obligates the audience to recognize its own potential for vice and folly. The verse is highly functional, varied appropriately with each character, who are finely executed caricatures rather than fully developed human beings. The play is one bit of evidence for deep and widespread interest in alchemy, a science which Jonson took as seriously as anyone else. His satire is aimed at human nature. The text (based on the 1616 Folio) and the notes are almost identical with those of Mares' Revels edition of 1967 (*see* 54).

61 Alvin B. Kernan, ed. New Haven: Yale University Press, 1974. 255 pp.

A professional mocker of Renaissance London, Jonson creates a mirror opposite to Marlowe's heroic world. *The Alchemist* ranks as his best conversion of heroic material to comedy. Its characters are both universal and reflective of a cross-section of 17th-century London. With their wit and quickness, Face and Subtle are true alchemists. The play incorporates Renaissance views of life, great dramatic heroes, fools, aspirations, and the magus (a kind of philosopher-scientist-magician). The text is based mainly on the 1616 Folio; the edition includes a glossary of alchemical terms.

Reviewed by I. Donaldson in N&Q 220 (1975):283-84; B. Harris and B. Gibbons in YWES 55 (1974):231; R. B. Parker in YES 6 (1976):244-45.

See also 17a.

The Alchemist: Translations and Adaptations

62 London: Davis-Poynter, 1973. [133 numbered pages, each verso blank.]
A playscript "devised for practical use in the theatre, in schools and by drama groups."

63 HODEK, BŘETISLAV. Alchymista. Prague: Československé Divadelní a Literární Jednatelství, 1956. 131 pp. (Czech translation.)

*63a _____. Prague: Orbis, 1956. 359 pp. (Czech translation. See 844.)

64 MÉLÈSE, MADELEINE. "L'Alchimiste," in Les Contemporains de Shakespeare. Edited by Pierre Mélèse. Paris: La Renaissance du Livre, 1932, pp. 4-7, 3-133. (French translation.)
Summarizes Jonson's life, his classical learning, his dramatic theory and practice. Difficult to determine whether Volpone or The Alchemist is his masterpiece; the latter is a work of great strength, and renders Jonson comparable to Molière in every respect.

65 _____. "L'Alchimiste de Ben Jonson." Cahiers du Sud 10 (June 1933):137-41.
French translation of Act I, Scene iii.

*66 MOUSSY, MARCEL. L'Alchimiste. Paris: L'Arche, 1957. 90 pp. (French adaptation.)

67 _____. Paris: L'Arche; Lausanne: La Cité, 1962. 130 pp. (French adaptation.)

68 OBERTELLO, ALFREDO. Ben Jonson: "The Alchemist." Florence: G. C. Sansoni, 1948. 637 pp. (Italian translation, with English on facing pages.)
The first Italian translation of the play. Jonson may have been influenced by Giordano Bruno's Il Candelaio (1582) but another possible source is Bernardino Lombardi's L'Alchemista (1583).

The Alchemist

The Alchemist: Criticism and Commentary

69 ALLEN, HOPE EMILY. "'Dicing Fly' and The Alchemist." TLS, 27 June 1935, p. 416.

Seventeenth-century correspondence regarding M. Adam Squire suggests that the "dicing fly" refers to "a familiar demon which can be bought and sold" (OED, 5a).

70 ANON. "In the Bag." Newsweek, 28 September 1964, pp. 91-92.

Review of New York Gate Theatre production. One of Jonson's lesser works, the play combines pratfalls and wit in equal measure.

71 ARNOLD, JUDD. "Lovewit's Triumph and Jonsonian Morality: A Reading of The Alchemist." Criticism 11 (1969):151-66.

Critics err in considering Lovewit a deus ex machina, for the "venter tripartite" is doomed from the beginning. His triumph is that of a Cavalier gallant, a type appealing to Jonson, who was not simply committed to a general reform of mankind. The image of a voyage proves effective for conveying the play's movement.

72 BLISSETT, WILLIAM. "The Venter Tripartite in The Alchemist." SEL 8 (1968):323-34.

Explores the world of The Alchemist against the background of the morality tradition. Identifies the "venter tripartite" tempting humanity as the Flesh (Dol) and the Devil (Subtle). The World is not so easily identifiable. Sir Epicure Mammon, although he has many characteristics of this vice-figure, comes closer to Carnal Imagination. Face, at first not fully delineated, takes on the characteristics of "the clever worldling" by outdoing Subtle and proving that the truly worldly man can excel the devil at any time. But Lovewit proves to be even more worldly-wise than Face as he commends his unjust servant and, while breaking no law, takes the profit and the wealthy widow.

73 BOAS, F. S. "Othello and The Alchemist at Oxford in 1610." TLS, 31 August 1933, p. 576.

Audited accounts of the city of Oxford show that the King's Men received payment from the mayor and hence gave performances under municipal, not academic, sponsorship. Diary entries suggest an association of the town with touring companies.

74 BRIGGS, KATHERINE MARY. The Anatomy of Puck: An Examination of Fairy Beliefs among Shakespeare's Contemporaries and Successors. London: Routledge and Kegan Paul, 1959, pp. 73-75, 106-12.

Provides background for The Alchemist and The Devil is an Ass.

75 DAVIES, ROBERTSON. "Ben Jonson and Alchemy," in Stratford Papers 1968-69. Edited by B. A. W. Jackson. Hamilton, Ont.: McMaster University Press; Shannon, Ireland: Irish University Press, 1972, pp. 40-60.

That Jonson's characters are not likable is a consequence of his "classical" concern with exposing and scourging follies. Alchemy was a serious science, which Jonson may or may not have believed in. He knew of its "relevance to medicine and speculative thought," but his primary use of it in The Alchemist was to expose human folly.

76 DAVIS, HERBERT. "Notes on a Cancel in The Alchemist, 1612." Library, 5th series 13 (1958):278-80.

At II.iii.221-24, the Folio transposes lines of the 1612 Quarto text. Discovery of an original E_{2v} indicates that the Folio editor made a careful correction in his copy text and placed the lines properly.

77 DESSEN, ALAN C. "The Alchemist: Jonson's 'Estates' Play." RenD 7 (1964):35-54.

Illustrates "how the characteristic dramatic structure of a group of late moralities provides a valuable key to Jonson's intent and achievement in The Alchemist." Analyzes the "thesis-and-demonstration structure" of a typical play of the genre in which characters represent social types or "estates" who enact vices representing their areas of society. Jonson's sophisticated adaptation of the "estates" morality plot embodies the anti-social forces in Subtle, Face, and Dol; the gulls represent the estates. The same elements occur in Volpone and Bartholomew Fair.

78 DIRCKS, RICHARD J. "Garrick and Gentleman: Two Interpretations of Abel Drugger." RECTR 7 (November 1968):48-55.

Garrick played Drugger as a fool and simpleton. Through textual changes he expanded the part but kept it restrained. Thomas Weston, standing in for Garrick in two of the seventy-two performances of the play at Drury Lane, used the role as a springboard into the Drugger of The Tobacconist (1770) by Francis Gentleman. The latter is a prose farce and presents Drugger as a central, broadly comic figure.

The Alchemist

79 DONALDSON, IAN. "Language, Noise and Nonsense: The Alchemist," in Seventeenth-Century Imagery: Essays on Uses of Figurative Language from Donne to Farquhar. Edited by Earl Miner. Berkeley: University of California Press, 1971, pp. 69-82.
Images of division underscore the separateness which marks characters at the end of Jonson's comedies. The emphasis on and varieties of language in The Alchemist force characters into opposing camps and give an index of their low moral and intellectual health. Many characters are overtly interested in language, but few have any awareness of sense being the soul of speech.

80 DUNCAN, EDGAR HILL. "Jonson's Alchemist and the Literature of Alchemy." PMLA 61 (1946):699-710.
Comparison of speeches from Jonson's play with medieval and Renaissance alchemical treatises both enriches understanding of the play and proves that Jonson did not essentially alter or exaggerate his characters' conceptions about alchemy.

81 _____. "Jonson's Use of Arnald of Villa Nova's Rosarium." PQ 21 (1942):435-38.
Three speeches in The Alchemist point to the Rosarium Philosophorum, an alchemical tract attributed to Arnald of Villa Nova, as Jonson's source. Agrees that these speeches (II.i.63-68, II.iii.102-14, II.v.36-40) evince elementary alchemical theory found in many sources, but emphasizes that Jonson did follow alchemical authority in the play and did not distort or exaggerate what was actually believed about alchemy.

82 EMPSON, WILLIAM. "The Alchemist." HudR 22 (1969-1970): 595-608.
Jonson's statements about improving the theatre report only part of his artistic goal. He depends on rogues and the audience's sympathy with tricksters. The comic and apparently immoral figure can have elements of respectability. The play reflects both Jonson's anti-Puritan and anti-Cavalier point of view and his attitude toward money.

83 ERVINE, ST. JOHN. "The Alchemist." Observer (London), 25 March 1923, p. 11.
Review of Phoenix Society production. Despite good individual scenes, the play remains dull. Jonson overworked the humours and should have devoted himself to tragic drama.

84 F., L. "Central City Actors Open New Season with Production of Ben Jonson's Alchemist." New York Times, 7 May 1948, p. 31.

Review of New York City Theatre Company production. No performance can bring the play back to life. Coleridge erred in citing it as a masterpiece of invention.

85 FERGUSSON, FRANCIS. "A Month of the Theatre: The Old and the New." Bookman 73 (1931):632.

Review of Fortune Players Production, New School for Social Research. The situations themselves are not the point, as in a Broadway farce, "but rather a device for revealing the deeper humour of character"; language is its most important element.

86 GOODMAN, PAUL. "Comic Plots: The Alchemist," in his The Structure of Literature. Chicago: The University of Chicago Press, 1954, pp. 82-103. [Reprinted as a Phoenix Book, 1962. Essay reprinted in Ben Jonson: A Collection of Critical Essays (1963), pp. 106-20 (see 3).]

Applies his method of "inductive formal analysis" to The Alchemist. States that the inductive critic, unlike the generic critic who imposes a definition, persists in his analysis until he can reach a "definition," but he begins discussion of comic plots by supplying definitions.

87 GRAVES, THORNTON S. "Notes on Elizabethan Plays." MP 23 (1925):1-2.

In his Prologue to a revival of Tomkis' Albumazar, Dryden wrongly suggests that Albumazar was written before The Alchemist.

88 H., J. "The Alchemist Diverting." New York Times, 5 June 1931, p. 27.

Review of Fortune Players' production. The play's merit rests in the simplicity of its argument.

89 HOLLERAN, JAMES V. "Character Transmutation in The Alchemist." CLAJ 11 (1968):221-27.

Shows a thematic parallel between "the scientific inadequacy of alchemy" and "the psychological inadequacy of the characters." Efforts at transmutation fail: the crooks and gulls alike eventually revert to their real selves, and even Lovewit does not succeed in transmuting himself.

The Alchemist

90 HOWARTH, R. G. "The Alchemist and Epicoene." TLS, 3 May 1934, p. 322.

Slight similarities link The Alchemist and the subplot of Northward Ho. Jonson offers hints about Epicoene's sex prior to play's conclusion.

91 HOY, CYRUS. "The Pretended Piety of Jonson's Alchemist." RenP 1957:15-19.

Points out the irony in the pretended piety of Subtle, Sir Epicure Mammon, and others in The Alchemist. All of the contemporary literature on alchemy stressed the need for piety in those who were seeking after gold, yet the play's most pervasive irony lies in the fact that "those who are most frantically seeking the means to turn base metals to gold are precisely those who vulgarize and profane all they touch."

92 HUSSEY, MAURICE. "Ananias the Deacon: A Study of Religion in Jonson's The Alchemist." English 9 (1953):207-12.

Besides satirizing hypocritical Puritanism, Jonson denounced personifications of the virtues and vices condemned in the sermons of the nonconformist preacher Thomas Adams. The sermons offered a guide to Christian thought, a norm implicit in the play. Ananias "provides the answer to many questions which we may ask about Jonson's dealing with organized religion."

93 _____. "An Oath in The Alchemist." N&Q 196 (1951):433-34.

Points out Jonson's subtle commentary on censorship in I.ii. The "By Gad" of the original edition was changed to "By Jove"; but Subtle's "No, no, he did but jest," Hussey suggests, is an aside which Jonson's audience would have caught as a twit aimed at the censors.

94 JONES, MYRDDIN. "Sir Epicure Mammon: A Study in 'Spiritual Fornication.'" RenQ 22 (1969):233-42.

Renaissance audiences would have immediately recognized and condemned Sir Epicure's caricature of religion. He consciously associates himself with Solomon's sensuality, wealth, and power but fails to recognize that these lead to the king's downfall. The homilies given on I Kings, by order of Queen Elizabeth, emphasized Solomon's idolatry as spiritual fornication and can be recognized in some of Surly's questions to Mammon, who exemplifies the evil at the heart of an acquisitive society.

95 KNOLL, ROBERT E. "How to Read The Alchemist." CE 21 (1960):456-60.

The play demands that students understand the nature of its dramatic satire and its peculiar virtue. Structurally, Jonson employs duplication; Surly provides cross-plotting but successive treatment of characters dominates. Essentially Christian, the play shows how false gods may usurp the very name and ritual of the true God. Jonson reworks the parable of the talents according to a Puritan reading of scripture, in which wealth is proof of God's favor, in order to show the shabbiness of the Puritan ethic.

96 LARDNER, JACK. "Something Silly, Something Old." NY, 15 May 1948, pp. 48-49.

Review of New York City Theatre Company production. Performance shows Jonson as a wise and entertaining, as well as a gross, writer. The complex plot moves too quickly for effectiveness; too much slapstick weakens the comic.

97 LEECH, CLIFFORD. "Caroline Echoes of The Alchemist." RES 16 (1940):432-38.

Details imitations, both in language and in certain scenes and situations, of The Alchemist by several Caroline dramatists.

98 LEVIN, HARRY. "Two Magian Comedies: The Tempest and The Alchemist." ShS 22 (1969):47-58.

Although closely related in theme and produced under similar auspices, the plays differ in dramatists' attitude toward human nature, characters' concerns, and magic's effects.

99 LEVIN, RICHARD. "'No Laughing Matter': Some New Readings of The Alchemist." SLitI 6 (April 1973):85-99. (See 40.)

Critics err in over-serious approaches to the play. Jonson's comic spirit is essential to his intention and significance.

100 MacCARTHY, DESMOND. "Ben Jonson's Laughter." New Statesman, 24 March 1923, pp. 722-23.

Review of Phoenix Society production. Finds similarities between Jonson's and Balzac's worlds, both "phantasmagorias of monomaniacs, crammed to the muzzle with will and appetite . . ." The tough-minded, Catholic Jonson, "if his experience reports that the world is damned, can afford to envisage human nature's vileness with scornful and possibly quite outrageous gaiety." Hazlitt's desire that Jonson be sympathetic misses the essence of Jonson's comic intentions.

The Alchemist

101 McCULLEN, JOSEPH T., JR. "Conference with the Queen of Fairies: A Study of Jonson's Workmanship in *The Alchemist*." *SN* 23 (1950):87-95.

Jonson drew suggestions for the play from well-known London law cases. Three suits attempted to determine ownership of estates originally possessed by a Rogers family in Dorset. Thomas Rogers, one claimant, may be the prototype of Dapper. Slight differences between Rogers and Dapper illustrate Jonson's method of adapting topical ideas to drama.

102 NOWAK, LOTHAR. *Die Alchemie und die Alchemisten in der englischen Literatur*. Breslau: n.p., 1934, pp. 63-71.

Jonson was the most original of the English writers who satirized alchemy. In *The Alchemist* he differs from previous writers by focusing more on the dupes than on the charlatans. Unusually realistic, the play reflects both Jonson's great knowledge of alchemy and his aversion to it.

103 OLIVER, EDITH. "O Quite Well-Done Ben Jonson!" *NY*, 26 September 1964, pp. 160-63.

Review of off-Broadway production at The Gate. *The Alchemist* omits no aspect of human baseness and gullibility.

104 PARR, JOHNSTONE. "Non-Alchemical Pseudo-Sciences in *The Alchemist*." *PQ* 24 (1945):85-89. [Reprinted in his *Tamburlaine's Malady and Other Essays on Astrology in Elizabethan Drama*. University: University of Alabama Press, 1953, pp. 107-11. Reprint. Westport, Conn.: Greenwood Press, 1971.]

Subtle's references to metoposcopy, physiognomy, chiromancy, and astrology are in accord with accounts of these pseudosciences in Richard Saunders' *Physiognomie, and Chiromancie, Metoposcopie . . . the Art of Memory* (1670-71). Subtle's mistaken association of the sign of Libra with the planet is explained by his wanting Drugger's horoscope to reflect riches and success in business.

105 PEARSON, LU EMILY. "Elizabethan Widows," in *Stanford Studies in Language and Literature*. Edited by Hardin Craig. Stanford: Stanford University Press, 1941, pp. 124-42. [Reprint. Folcroft, Pa.: Folcroft Editions, 1976.]

The Elizabethan widow, due to influences like the Pauline doctrine and contemporary writers like Vives, suffered from many prejudices. To protect reputation and fortune, many young widows submitted to a male guardian's choice of a husband and early remarriage. Ben Jonson draws on the "merry widow" theme in *The Alchemist* when he satirizes the helplessness of Dame Pliant.

106 PETRONELLA, VINCENT F. "Teaching Ben Jonson's The Alchemist: Alchemy and Analysis." HAB 21 (Spring 1970):19-23.

Provides suggestions for using information about alchemical lore in teaching the play. Includes a chart showing the general stages in the alchemical process, and discusses some of the metaphorical uses of alchemical terminology.

107 READ, JOHN. "An Alchemist in Jacobean London," in his The Alchemist in Life, Literature, and Art. London: Thomas Nelson and Sons, 1947, pp. 39-46.

Chaucer's Canon's Yeoman's Tale had little influence on Jonson's play; Chaucer's characters had worked at and been concerned about alchemy while Face and Subtle merely put on its vocabulary to seize an immediate opportunity. The two may be reflections of Dr. John Dee and his associate, Edward Kelly. Jonson demonstrates excellent command of alchemical vocabulary and more than mere acquaintance with the practical operation of an alchemical laboratory. The play should be read in the spirit of Mammon's opening admonition.

108 SCHELLING, F. E. "William Lilly and The Alchemist." MLN 26 (1911):62-63.

Direct parallels exist between Jonson's play and William Lilly's History of his Life and Times (ca. 1681).

109 SHAABER, M. A. "The 'Vncleane Birds' in The Alchemist." MLN 65 (1950):106-09.

Disagrees with various editors of The Alchemist who think that the "vncleane birds, in seventy seven" (IV.vii.53) refer to Spanish soldiers. Quotes from a tract in the British Museum dealing with "diverse unknowne Foules: having the fethers about their heads, and neckes like . . . great Ruffes, now in use among men and women . . . in Lincolnshire," which warns about such abuses in dress. Concludes that it was in keeping with the character of Ananias to denounce Surly's Spanish costume in like manner. Does not say Jonson knew the tract, but suggests that the sermon helps to explain the lines in the play.

110 SHANKS, EDWARD. "The Drama." Outlook (London), 24 March 1923, p. 249.

Review of Phoenix Society production. The Alchemist ranks second to Volpone in the Jonson canon, containing little that is universal. Performance indicates that the work is superior to modern plays only in language.

Bibliography

The Alchemist

111 SHEED, WILFRID. "Housebroken Satire." *Commonweal*, 9 October 1964, p. 73.

Review of New York Gate Theatre production. The printed text often conceals the comedy. The play depends on a single joke: "the scatology of avarice."

112 SISSON, C. J. "The Magic of Prospero." *ShS* 11 (1958):70-77.

Refers to Jonson's use of magic in *The Alchemist* and *The Devil is an Ass*. Finds Jonson's approach always "resolutely satirical, [and] destructive."

113 _____. "A Topical Reference in *The Alchemist*," in *Joseph Quincy Adams Memorial Studies*. Edited by James G. McManaway, Giles E. Dawson, and Edwin E. Willoughby. Washington: The Folger Shakespeare Library, 1948, pp. 739-41.

The archives of the Public Record Office, in particular in Star Chamber and in Chancery, have been neglected as a possible source of information on topical references in Elizabethan plays. Jonson drew on actual cases for the Dapper scenes in *The Alchemist* and the character of Savory in *The Devil is an Ass*.

114 SOUTH, MALCOLM H. "The 'Vncleane Birds, in Seventy-Seven': *The Alchemist*." *SEL* 13 (1973):331-43.

Ananias' complaint about Surly's ruff brings together scriptural sources, fashions of disguised priests entering England, a work written anonymously by Robert Persons, S.J., and growing fears about Catholics.

115 SPRAGUE, ARTHUR COLBY. "*The Alchemist* on the Stage." *TN* 17 (1963):46-47.

The play has been performed rather consistently since 1610 with the exception of a period after David Garrick's retirement from the stage (1776).

116 SUMMERS, MONTAGUE. "*The Alchemist* at Oxford." *TLS*, 7 September 1933, p. 592.

"After the Restoration the famous John Lacy sustained Ananias." Michael Wright's painting at Hampton Court, it is suggested, shows Lacy in this role.

117 TARGAN, BARRY. "The Dramatic Structure of *The Alchemist*. *Discourse* 6 (1963):315-24.

Compares *The Alchemist* with David W. Maurer's *The Big Con* and concludes that the con game has changed very little in the last hundred years. Jonson uses its devices not to make moral judgments, "but rather, to reveal moral truths" and to expound the theme of the play--ingenuity. He does this through the classical structure of protasis, epitasis, and catastrophe.

118 THAYER, CALVIN G. "Theme and Structure in The Alchemist." ELH 26 (March 1959):23-35.

Employing but not slavishly imitating Old Comedy, The Alchemist exhibits both classical and symbolic structure. Jonson carefully combines the Greek parabasis and agon in II.iii.125-210, indicating the association of the play with art and demonstrating that not only Subtle but the play itself and Jonson are alchemists. Locating Lovewit's house in the Blackfriars district and having the gulls come from all over images the theatre itself, whose patrons come from all areas.

119 TILLOTSON, GEOFFREY. "Othello and The Alchemist at Oxford in 1610." TLS, 20 July 1933, p. 494.

Henry Jackson's Latin correspondence suggests he may have attended The Alchemist at Oxford in 1610; the exact composition of the audience remains uncertain. Oxford's bestowal of a degree on Jonson in 1619 suggests its longstanding support, which may have extended to allowing The King's Men to perform both Volpone and The Alchemist on the Christ's College stage. Internal evidence and records of The King's Men indicate that The Alchemist was written between the early months of 1610 and July-September.

120 VAN DAM, B. A. P. "A Prompt-book Text of The Alchemist and Its Important Lesson." Neophil 19 (1934):205-20.

Compares Jonson's Folio edition of The Alchemist with a prompt-book edition of 1794 printed in Bell's British Theatre to determine what changes had to be made by the adapter for stage purposes, including both excisions and additions. The adapter ruined Jonson's blank verse but made the play's dialogue more lively.

121 WEISS, WOLFGANG. "Jonson: The Alchemist," in Das Englische Drama von Mittelalter bis zur Gegenwart. Vol. 1. Edited by Dieter Mehl. Düsseldorf: August Bagel, 1970, 262-73.

Investigates the reciprocal relationship between satiric intent and dramatic content. The Alchemist is an excellent example of satiric intent providing the organizing principle of a play, determining its structure, theme, plot, characters, and language, and being revealed by them.

The Alchemist

122 WILLIAMS, FRANKLIN B., JR. "Thomas Rogers as Ben Jonson's Dapper." YES 2 (1972):73-77.
Facts about the life of Thomas Rogers of Bryanston (1574-1609?) support the view that he provided the model for Dapper in The Alchemist. Contemporary documents show that he had been induced "to beleeve that he should have conference with the queene of the fairies, and that he should marrie with hir."

123 WYATT, EUPHEMIA VAN RENSSELAER. "The Fortune Players." Catholic World 133 (July 1931):465.
Review of Fortune Players production, New School for Social Research. Coleridge erred in considering the play as exhibiting one of the three best plots in literature.

The Alchemist: Performance Reviews

124 ARMSTRONG, MARTIN. "The Phoenix Society--Ben Jonson's The Alchemist." Spectator (London), 24 March 1923, p. 513.

125 CLURMAN, HAROLD. "The Alchemist and King Lear, 1963," in his The Naked Image: Observations on the Modern Theatre. New York: Macmillan, 1966, pp. 178-81.

126 FISHER, H. K. "The Theatre Reviewed." Life and Letters 54 (July 1947):63-64.
Old Vic production.

127 H., I. "The Alchemist." Manchester Guardian Weekly, 23 January 1947, p. 9.
Old Vic production.

128 S., F. "The Alchemist." Theatre World (London) 43 (February 1947):8.
Old Vic production.

129 STOKES, SEWELL. "The English Spotlight: Reviewers and Reviews." Theatre Arts 31 (April 1947):58.
Old Vic production.

130 ANON. "Old Play in Manhattan: The Alchemist." Time, 17 May 1948, p. 88.

131 NATHAN, GEORGE JEAN. Theatre Book of the Year, 1947-48. New York: Knopf, 1948, pp. 12-14, 217-19.
The New York City Theatre Company productions of The Alchemist and Volpone.

132 PHELAN, KAPPO. "The Alchemist." Commonweal, 21 May 1948, p. 139.
New York City Theatre Company production.

133 WYATT, EUPHEMIA VAN RENSSELAER. "The Alchemist." Catholic World 167 (June 1948):267.

134 HORN, ROBERT D. "Shakespeare and Ben Jonson--Ashland." SQ 12 (1961):415-18.
Oregon Shakespeare Festival production.

135 ANON. "Pickpocketing a Classic." Time, 21 October 1966, p. 85.
New York Lincoln Center production.

136 BRUSTEIN, ROBERT. "Sepulchral Odors at Lincoln Center." New Republic, 29 October 1966, pp. 32-33. [Reprinted in his The Third Theatre. New York: Simon and Schuster, 1969, pp. 173-77.]
New York Lincoln Center production.

137 CLURMAN, HAROLD. "Theatre." Nation, 31 October 1966, p. 460.
New York Lincoln Center production.

138 GILMAN, RICHARD. "Olsen and Jonson." Newsweek, 24 October 1966, p. 108.
New York Lincoln Center production.

139 HEWES, HENRY. "O, for a Philosopher's Stone!" SatR, 29 October 1966, p. 49.
New York Lincoln Center production.

140 LEWIS, THEOPHILUS. "The Alchemist." America, 19 November 1966, p. 688.
Vivian Beaumont Theatre production.

141 McCARTEN, JOHN. "Overwrought." NY, 22 October 1966, p. 83.
New York Lincoln Center production.

142 WEST, ANTHONY. "The Alchemist: Gropings in the Dark." Vogue, December 1966, p. 161.
New York Lincoln Center production.

Bibliography

Bartholomew Fair

Bartholomew Fair: Editions

143 *Acting Text for the Old Vic Theatre Company of London*. Introduction by Alexander Scott. Edinburgh: The Scots Review, 1950. 80 pp.

Explains the term "humour" as "strongly marked characteristic." The dramatis personae of Jonson's plays are "caricatures, personifications of abstract qualities." But Jonson succeeds in creating an illusion of reality. *Bartholomew Fair*, exceptional in its scope, is "an allegory of human life." Men easily deceive others and themselves.

144 E. A. Horsman, ed. Cambridge, Mass.: Harvard University Press, 1960. 211 pp.

Presents the play as a "discovery of certain relations between would-be moralists and those people or habits they attack." The former fail because their knowledge of human nature--their own and those they attack--is deficient. Sees the fair as embodying the iniquitous forces which the visitors "encounter to their pain and profit."

Reviewed by J. B. Bamborough in *RES* 14 (1963):197-98; A. Brown in *YWES* 41 (1960):128-29; K. Palmer in *MLR* 56 (1961):584.

145 Eugene M. Waith, ed. New Haven: Yale University Press, 1963. 239 pp.

The success of the play depends on its "superbly ordered multiplicity . . . [and] outstanding vitality." Discusses groupings of the characters and the function of these groupings in the structure of the play, and Jonson's use of discontinuity and amplification. Contains two appendixes--one on the text, the second on the staging of the play (basically the material which appeared in his "The Staging of *Bartholomew Fair*." *See* 188.)

Reviewed by M. N. Proser in *SCN* 22 (1964):10-11.

146 Maurice Hussey, ed. London: Ernest Benn, 1964. 159 pp.

Comments on the characters: Bartholomew Cokes is "a perfect jest-book type"; Ursula the greatest female comic role in contemporary drama.

Reviewed by F. Lagarde in *EA* 18 (1965):179-80.

147 Edward B. Partridge, ed. Lincoln: University of Nebraska Press, 1964. 207 pp.

The play, as well as the fair, represents "the endless voracity of man for food and money and sensuous pleasure." Carefully analyzes the folly of each of the main characters and groups of characters, and the significance of the puppet play.

Reviewed by R. Davril in EA 18 (1965):415; I. Donaldson in EIC 15 (1965):453-58; J. W. Jesse in SCN 23 (1965):4, 6; B. L. Rubin in SCN 22 (1964):27; N. Sanders in MLR 61 (1966):279-81.

148 Douglas Duncan, ed. Berkeley: University of California Press, 1972. 159 pp.

The play recalls Every Man out of his Humour and Cynthia's Revels in its fools' gallery and its satire of judgment and folly. Jonson provides no mouthpiece, but does give earthy characters some metaphoric significance. Working in the tradition of the "great stage of fools," he develops an ambiguous attitude: characters are witless but have a simple appeal. Although popular in the 18th century, the play has lost much of its appeal. History of the text indicates that Jonson was probably not responsible for any corrections made. Copy text for this edition is that of the Folger Shakespeare Library.

149 David McPherson, ed., in his Ben Jonson: Selected Works. New York: Holt, Rinehart and Winston, 1972, pp. 137-272.

Suggests the main theme is judgment; "Jonson demonstrates throughout the play that one's judgment of art is a crucial indication of one's judgment in general." Proposes that Jonson exhibits in the play "a genuine sympathy for human weakness and a grudging recognition that in the real world even the best examples of virtue fall short of the ideal." Text based on 1631 edition.

Bartholomew Fair: Translations and Adaptations

150 Prompt Copy Used by the Folger Theatre Group for Production in Folger Theatre. Washington: Folger Shakespeare Theatre, 1972-73.

The production cut and, in some spots, updated the text.

151 BENEDEK, ANDRÁS. Bertalannapi vásár, in Angol Reneszánsz Drámák. Vol. 3. Edited by Miklós Szenczi. Budapest: Európa Könyvkiadó, 1961, pp. 311-435. (Hungarian translation.)

See also 657.

Bartholomew Fair: Criticism and Commentary

152 BARISH, JONAS A. "Bartholomew Fair and Its Puppets." MLQ 20 (1959):3-17.

The puppet show is a microcosm of the fair and functions as a corrective instrument. The concept of "vapors" runs throughout the play, climaxing with the puppets.

Bartholomew Fair

153 BARTLEY, J. O. "The Development of a Stock Character: II. The Stage Scotsman; III. The Stage Welshman (to 1880)." MLR 38 (1943):279-88.

In Bartholomew Fair Northern "speaks in a way which, if not Scottish, is near to it." Haggise "may be a Scot, but does not show it." The language of Captain Jamy (Henry V) and Northern differs from English only in pronunciation. The Welsh nationality of Bristle is shown by "slight but definite references."

154 BENNEWITZ, FRITZ. "Der Bartholomäusmarkt am Deutschen Nationaltheater Weimar." SJW 109 (1973):40-46.

Several unrelated observations and questions about the play and its performance at Weimar, offered at a "Shakespeare-Day" colloquium at Weimar, 23 April 1972.

154a BLISSETT, WILLIAM. "Your Majesty is Welcome to a Fair," in The Elizabethan Theatre IV (1974):80-105. (See 22.)

Performed at court the day after its public theatre performance, Bartholomew Fair was written for both audiences. Elements geared to the court include: mockery of Puritans, vivid recreation of Smithfield, harangues against tobacco, and the figure of Overdo wandering through public places to identify evil. The play juxtaposes the opposite moral bearings and outcomes presented singly in Volpone and The Alchemist. Bringing together life and the theatre, Jonson reaches the goal of Renaissance art: delighting and educating.

155 BROWN, ARTHUR. "The Play within a Play: An Elizabethan Dramatic Device." E&S 13 (1960):36-48.

Variations on the device of the play within a play are found in Bartholomew Fair and Every Man out of his Humour.

156 COLLEY, JOHN SCOTT. "Bartholomew Fair: Ben Jonson's 'A Midsummer Night's Dream.'" CompD 11 (1977):63-72.

"Bartholomew Fair presents a vision of comic release and comic transformation . . . unique in Jonson's canon," its transformations resembling the magical ones in A Midsummer Night's Dream. Like Shakespeare, Jonson follows St. Paul in valuing apparent folly over apparent wisdom. Besides showing the cleansing power of madness, Bartholomew Fair suggests a connection between "the mysterious power of comic love and harmony and the mysterious power of Christian Grace," seen especially in Grace Wellborn. Jonson may have been influenced by the morality tradition and other earlier literature in presenting debates between Justice and Grace.

157 COPE, JACKSON I. "Bartholomew Fair as Blasphemy." RenD 8 (1965):127-52.

Bartholomew Fair "probes the wellsprings of religious consciousness to discover absurdity in the fullest sense of the word in both conscience and providence, in works and in grace--indeed, in all varieties of view which focus in the implicit axiom that there obtains some teleological relation between creator and creation, between God and the world." With attention to Jonson's use of the Bible, illustrates how Jonson's fair, evincing all aspects of the world, the flesh, and the devil, becomes a microcosm of the evil of the world.

158 FROSCH, THOMAS R. "Bartholomew Fair, or What You Will." SchoIS 2 (1976):3-23.

The play delights in refuting itself and focuses on the aesthetic. Feigning provides comic anarchy as characters open themselves to victimization. Affirmation occurs only after the theatre and comedy have been assaulted.

159 GARDINER, JUDITH K. "Infantile Sexuality, Adult Critics, and Bartholomew Fair." L&P 24 (1974):124-32.

Reviews Edmund Wilson's psychoanalytic appraisal of Jonson and the "vitalist" and "moralist" schools of criticism regarding Bartholomew Fair. Sees the play as built on, and the audience gratified by, "several parallel variations on Oedipal triangles," with the rebellious "son" punishing and humiliating an old "stepfather" and marrying the old "mother." "Much of the verbal wit of the play springs from the free expression of infantile views of sexuality, and the audience may be protected from guilt for its fantasies by a wide variety of comic distortions and displacements."

160 GILBERT, ALLAN H. "The Qualities of the Renaissance Epic." SAQ 53 (1954):372-78.

Bartholomew Fair puts a modern reader in better touch with the Renaissance than do the works of many historians.

161 HAMEL, GUY. "Order and Judgement in Bartholomew Fair." UTQ 43 (1973):48-67.

Two main patterns emerge from the presentation of disorder. Grace Wellborn and Quarlous play highly significant roles. The play balances perceptions of evil and attempts to correct it.

Bartholomew Fair

162 HIBBARD, G. R. "Ben Jonson's Use of 'Pimp'." *N&Q* 222 (1977):522.

Hibbard's emendation of "pimp" as "puny" in his edition of *Bartholomew Fair* is unnecessary. Jonson used the word in *The Alchemist* in its recognized sense and in the sense needed.

163 JANICKA, IRENA. "Figurative Language in *Bartholomew Fair*." *SJW* 111 (1975):156-67.

Verbal images and staging shed light on Jonson's technique as a satirist somewhat indebted to popular traditions. Jonson regularly dehumanizes characters, including enemies of the fair who burlesque heroic values. Purification occurs through ridicule.

164 KAPLAN, JOEL H. "Dramatic and Moral Energy in Ben Jonson's *Bartholomew Fair*." *RenD* NS 3 (1970):137-56.

Contrasts *The Shoemakers' Holiday* and *Bartholomew Fair* in terms of structure, themes, metaphors, characters' ways of imposing order, and audience response. The fair should be taken as Jonson intended it, without simplifying its moral issues.

165 LATHAM, JACQUELINE E. M. "Form in *Bartholomew Fair*." *English* 21 (1972):8-11.

The play offers four levels of reality; the puppets serve as a microcosm of the play.

166 LEE, UMPHREY. "Jonson's *Bartholomew Fair* and the Popular Dramatic Tradition." *Louisburg College Journal of Arts and Sciences* 1 (June 1967):6-16.

Developing further an observation of similarities made by C. R. Baskervill, claims that parts of *Bartholomew Fair* parody and burlesque Chettle and Day's *The Blind Beggar of Bednal-Green* (1600), and that the structure of the earlier plays helps elucidate the structure of Jonson's. Especially in his later comedies, Jonson used the audience's knowledge of earlier popular plays as an organizational device.

167 LEVIN, RICHARD. "The Structure of *Bartholomew Fair*." *PMLA* 80 (1965):172-79.

Explains the unity of the play by assuming that the visitors to the fair are the heroes and that Jonson arranges the characters in clearly defined groups. Points out as the first major division the people who make up the fair and those who visit it, and outlines in detail the further groupings and regroupings and the significance of the relationships of the characters in each group.

168 M., H. W. "Bartholomew Fair." Nation & Athenaeum, 2 July 1921, p. 520.

Performance review. Productions of Jonson, including the poor one given by the Phoenix Society, are important to the revival of historic English drama. Jonson was not a dramatist of the soul but an attentive showman of contemporary fashion.

169 MacCARTHY, DESMOND. "A Surfeit of Pig." New Statesman, 2 July 1921, p. 357.

Review of Phoenix Society production. The play is "a lumbering affair" too gross for modern taste.

170 McCOLLOM, WILLIAM G. "On the Edge of Comedy: Jonson's Bartholomew Fair," in his The Divine Average: A View of Comedy. Cleveland: The Press of Case Western Reserve University, 1971, pp. 153-64.

Bartholomew Fair departs from Volpone's moral acerbity but not from its moral assertiveness. Disguise emphasizes the play's numerous social elements and structures. More ironic than festive, the play presents a basically sobering experience.

170a McPEEK, JAMES A. S. The Black Book of Knaves and Unthrifts in Shakespeare and Other Renaissance Authors. Storrs: University of Connecticut, 1969, pp. 78, 93-100, 206-10.

Jonson clearly follows the tradition, and perhaps used the text, of The Hye Way to the Spyttel House in Bartholomew Fair. The play contains the same cross-section of rogues as the verse narrative, and both the Stagekeeper and Overdo resemble the Porter. The Thirde and last Part of Conny-catching provided Jonson with useful material on rogues and models of warning ballads. Jonson's emphasis on deformity at court (Cynthia's Revels) is also part of the tradition.

171 McPHERSON, DAVID. "The Origins of Overdo: A Study in Jonsonian Invention." MLQ 37 (1976):221-33.

Besides developing Justice Overdo from the disguised-duke figure popular in the Renaissance, Jonson incorporates topical satire. Traits, interests, and phrases of Thomas Middleton (a former Lord Mayor) as well as of Richard Johnson and George Whetstone (zealous pamphleteers) are carefully incorporated into the character.

Bibliography

Bartholomew Fair

172 MAGER, DON. "The Paradox of Tone in *Bartholomew Fayre*." *Thoth* 9 (Spring 1968):39-47.

The play successfully fuses moralistic ideas with dramatic texture, attitudes toward audience and toward material. Primary images--fair, seeking for permission, puppet show--grow throughout the play.

173 MAROTTI, ARTHUR F. "Donne's 'Loves Progress' ll. 37-38, and Renaissance Bawdry." *ELN* 6 (1968):24-25.

Quarlous and Winwife use a common topos--a bottomless vagina associated with a lover's pleasure--when they insult Ursula.

174 OLIVE, W. J. "A Chaucer Allusion in Jonson's *Bartholomew Fair*." *MLQ* 13 (1952):21-22.

Calls attention to an allusion to Chaucer's physician and apothecary in *Bartholomew Fair* which has been overlooked by editors of this play who have recognized it in *The Magnetic Lady*. Because in both plays "now" is changed by Jonson to "new," Olive concludes Jonson is emending Chaucer.

175 PARKER, R. B. "The Themes and Staging of *Bartholomew Fair*." *UTQ* 39 (1970):293-309.

Staging helps present the triple influence of the fair on appetite, law, and art. Through the puppet show Jonson comments on threatre, audience, and values of satire.

176 PEERS, E. A. *Elizabethan Drama and Its Mad Folk*. Cambridge: W. Heffer and Sons, 1914, pp. 53-54, 113-17. [Reprint. Folcroft, Pa.: Folcroft Library Editions, 1978.]

Trouble-all's humorous situations are essential for enjoyment of *Bartholomew Fair*. Jonson is technically correct in his presentations of madness.

177 PETRONELLA, VINCENT F. "Jonson's *Bartholomew Fair*: A Study in Baroque Style." *Discourse* 13 (1970):325-37.

Baroque style encourages the play's movement. Jonson employs a variety of prose techniques, reaching the ultimate in linguistic license in the puppet show.

178 POTTER, JOHN M. "Old Comedy in *Bartholomew Fair*." *Criticism* 10 (1968):290-99.

Jonson drew on Old Comedy for his structure, theme, and style of language. The play's episodes illustrate its theme and relate to it rather than to each other.

179 REID, J. S. "Imitation by Ben Jonson of a Passage in Cicero." PQ 2 (1923):142-43.

Draws notice to one of the rare instances when Jonson imitates little-known passages--two references to Cicero which say in effect "that the pig has only just enough of the life principle (anima) to keep its flesh from rotting." Jonson alludes to this dictum twice in Bartholomew Fair.

180 ROBINSON, JAMES E. "Bartholomew Fair; Comedy of Vapors." SEL 1 (Spring 1961):65-80.

Opposes critics who claim that the play lacks classical unity by demonstrating that its unity "lies in the symbolism of vapors that pervades the play's imagery, characterization, and action," and that Jonson's purpose was that of any good classicist: to instruct and delight. Presents the theory of "vapors" and details Jonson's use of it to present a universal comic truth and to produce a structure "compatible with Renaissance classical principles of dramatic unity."

181 SAVAGE, JAMES E. "Some Antecedents of the Puppet Play in Bartholomew Fair." UMSE 7 (1966):43-64. [Reprinted in his Ben Jonson's Comic Characters and Other Essays (1973), pp. 145-64 (see 36).]

Proposes Nashes Lenten Stuffe as a possible literary antecedent of the puppet play in Bartholomew Fair, based on Jonson's treatment of Dionysius, his association of Hero with herring, and the injection of the word "Fabian" into the dialogue. Suggests that the puppet play alludes to the divorce of the Earl of Essex.

182 SMITH, CALVIN C. "Bartholomew Fair: Cold Decorum." SAQ 71 (1972):548-56.

A figure of wisdom, Grace Wellborn is central to the play's action and imagery, measuring and correcting the enormity of its opposed worlds.

183 TARGAN, BARRY. "The Moral Structure of Bartholomew Fair." Discourse 8 (1965):276-84.

In Bartholomew Fair Jonson "moves from his strident concern with the particular follies and foibles of men to the urbane comic vision that deals with the folly of man," presenting what human conduct is rather than a judgment on it. The play is a dance in three movements with two groups of participants, the inhabitants of the fair and its visitors.

Bartholomew Fair

184 TARN. "Bartholomew Fair Produced by the Phoenix Society." Spectator (London), 2 July 1921, p. 15.

Performance review. The play is essentially dull, even in performance, and unworthy of revival.

185 THALER, ALWIN. "Was Richard Brome an Actor?" MLN 36 (1921):88-91.

Evidence points to possibility that Brome acted in Lady Elizabeth's Men's performance of Bartholomew Fair in 1614.

186 THAYER, C. G. "Ben Jonson, Markham, and Shakespeare." N&Q 199 (1954):469-70.

Agrees with Herford and Simpson that Jonson may have borrowed his details for Jordan Knockem's description of Win-the-Fight Littlewit from Markham's "picture of a perfect horse" in Cavelarice (1607). Suggests that although the passage (IV.v.21-27) may have drawn its detail from Markham, it is so evidently a parody of Venus and Adonis, ll.295-300, that the reader may "suspect that Jonson was using Markham to club Shakespeare."

187 WAITH, EUGENE M. "A Misprint in Bartholomew Fair." N&Q 208 (1963):103-04.

All editions incorrectly assign V.v.50-51 to Quarlous, who should not be on stage at the time. The lines belong to Grace Wellborn. The error may be due to a printer's confusion of "G" and "R" with "Q" and "U" in the speech headings.

188 _____. "The Staging of Bartholomew Fair." SEL 2 (1962): 181-95.

Reconstructs the staging and many of the properties of Bartholomew Fair by drawing on the text and concludes that the play "is one of the clearest examples of the survival in the Elizabethan public theatre of the essentially medieval tradition of staging. Though the 'Speciall Decorum' of the Fair relates the spectacle closely to Smithfield, the stage forms are those of the old mansions and the conception of space is that of the mysteries." Also, the play illustrates the Elizabethan concept of dramatic reality: the world of imagination is created with an awareness of the audience always in mind.

189 WILLIAMS, MARY C. "Ben Jonson's 'Apology' for Bartholomew Fair." ELN 10 (1973):180-85.

The "Apology" probably focused on satire, not poetic freedom. It relates to Donne's works and emphasizes Jonson's stress on critical authority.

Bartholomew Fair: Performance Reviews

190 ANON. "Bardelmy Fair." Observer (London), 26 June 1921, p. 9; 3 July 1921, p. 11.
Phoenix Society production.

191 WORSLEY, T. C. "Bartholomew Fair." New Statesman and Nation, 30 December 1950, p. 676.
Old Vic production.

192 HARTNOLL, PHYLLIS. "Library Drama Comes to Life." Theatre Arts 43 (December 1959):79, 83.
Oxford University Experimental Theatre Club production.

193 TYNAN, KENNETH. Curtains. New York: Atheneum, 1961, pp. 3-4, 35.
Old Vic production, 1951. Also reviews Volpone at Stratford-on-Avon, 1952.

194 HUNTER, G. K. "Renaissance Drama Productions." RORD 19 (1976):85-86.
Nottingham Playhouse production.

The Case is Altered: Editions

195 William Edward Selin, ed. Yale Studies in English, 56. New Haven: Yale University Press; London: Oxford University Press, 1917. 286 pp.
Detailed study of much internal evidence identifies the play as part of the Jonson canon preceding Every Man in his Humour. Sources include the Captivi and Aulularia of Plautus, as well as aspects of the person and career of Anthony Munday. The variety of plots included detracts somewhat from the work's dramatic unity. It was well received in its own time. The edition reproduces an original 1609 Quarto and presents variants.
Reviewed by P. Simpson in MLR 14 (1919):114-16.

The Case is Altered: Criticism and Commentary

196 ENCK, J. J. "The Case is Altered: Initial Comedy of Humours." SP 50 (1953):195-214.
The play offers a preliminary sketch for comedies of humours and is not a romantic work. It is self-contained.

197 HUNTLEY, FRANK L. "Ben Jonson and Anthony Munday, or The Case is Altered Altered Again." PQ 41 (1962):205-14.
Jonson created The Case is Altered from an old play written by his enemies, in order to achieve revenge, especially against Anthony Munday who, Huntley concludes,

The Case is Altered

contributed most to the original play. Proposes that The Case is Altered was a popular Henslowe play; that Jonson's critics rewrote part of Valentine's character satirizing Jonson's use of Asper to criticize London audiences in Every Man out of his Humour; that then Jonson grafted onto the character of Valentine a satire on Anthony Munday.

198 LAMBRECHTS, GUY. "Love's Labour's Lost et The Case is Altered." RANAM 4 (1971):130-40.
Proposes that there were three versions of The Case is Altered--1590, 1598, and 1608--and that the 1598 version was influenced by Love's Labour's Lost.

199 NOSWORTHY, J. M. "The Case is Altered." JEGP 51 (1952):61-70.
Although The Case is Altered was printed in 1609 with only Jonson's name on the title page, it was never acknowledged by Jonson to be his. Suggests that Henry Porter collaborated with Jonson in writing the play, and sees similarities to Porter's The Two Angry Women of Abingdon (1589). Drawing proof for his thesis from exterior evidence, Nosworthy establishes the time for the writing of the play as 1598 during the months that Jonson was working for Henslowe. Since Henslowe did not have an entry for The Case is Altered but did pay Porter, Chettle, and Jonson for a book called "hoote anger sone cowld," Nosworthy suggests that Jonson changed the title Hot Anger Soon Cold to The Case is Altered when he broke with Henslowe.

200 SCHRICKX, W. "Onion, A Sobriquet Relevant to Thomas Nashe?" RLV 27 (1961):322-28.
Supports the view of H. C. Hart (N&Q 9th Series, 12 [21 November 1903]:404) that, in The Case is Altered, Anthony Munday is represented by Antonio Balladino, Gabriel Harvey by Juniper, and Nashe by Onion. Believes that there is no evidence to support Jonson's opinion that Nashe was worsted by Martin Marprelate, an event represented in the play by the breaking of Onion's head.

Cynthia's Revels: Editions

201 Alexander Corbin Judson, ed. Yale Studies in English, 45. New York: Henry Holt, 1912. 346 pp.
Formless, complex, and allegorical, this play yields less to the Jonson reader than other parts of the canon. The edition sorts out and analyzes the dramatic elements, explains obscurities and allusions, and offers a critical analysis of the satire involved. Much of the play is highly conventional; it relates also to the War of the Theatres. Jonson's strong emphasis on the contemporary

political situation and his creation of masque-like effects indicate his use of John Lyly more than of the classics. The basic text of the edition is that of the 1616 Folio.
Reviewed in Nation, 26 September 1912, pp. 289-90.

Cynthia's Revels: Criticism and Commentary

202 BABB, LAWRENCE. "On the Nature of Elizabethan Psychological Literature," in Joseph Quincy Adams Memorial Studies. Edited by James G. McManaway, Giles E. Dawson, and Edwin W. Willoughby. Washington: Folger Shakespeare Library, 1948, pp. 509-22.
Although moral rather than scientific, Renaissance psychological treatises were scholarly works and offer important criteria for evaluating the drama of the time. The character Crites, through the psychological comments offered, would have been recognized as one with a perfectly balanced temperament.

203 BERRINGER, RALPH W. "Jonson's Cynthia's Revels and the War of the Theatres." PQ 22 (1943):1-22.
Cynthia's Revels should not be included in the War of the Theaters. Hedon is only a conventional gallant and not a satiric portrait of Daniel or Marston. Offers new evidence that the Folio additions to Cynthia's Revels were composed after 1605.

204 BRIGGS, WILLIAM DINSMORE. "Cynthia's Revels and Seneca." Flügel Memorial Volume. Stanford, Calif.: Stanford University Press, 1916, pp. 59-71.
Much of I.v.33-39 and II.iii.123-49 of Cynthia's Revels (relating to the character of Crites) is taken directly from Seneca, whose influence is also seen in Every Man out of his Humour and Poetaster. Baskervill was wrong to see Aristotle as the chief source of Jonson's ethical thinking, which is "basically Stoic and more especially Senecan." Nor is Crites the ideal courtier, but rather a member of Jonson's own social group, conforming to the Stoic ideal.

205 CHAN, MARY. "Cynthia's Revels and Music for a Choir School: Christ Church Manuscript Mus 439." SRen 18 (1971):134-72.
Study of the manuscript, as representative of the repertoire of Children of the Chapel, clarifies some points the play makes about the moral value of rhetoric.

Cynthia's Revels

206 CRANE, THOMAS FREDERICK. Italian Social Customs of the Sixteenth Century and Their Influence on the Literatures of Europe. New Haven: Yale University Press, 1920, p. 534. [Reprint. New York: Russell and Russell, 1971.]

Comments on the failure of editors of Jonson to recognize the two parlor games in the fourth act of Cynthia's Revels, the Game of Substantive and Adjective and "A thing done, and who did it," as parlor games of a type familiar in Italy during the 16th century.

207 FABIAN, BERNHARD. "'Cynthia' in the O.E.D." N&Q 204 (1959):356.

The earliest illustration of the first use of the word "Cynthia" in the OED is the citation from Milton's Il Penseroso. Two occurrences of the word--one from Marlowe and two from Jonson's Cynthia's Revels--which appeared forty years earlier, should supplement the present entry.

208 GIBSON, C. A. "'Behind the Arras' in Massinger's The Renegado." N&Q 214 (1969):296-97.

The phrase, "Behind the Turkish hangings," in Massinger's The Renegado (II.vi.6), is equivalent in connotation to "behind the arras" in Cynthia's Revels (IV.i.142). Similar phrases occur in other plays. They "almost invariably connoted duplicity and sexual immorality. . . . the dominant Jacobean and Caroline association of the phrase is with court lechery."

209 GILBERT, ALLAN H. "The Function of the Masques in Cynthia's Revels." PQ 22 (1943):211-30.

Understanding the play demands familiarity with Jonson's view of royalty and the function of the court. His perspective reflects traditional Renaissance ideas. The masques in Act V illustrate how vices disguised as virtues can flatter and deceive rulers. Crites, possessing the "sterner virtues," rightly has the responsibility of punishing the follies unmasked.

210 HIBERNICUS. "A Piece of Perspective." TLS, 28 July 1932, p. 545.

The play should be viewed as Jonson states: "directly." It can be imaged as a set of multiple pictures painted on pieces of cardboard, the aspect of which varies according to the viewing angle.

211 HONIG, EDWIN. "Examples of Poetic Diction in Ben Jonson." Costerus 3 (1972):121-62.

"Hymn to Cynthia" and "Echo's Song" (Cynthia's Revels), and "Hermogenes' Song" (Poetaster) are analyzed in terms of their metrical design and lyrical qualities. They "share alike a movement and rhythm which is musical rather than rhetorical."

212 LAWRENCE, W. J. "A Piece of Perspective." TLS, 21 July 1932, p. 532.

Offers an explanation of the term "a piece of perspective" used by the boy in the Induction to Cynthia's Revels. Lawrence disagrees with Judson's gloss in his edition of the play--"a drawing or painting in perspective used as stage scenery"--because scenery of this nature was unknown in England in 1600. Of two kinds of perspective pictures known in England at this time, Lawrence thinks that Jonson had the second type in mind: "a unified painting which appeared wholly or partly distorted when viewed in the normal way and only assumed a proper aspect when looked at through a hole slantingly."

213 Le COMTE, EDWARD SEMPLE. Endymion in England: A Literary History of a Greek Myth. New York: King's Crown Press, 1944, pp. 69-70. [Reprint. Folcroft, Pa.: Folcroft Library Editions, 1978.]

In Cynthia's Revels, V.xi.14-15, Jonson shows his approval of the imprisonment of Essex by Elizabeth.

214 McPEEK, JAMES A. S. "The Thief 'Deformed' and Much Ado about 'Noting'." Boston University Studies in English 4 (1960):65-84.

A central device of Shakespeare's appearance-reality theme is the gentleman thief, "Deformed." Jonson also uses the figure in Cynthia's Revels, a much more obvious dramatic treatment of the theme, in which all the characters except Arete, Crites, and Cynthia are deformed.

215 PALMER, RALPH GRAHAM. Seneca's "De Remediis Fortvitorvm" and the Elizabethans. Institute of Elizabethan Studies, 1. Chicago: Institute of Elizabethan Studies, 1953, p. 21.

Jonson borrowed from Seneca to describe the evil in the world in Cynthia's Revels.

216 POTTS, ABBIE FINDLAY. "Cynthia's Revels, Poetaster, and Troilus and Cressida." SQ 5 (1954):297-302.

A knowledge of the two Jonson plays assists in interpreting the Shakespeare play.

Cynthia's Revels

217 SABOL, ANDREW J. "A Newly Discovered Contemporary Song Setting for Jonson's Cynthia's Revels." N&Q 203 (1958):384-85.
Announces the discovery of a contemporary song setting for Jonson's Cynthia's Revels in Christ Church Oxford MS. 439. The song entitled "the Kisse" (IV.iii) is sung in the drama by an affected gallant, Hedon, and is intended by Jonson to satirize the formalized love-making "by book and by fashion practiced by the genteel and punctilious courtier."

218 _____. "Two Unpublished Stage Songs for the 'Aery of Children.'" Renaissance News 13 (1960):222-32.
Presents settings for two songs, one from Cynthia's Revels and the other from Marston's Dutch Courtezan. Explains Jonson's subtle defense of song in Cynthia's Revels; then analyzes the methods the composer used to realize his intention in writing the song: to furnish an excessively "sweet" lyric to ridicule the decadent courtier.

219 SHIBATA, TOSHIHIKO. "On the Palinodial Ending of Cynthia's Revels." ShStud 10 (1974):1-15.
The palinode that concludes Cynthia's Revels was ridiculed by contemporary playwrights as "a most pretentious piece of pedantry." It fails as a dramatic device because the corrective tone of the conclusion is not at variance with the tone of the rest of the play.

220 TALBERT, ERNEST WILLIAM. "The Classical Mythology and the Structure of Cynthia's Revels." PQ 22 (1943):193-210.
Critics have overlooked much of the play's unity by not recognizing Jonson's use of classical myths found in popular Renaissance handbooks and dictionaries. In Echo, Narcissus, Niobe, and Actaeon, Jonson drew upon the version of each myth dealing with presumption. This theme and that of self-love are shown through the courtiers.

221 THRON, E. M. "Jonson's Cynthia's Revels: Multiplicity and Unity." SEL 11 (1971):235-47.
Play offers intellectual delight from spectacle, not theatrical excitement; it has multiple, not dramatic, unity.

222 VOCHT, HENRY de. Comments on the Text of Ben Jonson's "Cynthia's Revels": An Investigation into the Comparative Value of the 1601-Quarto and the 1616-Folio. Materials for the Study of the Old English Drama, Series 2, Vol. 21. Louvain: Uystpruyst, 1950. 295 pp. [Reprint. Vaduz: Kraus, 1963.]

Uncertainty about press corrections in the Quarto reduces the significance of many 1616 Folio readings. The superiority of the Quarto over the Folio is demonstrated by textual analysis. Jonson did not supervise the printing of the Folio.

223 WREN, ROBERT M. "Ben Jonson as Producer." ETJ 22 (1970): 284-90.

Examines Cynthia's Revels as a source of information about Jonson's role as a play director, proposing that various pieces of dialogue reveal his method of teaching acting techniques to the boys' company. Conjectures that Jonson began a play with basic movements and important dialogue established, and then let improvisation develop the final script, which was rehearsed thoroughly and exactly for performance.

The Devil is an Ass: Editions

224 Maurice Hussey, ed. London: University Tutorial Press, 1967. 190 pp.

The play should not be considered a work of Jonson's dotage. Notes modern interest in the treatment of greed, the bird imagery, the extended metaphor related to ass and other animal images, and imagery drawn from food, money, and sex. Though his verse lacks Shakespeare's sensuous charm, Jonson is Shakespeare's equal in the "speed and power of conveying thought." Sources include several plays using devils: Grim the Collier of Croydon, Wily Beguiled, The Merry Devil of Edmonton, and Barnabe Barnes' The Devil's Charter. Some of Jonson's masque techniques appear.

Reviewed by B. Harris in YWES 48 (1967):180.

225 Gāmini Salgādo, ed., in his Four Jacobean City Comedies. Harmondsworth, Middlesex, England: Penguin Books, 1975, pp. 9-27 passim, 188-310.

Eastward Ho was the first city comedy to show harsh criticism of London life. The Devil is an Ass is typical of Jacobean city comedy in its satire on bought titles, corrupt courtiers, and cupidity, and in its fascination with London life. Jonson generally is more moralistic than other writers of city comedy, but in The Devil is an Ass his satire is less harsh than usual. The Alchemist is "the finest of all city comedies"; in it, alchemy becomes a metaphor for the kinds of financial and social transformation that "projecting" brought about. Text based on 1631 Quarto.

The Devil is an Ass

The Devil is an Ass: Criticism and Commentary

226 BRY, ANDRÉ. "Middleton et le public des 'City Comedies.'" *Dramaturgie et Société: Rapports entre l'oeuvre théâtrale, son interprétation et son public aux XVIe et XVIIe siècles.* Vol. 2. Edited by Jean Jacquot et al. Paris: Editions du Centre National de la Recherche Scientifique, 1968, 705-27.

The acquisition of noble titles by parvenus is denounced by Jonson in *The Devil is an Ass* (II.iv.20-21), *The Alchemist* (II.vi.52-54) and *The Staple of News* (II.iv.150-59; IV.iii.23-26).

227 GAGEN, JEAN E. *The New Woman: Her Emergence in English Drama 1600-1730*. New York: Twayne Publishers, 1954, pp. 102-04.

Through Lady Tailbush, Jonson adds to the body of female characters who have significant business ambitions outside their homes.

228 JOHNSON, W. NOEL. "The Devil as a Character in Literature." *Manchester Quarterly* 31 (1912):324-41.

The amiable devil, concerned with the family honor, whom Jonson presents in *The Devil is an Ass*, is part of a long literary tradition which casts Satan in a quaint, non-repulsive role.

229 KITTREDGE, GEORGE LYMAN. "King James I and *The Devil is an Ass*." *MP* 9 (1911):195-209.

I.i.12-23 alludes to actual witchcraft trials in Middlesex in 1615; the pretended demoniacal possession of Fitzdottrel, V.viii, is based on an actual occurrence in Leicestershire in 1616, which helps date the play. Since James I was a detector of false demoniacs, and since the latter scene is unnecessary to the plot, Jonson probably used it as a means of "paying a well-deserved compliment to his royal patron."

230 LLOYD, BERTRAM. "Jonson and *Thomas of Woodstock*." *TLS*, 17 July 1924, p. 449.

The reference in *The Devil is an Ass*, II.i., to *Thomas of Woodstock* is probably to the play in Egerton ms. 1994, and suggests a date for it "at least as early as 1616, and perhaps considerably earlier."

231 MILLS, LLOYD L. "The Devil is Indeed an Ass; Or Cosmic Optimism Verified." *SLM* 1 (1975):40-52.

"The contrast between the creative potency of God and the cunning impotency of Satan" is elaborated into an allegorical fable controlling the play "through a double analogy with Christ's incarnation (through parody) and the activities of London confidence men and their gulls (through similarity)."

232 POTTER, RUSSELL. "Three Jacobean Devil Plays." SP 28 (1931): 730-36.
Although The Devil is an Ass added nothing to Jonson's fame, it marks his participation in a popular literary tradition. A trenchant satire, the play focuses on prominent beliefs, values, and projectors of London in the early 17th century.

233 REED, ROBERT R., JR. "Ben Jonson's Pioneering in Sentimental Comedy." N&Q 195 (1950):272-73.
The sentimentalism of the subplot of The Devil is an Ass has been overlooked by critics studying the origins of Restoration sentimental comedy. Jonson anticipates the well-known sentimental formula used by Cibber and other 18th-century dramatists. The concluding lines of the play, spoken by Manly, are unmistakably a "noble sentiment." The Jonsonian formula used in the play--the reform of the intended seducer by an appeal to his subconscious moral goodness--was popular in Caroline comedy, especially Shirley's.

234 SAVAGE, JAMES E. "The Cloaks of The Devil is an Asse." UMSE 6 (1965):5-14. [Reprinted in his Ben Jonson's Comic Characters and Other Essays (1973), pp. 165-75 (see 36).]
The truth of Jonson's play is the reverse of the title: extreme folly accompanied by greed is the extreme vice. This folly is evident in the play each time a character accepts the cloak for the man, thus mistaking appearance for reality. Fitzdottrel consistently errs in this way.

235 SERONSY, CECIL C. "A Skeltonic Passage in Ben Jonson." N&Q 198 (1953):24.
Skeltonic language appears in V.vi.25 ff.

236 ZITNER, S. P. "The Revenge on Charis," in The Elizabethan Theatre IV (1974):127-42 (see 22).
The ironic intentions of the second and third stanzas of "Her Triumph," a part of Jonson's "A Celebration of Charis," are illuminated by their appearance in a comic context in The Devil is an Ass (II.vi).

The Devil is an Ass

The Devil is an Ass: Performance Reviews

237 OLIVER, CORDELIA. "Isolated Marvels." Plays and Players 24 (November 1976):18-19.
Birmingham (England) Repertory Theatre production.

Eastward Ho: Editions

238 John S. Farmer, ed. Tudor Facsimile Texts. Amersham, England: "Issued for subscribers by John S. Farmer," 1914. 64 pp.
Facsimile of the 1605 edition of the play, using the copy in the British Museum.

239 Thomas Marc Parrot, ed., in his The Plays and Poems of George Chapman: The Comedies. London: George Routledge and Sons; New York: E. P. Dutton, 1914, pp. 463-535. Introduction and notes, pp. 835-67. [Reprint. New York: Russell and Russell, 1961.]
Discusses the history and sources of the play, the scandal it caused, its relationship to other plays, and its composite authorship. Proposes that Jonson's contribution "is confined to insertions in the second and fourth acts, to the completion of Marston's work in the fourth and fifth acts, and to the four last scenes of the play." Besides giving advice, Jonson "did little more than revise and finish the work of his collaborators."

240 Julia Hamlet Harris, ed. Yale Studies in English, 73. New Haven: Yale University Press; London: Oxford University Press, 1926. 249 pp.
The play is part of the popular prodigal-son tradition and is most closely related to Gascoigne's Glasse of Government. Little external evidence exists for determining the division of authorship. Act V, usually attributed to Jonson, lacks his tone, manner, economy of characterization, and organization. Jonson's main contributions were probably the play's overall organization and the interpretation of contemporary life within the conventions of the genre. Text for the edition is a reproduction based on the 1605 copy in the Dyce Collection (South Kensington Museum).
Reviewed by F. S. Boas in YWES 7 (1926):141-42; W. W. Greg in MLR 23 (1928):76; in TLS, 21 July 1927, p. 500.

241 C. G. Petter, ed. London: Ernest Benn, 1973. 136 pp.
Reviews previous efforts to assign parts of the play to specific collaborators; suggests Jonson planned the work and was the author of most of Acts IV and V. Discusses date, sources, King James's displeasure, and the

imprisonment of Jonson and Chapman. Appendix reproduces documents related to the imprisonment.

Reviewed by B. Gibbons and B. Harris in YWES 54 (1973): 186; J. C. Maxwell in N&Q 220 (1975):284-86.

See also 17a.

Eastward Ho: Criticism and Commentary

242 BRETTLE, R. E. "Eastward Ho, 1605, by Chapman, Jonson, and Marston: Bibliography, and Circumstances of Production." Library, 4th series 9 (1929):287-302.

On the question of whether the trouble over the play was due to production or publication, Brettle claims that the offensive passages referring to the Scots and James's practice of granting knighthoods appeared in the production and a few copies of the first edition. One chief offending passage was later cancelled in the printed copies, and the type was reset.

243 CLARK, ANDREW. Domestic Drama: A Survey of the Origins, Antecedents and Nature of the Domestic Play in England, 1500-1640. JDS 49, 1975, 2:280.

With its tone alienating it from domestic drama, Eastward Ho is an obvious burlesque of the prodigal-son tradition common to that genre. It offers no protest against the middle-class morality of Westward Ho and is a comic triumph of virtue over vice. Its burlesque quality was enhanced by its dedication to the city and its being staged first at Blackfriars.

244 COHEN, RALPH A. "The Function of Setting in Eastward Ho." RenP (1973):85-96.

Locale inexorably binds together the play's humor, theme, and structure. The Thames acts as an agent of London, offering a warning against social climbing.

245 COOPER, LANE. "A Note on Eastward Ho, I.ii.178." MLN 43 (1928):324-25.

Offers "more illuminating allusions to the elephant and castle" passage than Robert Withington (see 257).

246 COPE, JACKSON I. "Volpone and the Authorship of Eastward Ho." MLN 72 (1957), 253-56.

The similarity of speech between Security (II.ii) and Volpone (I.i.33-39) indicates that Jonson probably wrote that scene of Eastward Ho.

Eastward Ho

247 FARMER, A. J. "Une source de Eastward Hoe: Rabelais." EA 1 (1937):325.

Touchstone's speech on cuckolds (V.v.183-96) is generally attributed to either Jonson or Chapman. Whoever wrote the passage was evidently inspired by a similar passage in Rabelais' Pantagruel, Book III, Chapter 28. Possibly Marston was the author.

248 GILBERT, ALLAN H. "Virginia in Eastward Hoe." MLN 33 (1918):183-84.

Jonson uses travelers' accounts of Virginia from Hakluyt's Principal Navigations.

249 GREG, W. W. "Eastward Ho, 1605." Library, 4th series 9 (1929):303-04.

The printed, rather than the performed, version of the play probably caused Jonson's trouble with the law.

250 HORWICH, RICHARD. "Hamlet and Eastward Ho." SEL 11 (1971): 223-33.

Draws parallels between the two plays. A parody which both intensifies and undercuts Hamlet, Eastward Ho gains an emotional impact by its resonances of Shakespeare's play.

251 LAWRENCE, W. J. Speeding Up Shakespeare. Studies of the By-gone Theatre and Drama. London: Argonaut Press, 1937, pp. 76-86, 103-13. [Reprint. New York: Benjamin Blom, 1968.]

Jonson's usual composition habits and those associated with Eastward Ho show that he did no more than plot out and supervise the play, perhaps writing the Prologue. The same is true of The Widow, which carries his name as a collaborator and from which he may have borrowed parts of The New Inn.

252 LEECH, CLIFFORD. "Three Times Ho and a Brace of Widows: Some Plays for the Private Theatre," in The Elizabethan Theatre III. Papers given at the Third International Conference on Elizabethan Theatre held at the University of Waterloo, Ontario, in July 1970. Edited by David Galloway. Hamden, Conn.: The Shoe String Press, Archon Books; Toronto: Macmillan, 1973, pp. 14-32.

Eastward Ho provides evidence about staging at private theatres. The opening should be taken at face value as Jonson's using what had been successful theatre in his own time. A good-humoured satire, the play is highly unified and incorporates many "in" jokes along with allusions to Shakespeare's works.

253 PEERY, WILLIAM. "Eastward Ho! and A Woman is a Weathercock." MLN 62 (1947):131-32.
A line in Nathan Field's A Woman is a Weathercock (1609) is reminiscent of a passage in Eastward Ho, a play in which Field may well have performed.

254 SCHOENBAUM, S. Internal Evidence and Elizabethan Dramatic Authorship: An Essay in Literary History and Method. Evanston, Ill.: Northwestern University Press, 1966, pp. 100, 168, 173, 225.
Harris' critical edition of Eastward Ho (see 240) lacks sufficient evidence to support her hypotheses about which parts are the work of Chapman, of Jonson, and of Marston. The play is a remarkably consistent piece produced by three highly individualistic authors. Cuts were made by the printers, not by Jonson.

255 SIMPSON, PERCY. "The Problem of Authorship of Eastward Ho!" PMLA 59 (1944):715-25.
Knowledge of the authors' styles indicates that Marston originated the play's idea and worked out the opening scene. Jonson may have done the Prologue and most probably did III.i.1-39; III.ii.83-200; IV.i.185-283; IV.ii; V.i-iii; V.v.1-205. The play, written quickly, reflects Jonson's clear, direct style.

256 SYKES, H. DUGDALE. "The Prologue to Jonson, Chapman, and Marston's Eastward Hoe." N&Q 131 (2 January 1915):5-6.
Chapman, not Jonson, probably wrote the Prologue.

257 WITHINGTON, ROBERT. "A Note on Eastward Ho, I.ii.178." MLN 43 (1928):28-29.
Expands Schelling's notes on Golding's elephant with a "castle on his backe" in the Belles-Lettres edition of Eastward Ho (1910), giving several references from pageantry to illuminate the passage. (See 245.)

Epicoene: Editions

*258 (The Silent Woman). London: Holerth Press, 1924. 126 pp.

*259 W. R. Macklin, ed. London: A. & C. Black, 1926. 95 pp.

260 L. A. Beaurline, ed. Lincoln: University of Nebraska Press, 1966. 182 pp.
Analyzes the complicated plot from the viewpoint of the "varieties of sexual metamorphosis" evident in the characters and in the manoeuvres of Truewit.

Epicoene

261 Edward Partridge, ed. New Haven: Yale University Press, 1971. 216 pp.

Although unique, the play depends on many typical Jonsonian techniques: exposure, baiting, and ironic reversals. Its grim comedy depends on both the gamesmanship of the heroes and the aggressive impulses of the audience. Jonson's concepts of the natural and decorous appear most strongly in the characters' violations through diction and individualized kinds of speech. The epicoene occurs throughout literature, but Jonson drew most heavily from Libanius, Aretino, and Plautus. The audience is called upon to judge all the characters and recognize that the play's greatest achievement comes from the comic life. The text is basically that of Herford and Simpson.

Reviewed by B. Gibbons and B. Harris in YWES 53 (1972): 194-95; R. Gill in N&Q 219 (1974):311-12; A. Rendle in Drama (Summer 1972), p. 77; J. J. Yoch, Jr., in SCN 32 (1974):19.

See also 17a

Epicoene: Translations and Adaptations

*262 ACHARD, MARCEL. La femme silencieuse, in Je ne vous aime pas, comédie en trois actes. La femme silencieuse, comédie en quatre actes, d'après Ben Jonson. Paris: Editions de la Nouvelle Revue Française, 1926. 252 pp. (French adaptation.)

263 BLOX, E., and BLOX, R. Èpisin ili molčalivaja ženščina [Epicoene or the silent woman]. Edited by S. K. Bojanus and J. N. Blox. Peterburg [sic]: Petropolis, 1921. 213 pp. (Russian translation.)

*264 KOENIGSGARTEN, HUGO F. Lord Spleen: Die Geschichte vom lärmscheuen Mann. Komische Oper in 2 Akten. Text von Hugo F. Koenigsgarten. Musik von Mark Lothar. Op. 17. Klavierauszug mit Text. Berlin: A. Fürstner, 1930. (German adaptation.)

265 ZWEIG, STEFAN. Die schweigsame Frau: Komische Oper in drei Aufzügen. Frei nach Ben Jonson von Stefan Zweig. Musik von Richard Strauss. Opus 80. Berlin: Adolph Furstner, 1935. 111 pp. (German adaptation.)

Libretto only.

266 _____. Musik von Richard Strauss. Opus 80. Klavierauszug mit Text von Felix Wolfes. Mainz: B. Schott's Sohne; London: Boosey & Hawkes, 1935. 460 pp.
Vocal score with piano reduction of orchestral score.

Epicoene: Criticism and Commentary

267 ANDERSON, MARK A. "The Successful Unity of Epicoene: a Defense of Ben Jonson." SEL 10 (1970):349-66.
Epicoene provides the key to the play, which emphasizes deceptions and misjudgments in society. Deception of the audience is Jonson's way of equating audience and characters.

268 ANON. "The Silent Woman." The New Statesman and Nation, 6 August 1938, p. 220.
Review of Oxford Playhouse production. Modern audiences are too ignorant and nice to enjoy this play.

269 ARNAUD, LUCIEN. Charles Dullin. Preface by Jean Vilar. Théâtre National Populaire: Collection "Le Théâtre et les Jours," 12. Paris: L'Arche Editeur, 1952, pp. 79-80, 90-93.
Dullin's production of La Femme silencieuse, adaptation by Marcel Achard, was the Atelier's chief success in the 1925-26 season. Jules Romains' version of Stefan Zweig's adaptation of Volpone proved to be a major success in 1929, running over 300 performances.

270 BARISH, JONAS A. "Ovid, Juvenal, and The Silent Woman." PMLA 71 (1956):213-24.
Popular in its own time, the play now sparks great debate. Barish roots its ambiguity in its transitional position, evidenced in the treatment of material from Ovid's Ars Amatoria and Juvenal's Sixth Satire against women. Jonson favors Juvenal's point of view but allows Ovid to prevail in such a way as to distort the original, even while treating Juvenal more directly.

271 BIRRELL, FRANCIS. "The Drama: The Triumph of Ben Jonson." Nation and Athenaeum, 22 November 1924, pp. 295-96.
Review of Phoenix Society production. Praises Jonson's play construction, and states that he is the most underestimated of England's great writers because he "wrote emphatically for the stage, and the stage has hardly existed in England for a hundred and fifty years." Epicoene is "the first English play with the genuine 'Restoration' ring, revealing Ben Jonson as the father of Dryden and Congreve . . . [and] of the modern stage."

Epicoene

272 BOUGHNER, DANIEL C. "Clizia and Epicoene." PQ 19 (1940): 89-91.

Cites Aretino's Il Marescalco and Machiavelli's Clizia as close analogues to Epicoene and agrees with Campbell that Plautus' Casina has little value in studying the sources of Jonson's play. (See 275.)

273 BRADBROOK, M. C. "Dramatic Role as Social Image: A Study of the Taming of the Shrew." Shakespeare-Jahrbuch 94 (1958):132-50.

With the exception of Morose, all the characters in Epicoene "are static, inflexible, all equally interconnected in a web of purely external relationships." The satiric approach represented by Jonson "offers the audience a direct and assured moral judgment."

274 BROWN, IVOR. "The Theatre. Too Rare Ben Jonson." Saturday Review (London), 22 November 1924, pp. 518-19.

Review of Phoenix Theatre production. Finds the play farcical and cruel, and not up to the level of Jonson's best comedies. "The real point of this play, and indeed of most of Jonson's work, is that the life of the town comes bubbling out of the town and on to the stage."

275 CAMPBELL, OSCAR JAMES. "The Relation of Epicoene to Aretino's Il Marescalco." PMLA 46 (1931):752-62.

Jonson's comic motif of the boy disguised as a woman more closely resembles material in Aretino's work than that in Plautus' Casina. In both plays the trick is the central idea of the plot, the woman is impersonated by the boy with a comic intent, and once the disguise scheme has been begun the butt of the joke is forced repeatedly into despair. References in Volpone indicate Jonson's knowledge of Aretino's work.

276 CARPENTER, CHARLES A. "Epicoene Minus Its Secret: Surprise as Expectation." Xavier University Studies 7 (1968):15-22.

Jonson wrote both for audiences that did not anticipate Epicoene's being a boy and those that did. The latter has a joy of expectation fulfilled, can delight more in reactions of other characters, and gains a feeling of being enlightened.

277 D., A. "The Genesis of Jonson's Epicoene." N&Q 193 (1948): 55-56.

Jonson may have been influenced in the creation of Epicoene by Satyrus Peregrinans, a satire appended to a collection of pious poems, Seauen Satyres Applyed to the Weeks (1598), by William Rankins.

278 DONALDSON, IAN. "'A Martyrs Resolution': Jonson's Epicoene." RES 18 (1967):1-15.

The unity of Epicoene is best understood if the drama is related to "festive comedy." The central action is Morose's misanthropy, the harassment that it invites, and its final punishment; this major theme is developed in the context of a parody of a courtly wedding masque. Other themes of the play--the lack of harmony between the public and private worlds of the characters, between appearance and reality, between individuals--are developed in a similar manner.

279 FERNS, JOHN. "Ovid, Juvenal, and The Silent Woman: A Reconsideration." MLR 65 (1970):248-53.

Jonson exercises control over material borrowed from both authors, compressing that from Ovid and expanding that from Juvenal, and introduces contemporary references into it.

280 GRAVES, T. S. "Jonson's Epicoene and Lady Arabella Stuart." MP 14 (1917):525-30.

Lady Arabella took offense at V.i. A pause in delivery could have cast her as a mistress of Stephen Bogdan, pretender to the Moldavian throne.

281 GREG, W. W. "Was There a 1612 Quarto of Epicoene?" Library, 4th series 15 (1934):306-15. [Reprinted in W. W. Greg, Collected Papers. Edited by J. C. Maxwell. Oxford: The Clarendon Press, 1966, pp. 314-21.]

Existence of the Quarto, which Gifford claims to have seen, is doubtful but possible.

282 GRUBBS, HENRY A. "An Early French Adaptation of an Elizabethan Comedy: J. B. Rousseau as an Imitator of Ben Jonson." MLN 55 (1940):170-76.

Jean-Baptiste Rousseau's L'Hypocondre, ou la femme qui ne parle point, based on Epicoene, was "the first French adaptation of a play by Ben Jonson." It was written ca. 1733 but not published until 1751. Although a "respectable adaptation," it received little critical acceptance, was not performed, and fell into obscurity.

283 H., H. "Epicoene, or The Silent Woman!" Observer (London), 23 November 1924, p. 11.

Review of Phoenix Society production. Jonson is a rare, but not insinuating writer, who stuns rather than charms an audience. Although enjoyable as it goes along, Epicoene ends up being rather poor sport.

Epicoene

284 HENRY, HÉLÈNE. "Charles Dullin et le théâtre élisabéthain." *EA* 13 (1960):197-204.

Briefly describes Dullin's 1925 production of Marcel Achard's adaptation of *Epicoene* and his 1928 production of the Zweig-Romains *Volpone*. Reviews some of the artistic debate that arose over the latter.

285 HOGAN, ROBERT, and MOLIN, SVEN ERIC. "Discussion of The *Silent Woman*," in their *Drama: The Major Genres*. New York: Dodd, Mead, 1963, pp. 265-71.

Epicoene exemplifies comedy in the text. Using Dryden's *Essay on Dramatic Poesie*, they draw from his passages on characterization, expand his few hints on comic language, and disagree with his assumption that a well-made comic plot, like that of tragedy, should have no extraneous incidents.

286 KRANIDAS, THOMAS. "Possible Revisions or Additions in Jonson's *Epicoene*." *Anglia* 83 (1965):451-58.

Argues that Jonson revised or added to the script of *Epicoene* during or after 1613 to include two passages that parody incidents in the Essex divorce trial of that year: 1) Morose's impotence (V.iii), and 2) the suggestion that the Ladies Collegiate act as a jury to examine him to attest to his impotence (V.iv).

287 Le COMTE, EDWARD SEMPLE. *The Notorious Lady Essex*. New York: Dial Press, 1969, pp. 206-08.

Epicoene V.iv.33-60, in which Morose states he is impotent, may allude to the Howard-Essex annulment of 1613. The play contains a reference to Simon Forman and possibly an allusion to Thomas Overbury.

288 MacCARTHY, DESMOND. "*The Silent Woman*." *The New Statesman*, 22 November 1924, p. 203.

In reviewing Phoenix performance, finds the play on the whole "mirthless."

289 MERCHANT, PAUL. "Another Misprint in *Epicoene*?" *Library*, 5th Series 27 (1972):326.

"Does" (I.iv.46) should probably read "Doues."

290 PARTRIDGE, E. B. "The Allusiveness of *Epicoene*." *ELH* 22 (1955):93-107.

Much of the comic effect results from juxtaposition of the world of the characters and that suggested by allusions, especially to prodigies, the strange, and to dress. The play is fundamentally concerned with deviations from a norm and stresses decorum. It offers no answers to any of the questions it raises, but suggests that the answers will be comic. George Coleman's acting version (1776) eliminates much of the rich allusiveness.

291 SALINGAR, L. G. "Farce and Fashion in The Silent Woman." E&S 20 (1967):29-46.

Epicoene is a farce combined with some elements of what was to become the comedy of manners. Reviewing the qualities and characteristics of medieval farce, Salingar explicates the play, with reference to Aristotle's conjectured definition of comedy. Defending Truewit as "farceur," Salingar argues against Barish's view of the work as satire. The play is highly topical.

292 SAWIN, LEWIS. "The Earliest Use of 'Autumnal.'" MLN 69 (1954):558-59.

Points out the use of "autumnal" in the sense of "past the prime (of life)" in Epicoene, I.i.83-85, thus providing proof of one use of "autumnal" forty-six years earlier than OED entry.

293 SHAPIRO, MICHAEL. "Audience vs. Dramatist in Jonson's Epicoene and Other Plays of the Children's Troupes." ELR 3 (1973):400-17.

Playwrights for private theatres and children's troupes incorporated exhortations to acceptable theatre behavior into their plays. Epicoene, the most ambitious, rewarding attempt to control audience behavior, ridicules vanities of upper social classes and offers models of differing degrees of social detachment.

294 SLIGHTS, WILLIAM W. E. "Epicoene and the Prose Paradox." PQ 49 (1970):178-87.

The play includes many types of the prose paradox, a popular Renaissance genre. The barrage of language may alienate modern audiences.

295 TAYLOR, MARION A. "Lady Arabella Stuart and Beaumont and Fletcher." PLL 8 (1972):252-60.

Although scholars have generally agreed that Lady Arabella's anger at being slandered in a contemporary play was directed toward Epicoene, there are more allusions to her in The Knight of the Burning Pestle.

296 TAYLOR, MICHAEL. "Jonson's Epicoene: Art for Nature's Sake." HAB 20 (1969):56-67.

The play explores the interdependency of great art and superior morality through shades of differences rather than confrontation of good and evil. Characters' inconsistencies become part of the total design; the subplot offers burlesque on theme of art-nature.

Epicoene: Performance Reviews

297 CAPELL, RICHARD. "Richard Strauss's Silent Woman." Monthly Musical Record 65 (1935):156-57.
Reviews the performance of the Zweig-Strauss Die schweigsame Frau at Dresden on 24 June 1935. Notes lack of similarity to Jonson's original.

298 TWOMBLEY, ROBERT. "Jonson's Epicoene: Departmental Play Delightfully Absurd." The Daily Texan, 26 March 1976.

Every Man in his Humour: Editions

299 Percy Simpson, ed. Oxford: Clarendon Press, 1919. 239 pp.
Jonson considered the play the starting point of his dramatic achievement and reworked it in great detail; it took final shape when he began work on the Folio. The tradition of "humours" had already been overused in Renaissance England; Jonson's contribution consisted in the additional concept of mirroring and anatomizing. The basic text of the edition is the 1601 Quarto.

300 Henry Holland Carter, ed. Yale Studies in English, 52. New Haven: Yale University Press; London: Oxford University Press, 1921. 553 pp.
Comparison of the Quarto and Folio texts shows Jonson's process of reflection, his stripping away of the Italian and his emphasis on England--his traditional mental background. The Quarto text was both expanded and condensed, with many changes in expression and syntax. Evidence about dating remains uncertain. The edition lists actors for performances between 1767 and 1825. Quarto and Folio texts are printed on opposite pages.
Reviewed by A. Nicoll in YWES 3 (1922):95-96.

301 R. S. Knox, ed. London: Methuen, 1923, 145 pp. ["Second edition," 1949, appears identical to 1923 edition.]
Summarizes Jonson's comic theory and practice as evidenced in the Prologue and the play itself. Briefly discusses questions of date of first performance and of revisions appearing in the 1616 Folio, which is the basis of the text. Examines construction, characters, and style.

302 G. B. Harrison, ed. London: Robert Holden, 1926. 154 pp.
Notes as Jonson's contribution to English drama his development of critical theory which shaped all the "mongrel" elements that contributed to English comedy--Latin comedy, the old interlude, and the extemporaneous wit of the clown--and his comedies written according to his theory.
Reviewed by F. Birrell in Nation & Athenaeum, 5 March 1927, p. 764.

303 John Kennair Peel, ed. The Borzoi Acting Versions of English Dramatists. London: Knopf, 1928. 161 pp.
Based on the thesis that Jonson's plays are unactable as written for publication, the edition expurgates and cuts the text for acting purposes on a non-commercial stage. The edition offers a popularized life of Jonson and adds stage directions within the play.

*304 Arthur Sale, ed. Second edition. London: University Tutorial Press, 1949. 152 pp. [Introduction reprinted in Ben Jonson: A Collection of Critical Essays (1963), pp. 75-81 (see 3).]

305 Martin Seymour-Smith, ed. London: Ernest Benn, 1966. 160 pp.
Discusses Jonson's theory of humours, his characterization, and the reasons for and the effect of revisions in the play. Only Kitely, Old Kno'well and, to some extent, Downright qualify as humours characters. Critics have misunderstood Jonson's moral intent; he was anti-establishment and often ignored Sidney and critical principles in the plays. The text follows the 1616 Folio in everything but spelling.
Reviewed by G. R. Proudfoot in N&Q 213 (1968):154-55; in TLS, 16 March 1967, p. 225.

306 Gabriele Bernhard Jackson, ed. New Haven, London: Yale University Press, 1969. 259 pp.
Jonson presents, in embryo, the major topics and methods employed in his dramatic canon. A comedy of interaction, the play moves from varied points to accidental rather than essential meeting points. It illustrates the natural conclusion of Jonsonian comedy: fragmentation of an arbitrary reconstruction of society. The primary action stems from the characters' fear of developing unmediated relationships; they cohere by contrast and parody each other's behavior. The 1616 Folio text is employed.
Reviewed by N. W. Bawcutt in YES 2 (1972):256; R. Gill in N&Q 217 (1972):279-80; B. Harris in YWES 51 (1970): 185-86; W. D. Kay in MP 69 (1972):339-41; M. Mincoff in ES 53 (1972):557-58.

Every Man in his Humour

307 J. W. Lever, ed. Lincoln: University of Nebraska Press, 1971. 324 pp.

Jonson's first clear success, the play offers a fine coordination of the basic elements of comedy. Jonson uses "humour" as a current, vogue word rather than as it is used in later works; "gentleman," however, is the work's essential word. The play's second version reshapes almost every aspect: structure, setting, and language; characterization is deepened and made complex. The date of the revision remains uncertain. The edition presents the 1601 Quarto and the 1616 Folio texts on facing pages.

Reviewed by B. Harris and B. Gibbons in YWES 52 (1971): 194.

308 Claude J. Summers, ed. Menston, Yorkshire: Scolar Press, 1972. 92 pp.

The play was Jonson's "first undisputed success"; evidence shows that it was performed initially in the late summer of 1598. Briefly reviews early publication history, and mentions several notable stage performances. Text is a facsimile of the 1601 Quarto.

Reviewed in SCN 31 (1973):91.

See also 17a

Every Man in his Humour: Criticism and Commentary

309 AYLWARD, J. D. "The Inimitable Bobadill." N&Q 195 (1950): 2-4, 28-31.

Suggests Rocco Bonetti, a famous Italian master of the rapier, as the origin of Bobadill in Every Man in his Humour. (See 314.)

310 BOAS, FREDERICK S. "The Soldier in Elizabethan and Later English Drama." EDH 19 (1942):121-56.

Brainworm's pretense of being a soldier returned from the wars reflects actual practice, as seen in government documents of the 16th century. Bobadill, however, and Captain Tucca of Poetaster, depend on the literary prototype of the miles gloriosus, rather than historical reality, and are "essentially un-English in their blending of boastfulness and cowardice."

311 BROWN, IVOR. "Every Man in his Humour." Observer (London), 8 August 1937, p. 11.

Review of Stratford performance. There is little plot in the play; "nowadays the text seems long and heavy."

312 BRYANT, J. A., JR. "Jonson's Revision of Every Man in his Humor." SP 59 (1962):641-50.
Discusses Jonson's adaptation of Roman comedy structure from The Case is Altered to Bartholomew Fair. Intrigue is consistently used for more than gaining audience attention. Distracted by the humours theory in Every Man out of his Humour, Jonson demanded too much of it and ended up moralizing. Therefore, he reshaped the play in his Works chiefly by converting the stereotypes into convincing characters and using a design comparable to "the predictable course of a disease, moving from symptoms to aggravation to crisis to cure."

313 BURTON, ANTHONY. "Forster on the Stage." Dickensian 70 (1974):171-84.
Dickens played Bobadill in his amateur company's production; John Forster played Kitely.

314 BUTLER, K. T. "Some Further Information about Rocco Bonetti." N&Q 195 (1950):95-96.
Adds details to J. D. Aylward's account of Rocco Bonetti (suggested model for Bobadill) and, drawing on state papers, corrects some of Aylward's data. (See 309.)

315 CAMDEN, CARROLL. "The Mind's Construction in the Face." PQ 20 (1941):400-12.
Although Edward Kno'well expresses a belief in the theory of physiognomy (I.iii.122-27), Jonson "gives the lie to physiognomy" in Amorphus' speech to Asotus (Cynthia's Revels, II.iii.11-69), where the theory is refuted.

316 COLLEY, JOHN S. "Opinion, Poetry, and Folly in Every Man in His Humor." SAB 39 (November 1974):10-21.
The Quarto edition of the play emphasizes Jonson's belief in the relationship between poetry and right reason and his fascination with Opinion--a 16th-century emblem of self-deception and moral blindness. Victims of Opinion, the play's characters pervert normal approaches to parenthood, marriage, and literature. The formula proves workable in later plays, also, but in them the satiric pattern becomes more subtle and characters' violations more extreme.

317 DENT, ALAN. "Rare Ben," in his Preludes and Studies. London: Macmillan, 1942, pp. 130-36. [Reprint. Port Washington, N.Y.: Kennikat Press, 1970.]
The only event marking the tercentenary of Jonson's death took place in 1937 at Stratford, where the Festival Company played four performances of Every Man in his Humour. The play, like much of Jonson, is beyond the

comprehension and interest of modern audiences, which prefer sentiment and romance. The 1938 revival of Volpone at the Westminster Theatre was "well enough done to remind us that this great comedy is larger than life and twice as unnatural."

318 DUTTON, A. RICHARD. "The Significance of Jonson's Revision of Every Man in His Humour." MLR 69 (1974):241-49.
Important elements in major plays can be traced to the revision of Every Man in his Humour. Jonson underwent a change in 1605.

319 EATON, WALTER PRICHARD. The Drama in English. New York: Charles Scribner's Sons, 1930, pp. 110-22.
The great influence that the dull, flat, clumsily developed Every Man in his Humour had on the theatre for 200 years was pernicious because it fostered the imitation of Jonson's superficial realism, and his dependence on exaggerated, easily acted characters and easily grasped stock effects.

320 EEKHOUD, GEORGES. "La Plēiade Shakespearienne: Ben Jonson." La Sociētē Nouvelle 17 (1911):71-89.
In a brief review of Jonson's life and works, notes a "mediocre" French translation of Every Man in his Humour written by Mennechet in 1827.

321 FIJN VAN DRAAT, P. "Sheridan's Rivals and Ben Jonson's Everyman in His Humour." Neophil 18 (1933):144-50.
Sheridan's dependence on Jonson amounts to plagiarism.

322 FOLTINEK, HERBERT. "Uber die Methode des Motivvergleichs: Dargestellt an englischen Literatur-werken." EM 15 (1964): 103-33.
In studying the treatment of similar motives in pieces of literature from the same era, compares the Kno'well Senior and Junior relationship in Every Man in his Humour to the Polonius-Laertes-Ophelia relationship in Hamlet.

323 GARDNER, THOMAS. "'A Parodie! A Parodie!': Conjectures on the Jonson-Daniel Feud," in Lebende Antike: Symposion für Rudolf Sühnel. Edited by Horst Meller and Hans-Joachim Zimmermann. Berlin: Erich Schmidt Verlag, 1967, pp. 197-206.
Daniel's attack on Jonson via his masque Tethys' Festival, particularly its parody of "Come my Celia," may account for Jonson's change in the 1601 Quarto of Every Man in his Humour (V.iii.289) to incorporate an attack on Daniel and his practices.

324 HARDISON, O. B. "Three Types of Renaissance Catharsis." *RenD* NS 2 (1969):3-22.
Nonacademic theories of catharsis, which influenced dramatists, were mainly moral, religious, and literal. *Every Man in his Humour* embodies the religious theory, in which the punishment closely fits the crime.

325 HERRICK, MARVIN T. *Italian Comedy in the Renaissance*. Urbana: University of Illinois Press, 1960, pp. 117-19, passim. [Reprint. Freeport, N.Y.: Books for Libraries Press, 1970.]
Kitely may have been inspired by the jealous husband in Ercole Bentivoglio's *The Jealous Man*, and Bobadill by the soldier Brandonio from the same play.

326 HIBERNICUS. "A Jonson Crux." *TLS*, 4 February 1932, p. 76.
An additional possibility exists of explaining *Every Man in his Humour* IV.vi.: the voices were voices when the speakers were unseen, men when they were seen.

327 HILLEBRAND, HAROLD NEWCOMB. *Edmund Kean*. New York: Columbia University Press, 1933, pp. 161-62. [Reprint. New York: AMS Press, 1966.]
Kean's two performances as Kitely in 1861 contained nothing remarkable.

328 KALLICH, MARTIN. "Unity of Time in *Every Man in his Humor* and *Cynthia's Revels*." *MLN* 57 (1942):445-49.
In revising Quarto versions of his plays for the 1616 Folio, Jonson changed *Every Man in his Humour* to conform to the neoclassical rule of action being completed within twelve hours. He exhibited carelessness in this regard in *Cynthia's Revels*.

329 LAWRENCE, W. J. "The Casting-Out of Ben Jonson." *TLS*, 8 July 1920, p. 438.
The masque Jonson told Drummond he had been ousted from was Daniel's *Vision of the Twelve Goddesses*; connects this event with a suggestion that Daniel was satirized as Matheo in *Every Man in his Humour* (1598) and as Fastidious Brisk in *Every Man out of his Humour*. (*See* 330, 338, 339.)

330 _____. "The Casting-Out of Ben Jonson." *TLS*, 22 July 1920, p. 472.
Quotes J. H. Penniman in support of his opinion that Daniel is satirized as Matheo in *Every Man in his Humour* (1598) and Fastidious Brisk in *Every Man out of his Humour*. (*See* 329, 338, 339.)

Every Man in his Humour

331 LEVIN, LAWRENCE L. "Clement Justice in Every Man in his Humour." SEL 12 (1972):291-307.
Clement embodies Jonson's idea of a justice and functions as a poet-reformer.

332 LEWIS, C. S. "Variation in Shakespeare and Others," in his Rehabilitation and Other Essays. London: Oxford University Press, 1939, pp. 159-80. [Reprint. Freeport, N.Y.: Books for Library Press, 1972.]
"Construction" differs from "variation" in that it does a thing as well as possible and moves to another while "variation" repeats the same thing several times. Every Man in his Humour (III.i) relies strongly on the popular Elizabethan variation.

333 McGLINCHEE, CLAIRE. "Still Harping. . . . " SQ 6 (1955): 362-64.
Since Shakespeare acted in Every Man in his Humour, and was, consequently, familiar with the lines of Elder Kno'well's advice to his nephew Stephen, those lines may have influenced him in writing the "precepts" speech of Polonius.

334 MAXWELL, J. C. "Comic Mispunctuation in Every Man in his Humour." ES 33 (1952):218-19.
Simpson missed the small joke in Jonson's intentional mispunctuation of Every Man in his Humour, III.iv.61-62, 66-67, in the Quarto text.

335 ROLLIN, ROGER B. "Images of Libertinism in Every Man in His Humor and 'To His Coy Mistress.'" PLL 6 (1970):188-91.
Marvell possibly read or saw Jonson's play and drew on it for images and the witty, philandering hero. Both authors use the invitation-to-love tradition.

336 SCOUFOS, ALICE LYLE. "Nashe, Jonson, and the Oldcastle Problem." MP 65 (1968):307-24.
Lord Cobham, a member of the Oldcastle-Cobham family, which attracted much satire, may have been satirized in Jonson and Nashe's lost play, The Isle of Dogs (1597), for which the dramatists were severely punished. Jonson revenged himself in Every Man in his Humour by creating the water-carrier Cob, by whom he probably meant to satirize the younger Lord Cobham, who held the post of Lord Warden of the Cinque Ports.

337 SEWELL, SALLIE. "The Relation between The Merry Wives of Windsor and Jonson's Every Man in His Humour." SAB 16 (1941):175-89.
Shakespeare was following Every Man in his Humour in writing The Merry Wives of Windsor, as seen in plot, characters, characterization, and objects of satire.

338 SIMPSON, PERCY. "The Casting-Out of Ben Jonson." TLS, 15 July 1920, p. 456.
Without offering an alternative, disagrees with Lawrence's claim that Jonson satirized Daniel in Every Man in his Humour (1598) and Every Man out of his Humour. (See 329, 330, 339.)

339 _____. "The Casting-Out of Ben Jonson." TLS, 5 August 1920, pp. 504-05.
The portrait of Matheo in Every Man in his Humour (1598) is that of a typical gull, and cannot be connected specifically to Daniel. (See 329, 330, 338.)

340 SPENCER, THEODORE. "The Elizabethan Malcontent," in Joseph Quincy Adams Memorial Studies. Edited by James G. McManaway, Giles E. Dawson, Edwin E. Willoughby. Washington: Folger Shakespeare Library, 1948, pp. 523-35.
Mathew's teasing (Every Man in his Humour III.i) is in terms of artificial melancholy, a type associated with satire and social climbing.

341 STRATMAN, CARL J. "Scotland's First Dramatic Periodical: The Edinburgh Theatrical Censor." TN 17 (Spring 1963): 83-86.
Every Man in his Humour was performed in Scotland between 21 March and 30 July 1803.

342 TAYLOR, GEORGE C. "Did Shakespeare, Actor, Improvise in Every Man in His Humour?" in Joseph Quincy Adams Memorial Studies. Edited by James G. McManaway, Giles E. Dawson, Edwin E. Willoughby. Washington: Folger Shakespeare Library, 1948, pp. 21-32.
Evidence indicates Shakespeare played, and extemporized, in this play. He probably took the part of Kitely.

Every Man out of his Humour

Every Man out of his Humour: Editions

343 F. P. Wilson and W. W. Greg, eds. Malone Society. London: Oxford University Press, 1921. 141 pp.
The edition is based on the pre-1600 Quarto owned by the British Museum; doubtful and irregular readings are listed.
Reviewed by F. S. Boas in YWES 2 (1920-21):87-88.

Every Man out of his Humour: Criticism and Commentary

344 BISHOP, DAVID H. "Shylock's Humour." SAB 23 (1948):174-80.
Shylock's use of the word "humour" (Merchant of Venice IV.i.44) is essentially equivalent to that intended by Jonson in the Induction.

345 BLEIBTRAU, KARL. Shakespeares Geheimnis. Bern: Bircher, 1923, pp. 119, 121.
Sees Sogliardo as a take-off on Shakespeare.

346 COPE, JACKSON I. The Theater and the Dream: From Metaphor to Form in Renaissance Drama. Baltimore: Johns Hopkins University Press, 1973, pp. 226-36.
Every Man out of his Humour offers a paradigm of Mazzoni's argument relating to the paradox of illusion and the presence of the author as a character in his play. By linking Asper, Macilente, Buffone, and himself, Jonson expands the concept of the satiric figure and offers simultaneous acting and watching. The central metaphor and effect of the play is dissolution. Macilente does for the play world what Jonson wished to do for the real world: dissolve it and have himself remain. The dream becomes an anti-structure.

347 ELIOT, SAMUEL A., JR. "The Lord Chamberlain's Company as Portrayed in Every Man Out of His Humour," in Essays Contributed in Honor of President William Allan Neilson. Edited by Caroline B. Bourland et al. Smith College Studies in Modern Languages, 21, nos. 1-4. Northampton, Mass.: Department of Modern Languages of Smith College, 1939, pp. 64-80.
Jonson expressly designed Every Man out of his Humour for the Lord Chamberlain's Company as it was playing Every Man in his Humour. Much of the characterization for the latter came to Jonson as the Admiral's Company performed Chapman's An Humorous Day's Mirth. Distribution of parts for Every Man in his Humour, best done by looking backwards from other parts written for the actors, indicates Shakespeare played "Old" Lorenzo (Kno'well) and Richard Burbage took the part of Musco (Brainworm). Disagrees with T. W. Baldwin's attribution of roles.

348 GILBERT, ALLAN H. "The Italian Names in Every Man out of his Humour." SP 44 (1947):195-208.
Names of the characters in Every Man out of his Humour are transparencies which tell the spectators something about each character; they were probably drawn from John Florio's A Worlde of Wordes (1598).

349 GRAY, ARTHUR. "Shakespeare's 'Purge' of Jonson." TLS, 10 May 1928, p. 358.
Opposes view that Shakespeare's Nym is supposed to represent Jonson, and claims "rather palpable evidences of the similarity between Jaques and Jonson." There are "unmistakable echoes of Every Man out of his Humour in As You Like It." (See 363.)

350 GRUND, GARY R. "Ben Jonson, John Hoskyns, and the Anti-Ciceronian Movement." SELit 54 (1977):33-53.
Points out that the satirical characterization of Fastidious Brisk, "who made the Arcadia the standard in pure phrases and choice figures," is not aimed at Arcadianism but at the kind of linguistic behavior Brisk represents.

351 HOOKHAM, GEORGE. "Corporal Nym and Ben Jonson." TLS, 26 January 1922, p. 61.
Arthur Quiller-Couch and J. D. Wilson's tentative identification of Nym as Jonson would be confirmed if Jonson intended Sogliardo, of Every Man out of his Humour, as Shakespeare, indicating an extended quarrel between them. Possibly Carlo Buffone "is meant for Falstaff."

352 HUNTER, G. K. "English Folly and Italian Vice: The Moral Landscape of John Marston." Jacobean Theatre. Stratford-upon-Avon Studies, 1 (1960):85-111.
Refers to Jonson's Every Man out of his Humour as possessing "comic logic coupled to an unsparing social realism, and an insistence on judgement, which is completely new in Elizabethan comedy."

353 KITTLE, WILLIAM. Edward de Vere, 17th Earl of Oxford, and Shakespeare. Baltimore: Monumental Printing Co., 1942, pp. 187-92.
The play is, in part, Jonson's burlesque of the grant of a coat of arms to John Shakespeare in 1596. The fact that Shakespeare is listed among the actors in Every Man out of his Humour in 1598 and Sejanus in 1603 proves that Shakespeare was in London between those dates.

Every Man out of his Humour

354 LAWRENCE, EDWIN DURNING. "The Player in Ratsei's Ghost and Sogliardo." Baconiana 10 (1912):207-09.
Every Man out of his Humour, III.iv.46-87, glances at Shakespeare's obtaining a grant of arms. Sogliardo is Shakespeare; Puntarvolo "undoubtedly is Bacon."

355 LEGOUIS, ÉMILE. "La littérature anglaise au XVIIe siècle: Ben Jonson." Revue des Cours et Conférences, 11 May 1911, pp. 397-406.
Jonson presents some characters in his Epigrams as he does "The Character of the Persons" at the beginning of Every Man out of his Humour.

356 McNEAL, THOMAS H. "Every Man out of his Humour and Shakespeare's Sonnets." N&Q 197 (1952):376.
Jonson borrowed the conceit of the "tickling" of the viola da gamba from Shakespeare's Sonnet 128 and the opening speech from Sonnet 29.

357 MAIN, WILLIAM W. "'Insula Fortunata' in Jonson's Every Man out of his Humour." N&Q 199 (1954):197-98.
"The fortunate island" where Jonson lays the scene for Every Man out of his Humour probably refers to the birthplace of Folly in Erasmus' In Praise of Folly. The Erasmian allusion would have enhanced the satire for contemporary Elizabethans.

358 MATCHETT, WILLIAM H. The Phoenix and the Turtle: Shakespeare's Poem and Chester's "Loves Martyr." The Hague: Mouton, 1965. 213 pp., passim.
Jonson's praise of Elizabeth and bids for favor in Every Man out of his Humour and Cynthia's Revels stem, in great part, from his desire to clear himself from any disfavor caused by his pro-Essex poems appended to Loves Martyr. In Poetaster Jonson hoped to defend himself by ridiculing anyone suspecting the real interpretation of Chester's poem.

359 MATHEW, FRANK. An Image of Shakespeare. London: Jonathan Cape, 1922, pp. 317-51. [Reprint. New York: Haskell House, 1972.]
Jonson drew a friendly picture of Shakespeare in Every Man out of his Humour (Cordatus) and offered a humourous description in the Induction to Cynthia's Revels.

360 SELBY, ROBERT H. "The Italian Names in Ben Jonson's Every Man Out of His Humour." Of Edsels and Marauders, Publication 1, South-Central Names Institute. Commerce, Texas: Names Institute Press, 1971, pp. 97-106.

Every Italian name in the play is an Italian word taken from John Florio's A Worlde of Wordes (1598). A comparison between Florio's definitions and Jonson's explanations of the "humours" of his characters show Jonson's dependence on the definitions (supplied in an appendix).

361 SNUGGS, HENRY L. "Fynes Moryson and Jonson's Puntarvolo." MLN 51 (1936):230-34.
Moryson's description of his trip to Constantinople in 1595 refers to speculating upon travel abroad, thus providing an historical reference to the practice Jonson satirizes in Puntarvolo. Although Jonson claimed he did not satirize specific individuals, he did so in The Case is Altered, Every Man out of his Humour, and Poetaster.

362 _____. "The Source of Jonson's Definition of Comedy." MLN 65 (1950):543-44.
Jonson's definition of comedy, spoken by Cordatus in Every Man out of his Humour, draws upon that attributed to Cicero by Donatus but also translates and paraphrases Minturno's definition in the Fourth Book of De Poeta.

363 TILLEY, M. P. "Shakespeare's 'Purge' of Jonson." TLS, 11 October 1928, p. 736.
Discounts the claim that there are specific, deliberate echoes of Every Man out of his Humour in As You Like It, and that Jaques is Jonson. (See 349.)

364 VOCHT, HENRY de. Comments on the Text of Ben Jonson's "Every Man Out of His Humour." Materials for the Study of the Old English Drama, Series 2, Vol. 14. Louvain: Uystpruyst, 1937. 175 pp. [Reprinted. Vaduz: Kraus, 1963.]
While the printers of Jonson's original Quarto presented his manuscript as faithfully as possible, printers of the 1616 Folio distorted the Quarto's text by changes in spelling, orthography, and stage directions. How or why Jonson allowed such changes remains unknown. Mrs. Simpson, in disagreeing with the thesis that Jonson did not supervise the printing of the Folio, has not presented sufficient evidence to negate it.

The Magnetic Lady: Editions

365 Harvey W. Peck, ed. Yale Studies in English, 47. New York: Henry Holt and Co., 1914. 268 pp.
Although it contains only a slight allegory and lacks the unifying force of a central satiric motive, the play should not be dismissed as simply a work of Jonson's dotage. Jonson drew upon Chaucer, Plato, and Aristotle as well as his

own earlier works; many of the play's characters resemble those he had previously created. The topics presented are those popular in the non-dramatic satires. The play belongs to the class which represents character mainly through speech: it errs by having too much monologue. The basic text for the edition is that of the 1640 Folio; variants are noted.

The Magnetic Lady: Criticism and Commentary

366 CHAMPION, LARRY S. "The Magnetic Lady: The Close of Ben Jonson's Circle." SHR 2 (1968):104-21. [An abridgement of Chapter VI of his Ben Jonson's "Dotages" (see 8).]
The play is "a dramatic portrayal of [Jonson's] ars poetica. . . . it illustrates a remarkable summation of Jonson's comic technique." Though in comic intention the play is "manifestly consistent" with his earlier work, it is "by no means merely a repetition of earlier creation."

367 COPE, JACKSON I. "Jonson on the Christ College Dons." MLN 74 (1959):101-02.
Identifies an allusion in The Magnetic Lady to Cambridge religious quarrels involving three rival parties during the twenties and early thirties.

368 FOREY, MARGARET. "Cleveland's 'Square-Cap': Some Questions of Structure and Date." DUJ 36 (1975):170-79.
In connection with John Cleveland's use of the term "calot" or "callot," cites Jonson's use of it in The Magnetic Lady, I.vii.68. Believes Herford and Simpson are wrong in identifying a callot as the coif of a sergeant-at-law; it was, rather, a leather cap worn for fashion's sake in court circles.

369 McFARLAND, RONALD E. "Jonson's Magnetic Lady and the Reception of Gilbert's De Magnete." SEL 11 (1971):283-93.
Jonson's play offers a commentary on what an educated Englishman would have known about magnetism thirty years after Gilbert's work. The scientific metaphor provides the only unique device in an otherwise weak play. The magnet conceit gives the drama a compact, coherent structure and appears in names, puns, technical word play, and theme (the power of money to attract).

The New Inn: Criticism and Commentary

370 ARONSTEIN, PHILIPP. "Fletchers Love's Pilgrimage und Ben Jonsons The New Inn." Englische Studien 43 (1911):234-41.

Concludes, in connection with similarity of passages in Love's Pilgrimage (I.i) and The New Inn (II.i and III.i), that Jonson wrote the passage in the former play and later took it over, partially improved it, and used it for The New Inn.

371 BRIGGS, WILLIAM DINSMORE. "Ben Jonson: Notes on Underwoods XXX and on The New Inn." MP 10 (1913):573-85.
Lovell's discourse on "true valour" in the play relates directly to parallel passages in the poem, which has its roots in Aristotle, Seneca, and Cicero. The Aristotelian philosophy offered does not blend well with the Senecan, but Jonson was more interested in presenting the art of life than a congruent philosophical unit.

372 CHAMPION, L. S. "The Comic Intent of Jonson's The New Inn." WHR 18 (1964):66-74.
A parody of false love and valor, the play is a highly imaginative romantic comedy with a plot too complex for successful staging. Jonson intends to expose hypocrisy and pretension.

373 DUNCAN, DOUGLAS. "A Guide to The New Inn." EIC 20 (1970): 311-26.
Spoofing romantic comedy, Jonson contrasts idealism committed to disappointment and irony dedicated to good cheer. Play fails by being too much of a game on Jonson's terms.

374 FOAKES, R. A. "Mr. Levin and 'Good Bad Drama'." EIC 22 (1972):327-29.
Although erring in many points, Levin points out an important danger in his criticism of The New Inn: most Renaissance plays exist only in texts, not performances, and a variety of interpretations is therefore possible. Many of the plays tend toward being burlesques. (See 377.)

375 HAWKINS, HARRIETT. "The Idea of Theater in Jonson's The New Inn." RenD 9 (1966):205-26.
Jonson's "highly experimental" use of the theatrum mundi commonplace in The New Inn was too demanding for his audience but makes the play of continuing interest to scholars. He "constantly stresses, for comic purposes, the feigning and teaching themes which the theatrum mundi commonplace had acquired."

The New Inn

376 HOTSON, LESLIE. Shakespeare by Hilliard. Berkeley and Los Angeles: University of California Press; London: Chatto and Windus, 1977, pp. 175-76.

Prudence, "in Ben Jonson's leap-year play The New Inn," resembles "Shakespeare's leap-year gentlewoman Maria. . . ."

377 LEVIN, RICHARD. "The New Inn and the Proliferation of Good Bad Drama." EIC 22 (1972):41-47.

Laetitia's transformations are important not for their number but for the reversals they allow when revealed. Had Jonson been spoofing romantic comedy in his ending, he would have indicated such in his many comments reacting to the play's poor reception. Labeling defective Elizabethan dramas as spoofs or parodies can indicate failure to believe playwrights had either apprenticeships or dotages.

378 LODGE, OLIVER. "A Ben Jonson Puzzle," TLS, 13 September 1974, p. 465.

Jonson changed the Chambermaid's name from "Cis" to "Pru" in The New Inn because the original name suggested hissing, especially when pronounced frequently as it is in Act II by Lady Frances Frampul. Since the play was a "first-night" failure, Jonson probably did not wish to give other audiences any onomatopoetic suggestions.

379 MAXWELL, BALDWIN. "The Date of Love's Pilgrimage and its Relation to The New Inn." SP 28 (1931):702-09. [Reprinted in his Studies in Beaumont, Fletcher, and Massinger (1939), pp. 107-115 (see 1189).]

Accounts for lines common to the two plays by suggesting that Jonson borrowed from Fletcher.

380 MOORE, RAYBURN S. "Some Notes on the 'Courtly Love' System in Jonson's The New Inn," in Essays in Honor of Walter Clyde Curry. Edited by Richmond C. Beatty. Nashville: Vanderbilt University Press, 1954, pp. 133-42.

Jonson's treatment of the "courtly love" conventions in The New Inn was influenced by the Platonic love doctrine as sponsored and practiced at court by Queen Henrietta Maria. Jonson uses the court of love and other "courtly love" conventions for satiric purposes.

381 PARTRIDGE, E. B. "A Crux in Jonson's The New Inne." MLN 71 (1957):168-70.

Looked at in context, V.ii.15-16 is an example of Jonson's dramatic irony. Lady Frampul sees the incident of the soiled gown as an opportunity for Pru to revive Lovel's love for her by asking him to rescue her clothes that had been soiled by the fat body of a boor. The reasoning is comic enough in itself; the concept is a facet of the underlying motif that clothes have a religious value and independent existence.

382 ROSS, ALAN S. C., and REES, D. G. "Face It Out with a Card of Ten." N&Q 211 (1966):403-07.
The lines, "Some must be knaues, some varlets, baudes and ostlers,/As aces, duizes, cards o' ten, to face it/Out, i' the game, which all the world is" (The New Inn, I.iii. 105-107), refer to the game of primero, in which a card worth only ten points was of the lowest value. "Facing it out" suggests the possibility of continuing play, as in modern poker, in the hopes of improving one's hand. "I have fac'd it with a card of ten" occurs in The Taming of the Shrew, II.i.397.

383 SENSABAUGH, G. F. "Love Ethics in Platonic Court Drama, 1625-1642." HLQ 1 (1938):277-304.
Queen Henrietta Maria's interest in "Platonic love" is related to Jonson's treatment of the doctrine in The New Inn, where "the typical Platonique appears in Lady Frances Frampul."

Poetaster: Editions

384 Josiah H. Penniman, ed., in his "Poetaster," by Ben Jonson, and "Satiromastix," by Thomas Dekker. Boston and London: D. C. Heath, 1913. 526 pp.
Poetaster played an important role in the War of the Theatres, with its characters representing specific people in the theatrical world. Text of the edition is that of the 1616 Folio.
Reviewed by J. Q. Adams, Jr. in JEGP 13 (1914):613-24.

385 Henry de Vocht, ed. Materials for the Study of the Old English Drama, Series 2, Vol. 9. Louvain: Uystpruyst, 1934. 143 pp. [Reprint. Vaduz: Kraus, 1965.]
Uses 1602 Quarto. Comparison with the Folio indicates the dependence of the latter on the former, and the latter's superiority. The edition does not include several lengthy passages probably composed about 1602, missing from the Quarto but added to the Folio.

Poetaster: Criticism and Commentary

386 ADAMS, JOSEPH QUINCY, JR. "The Source of the Banquet Scene in The Poetaster." MLN 27 (1912):30.
The scene owes more to Lucian (Zeus the Tragedian and The Conversation of the Gods) than to Homer (Iliad I,

493-611) for its spirit and its way of representing Greek gods.

387 ANDERSON, DONALD K. "The Banquet of Love in English Drama (1595-1642)." JEGP 63 (1964):422-32.
Based on scripture as well as Renaissance Italian painting and literature, the sensuous and sensual love banquet was a typical scene in the period's English drama. Jonson employs it mainly in Poetaster (IV.iii). To the traditional banquet he adds that of the gods and that of the senses.

388 BOWERS, FREDSON T. "Ben Jonson the Actor." SP 34 (1937): 392-406.
Jonson's roles included Zulziman, Hieronimo, and Christopher Sly. Although the acting profession united in speeding his release from prison, he satirized it in Poetaster.

389 CAMPBELL, OSCAR J. "The Dramatic Construction of Poetaster." Huntington Library Bulletin 9 (April 1936):37-62.
A social satire, the play presents Ovid as a doomed sensualist and offers Jonson's judgments about society and its views of art. Modern audiences lack the intense ethical interests needed to like the play.

390 EAGLE, R. L. "Ben Jonson and Shakespeare." Baconiana 27 (January 1943):28-29.
In Poetaster, "the lawyer-poet [Ovid] is clearly meant to represent Francis Bacon." Luscus, the servant, "seems to represent Shakespeare," as does Sogliardo in Every Man out of his Humour.

391 FELDMAN, ABRAHAM B. "Playwrights and Pike-Trailer in the Low Countries." N&Q 198 (1953):184-87.
Jonson's military experience in the low countries did not have a profound influence on his dramas. There are only slight references to his plays to his career as a soldier--in the Epilogue to Poetaster and in The Case is Altered, I.i.

392 GRAY, HENRY DAVID. "The Chamberlain's Men and The Poetaster." MLR 42 (1947):173-79.
Jonson mocks many of the company, including Shakespeare (as Aesop), in III.iv. The slur may have resulted from their thwarting of a court performance of Cynthia's Revels. (See 393 and 855.)

393 GRAY, HENRY DAVID, and SIMPSON, PERCY. "Shakespeare or Heminge? A Rejoinder and a Surrejoinder." MLR 45 (1950):148-52.

Gray reopens the controversy on whether the Aesop in Poetaster is Shakespeare by restating his former argument under five headings. Desires stronger proof from Simpson in favor of identifying Aesop as Heminge. Simpson's reply strengthens the points already made in his earlier reply (see 392 and 855), but does not answer Gray's challenge to make a stronger case for identifying Aesop as Heminge.

394 HALIO, JAY L. "The Metaphor of Conception and Elizabethan Theories of the Imagination." Neophil 50 (1966):454-61.

Cites Poetaster, "To the Reader," 11.209-15, as an example of the Elizabethan use of human conception as a metaphor for imaginative invention.

395 JONES, ROBERT C. "Satirist Retirement in Jonson's 'Apologetical Dialogue'." ELH 34 (1967):447-67.

The "dialogue" at the conclusion of Poetaster is ambivalent because the dramatist says, in effect, that the good poet must be an effective, ethical teacher, yet claims he will no longer address those most needing learning and reform. Jones identifies Jonson's concept of the poet-world relationship and traces the function of the poet figures in the comical satires, which he considers one drama. Jonson came to realize that the poet cannot change the world but must content himself with affecting only a judicious few. The ambivalence of his position appears in the statements of the poet-satirists and their supporters regarding the purpose and power of poetry.

396 KING, ARTHUR H. The Language of Satirized Characters in "Poëtaster": a socio-stylistic analysis 1597-1602. Lund Studies in English, 10. Lund: C. W. K. Gleerup, 1941. 293 pp. [Reprint. Nendeln, Liechtenstein: Kraus, 1968.]

Poetaster, philologically Jonson's most important play, exemplifies the linguistic movements and norms of Renaissance England. By careful creation of identifiable vocabulary and language patterns for Crispinus, the court, and the street characters, and the subsequent satirization of each, Jonson emphasizes the power of the class and group tones of language. Analysis of Crispinus's language and that appearing in Marston's works suggests that Jonson satirized little more than Marston's crude diction and the general tendency of pedantic, courtly affectation. King finds Ovid, not Julia, the most important dramatic figure of the court and Tucca the most important figure of the play, the main object of satire. Jonson employed a great variety of the stylistic figures popular at the time but satirized mainly schemes in the play.

Reviewed by N. E. Eliason in MLN 57 (1942):392-94; G. D. Willcock in MLR 37 (1942):205-07; R. W. Zandvoort in ES 25 (1943):51-53; in TLS, 17 July 1943, p. 347.

397 _____. "A Note on the Virgil Translation in Poetaster, V.ii." ES 23 (1941):75-80.

Jonson used the Tottel and Hargrave ms. versions of Surrey's translation of The Aeneid as the basis of the passage on rumor. Defends Jonson against the charge of plagiarism by arguing that Jonson used Surrey's version because it was well known and that Jonson believed that heroic couplets were preferable to blank verse for translations from Virgil. Points out the improvements Jonson made on the Surrey translation.

398 _____. "'Swell mee a bowle': Notes on Jonson's Poetaster, III.i.8-12." SN 11 (1938):267-76.

Examines Jonson's lyric beginning "Swell mee a bowle" in Poetaster, III.i.8-12, and a similar song in Marston's Antonio and Mellida; concludes that Jonson is not imitating Marston but offering his song in contrast, and as an improvement. Claims further that the sense in which Jonson uses such terms as "flowing measure" and "Flame" looks forward to the lyric style of the Age of Dryden.

399 MARCKWARDT, ALBERT H. "A Fashionable Expression; Its Status in Poetaster and Satiromastix. MLN 44 (1929):93-96.

Traces the use of the expression "in" (or "out" of) one's "element" through its use in five contemporary plays, including Poetaster and Cynthia's Revels.

400 NASH, RALPH. "The Parting Scene in Jonson's Poetaster (IV.ix)." PQ 31 (1952):54-62.

The parting scene between Ovid and Julia is structurally significant and must be studied in relation to the action that goes before and follows. "The serious concern of the parting scene seems to be the nature of true virtue (and virtuous love) and its prerogative of place."

401 PEMBERTON, HENRY, JR. Shakspere and Sir Walter Ralegh. Philadelphia: Lippincott, 1914, pp. 188-93. [Reprint. New York: Haskell House, 1971.]

Jonson "scornfully portrayed Shakespere [sic] as Histrio in The Poetaster . . . as an actor, a usurer, and an employer of dramatists and other actors, and does not rank him with poets or dramatists."

Poetaster

402 PLATZ, NORBERT H. Jonson's "Ars Poetica": An Interpretation of "Poetaster" in Its Historical Context. ElizS 12, 1973, 42 pp.

Poetaster allowed Jonson to present, dramatically, his views about the relationship between society and poetry, the state and literature. A skillful work, the play builds a case for satire as an important poetic genre.

Reviewed by R. B. Parker in MLR 70 (1975):145-48.

403 REIMAN, DONALD H. "Marston, Jonson, and the Spanish Tragedy Additions." N&Q 205 (1960):336-37.

Jonson's parody on Antonio's Revenge (V.iii.1-4), appearing in the 1602 Quarto of Poetaster (III.ii.230-35), reinforces the theory that the "additions" to the Spanish Tragedy were written earlier than those for which Henslowe paid Jonson in 1601 and 1602.

404 SYKES, H. DUGDALE. "Identification of Lines Quoted in Jonson's Poetaster." N&Q, 11th Series 10 (11 July 1914):26.

It is generally thought that Poetaster III.iv.236-43 parodies the murder of Horatio in The Spanish Tragedy, but line 242, "Who calls out murder? lady, was it you?" is intended to parody a line in Chapman's Blind Beggar of Alexandria: "Who calls out murther, Lady, was it you?" (See 405.)

405 _____. "Lines Quoted in Jonson's Poetaster." N&Q, 11th Series 10 (3 October 1914):266.

Poetaster III.iv.242, "Who calls out murder? lady, was it you?" occurs in slightly different form in Eastward Ho II.i.110. Both are jesting allusions to a line in Chapman's Blind Beggar of Alexandria; Poetaster comes closer to the original. (See 404.)

406 TALBERT, ERNEST WILLIAM. "The Purpose and Technique of Jonson's Poetaster." SP 42 (1945):225-52.

Not merely of interest because of the Poetomachia nor primarily concerned with the Ovid-Julia relationship, the play is "primarily a defence of poetry." The two prologues set the motif: immortal poetry can withstand all detractors. The actions of major and minor characters illustrate the theme. Ovid's soliloquy prior to the parting scene reveals Jonson's central idea concerning poetry: poetry and the court relate intimately.

Poetaster

407 TERR, LEONARD B. "Ben Jonson's Ars Poetica: A Reinterpretation of Poetaster." Thoth 11 (1971):3-16.
The play's stance toward imagination makes it central to Jonson's canon. Although speaking little, Ovid occupies a central role in the development of related ideas about poetry and the poet.

408 VOCHT, HENRY de. Studies on the Texts of Ben Jonson's "Poetaster" and "Seianus." Materials for the Study of the Old English Drama, Series 2, Vol. 27. Louvain: Uystpruyst, 1958. 63 pp. [Reprint. Vaduz: Kraus, 1963.]
Poetaster ranks as the drama most intimately connected with Jonson's character and work, and clearly indicates his superior wit, learning, and able presentation of the manners of the time. Sejanus, very unpopular because of its espousal of authoritative measures and harsh blame on excesses, presented significant difficulties in performance. Jonson edited the text to emphasize its classical roots; he invented strictly accurate historical drama in England. For both plays, the Quarto edition is generally superior to the Folio. Textual examination indicates that Jonson did not oversee the printing of the 1616 Folio.

409 WAITH, EUGENE M. "The Poet's Morals in Jonson's Poetaster." MLQ 12 (1951):13-19.
The play presents the poet's social responsibilities, brought out "by Horace in the third act, by Caesar in the fourth act, and by Horace, Virgil and Caesar in the fifth act." The defense of poetry in III.v contrasts greatly with Ovid's in Act I. The entire play's structure witnesses Jonson's tenet: the good poet must be a good man.

410 ZENDER, KARL F. "The Function of Propertius in Jonson's Poetaster." PLL 11 (1975):308-12.
Propertius serves as an image of grief, establishing a contrast between himself and Ovid and foreshadowing Ovid's view of relations among art, life, and moral order. Augustus, Horace, and Vergil have correct views of these relations.

The Staple of News: Editions

411 Devra Kifer, ed. Lincoln: University of Nebraska Press, 1975. 196 pp.
Although it does not represent Jonson at his best, the play enjoys a prominent place among the satires of newsmongering common in the 17th century. Jonson draws on the morality tradition, making Penniboy Junior into Every-Heir and Penniboy Senior into an antithesis of Mistress Mirth.

The play's festive ritual, as well as its performance at Shrovetide, emphasizes its holiday nature. The number of marginal notes merely restating the action or dialogue is unusual. The text of the edition is based on the 1631 Folio.

Reviewed by B. Gibbons and B. Harris in YWES 57 (1976): 147; A. B. Kernan in YES 9 (1979):329-30.

412 No Entry

The Staple of News: Criticism and Commentary

413 DESSEN, ALAN C. "Jonson's 'Knave of Clubs' and The Play of the Cards." MLR 62 (1967):584-85.

Jonson claims that he rejects the old morality tradition and attires his Vices "like men and women o' the time." The old morality tradition alluded to in The Staple of News may be represented by the lost Play of Cards described by Sir John Harington in his defense of drama. In this tradition, the knaves in a play related metaphorically to their counterparts in a deck of cards.

414 EMERY, CLARK. "A Further Note on Drebbel's Submarine." MLN 57 (1942):451-55.

Kuethe's citing of The Staple of News (III.ii) in relation to 17th-century submarines is ill-founded, for Jonson is being satirical. (See 420.)

415 ENDERS, JOHN F. "A Note on Jonson's Staple of News." MLN 40 (1925):419-21.

"Naometry" (III.i) refers to the Naometria by the German antiquary and mystic Simon Studion, who represented the doctrines of extreme Protestantism, which Jonson connects with the Brownists. Jonson would not have seen Studion's work, which remained in manuscript, but probably gained his knowledge of it through travelers' tales of the "saints of Amsterdam."

416 JANICKA, IRENA. "Jonson's Staple of News: Sources and Traditional Devices." KN 15 (1968):301-07.

Jonson may have drawn from The Trial of Treasure. He uses devices of the masque, Dance of Death, and sottie.

417 JONES, ROBERT C. "Jonson's Staple of News Gossips and Fulwell's Like Will to Like: 'The Old Way' in a 'New' Morality Play." YES 3 (1973):74-77.

The Staple of News draws on both old and new satiric methods. Mirth's reference to the Knave of Clubs recalls Fulwell's scene of Satan carrying off a Vice on his back and the common emblem of card knaves as Vices.

The Staple of News

418 KIFER, DEVRA ROWLAND. "*The Staple of News*: Jonson's Festive Comedy." *SEL* 12 (1972):329-44.

The play balances traditions of morality, allegory, satire, and festive comedy. It is more gentle than most of Jonson's comedies.

419 _____. "Too Many Cookes: An Addition to the Printed Text of Jonson's *Staple of Newes*." *ELN* 11 (1974):264-71.

Jonson added V.vi.42-48 when the play was printed to protect himself against charges of slandering Sir Edward Coke. Although Penniboy Senior resembles Coke, Jonson overtly identifies the jurist with Lickfinger in the printed version, thus putting discretion before conviction.

420 KUETHE, J. LOUIS. "Mechanical Features of a Seventeenth-Century Submarine." *MLN* 56 (1941):202-04.

The Staple of News reviewed events of its day much as a modern newspaper does. In III.ii, the characters provide a helpful picture of Cornelius Van Drebel's submarine: a self-moving war vessel equipped with a ram. (*See* 414.)

421 LEVIN, RICHARD. "*The Staple of News*, The Society of Jeerers, and Canters' College." *PQ* 44 (1965):44-53.

In terms of theme and the relationship of character and incident, the Staple relates more closely to the jeerer and the Canters' College than to Pecunia. Jonson's main themes are the prodigality of Penniboy and the abuse of language (of the Staple, the jeerers, and the Canters' College) rather than greed, as most critics suppose.

422 McKENZIE, DONALD F. "*The Staple of News* and the Late Plays," in *A Celebration of Ben Jonson* (1973), pp. 83-128. (*See* 5.)

Jonson's late plays are his reactions to the popular success of his middle comedies and his final attempt to support his own judgment. *The Staple of News* makes literal the implications in *The Devil is an Ass* and marks the defeat of the dramatic poet as rhetor to the journalist. Although committed to the court, Jonson felt it would not be improved by plays but could be corrupted by them.

423 MAXWELL, J. C. "Dryden's Paraphrase of Horace and *The Staple of News*." *N&Q* 197 (1952):389.

In paraphrasing Horace (*Odes* III.xxix.87), Dryden probably had Jonson's play (IV.iv) in mind.

424 MILLS, LLOYD L. "A Clarification of Broker's Use of 'A Perfect Sanguine' in The Staple of News." N&Q 212 (1967): 208-09.

Editors incorrectly gloss "a perfect sanguine," II.ii.39-43, as a reference to Piedmantle's complexion. These words suggest a gold piece; Piedmantle is bribing Broker to arrange a meeting with Lady Pecunia.

425 MOTT, FRANK LUTHER. Ben Jonson's 1625 Satire on News: Excerpts from "The Staple of News." Oldtime Comments on Journalism, edited by Frank Luther Mott, No. 1. Columbia: Press of the Crippled Turtle, 1953. 12 pp.

Reproduces extracts from The Staple of News that refer to news and news-publication, with explanatory notes in the margins.

426 NICOLSON, MARJORIE. "The 'New Astronomy' and English Literary Imagination." SP 32 (1935):428-62.

Reference to the new astronomy is fairly common in Ben Jonson's works. The Staple of News, III.i, provides an example.

427 PARR, JOHNSTONE. "A Note on Jonson's The Staple of News." MLN 60 (1945):117.

Drawing on Ptolemy, explains that Hercules, like Mars, causes all types of violence and disaster; hence, it is natural that Penniboy Senior, born under "Hercules starre," is oppressed with "trouble and tumult" (III.iv.1-3).

428 POTTLE, FREDERICK A. "Two Notes on Ben Jonson's Staple of News." MLN 40 (1925):223-26.

The line, "Look to me, wit, and look to my wit, Land" (I.i.3), is a parody of the first line of Donne's "Elegy upon the Untimely Death of the Incomparable Prince Henry." The three inventions mentioned in III.ii.54-57, 106-08, may have been suggested by a patent granted Drummond of Hawthornden for the making of military machines.

429 SALTER, KEITH W. "Of the Right Use of Riches." E&S 16 (1963):101-14.

Ben Jonson's view of riches in The Staple of News, III.ii, seems both to draw upon a classical tradition and embody the medieval Christian doctrine that there can be no absolute possession in a life which terminates in death.

The Staple of News

430 SAVAGE, JAMES E. "Ben Jonson and Shakespeare; 1623-1626." UMSE 10 (1969):25-48. [Reprinted in his Ben Jonson's Comic Characters and Other Essays (1973), pp. 176-99 (see 36).]
The Staple of News is more Shakespearean than Jonson's other plays, with Jonson indebted to Shakespeare and paying him tribute in it. The play also draws on Timon of Athens which, itself, draws on Sejanus.

431 STONEX, ARTHUR BEVINS. "The Sources of Jonson's The Staple of News." PMLA 30 (1915):821-30.
Jonson drew on English morality plays and contemporary works as well as the works of Greek satirists.

A Tale of a Tub: Editions

432 Hans Scherer, ed. Materials for the Study of The Old English Drama, Series 1, Vol. 39. Louvain: Uystpruyst, 1913, 65-113. [Reprint. Vaduz: Kraus, 1963.]
Although its date is disputed, the play seems to have been written in 1599 or 1600, between Every Man out of his Humour and Cynthia's Revels. Conclusions regarding the text are rendered difficult by the fact that the earliest extant version is 1640. Source investigation is complicated by the confusion over date of composition. Text based on 1640 Folio. (Introduction in German.)

433 Florence May Snell, ed. London and New York: Longmans, Green, 1915. 238 pp.
Writing the play about 1633, Jonson intended to create an atmosphere of Elizabethan times. It reflects his study of mid-16th-century literature in its satire of contemporary life. Comparison with Teniers' painting provides an apt insight: the play is vital but lacks unity. The text for the edition is the 1640 Folio.
Reviewed by S. G. C. in MLN 31 (1916):128; P. Simpson in MLR 11 (1916):474-77.

A Tale of a Tub: Criticism and Commentary

434 BROWN, E. R. "Jonson's A Tale of a Tub." TLS, 10 May 1928, p. 358.
Disagrees with Herford and Simpson's view (in Introduction to the Oxford edition) that the play was probably performed by the Queen's Men at Blackfriars, suggesting the Cockpit instead. (See 439.)

A Tale of a Tub

435 BRYANT, J. A., JR. "A Tale of a Tub: Jonson's Comedy of the Human Condition." RenP (1963), pp. 95-105.

The play is a much more mature work than "the customary Christian adaptation of classical comedy." It presents "the victory of man's genuine impulses over the shaky institutions that man has devised for the purpose of organizing his impulses: that is, the victory of nature over man's social order." Since this type of penetration of thought was beyond the young Jonson, the play could not have been written before 1605, when he was moving toward the thinking of Bartholomew Fair.

436 COOK, ALBERT S. "An Emendation." Nation, 7 January 1915, p. 18.

Placing the stress on the second syllable of "Pancrace," in IV.i.82, makes the line in question metrical. In the following line, "not" should be read with its possible Old English meaning of "know not."

437 PALME, PER. Triumph of Peace: A Study of the Whitehall Banqueting House. Stockholm: Almqvist & Wiskell, 1956; London: Thames and Hudson, 1957, pp. 291-92.

Explains lines 1-3 and 45-47 of "The Scene interloping" in Act IV of A Tale of a Tub as aimed at Inigo Jones' lack of theoretical consistency.

438 PENNANEN, ESKO. "On the Date of Ben Jonson's A Tale of a Tub." NM 53 (1952):224-40.

Reviews arguments on the problem of dating the play. Some critics hold that it was written, and perhaps even acted, by 1601, and that Jonson revised it for a court production in 1634; other contend that it was written for court production and hence can be considered one of the works of his later period. The arguments of both schools of thought rest chiefly on two considerations: the allusions and the internal evidence (the style and the verse). Pennanen concludes that the early dating of A Tale of a Tub is "practically certain, for not only its motive, style, verse, and plot-structure, characters and chronological allusions but also its language and diction show decidedly early features."

439 SIMPSON, PERCY. "Jonson's A Tale of a Tub." TLS, 17 May 1928, p. 379.

In reply to E. R. Brown (see 434), agrees that the play was performed at the Cockpit and notes that the correction is made in the third volume of the Oxford Ben Jonson. Since this performance, no production of A Tale of a Tub has been recorded.

A Tale of a Tub

440 SNELL, FLORENCE M. "The Date of Jonson's *Tale of a Tub*." *MLN* 30 (1915):93-94.
Versification and other internal evidence indicate that the drama was written as a unit about 1633, the time of its presentation.

441 SWAEN, A. E. H. "Two Notes on Ben Jonson's *Tale of a Tub*." *Neophil* 7 (1922):279-80.
Identifies two references to contemporary songs in the play.

442 WILLIAMS, MARY C. "*A Tale of a Tub*: Ben Jonson's Folk Play." *NCarF* 22 (1974):161-68.
Jonson builds a tale of the folk through setting, plot, characters, imagery, and speech.

Volpone: Editions

*443 Calcutta: University of Calcutta, 1917. 132 pp.

444 John D. Rea, ed. Yale Studies in English, 59. New Haven: Yale University Press, 1919. 305 pp.
Compares Jonson's method of composition to that of a mosaic-maker, questions Jonson's scholarship, and claims that his knowledge of classical authors has been exaggerated. Disagrees with earlier writers on the play by arguing that the source of the play as a whole is Erasmus' *In Praise of Folly*. Argues for identifying Sir Politic Would-be with Sir Henry Wotton.
Reviewed by M. Summers in *YWES* 1 (1919-1920):75.

445 Henry de Vocht, ed. Materials for the Study of the Old English Drama, Series 2, Vol. 13. Louvain: Uystpruyst, 1937. 261 pp. [Reprint. Vaduz: Kraus, 1963.]
Describes copies of the 1607 Quarto and Folio editions, text, notes variants among the Quarto and Folio editions, and provides analysis of the verse. Argues that Jonson could not have overseen the printing of the Folio, on the basis of its many errors.

446 Introduction by Louis Kronenberger. Oxford: The Limited Editions Club, 1952. 188 pp.
Jonson, "supremely un-Shakespearian," has "a gift for the intense and grotesque" that helps make him great. But he "lacks the *vox humana*: so far from possessing sentiment, he actually seems to recoil from it." Despite its greatness, *Volpone* has some weaknesses: the sameness of the vicious legacy-hunters, the unconvincingness of Celia and Bonario, the detracting offensiveness of Volpone's

grotesque children, and the poor subplot. Further, in considering the aesthetic problems arising from the play's conclusion, it seems that Jonson "from not blending his colours can find no satisfactory final tone."

447 Arthur Sale, ed. "Second edition." London: University Tutorial Press, 1956. 215 pp. [Originally published 1951.]

Contends with various criticisms of the play. Rebuts J. D. Rea's contention that Jonson patched together borrowings from other authors.

Reviewed by F. S. Boas in YWES 32 (1951):146-47.

448 Jonas A. Barish, ed. New York: Appleton-Century-Crofts, 1958. 123 pp.

Jonson is insufficiently valued for his theatrical inventiveness, a chief example of which is Volpone. Opposing the escapism of romantic comedy, he aimed at inculcating virtue by realistically exhibiting human folly. Though eclectic, Volpone is extremely original. The stock comic characters, now "humours," are engaged in conspiratorial action that "probes something far more deep-seated and malevolent . . . than mere eccentricity." The chief impression is that men are beasts and monsters, but the "double doublecross" of the conclusion restores our faith in the power of good, and dispels whatever wish-fulfilling identification we feel with the chief villains. The Zweig-Romains version of the play is "counterfeit"; it dilutes the original, ironically, "because of the venality of the box-office."

Reviewed by G. E. Nichols, III, in CE 22 (1960):56.

449 Vincent F. Hopper and Gerald B. Lahey, eds. With a note on the staging by George L. Hersey. Great Neck, N.Y.: Barron's Educational Series, 1959. 218 pp.

Discussion of the central theme (avarice) and a contemporary view of the seriousness of its corrupting influence. Study of chief criticisms of the play: lack of motivation for Volpone's tormenting those who have just defended him in court, too sudden overthrow of Volpone and Mosca, portrayal of virtue as powerless, borrowings from previous writers, and inappropriateness of introducing lyrical "Song to Celia" in a scene of high tension.

450 Henry G. Lee, ed. San Francisco: Chandler Publishing Company, 1961. 126 pp.

Provides a brief account of Jonson's life and contributions to drama; discusses the action and intent of the play. "Volpone is a forceful, but perverse comedy."

Volpone

451 David Cook, ed. London: Methuen, 1962; New York: Barnes and Noble, 1967. 256 pp.

Discusses Jonson's classicism as well as his deviations from it. Volpone demonstrates careful use of classical methods of structure and character presentation. The general plot is original, but passages from Lucian and Petronius may have been sources for the legacy-hunting theme.

Reviewed by N. W. Bawcutt in MLR 58 (1963):315-16.

452 Alvin B. Kernan, ed. New Haven: Yale University Press, 1962. 240 pp.

Discusses motifs and Jonson's method of structuring his meaning through irony. I.i.1-27 establish gold as the "dumb god" of the play's universe; infectious greed spreads into the lives of all who contact Volpone's household. By allusions, Jonson not only satirizes the materialism of the Renaissance but also points out the timelessness of greed and gullibility. Metamorphosis of character constitutes another major theme. Jonson presents his ethics implicitly by use of irony as Volpone inverts the world and men become animals, descending the Great Chain of Being. The text is basically that of Herford and Simpson, with modern spelling and punctuation.

Reviewed by A. Brown in YWES 43 (1962):134-35; C. G. Thayer in Books Abroad 38 (1964):187; in SCN 21 (1963):23.

453 J. B. Bamborough, ed. New York: St. Martin's Press; London: Macmillan, 1963. 159 pp.

Jonson's strength lay in his "realistic portrayal of contemporary life and manners." Argues that Jonson should be compared to Molière rather than Shakespeare, and that Volpone should be judged not as a comedy that comes too close to tragedy, but as belonging to a special genre of comedy associated with Molière and the Restoration playwrights. This type of comedy, in which all characters are ridiculed, and the audience is invited to laugh at rather than with the characters, complies with Renaissance critical theory, which proposes the exposure of folly in order for it to be remedied. Volpone is the best example of the genre in English.

454 Jay L. Halio, ed. Berkeley: University of California Press, 1968. 170 pp.

Explores the different degrees of avarice in the various characters and Volpone's and Mosca's "overreaching." Shows the relationship of the play to Sejanus, Epicoene, and The Alchemist. Text based on 1607 Quarto.

Reviewed by R. Gill in RES 20 (1969):491-94; in TLS, 23 April 1970, p. 450.

455 Menston, Yorkshire: Scolar Press, 1968. 124 pp.
Facsimile reprint of 1607 edition.

456 Philip Brockbank, ed. London: Ernest Benn; New York: Hill and Wang, 1969. 208 pp.
A play about virtuosity, Volpone is itself a feat of virtuosity in its language, postures, and demands placed upon performers. Venice offers a good theatrical model for an acquisitive society, but Jonson actually depended more on classical sources. His Epistle provides the appropriate platform for surveying the play. Actual staging demands special attention to the rhythm of the work. Both the Quarto and Folio texts have been used for this edition.
Reviewed by E. Bas in EA 22 (1969):312-33; R. Gill in RES 20 (1969):491-94; J. C. Maxwell in N&Q 214 (1969): 306-08; in TLS, 31 October 1968, p. 1234.

457 Louis B. Wright and Virginia A. LaMar, eds. New York: Washington Square Press, 1970. 175 pp.
Despite Jonson's considerable borrowing from numerous classical sources, the audience is not aware of any "mosaic" effect. He "digested his material thoroughly and made it completely his own." Volpone is like his other plays in its appeal to the mind, and not the heart. For modern audiences, it is the "most satisfactory" of his plays; except for a period during the 19th century, it has remained consistently popular. Text based on 1616 Folio.

458 David McPherson, ed., in his Ben Jonson: Selected Works. New York: Holt, Rinehart and Winston, 1972, pp. 1-136.
"The humor and the savagery [of the play] are controlled and kept subservient to the moral purpose. The moral theme . . . is that vice and folly are ultimately self-defeating." The central purpose of the play is to imitate poetic justice, the workings of which in a sense provide the humor of the play. The nasty comic language is "morally appropriate"; the tone is ironical. Text based on 1616 Folio.

Volpone: Translations and Adaptations

459 ARAQUISTAIN, LUIS. Ben Jonson: "Volpone o El Zorro." Madrid: Prensa Moderna, 1929. 88 pp. (Spanish adaptation.)
In exhibiting the triumph of rascality over rascals, Volpone reflects the picaresque morality that inspired

Volpone

Italian Renaissance literature, as well as the shift from feudal and theocratic to bourgeois norms. Jonson, closer to modern life than his contemporaries, is at his best in the comedies that ridicule human passions for the purpose of correcting them. Araquistain compares in some detail the Zweig-Romains adaptation with Jonson's original, and says that in his own version he has attempted not to distort the character and style of the original except when absolutely necessary. He justifies changes in character and plot, notably the conclusion, as suitable to modern notions of comedy.

460 BORRÁS, TOMÁS. "Volpone," el Magnifico. Adaptación Libre y Escenificación Nueva de Tomás Borrás. Madrid: Ediciones ALFIL, 1953. 64 pp. (Spanish adaptation.)

461 CASTELAIN, MAURICE. Volpone ou le Renard. Paris: Belles Lettres, 1934. 308 pp. (French translation, with English on facing pages.)

Jonson's Volpone, despite some prolixity, is a better play than the Zweig-Romains adaptation; this translation into blank verse attempts to be as true to the original as possible. Jonson claims to observe the unities of time, place, and characters, but his classicism is typical of the English Renaissance, to which the notion of unity was foreign. The play would benefit from cutting most of the mountebank scene, eliminating the servants' entertainments, and cutting most if not all of the subplot. Volpone does not fit into any arbitrary category of comedy. It is heavily indebted to classical and Renaissance sources, but is highly original and vigorous.

462 No entry

463 JARNES, BENJAMIN. Ben Jonson: "Volpone." Farsa en tres actos y cinco cuadres. Madrid: La Farsa, 1929. 62 pp. (Spanish translation and adaptation.)

A free translation, but accommodated to the spirit of its author.

*464 MELKOVOJ, P. B. Vol'pone; ili Xitryi lis [Volpone; or the sly fox]. Edited by A. A. Smirnov. Moscow: Iskusstvo, 1954. 188 pp. (Russian translation.)

465 MESSIAEN, PIERRE. Volpone ou le renard, in his Théâtre anglais, moyen âge et XVIe siècle. Desclée, Belgium: DeBrouwer, 1948, pp. 773-888. (French translation.)

Jonson preferred the presentation of eccentric types to the study of character. His comedies are maladroit, heavy, poorly made, and permeated with Latin erudition. But his sense of farce and the eloquent vigor of his satire compensate for his structural faults.

466 PRAZ, MARIO. *Volpone*. Florence: G. C. Sansoni, 1943. 358 pp. (Italian translation, with English on facing pages.)

The play is Aretinesque, superior to the comedies of Aretino himself, and anticipates the psychical dynamics of the Marquis de Sade. Jonson might have known of Aretino's work through his friendship with John Florio, whose *Worlde of Wordes* furnished Italian terms for *Volpone* and *Cynthia's Revels*. The play mixes tragedy and comedy to form a unity; Volpone is the perfect incarnation of the *titanico trasgessore*. Praz furnishes a list of translations and adaptations.

467 QUINTELA, PAULO. "*Volpone*" ou "*O Raposão*." Oporto: Imprensa Social, 1958. 144 pp. (Portuguese translation.)

468 ROMAINS, JULES. *Volpone en collaboration avec Stefan Zweig d'après Ben Jonson*. Théâtre de Jules Romains. Paris: Editions de la Nouvelle Revue Française, 1929. 144 pp. (French adaptation.)

469 ROMAINS, JULES, and ZWEIG, STEFAN. *Volpone*, in *Les Oeuvres Libres*, No. 91. Paris: Artheme Fayard, January 1929, pp. 5-82. (French adaptation.)

470 _____. Paris: Gallimard, 1965. 219 pp. (French adaptation; originally published 1950.)

471 SLOMCZYNSKI, MACIEJ. *Volpone albo lis*. Warsaw: Panstwowy Instytut Wydawniczy, 1962. 221 pp. (Polish translation.)

472 STEFANI, A. de. "*Volpone*." *NA*, 15 June 1930, pp. 428-51; 1 July 1930, pp. 53-71; 15 July 1930, pp. 157-77; 1 August 1930, pp. 315-28. (Italian translation.)

473 TASIS, RAFAEL. *Volpone*. Introduction by Joan Triadú. Palma de Mallorca: Editorial Moll, 1957. 128 pp. (Catalan adaptation.)

The play is reminiscent of masquerade and the old Latin comedy. It is above all a satire of egoism, a troubling divertissement. Jonson is a social dramatist of the first order.

Volpone

473a VAS, ISTVÁN. Volpone, in Angol Reneszánsz Drámák, Vol. 3. Edited by Miklós Scenczi. Budapest: Európa Könyvkiadó, 1961, pp. 173-310. (Hungarian translation.)

474 ZWEIG, STEFAN. Ben Jonson's "Volpone": A Loveless Comedy in 3 Acts. Freely adapted by Stefan Zweig. New York: Viking, 1928. 187 pp. (In English; translated from the German by Ruth Langner.)

*475 _____. "Volpone": Eine lieblose Komödie in drei Akten von Ben Jonson. Frei bearbeitet von Stefan Zweig. Berlin-Wilmersdorf: F. Bloch Erben, 1925.

This "edition," cited in the National Union Catalogue, seems to be a bibliographical ghost. The 1927 edition (see 476), apparently the first, carries the information that the play had been copyrighted by Felix Bloch Erben in 1925.

476 _____. "Volpone." Eine lieblose Komödie in drei Akten von Ben Jonson. Frei bearbeitet von Stefan Zweig. Potsdam: Gustav Kiepenheuer, 1927. 148 pp. (German adaptation.)

*477 _____. Frankfurt-am-Main: S. Fischer, 1950. 99 pp. [Originally published 1928.]

See also 657

Volpone: Criticism and Commentary

478 ALEXANDER, HENRY. "Jonson and Johnson." QQ 44 (1937):13-21.

"Humours" comedy reached its highest point in Volpone. A grim play that at times verges on tragedy, it is a masterly treatment of the theme of the misanthrope. Like all comedies of humour, "life has been somewhat distorted to serve the purposes of a dramatic theory."

479 ANDERSON, MARK A. "Structure and Response in Volpone." RMS 19 (1975):47-71.

Audience's divided response (admiration and condemnation) corresponds to division in man between morality and worldly wisdom. Volpone's relationships illustrate corruption at varied social levels. The comedy undercuts simplistic values and shows that evil threatens all.

480 ANON. "'O Rare.'" New York Times, 5 March 1929, p. 30.

Volpone, in adaptation, is popular theatre in New York, the Midwest, and Paris. London is ready for the original play.

481 ANON. "Volpone: Reducing All Wit to the Dung Cart." Dramatist 19 (April 1928):1365-66.
Review of Langner translation of Zweig adaptation, 1928 (see 474). Jonson tried to write a play about avarice, but strayed into "aimless dribble of irrelevant indecencies and obscenities." Zweig should have purified and refined the play for modern consumption, but has not.

*482 ARNAVON, J. "Volpone: de Ben Jonson (1605) à Jules Romains (1928)." France-Grande Bretagne, September 1929.

483 ARNOLD, JUDD. "The Double Plot in Volpone: A Note on Jonsonian Dramatic Structure." SCN 23 (1965):47-52.
The Would-be subplot is dramaturgically sound because it prepares for the important role that Lady Would-be plays in the dénouement.

484 ATKINSON, J. BROOKS. "Rare Ben: How Zweig's Adaptation of Volpone transforms Jonson's Text--Latest Intelligence of the Poets' War of 1600." New York Times, 22 April 1928, Sec. 9, pp. 1-2.
Review of New York Theatre Guild production of Zweig-Romains adaptation. Zweig's adaptation is funny but leaves audiences cold. Although remaining true to Jonson in central relations and the essence of characters, Zweig has produced a new play: a shorter, faster prose work with a final flourish that improves upon the original ending.

485 _____. "Some Rare Ben Jonson," in New York Theatre Critics' Reviews 8 (10 March 1947):449. [Originally published New York Times, 25 February 1947.]
Review of Century Theatre production. The play differs significantly from the modern ideas of comedy.

486 BANTA, MARTHA. "The Quality of Experience in What Maisie Knew." NEQ 42 (1969):483-510.
Compares the James novel to the most effective of Jonson's dramas in its merging of comic tone and "horrors." Unlike Maisie, the characters in Volpone cannot escape the bestial world.

487 BARISH, JONAS A. "The Double Plot in Volpone." MP 51 (1953):83-92. [Reprinted in Ben Jonson: A Collection of Critical Essays (1963), pp. 93-105 (see 3).]
The Politic Would-bes are beast-fable parrots who not only chatter, but mimic, and in so doing unknowingly travesty the actions of the main characters, thus fulfilling the usual function of a comic subplot. Sir Politic, as unsuccessful enterpriser, is a comic distortion of Volpone;

Lady Would-be caricatures the legacy hunters. The households of Corvino and Sir Politic illustrate the contrast between Italian vice and English folly, the latter mimicking the former. But the Italian vice is itself a mimicry, which Barish calls "metamorphosis," defined as "the folly of becoming, or trying to become, what one is not, the cardinal sin of losing one's nature."

488 _____. "Volpone": A Casebook. London: Macmillan, 1972. 255 pp.

Critics from 1662 to the present offer both general impressions of the play and detailed considerations of such aspects as the double plot, the catastrophe, sources, use of metempsychosis, and the individuality of characters. Most writers rank the play as Jonson's best even while they find flaws in it. Includes eight performance reviews.

489 BEAURLINE, L. A. "Volpone and the Power of Gorgeous Speech." SLitI 6 (April 1973):61-75. (See 40.)

Volpone's wooing of Celia is part of a long literary tradition and a fine example of good dramatic speech. His language and acting in the scene are highly appropriate, given his skill in role-playing. The failure of his verbal art in the seduction attempt moves him to other methods, where force and chance take over.

490 BELLAMY, FRANCIS R. "Lights Down: A Review of the Stage." Outlook, 25 April 1928, p. 665.

Review of New York Theatre Guild production of Zweig-Romains adaptation. Neither Jonson's Volpone nor Zweig's adaptation employs the delicate psychological strokes the play's situation demands. The comedy shows a childish sense of humor, is not funny, and is hardly unusual.

491 BENTLEY, ERIC. "A One-Man Dialogue on the Barrault Repertory." New Republic, 18 March 1957, pp. 20-22.

Review of New York Winter Garden production. Zweig and Romains ruined Volpone, particularly Mosca's role. Unable to accept Jonson's moral severity, they replaced his accusing finger with a shrug of the shoulder.

492 BLATT, THORA BALSEV. "Who Was Volpone's 'Danish Gonswart'?" ES 56 (1975):393-95.

Finds Herford and Simpson's suggested identifications unsatisfactory. Jonson probably referred to Cornelius Hamsforth (1509-80), a Danish doctor, and intended a compliment to Queen Anne.

493 BOAS, F. S. "Hamlet and Volpone at Oxford." Fortnightly Review, 16 May 1920, pp. 709-16.

Evidence shows that both plays were performed in the university town, but no evidence indicates that they received university sanction.

494 BOUGHNER, DANIEL C. "Lewkenor and Volpone." N&Q 207 (1962): 124-30.

Disagrees with Mario Praz that John Florio was Jonson's chief source in writing Volpone. Claims rather that Jonson's debt was to Lewis Lewkenor's The Commonwealth and Government of Venice (1599), a translation of Cardinal Catareno's Della Republica et Magistrati di Venetia (1564). After examining in detail Jonson's use of material in Lewkenor's book, Boughner concludes that he was Jonson's primary source for things Italianesque in Volpone, and that the work provided bibliographical assistance also.

495 BRADBROOK, F. W. "John Donne and Ben Jonson." N&Q 202 (1957):146-47.

Volpone's opening speech echoes Donne's "The Sunne Rising." If Jonson had the poem in mind, his intention must have been to contrast the sterile love of wealth of the Fox to the human passion celebrated in Donne's poem. Proposes another similarity to Donne ("Satire III") in Volpone, V.i.

496 BROWN, IVOR. "Volpone, or The Fox." Observer (London), 30 January 1938, p. 13.

The play's fierce satire results from the social situation at the time of its conception.

497 BROWN, JOHN MASON. "Valedictory to a Season." Theatre Arts Monthly 12 (1928):387-90.

Review of New York Theatre Guild production of Zweig-Romains adaptation. Compared to Zweig's sharply pointed adaptation, Jonson's work is a Sunday school lesson. Zweig allows no poetic justice to spoil the full irony of the ending and creates a loveless comedy about adult vices.

497a BRUNNER, K. "Die Quellen von Ben Jonsons Volpone." Archiv 152, NS 52 (1927):218-19.

Gower's Confessio Amantis (V.2643-2825, in Macaulay's Oxford edition) is the most likely source of the portion of the plot involving Corvino's bringing Celia to the "sick" Volpone.

Volpone

498 CANUTESON, JOHN. "Sir Politic Would-Be's Testudo." AN&Q 11 (1973):117-18.
The fact that, for Jonson and his audience, the word "tortoise" could have the same meaning as "testudo," part of the Roman war machine, helps deflate Sir Pol's pretensions. "He is no longer the statesman he would be, but the common foot-soldier inside an engine of war. And his engine is not really a testudo, but a tortoise-shell. . . ."

499 CLARK, BARRETT H. "Broadway Opens Shop Again." Drama 19 (October 1928):10.
Review of Theatre Guild production of Zweig-Romains adaptation. Sees Jonson's version as "ponderous and dull," the modern one as not much of an improvement. But the play is "an amusing bit of mockery."

500 CLARY, FRANK N., JR. "The Vol and the Pone: A Reconsideration of Jonson's Volpone." ELN 10 (1972):102-07.
Volpone's final disguise is appropriate if his name is understood as a compound, with "vol" indicating a lure and "pone" a writ. Jonson may have been blending two fables with the name.

501 CLOUDSLEY, ANNABELLA. "Volpone in Germany." Twentieth Century 168 (July 1960):66-69.
Francis Burt effectively presented Volpone in opera form. A. E. Eichmann collaborated with Burt to produce a German form of the play using a lower social scale than Jonson's.

502 COX, GERARD H., III. "Celia, Bonario, and Jonson's Indebtedness to the Medieval Cycles." EA 25 (1972):506-11.
The concept "dramatic," in the medieval period, did not demand that a character be active. Both Celia and Bonario, with their undeveloped characters, clearly relate to the medieval cycles.

503 CRAIK, T. W. "Volpone's 'Young Antinous.'" N&Q 215 (1970): 213-14.
Volpone probably associates himself (III.vii.157-64) with Penelope's chief suitor.

504 CREASER, JOHN. "The Popularity of Jonson's Tortoise." RES NS 27 (1976):38-46.
Sir Politic Would-be's posing as a tortoise is too wittily emblematic to be a mere farce and too dependent on popular lore to be esoteric. The animal's popular symbolism of prudence and persistence makes it stand in opposition to Peregrine's impulsiveness and testiness.

505 _____. "Vindication of Sir Politic Would-Be." ES 57 (1976): 502-14.
Modern audiences might appreciate the play more if they understood Renaissance attitudes toward travel, Jonson's delight with foolish characters, and the subplot's relation to the main plot.

506 _____. "Volpone: The Mortifying of the Fox." EIC 25 (1975):329-56.
Volpone's complexity and mental agility explain his fluctuating conduct, moving audiences to both condemn and admire him. The "justice" he receives at the end makes him a kind of tragic hero; his own "mortification" turns his legal defeat into an emotional triumph.

507 CREWE, J. V. "Death in Venice: A Study of Othello and Volpone." UCTSE 4 (1973):17-29.
Othello and Volpone, written around the same time, may be using Venice as suggestive of a particular moral environment: sinister, luxurious, commercial. Iago and Mosca are "fraternal twins" with similar manifestos. Both are Machiavels who invert the traditional moral scheme, and are "pre-revolutionary" in their intention to manipulate the existing order rather than define new ethical aims for themselves. Both plays hinge primarily on the theme of deception. Jonson has trouble enunciating a positive value system and betrays some ambiguity in his attitude towards Volpone, who, though a "sinister portent," is at the same time a "potential titan," who has to be thrown in prison so as not to run away with the play.

508 CROSSLEY, BRIAN, and EDWARDS, PAUL. "Spenser's Bawdy: A Note on The Fairy Queen 2:6." PLL 9 (1973):314-19.
As used in Volpone, "gondola" was associated with sexuality.

509 CUTTS, JOHN P. "Volpone's Song: A Note on the Source and Jonson's Translation." N&Q 203 (1958):217-19.
Disagrees with Herford and Simpson's conclusion that the source of Jonson's snatch of song following "Come, my Celia," is Catullus's seventh poem. The poem is derived from Catullus's fifth poem.

510 DAVISON, P. H. "Volpone and the Old Comedy." MLQ 24 (1963):151-57.
Jonson is indebted to Aristophanes, from whom he borrowed the characters of the impostor and the ironical buffoon. Volpone and Mosca each play both roles. Other aspects of Aristophanic comedy--savage satire, farce, and

burlesque--also appear in Volpone, but a major difference in the two dramatists is Jonson's "greater concern for moral issues."

511 DEAN, LEONARD F. "Three Notes on Comic Morality: Celia, Bobadill, and Falstaff." SEL 16 (1976):263-71.
Ensemble acting and theatrical elements are essential to the comic morality of the plays. Some of Jonson's best moral thinkers are social outsiders.

512 No entry

513 DE SILVA, DEREK. Jonson: Wit and the Moral Sense in "Volpone" and the Major Comedies. JDS 1, 1972, pp. 194-211. [Bound with John Webster's Imagery and the Webster Canon by Sanford Sternlicht.]
Volpone, The Alchemist, and Bartholomew Fair show Jonson's belief that, in art, aesthetic pleasure need not be identified with moral wholeness. The impudence and ingenuity of his major evil figures heighten their stage presence, giving them a kind of excellence.

514 DESSEN, ALAN C. "Volpone and the Late Morality Tradition." MLQ 25 (1964):383-99.
The main plot of Volpone draws on the late Elizabethan moralities (1560-1590) for theme, character, and structure. Jonson's chief theme, "the various ways in which Money or Lucre can dominate society," is found in many extant plays of the period. Jonson also adopts the three types of morality characters: Vices, Virtues, and "estates" (social types, each of which enacts the vice in his area of society). The structure of the play derives from a situation familiar to the late moralities: "the rescue of Heavenly Man from Worldly Man by Good Conscience."

515 DONALDSON, IAN. "Jonson's Italy: Volpone and Fr. Thomas Wright." N&Q 217 (1972):450-52.
Wright's book, The Passions of the minde in generall (1601), could have contributed to Jonson's presentation of Italians as corrupt, crafty figures and the English as simple, virtuous, but unwary people.

516 _____. "Jonson's Tortoise." RES 19 (1968):162-66.
The tortoise scene fails not, as some critics feel, because it is a pointless piece of farce, but because its humor is too esoteric. Jonson unites three emblematic motifs: the tortoise as an emblem of policy (a means to keep safe), of silence (in classical literature the tortoise is thought to be tongueless), of the two most important

qualities of a chaste woman (silence and keeping to her house). Combining these meanings, the scene in the subplot relates in several ways to the total meaning of the play.

517 _____. "Volpone." EIC 22 (1972):216-18.
Yeats finds a pathos in Celia and Bonario being united not in love but in innocence and going their separate ways. He is very alert to the surprise of the last act, but seems to have forgotten that the play is a comedy. Jonson's comic subversion of Bonario may be an attempt to lighten the work.

518 _____. "Volpone: Quick and Dead." EIC 21 (1971):121-34.
Critics frequently misinterpret the way the comedy's moral force operates. Celia and Bonario may represent Christian values, but they enjoy a very subordinate, relatively impotent role. Volpone and Mosca, however, are filled with energy, and constantly play off sickness and death against it. The play's excitement comes from the ways their energy slowly falls victim to law, sickness, and death. Feigning illness for mischief, Volpone must come to realize decay.

519 DOOB, P. B. R., and SHAND, G. B. "Jonson's Tortoise and Avian." Ren&R 10 (1974):43-44.
Avian's fable of the tortoise and other birds provides an analogue to the Peregrine-Sir Politic plot. The tortoise, image of foolish aspirations and personal enhancement, matches Sir Pol. Peregrine, like the eagle in the fable, arranges Pol's humiliation.

520 DRAPER, R. P. "The Golden Age and Volpone's Address to His Gold." N&Q 201 (1956):191-92.
Jonson deliberately recalls the Golden Age in the play's opening, with an emphasis on freedom from the need to work because of Nature's providence. Volpone's distortion of the concept and his rejection of normal means of making a living emphasize the contrast between his depravity and the innocence of man in the Ovidian Golden Age.

521 DREW, DAVID. "Volpone Above-Board." New Statesman, 28 April 1961, pp. 681-82.
Reviews the opera Volpone composed by Francis Burt and presented by the New Opera Company. Although Drew does not find the work of major importance, he finds that "it has some estimable virtues."

Volpone

522 DUNCAN, DOUGLAS. "Audience-Manipulation in Volpone." WascanaR 5 (1970):23-37.

Jonson borrowed mainly from Lucian's 9th Dialogue of the Dead for the method and content of Volpone. He failed, however, to separate the ironist from his characters, letting Mosca's and Volpone's selves reside wholly in their art. The audience is challenged to keep its moral bearings against the author's manipulations, particularly those of the Celia subplot and the Would-bes. Volpone's character gains its force not from any inner complexity but from his ability to change his attitudes and methods rapidly. The play does not present Jonson's vision of the world but rather a fable whose impersonality masks an inquisitorial purpose.

523 DUTTON, A. RICHARD. "Volpone and The Alchemist: A Comparison in Satiric Techniques." RMS 18 (1974):36-62.

Jonson anticipates a new relationship with his audiences in these equally serious satires. He implies a universal context, counting on each audience being susceptible to some folly.

524 ELLIS-FERMOR, UNA M. "Dramatic Notes." English 2 (1938): 41-43.

Review of Group Theatre production. The play is extremely difficult to stage. Successful performance requires abandoning strict Jacobean interpretations of drama.

525 EMPSON, WILLIAM. "Volpone." HudR 21 (1968-69):651-66.

Readers and critics need a more jovial approach to Volpone. The play shows the evil and the commercial importance of Venice, which produces characters like Volpone, whom English audiences would have themselves exonerated.

526 ENRIGHT, D. J. "Poetic Satire and Satire in Verse: A Consideration of Jonson and Massinger." Scrutiny 18 (1952): 211-23. [Reprinted in his The Apothecary's Shop. Philadelphia: Dufour, 1957, pp. 54-74. Reprint. Greenwich, Conn.: Greenwood Press, 1975.]

Study of Volpone and Massinger's plays shows that "Jonson wrote poetic satire, Massinger wrote satire in verse." Celia and Bonario are not the positive standards by which the rogues are judged; the standards rest within the play's plot structure and poetry. A subtle technique disposes of Volpone: he condemns himself through the imagery and rhythms of his poetic satire. His overreaching temperament, not Mosca's machinations, ruins him. Massinger's plays lack Jonson's demolishing poetry.

527 ERVINE, ST. JOHN. "Volpone, or, The Foxe." Observer (London), 6 February 1921, p. 9.
Review of Phoenix Society production. Volpone demonstrates Jonson's skill as a dramatic craftsman and the importance of robustness.

528 FARJEON, HERBERT. "Theatres." Graphic (London) 30 (January 1932):167.
Review of Venturers' Society production of Zweig adaptation. Zweig's adaptation ruined the play, but the original also palls, owing to lack of variety.

529 FITZGIBBON, G. "An Echo of Volpone in The Broken Heart." N&Q 220 (1975):248-49.
Corvino and Bassanes threaten their wives in similar ways.

530 FIZDALE, TAY. "Jonson's Volpone and the 'Real' Antinous." RenQ 26 (1973):454-59.
Volpone probably refers to Antinous of The Odyssey in III.vii.157-64.

531 FLEMING, PETER. "The Theatre. Volpone." Spectator (London), 30 January 1932, p. 141.
Review of Venturers' Society production of Zweig adaptation. Zweig has "stolen the theme, lost the spirit, and mangled the plot" of the original; "a shoddy transatlantic fustian has superseded Jonson's verse."

532 FREEMAN, ARTHUR. "The Earliest Allusion to Volpone." N&Q 212 (1967):207-08.
Henry Parrot's collection of epigrams, The Mous-Trap (1606), seems to contain the earliest datable allusion to the play.

533 FRIEDENREICH, KENNETH. "Volpone and the Confessio Amantis." SCB 37 (1977):147-50.
Cites several parallels between the play and Gower's poem. Karl Brunner's suggestion of one such parallel, made in 1927 (see 497a), has been ignored by modern editors of the play.

534 G., G. "Jonson and Fletcher." Saturday Review (London), 7 July 1923, pp. 10-11.
Review of Phoenix Society production. Jonson's "majestic intelligence is curiously and querulously at work" in Volpone--"learned, angry, metaphysical." The play depends too much on construction and not enough on the subtleties

of human nature. In performance, even the magnificent language is seen as subordinate to the action.

534a GARCÍA DENIZ, JOSÉ A. "Aspectos del Humor en Volpone de Ben Jonson." FMod 12 (1972):281-97.
If Jonson had presented only a world of evil, as has been claimed, his didactic purposes would have been defeated. He presents a world both good and evil by means of an equilibrium between "negative" humor, a species of ironic humor, and "positive" humor; the alternation between them contributes to a pattern of tension and release which governs the structure of the first four acts of Volpone.

535 GARLAND, ROBERT. "Volpone Presented at Century Theatre," in New York Theatre Critics' Reviews 8 (10 March 1947):448. [Originally published New York Journal American, 25 Febuary 1947.]
Century Theatre production. This first presentation of the real Volpone on a Broadway stage shows Jonson's intoxication with life, his loud, lusty humor.

536 GERTMENIAN, DONALD. "Comic Experience in Volpone and The Alchemist." SEL 17 (1977):247-58.
The first scene of each play both defines the issues of the dramas and suggests distinctions between them. Unlike Volpone, which maintains a balance between pleasure and uneasiness, The Alchemist immediately focuses on pleasure coming from appreciation of mere energy. Presenting a conflict of man against man, it skirts moral affirmation and forces the reader to let his judgment relax and conquer any dislike. The plays indicate Jonson's division between sheer energy and order; he enjoyed the former but did not trust it.

537 _____. "Volpone's Mortification." EIC 26 (1976):274-77.
In V.xii, Volpone becomes a moral exemplum as he awaits his punishment and, for the first time in the play, is subservient to the court. His apologetic epilogue comes from Jonson, not from his own character or final situation. Significant changes at the play's end create conflicting feelings in the audience: acceptance of justice but bewilderment at the denial of delight.

538 GIANAKARIS, C. J. "Identifying Ethical Values in Volpone." HLQ 32 (1968):45-57.
Volpone differs from other Jonsonian comedies because no trustworthy commentator exists. Characters fall into three groups according to their perceptiveness and function. Jonson counted on his audiences' conventional morality.

539 _____. "Jonson's Use of 'Avocatori' in Volpone." ELN 12 (1974):8-14.

Jonson's assigning a dual role to the avocatori shows his sophisticated grasp of Venetian judicial practices during the republican period, when such men did serve as both lawyers and judges.

540 GOLDBERG, S. L. "Folly into Crime: The Catastrophe of Volpone." MLQ 20 (1959):233-42.

Audiences' attraction to the villains during the drama leads to ambiguous feelings when they receive harsh punishments. The dilemma grows by the shift in Act IV from private to public folly and realization of the seriousness involved in inverting proper order. Jonson attempts to lighten the play's grim conclusion by Volpone's extra-dramatic reminder that all has been a play, but the problem remains. In contrast, Jonson preserves comic tone throughout The Alchemist, thus helping audiences to accept that play's diversities.

541 GRAHAM, C. B. "An Echo of Jonson in Aphra Behn's Sir Patient Fancy." MLN 53 (1938):278-79.

Behn's play borrows the opening lines of Volpone, but uses them for a very non-Jonsonian purpose.

542 GREENBLATT, STEPHEN J. "The False Ending In Volpone." JEGP 75 (1976):90-104.

The false ending (close of Act IV) tests the audience, questions the "natural," and shows the emptiness inherent in self-creation. By Act V, Volpone begins to fear real things, but then turns these into fiction. By the true end of the play he and Mosca are fixed as displaced figures, a fitting result of Volpone's initial displacement of God. Jonson wishes the audience to reject theatrical principles of displacement, mask, and metamorphoses, associating the claims of the poet as teacher with cant and hucksterism.

543 HALLETT, CHARLES A. "Jonson's Celia: A Reinterpretation of Volpone." SP 68 (1971):50-69.

Celia has a central, determining role in the play; she deserves and rewards seriousness of study given to other characters. Volpone causes his own downfall, but Jonson sees the events of Act V as providential, thus endorsing Celia's stance.

Volpone

544 _____. "The Satanic Nature of Volpone." PQ 49 (1970):41-55. Volpone employs and builds on both the fable and Christian tradition paralleling Satan and the fox. Letting Volpone damn himself, Jonson shows him as the incarnation of evil, deeply corrupt. Associating Volpone with Mammon also reinforces parallels with Satan. The potentially disturbing Act IV is fitting since the court is part of Volpone's world and hence subject to his control. Further, in the Christian context, good is rewarded in the next world.

545 _____. "Volpone as the Source of the Sickroom Scene in Middleton's Mad World." N&Q 216 (1971):24-26.
Parallels between the two plays include a feigned illness, duped visitors, an accomplice in deception, and use of a bawd.

546 HAN, PIERRE. "'Tabarine' in Ben Jonson's Volpone." SCN 28 (1970):4-5.
"Tabarine" was probably a nom de parade for improvisations undertaken by many travelling companies in Europe. Jonson seems to be referring not to an individual, but to "a whole tradition of improvised buffoonery that characterized the Italian commedia dell'arte."

547 HARTMAN, JAY H. "Volpone as a Possible Source for Melville's The Confidence Man." SUS 7 (1965):247-60.
Melville owned a copy of Volpone. Both authors lived in times when commercialism threatened traditional values. In view of striking similarities in theme, characterization, and structure, it seems possible that Volpone was a source of ideas for The Confidence Man.

548 HAWKINS, HARRIETT. "Folly, Incurable Disease, and Volpone." SEL 8 (1968):335-48.
Draws parallels between the worlds of the play and Erasmus' In Praise of Folly. The end of Volpone relates directly to thematic development of the plot, reinforcing the earlier ramifications of poetry and comic irony.

549 HEILMAN, ROBERT B. "Dramas of Money." Shenandoah 21 (Summer 1970):20-33.
Volpone proclaims that money will do anything and is a touchstone for many plays focusing on wealth.

550 HELTON, TINSLEY. "Theme as a Shaping Factor in Volpone and The Alchemist." EngR 13 (1963):38-46.

Explains the discrepancy in the punishments meted out by Jonson at the conclusions of the plays by stating that Jonson shaped his material in each to emphasize his major theme, greed in Volpone and fraud in The Alchemist. Greed, a personal sin, debases personal relationships and hence is more severely punished than fraud, "clearly a social vice."

551 HILL, W. SPEED. "Biography, Autobiography, and Volpone." SEL 12 (1972):309-28.

Jonson's autobiography may help solve some ethical ambiguities in Volpone. Creating a good world through the evil of Venice, Jonson illustrates his serious moral purpose, but the play does not conclude in a clear moral victory.

552 HOFFMANN, GERHARD. "Zur Form der satirischen Komödie: Ben Jonsons Volpone." DVLG 46 (1972):1-27.

Points out the difficulties of classification and interpretation of plays that combine comic and satiric intent. Analyzes, in Volpone, the relationship between comic and satiric structural elements, under four headings: characters, interpretation of the comic conflict, the picture of society, and plot structure. Notes that Volpone combines a "rise and fall" (comic) and "circular" (satiric) structure, and becomes gradually "darker" as the satiric tends increasingly to dominate the comic in the course of the play. Jonson's integration of the two modes is exceptionally successful in Volpone, a comedy whose "hermetic" qualities have been approached only in 20th-century drama.

553 JANICKA, IRENA. "The Subplot of Volpone and The Three Lords and Three Ladies of London." KN 15 (1968):306-07.

The subplot of Volpone burlesques the late morality play.

554 KRONENBERGER, LOUIS. "Les Liaisons Dangereuses." MQR 8 (1969):181-88.

Volpone, a model for some of Laclos's characters, belongs to the group of characters who gloat over making fools of others while pursuing evil themselves. He has a single motivating purpose and becomes more a symbol than a person.

Volpone

555 LEGGATT, ALEXANDER. "The Suicide of Volpone." UTQ 39 (1969):19-32.
Volpone's risk-taking and ultimate suicide stem not from overreaching but from his basic theatricality. The play cannot end in reconciliation because of its satiric nature. The epilogue deserves greater attention.

556 LEVIN, HARRY. "Jonson's Metempsychosis." PQ 22 (1943):231-39.
Volpone develops the prominent Jacobean theme of disinheritance and the broader theme of inherent evil in the world. The chorus of deformed servants relates to the theme which in turn relates to Jonson's age. Prefigured by Lucian's cobbler in Gallus, Volpone's suitors connect the interlude and play through the theme of transmigration. The theme, and the problem of evil, appear also in Donne (The Progress of the Soul) and Shakespeare (Hamlet).

557 LITT, DOROTHY E. "Unity of Theme in Volpone." BNYPL 73 (1969):218-26.
Charges brought against the play indicate the need to see it performed. Jonson emphasizes the human tendency to believe whatever flatters one's hopes, regardless of the truth. The two plots relate very directly, with the Would-bes imaging the would-be heirs.

558 LOKHORST, EMMY VAN. "Volpone." Gids 94 (January 1930): 137-41. (In Dutch.)
Comments on the demonic elements in Zweig's adaptation.

559 LYLE, ALEXANDER W. "Volpone's Two Worlds." YES 4 (1974): 70-76.
Contrasts Volpone's performance and success in his bedroom, where he functions as an artist, and in the outside world, where he is a real person and is subject to judgment. Jonson, placing him in the real world early in the play, calls on the audience to condemn him from the beginning.

560 M., L. "Volpone in den K.N.S." [Volpone at the Royal Dutch Theatre.] Het Tooneel (Antwerp), 16 March 1935, pp. 1-3; 23 March 1935, pp. 1-3, 7. (In Dutch.)
Review of Zweig version.

561 McCANLES, MICHAEL. "Mythos and Dianoia: A Dialectical Methodology of Literary Form." LMonog 4 (1971):1-88.
Plot, the Aristotelian "ultimate principle of coherent form," derives from "the attempt on the part of the agent of the plot to avoid and deny plot." Volpone is examined

in terms of a dialectic in which static theme (dianoia) and dynamic plot (mythos) not only mirror but oppose each other. The arrangement of the play's plot and its sub-themes is "rigidly controlled not by the play's dianoia directly, but by the attempts of the characters to deny this dianoia."

562 MacCARTHY, DESMOND. "Ben Jonson: An Object Lesson." New Statesman, 5 February 1921, pp. 530-32. [Reprinted in his Humanities. New York: Oxford University Press, 1953, pp. 54-59.]

Review of Phoenix Society production. Although the humor and the character drawings in Volpone are not first-rate, its figures have great vitality. Jonson's limitations are seen in the insipidity of Bonario and Celia, and in the fact that the overpowering quality of evil in the punished characters prevents the audience from experiencing relief at the end of the play.

563 _____. "Volpone Revived." New Statesman and Nation, 29 January 1938, pp. 164-65.

Review of Westminster Theatre production. Jonson's comic world resembles Balzac's; his period of Catholicism enabled him to rejoice in humanity even while seeing it as wicked.

564 McKENZIE, KENNETH. "Ben Jonson's Lombard Proverb." MLN 27 (1912):263.

A Piedmont or Lombard proverb uses "to have cold feet" in the same sense Volpone does in the mountebank scene: to retreat from one's position.

565 McPHERSON, DAVID. "Rough Beast into Tame Fox: The Adaptations of Volpone." SLitI 6 (April 1973):77-84. (See 40.)

Most major adaptations since 1771 tamed Volpone and recast Celia and Bonario. Productions since 1947 have moved back to the original text, which is hardly too indelicate for the modern stage.

566 MERCHANT, W. MOELWYN. Comedy. Critical Idiom Series, No. 21, London: Methuen, 1972, pp. 2, 3, 40, 41, 42-44, 70-72.

Jonson's claim that comedy sports with follies does not account for the darker side of his comical satires, making his intentions ambiguous. Volpone is closer to Aristophanes than to Shakespeare; "the hard edge of Jonson's irony cuts into the social evil."

Volpone

567 MILLER, JOYCE. "*Volpone*: A Study in Dramatic Ambiguity," in *Studies in English Language and Literature*. Edited by Alice Shalvi and A. A. Mendilow. Publications of The Hebrew University, 17. Jerusalem: The Hebrew University, 1966, pp. 35-95.

Conflicting critical statements result from the ambiguity in I.i. By eschewing the religious world, Volpone and Mosca immediately reveal their ignorance and corruption; the final scene is a natural result. The play is a highly unified satirical farce.

568 NARDO, A. K. "The Transmigration of Folly: Volpone's Innocent Grotesques." *ES* 58 (1977):105-09.

Innocent figures, Volpone's dwarf, hermaphrodite, and eunuch have no ruthless ambition or avarice but, rather, show positive qualities: they can entertain, and they have more creative self-knowledge than any other character. Mosca's setting them free at the end is appropriate and points to the broad tolerance Jonson will show in *The Alchemist* and *Bartholomew Fair*.

569 NASH, RALPH. "The Comic Intent of *Volpone*." *SP* 44 (1947): 26-40.

Argues against critics of *Volpone* who have ignored Jonson's statement of comic intent in the Prologue and see the play as grim and sardonic. The harsh punishment of wrongdoers would not have bothered the Elizabethan audience unless it was "insufficient."

570 NEWTON, GLORIA E. "Dramatic Imagery in *Volpone*." *The Manitoba Arts Review* 8 (1952):9-17.

Each Jonson play incorporates the theme that unrestrained self-assertion is wrong and must be punished. *Volpone*, high-point of the canon, gains power by skillful incorporation of intrinsic images.

571 NOYES, R. G. "Importing Jonson Via the North Sea." *New York Times*, 22 April 1928, p. 29.

Review of New York Theatre Guild production of Zweig-Romains adaptation. Zweig respects his chief source and creates a good work. Changes include giving all characters animal names; removing Volpone's household, the mountebank scene, the love song to Celia, and the entire subplot.

572 ______. "A Manuscript Restoration Prologue for *Volpone*." *MLN* 52 (1937):198-200.

Prints a previously unpublished anonymous prologue written about 1675.

573 _____. "'Volpone,' the Evolution of a Nickname." Harvard Studies and Notes in Philology 16 (1934):161-75.

Aesop's fables and Volpone enjoyed great popularity in the late 17th century and provided the nickname for Sidney Godolphin: Queen Anne's treasurer was known as "the old Volpone." The 18th-century political satires also found Jonson's play a rich source and helped make "Volpone" the name/term with the most varied history.

574 ORNSTEIN, ROBERT. "The Ethical Design of The Revenger's Tragedy." ELH 21 (1954):81-93.

The ethical design of Tourneur's play resembles that of Volpone: a world of evil governed by a detached moral order.

575 _____. "Volpone and Renaissance Psychology." N&Q 201 (1956): 471-72.

Jonson's audience did not consider Volpone a near-tragic figure, as many modern readers do. Rather, it would have recognized in Volpone the conventional vices of the "rich man" as he was portrayed by F. N. Coeffeteau in his Table of Human Passions.

576 P., A. "Volpone." Spectator (London), 7 July 1923, p. 14.

Review of Phoenix Society production. The play puts no strain on a company because it does not demand "getting inside" the dialogue. Jonson is conscienceless in making virtue so overwhelmingly triumphant but succeeds in producing a tightly constructed play.

577 PALUMBO, RONALD J. "Volpone, III.vii.100-105: A Mocking Allusion." AN&Q 13 (1975):98-99.

Corvino's threat to lash his wife to a dead slave recalls Antonio's Revenge, but Jonson makes the image purely comic.

578 PARFITT, GEORGE A. E. "Notes on the Classical Borrowings in Volpone." ES 55 (1974):127-32.

Approximately 10 percent of the play comes from the classics. Jonson never superimposes borrowed material but weaves it into his own dramatic context.

579 _____. "Virtue and Pessimism in Three Plays by Ben Jonson." SLitI 6 (April 1973):23-40. (See 40.)

Volpone, Bartholomew Fair, and Sejanus present three different kinds of virtuous characters, all of whom are significant figures but none of whom really triumphs over evil or foolishness.

Volpone

580 _____. "Volpone." EIC 21 (1971):411-12.
Discussing Jonson's intentions relating to the frailty and solitariness of Celia and Bonario is futile. Their impotence against corruption is not a defect in the play but part of reality, for evil characters also come to defeat. Volpone's pessimism results from its world, in which virtue fails to be operative.

581 PARKER, R. B. "Volpone and Reynard the Fox." RenD NS 7 (1976):3-42.
Careful study of the many forms of the Reynard story, as presented in both literature and iconography, reveals many elements directly presented in Volpone. Jonson could have counted on his audience to recognize the fox's feigning illness and death to attract the gulls, his desire to have the crow's wife, his attempt at rape, his manipulation of the court, and his role-playing as doctor and preacher. Jonson himself probably knew the fable's complexities better than did his audience, and drew on it for other less easily recognized details. The strong association of the play and the fable indicates another source of unity in the play and accounts for apparent contradictions in tone.

582 _____. "Wolfit's Fox: An Interpretation of Volpone." UTQ 45 (1976):200-20.
Compares Donald Wolfit's final London performance as Volpone with other artists' presentations. Pruning and relating the total play to himself, Wolfit offered a ruthless, highly virile Volpone and maintained a comic tone by balancing audiences' sympathy for and repudiation of the Fox.

583 PERKINSON, RICHARD H. "Volpone and the Reputation of Venetian Justice." MLR 35 (1940):11-18.
Accounts for Jonson's setting Volpone in Venice. To the Elizabethan mind, Italy was a land lawless enough to produce Volpone and Jonson's other realistic villains; the reputation for integrity and severity of the Venetian courts was strong enough to make the dénouement plausible. Jonson probably derived his knowledge from Lewis Lewkenor's translation of Contarini's De Magistratibus et Republica Venetorum.

584 PINEAS, RAINER. "The Morality Vice in Volpone." Discourse 5 (1961-1962):451-59.
Traces the influence of the morality-play figure Vice upon the arch-villains in Volpone. Volpone and Mosca evince the chief traits of the Vice by proclaiming love of evil for itself, by deceiving, and by using disguise.

Having the two villains turn upon and deceive each other is also characteristic of the morality play.

585 POTTER, ROBERT. "Volpone as a Jacobean Everyman," in his The English Morality Play: Origins, History and Influence of a Dramatic Tradition. London and Boston: Routledge and Kegan Paul, 1975, pp. 144-52.

Volpone is "a rich savage theatrical treatise on human nature, as defined by the eventuality of death." Jonson reverses the pattern of Everyman (withdrawal from the worldly concerns of Fellowship, Kindred, and Cousin), parodies the stage devices of mercy and despair, and draws on other morality devices such as Lady Lechery, Mercy, and the Vice. He brings his fictional sinners to their punishment and, in the spirit of the moralities, warns "the yet-unjudged audience."

586 RICHTER, HELENE. "Ben Jonsons Volpone und sein Erneuerer Stefan Zweig." Shakespeare-Jahrbuch 63 (1927):183-90.

In many ways, Zweig's adaptation suits modern audiences better than the original; it is more compactly constructed and goes beyond Jonson's more narrowly conceived notions of character types. Zweig's elimination of the subplot is of dubious value, and he allows Mosca to fall out of his role. Zweig's amoral conclusion fits modern times, when only the unimaginative ask about right and wrong.

587 SALINGAR, LEO. "Comic Form in Ben Jonson: Volpone and the Philosopher's Stone," in English Drama: Forms and Development. Essays in Honour of Muriel Clara Bradbrook. Edited by Marie Axton and Raymond Williams. Cambridge: Cambridge University Press, 1977, pp. 48-69.

Jonson's best plays, Volpone and The Alchemist, both employ the unifying symbol of alchemy and release the two sides of his personality: rational control and energetic fantasy. All characters in Volpone make (or attempt to make) something from nothing and thrive on others' hopes; Volpone himself incarnates the quintessence of his clients' vices. The play contains more references to health than to fraud and focuses on Jonson's concern about improvisation based on opportunism. The Alchemist depends upon and develops many of the methods and kinds of characters in Volpone. Jonson drew heavily from Plutus (Aristophanes) and Timon (Lucan) for the comedies.

<u>Volpone</u>

588 _____. "The Revenger's Tragedy: Some Possible Sources." MLR 60 (1965):3-12.
Volpone is mentioned as sharing characteristics with The Revenger's Tragedy, and as an example of a play "based on a moral idea for which the dramatist invented a situation, filling it out with originally disconnected items from his observations and his reading."

589 SCHEVE, D. A. "Jonson's Volpone and Traditional Folk Lore." RES NS 1 (1950):242-44.
Jonson interweaves the theme of legacy-hunting drawn from Petronius or Lucian with the story from animal lore of the fox feigning death in order to catch birds, found in Conrad Gesner's Historia Animalium, a book Jonson owned. Traces the story from Oppianus in the 1st century to the 17th century.

590 SERONSY, CECIL C. "Sir Politic Would-Be in Laputa." ELN 1 (1963):17-24.
Sir Politic resembles characters in Gulliver's Travels III, 5 and 6.

591 SIMMONS, J. L. "Volpone as Antinous: Jonson and Th'Overthrow of Stage-Playes." MLR 70 (1975):13-19.
The William Gager-John Rainolds controversy attracted Jonson's attention. Volpone's career ironically confirms a Rainolds argument against acting; moral idealism associated with Gager does not dispel the play's darkness.

592 SMITH, WINIFRED. "Italian Actors in Elizabethan England." MLN 44 (1929):375-77.
Scoto of Mantua, whose real name was Dionisio, is alluded to in Volpone. Although James I refers to his "juglarie trickes" and "false practicques" in Daemonologie, a letter written to the Grand Duke of Tuscany in 1602 provides evidence that Dionisio, also called "Scotto Mantovano," was both an actor and the leader of an acting troupe. The letter is reproduced.

593 SOUTH, MALCOLM H. "Animal Imagery in Volpone." TSL 10 (1965):141-50.
Jonson drew on the description of the fox and other animal imagery from the Bestiary and popular animal lore literature known in the Renaissance. Illustrates in detail how Jonson reinforces the characterization, tone, and action as well as structure, theme, and satire through his use of animal imagery and allusion.

594 STERNFELD, FREDERICK W. "Song in Jonson's Comedy: A Gloss on Volpone." Studies in the English Renaissance Drama in Memory of Karl Julius Holzknecht. Edited by Josephine W. Bennett, Oscar Cargill, and Vernon Hall, Jr. New York: New York University Press, 1959, pp. 310-21. [Reprint. London: P. Owen & Vision Press, 1961.]

For Jonson, music, like poetry, could be well used or misused. He tended to use little in his plays, but the setting of Volpone's song to Celia (presumably the one composed by Ferrabosco) "adds pungency to the comedy without descending to the level of . . . degenerate music." This version of Catullus's "Vivamus mea Lesbia" is compared with two attributed to Campion.

595 SWINNERTON, FRANK. "The Drama: Volpone." Nation (London), 5 February 1921, p. 633.

Review of Phoenix Society production. The play is sordid and revolting, and immersed in the evil it reveals, but saved by "a great strictness of characterization and invention, and a really notable ingenuity in the arrangement of successive climaxes." It reveals Jonson's tough, almost savage mind, which takes pleasure in reinforcing our knowledge of ugliness.

596 SYLVESTER, WILLIAM. "Jonson's 'Come, My Celia' and Catullus' 'Carmen V.'" Expl 22 (January 1964): item 35.

Catulus's song gives an attitudinal dimension to Jonson's lyric and relates directly to Volpone's action.

597 TARN. "Volpone at the Phoenix." Spectator (London), 5 February 1921, p. 170.

Review of Phoenix Society production. Volpone shows Jonson in his most railing mood and at his peak of dramatic construction. It is more a Restoration than an Elizabethan drama.

598 TULIP, JAMES. "Comedy as Equivocation: An Approach to the Reference of Volpone." SoRA 5 (1972):91-101.

Predicated on a world of play, Volpone is both its own subject and object. Jonson may refer to the Gunpowder Plot, but definitely refers to contemporary political events and issues.

599 WATTS, RICHARD, JR. "Wolfit Players at Their Best in Ben Jonson's Scornful Play," in New York Theatre Critics' Reviews 8 (10 March 1947):449. [Originally published New York Post, 25 Feburary 1947.]

Review of Century Theatre production. The play presents a lugubrious story of evil triumphant, but in a genuinely funny way.

Volpone

600 WELD, JOHN S. "Christian Comedy: Volpone." SP 51 (1954): 172-93.

Argues that the unifying theme of the play is the folly of worldliness, not avarice or greed. Defines "worldliness" as it was understood in contemporary sermons, emblem books, and devotional literature: "essentially an inversion or misdirection of love, toward the vain and fleeting delights of the earth instead of toward the only lasting and truly enjoyable object, God." Volpone's opening speech and actions, like the devices of a morality play, represent the inverted values of the chief character; the scenes and episodes in the play involving Volpone and all of the other fools are "built into a structure of layered parallels . . . [to] make the theme clear to the reader." The unmasking and punishment of all of the fools, including the arch-fool Volpone, is consistent with Jonson's intent of revealing the absurdity of the worldly, who are blinded by self-love and inordinate passions.

601 WELSH, JAMES M. "Shades of Ben Jonson and Stefan Zweig: Volpone on Film." SAB 39 (November 1974):43-50.

The French film (1939) significantly alters both Jonson's work (characterization and justice) and Zweig's adaptation (names and personalities). It aims at verisimilitude, offers a Marxist allegory, and possesses good visual style.

602 WESCOTT, ROBERT. "Volpone--or The Fox?" CR 17 (1974):82-96.

Compares Volpone's and Mosca's purposes and skills in playing. The constant exercise of animosity becomes associated with complex subversions of personality.

603 WHITING, GEORGE W. "Volpone, Herr Von Fuchs, and Les Héritiers Rabourdin." PMLA 46 (1931):605-07.

Zola borrowed only his theme from Volpone. Tieck remained closer to Jonson, but Herr Von Fuchs is a lighter play than Volpone.

604 YOUNG, STARK. "The Theater Guild's 'Volpone'." New Republic, 25 April 1928, pp. 295-96.

Review of Theatre Guild production of Zweig-Romains adaptation. Jonson is too far removed from modern theatrical capacities and powers of response for effective presentation; Zweig's work makes the play accessible while maintaining its humor, plotting, and characterization.

605 ZWAGER, N. H. M. "Ben Jonson's Religion." Tijdschrift voor Taal en Lettern (Amsterdam) 12 (1924):188-91.
In Sir Politic Would-be, Jonson is ridiculing Sir Henry Wotton and the gossip-mongering of anti-Catholic Protestants living abroad.

Volpone: Performance Reviews

606 BIRRELL, FRANCIS. "Volpone at Cambridge." New Statesman, 10 March 1923, p. 659.
Marlowe Society production.

607 ANON. "Two Guild Plays Face Police Watch." New York Times, 25 April 1928, p. 31.
New York City District Attorney Banton assigned an assistant district attorney to an investigation of the Theatre Guild's productions of Volpone and Strange Interlude to determine if they violated the Wales law against "objectionable performances."

608 ANON. "Banton Reads Guild Plays." New York Times, 26 April 1928, p. 29.
New York City District Attorney Banton was reported to be reading Volpone and Strange Interlude to determine if the Theatre Guild productions of these plays violated the Wales law.

609 ANON. "Wallace Sees Volpone." New York Times, 29 April 1928, Sec. 1, p. 13.
New York City Assistant District Attorney Wallace, accompanied by a representative of the Police Commissioner's office, attended a performance of Volpone on April 28. Jonson's play, and O'Neill's Strange Interlude, both Theatre Guild productions, had been cited as "improper and objectionable, and within the purview of the Wales Padlock law," according to complaints from the Shuberts, one of whose plays had been closed down.

610 ANON. "Strange Interlude Cleared by Banton. Volpone Also is Found Not to Violate Wales Law Against Objectionable Plays." New York Times, 2 May 1928, p. 16.
On the basis of visits of two of his assistants, New York City District Attorney Banton decided that "the [Theatre Guild] productions would not tend to corrupt the morals of youth or others, which is the test of the new law." He felt, however, that there were lines in the plays that offended against good taste.

Volpone

611 ANON. "Volpone." Life, 9 July 1945, pp. 93-94, 97.
Actors' Laboratory production.

612 ANON. "Shakespeare Outfoxed." Time, 10 March 1947, p. 44.
New York Century Theatre production.

613 HAWKINS, WILLIAM. "Wolfit's Volpone Hits Uneven Note," in New York Theatre Critics' Reviews 8 (10 March 1947):449. [Originally published New York World Telegram, 25 February 1947.]
New York Century Theatre production.

614 MORGAN, FREDERICK. "The Season on Broadway (II)." SR 55 (1947):517-20.
London Company production.

615 BEYER, WILLIAM. "The State of the Theater: Mid-Season High Lights." School and Society, 31 January 1948, p. 87.
New York City Theatre Company production.

616 GIBBS, WOLCOTT. "Rough Stuff." NY, 17 January 1948, pp. 40, 42.
New York City Theatre Company production.

617 KRUTCH, JOSEPH WOOD. "Drama." Nation, 24 January 1948, pp. 108-09.
New York City Theatre Company production.

618 McCARTHY, MARY. "Theater Chronicle: Modest Proposals." PR 15 (1948):477-80. [Reprinted in her Sights and Spectacles: 1937-1956. New York: Farrar, Straus and Cudahy, 1956, pp. 136-37; and Mary McCarthy's Theatre Chronicles: 1937-1962. New York: Farrar, Straus, 1963, pp. 136-37.]
New York City Theatre Company production.

619 WYATT, EUPHEMIA VAN RENSSELAER. "Volpone." Catholic World 166 (1948):457-58.
New York City Theatre Company production.

620 CLURMAN, HAROLD. "Theatre." Nation, 10 August 1964, p. 59.
Tyrone Guthrie Theatre production.

621 PENSA, CARLO MARIA. "Troppi nemici per Ben Jonson." FLe 48 (1972):26.
Olimpico di Vicenza production.

Volpone: Performance Reviews, Zweig Adaptation

622 SELLMAN, PRISCILLA M. "The Old Globe's Sixth Season in San Diego." SQ 7 (1956):419-22.

623 HEWES, HENRY. "The Westport Itch." SatR, 2 March 1957, p. 26.
Second Avenue Rooftop Theatre production.

624 LEWIS, THEOPHILUS. "Theatre." America, 16 February 1957, pp. 566-67.
Second Avenue Rooftop Theatre production.

625 SCOBIE, W. I. "England in Los Angeles." National Review, 4 August 1972, pp. 859-60.
Los Angeles Center Theatre Group production.

Volpone: Performance Reviews, Zweig-Romains Adaptation

626 ANON. "Volpone." Theatre Magazine 47 (June 1928):38-39.
New York Theatre Guild production.

627 ATKINSON, J. BROOKS. "Ben Jonson in Adaptation." New York Times, 10 April 1928, p. 32.
New York Theatre Guild production.

628 SELDES, GILBERT. "The Theatre." Dial 84 (June 1928):528-30.
New York Theatre Guild production.

629 ANON. "L'Atelier: The Theatre in which Paris Gives Hearty Welcome to Jules Romains' Production of Volpone." Theatre Magazine, 19 March 1929, p. 56.
A page of eight photographs of characters in the Paris production of Romains' adaptation of the Zweig version of Volpone.

630 BOWERS, FAUBION. "Renaud-Barrault Company." Theatre Arts 41 (April 1957):20-21.
New York Winter Garden production.

631 CLURMAN, HAROLD. "Theatre." Nation, 23 February 1957, p. 174.
New York Winter Garden production.

Volpone: Performance Reviews, Other Adaptations

632 ILUPINA, ANNA. "Muscovites Applaud Ben Jonson." SovL (April 1957):181-82.
Lithuanian Theatre Company production.

Volpone

633 GILL, BRENDAN. "The Triumph of Avarice." NY, 27 December 1976, p. 52.
Sly Fox, Larry Gelbart's adaptation of Volpone, at New York Broadhurst heatre.

Tragedies

Catiline His Conspiracy: Editions

634 Lynn Harold Harris, ed. Yale Studies in English, 53. New Haven: Yale University Press; London: Humphrey Milford, 1916. 297 pp.
Review of Jonson's very specific and deliberately included sources shows that the play follows the sources but is not true to history. Many passages are extremely well translated. The edition notes other dramatic works dealing with Catiline; the text employed is that of the 1616 Folio.
Reviewed by C. R. Baskervill in MP 18 (1921):174.

635 W. F. Bolton and Jane F. Gardner, eds. Lincoln: University of Nebraska Press; London: Edward Arnold, 1973. 229 pp.
Jonson created a highly unpopular play using a highly popular tradition: the "matter of Rome." Although it employs many of the preoccupations and techniques of Sejanus, it differs from that play in its chorus, prologue, tragic structure, and placing of evil. Catiline has few ties with Shakespearean or classical tragedy, but relates to Jonson's own comedies as well as to academic drama and chronicle plays. Language functions as an important subject matter and a source of unification. Ten copies of the 1616 Folio were collated for the edition.
Reviewed in TLS, 30 March 1973, p. 362.

Catiline His Conspiracy: Criticism and Commentary

636 BLISSETT, WILLIAM. "Caesar and Satan." JHI 18 (1957):221-32.
Catiline is part of a chain of evidence linking Caesar to Satan.

637 BRYANT, JOSEPH ALLEN, JR. "Catiline and the Nature of Jonson's Tragic Fable." PMLA 69 (1954):265-77. [Reprinted in Ben Jonson: A Collection of Critical Essays (1963), pp. 147-59. (See 3.)]
Jonson's presentation of Catiline as a real, present danger indicates his belief that tragedy should be judged according to "truth of argument." The Roman historians' lack of consensus about Caesar's position benefited Jonson's dramatic emphasis. Making the state his protagonist, Jonson attempted to extend the scope of history.

Catiline His Conspiracy

638 CABLE, CHESTER H. "Oldham's Borrowing from Buchanan." MLN 66 (1951):523-27.
John Oldham drew on Catiline for his first satire against the Jesuits but on George Buchanan for the third.

639 COOK, ALBERT S. "Ovid as a Source." Nation, 6 March 1913, pp. 229-30.
References to the sun's breeding powers in Catiline V.i.54-55 may have been derived from Metamorphoses I.416-40.

640 DE LUNA, BARBARA N. Jonson's Romish Plot: A Study of "Catiline" and Its Historical Context. Oxford: Clarendon Press, 1967. 415 pp.
A parallelograph, Catiline presents the Gunpowder Plot and is Jonson's attempt to justify his political action of 1605. Alert English theatre-goers recognized plot, character, diction, and image parallels, although Jonson deliberately distorted many components. Reading the play as a parallelograph demonstrates Jonson's artistic powers and his intense association with his own times. Although condemned and causing resentment when staged, Catiline was highly quoted by 17th-century writers and ranked as the main source of Jonson allusions.
Reviewed by B. Fitzgibbon in RES 20 (1969):494-97; B. Harris in YWES 48 (1967):182-83; M. T. Jones-Davies in EA 22 (1969):420-21; A. Leggatt in UTQ 39 (April 1970): 287-88; E. Partridge in RenQ 21 (1968):232-36; N. Platz in Anglia 87 (1969):259-61; L. Tennenhouse in SCN 28 (1970): 28-29; C. G. Thayer in ELN 5 (March 1968):212-16; P. Ure in N&Q 213 (1968):274-76; S. Warhaft in DR 47 (1967):413-16.

641 DORENKAMP, ANGELA G. "Jonson's Catiline: History as the Trying Faculty." SP 67 (1970):210-20.
The conspiracy, not Catiline, forms the play's essence. Jonson attempted to consolidate teleologies of history and drama and thus could not give up many historical details for the sake of drama. Closer to dramatized history than to historical drama, Catiline is concerned with larger issues than its events or persons adumbrate.

642 ECHERUO, MICHAEL J. C. "The Conscience of Politics and Jonson's Catiline." SEL 6 (1966):341-56.
Interested more in the processes than the ends of policy, Jonson demonstrates the fine distinction between those using "policy" for good and those using it for evil.

Catiline His Conspiracy

643 HARRIS, LYNN HAROLD. "Local Color in Ben Jonson's Catiline and Historical Accuracy of the Play." Classical Philology 14 (1919):273-83.
The classics provide Jonson's plot, dialogue, and choruses. Although the play is about one-fourth translation and follows the sources, it is not true to history.

644 _____. "Lucan's Pharsalia and Jonson's Catiline." MLN 34 (1919):397-402.
Lists, in parallel passages, Jonson's borrowings from Lucan.

645 _____. "Three Notes on Ben Jonson." MP 17 (1920):679-85.
The influence of Seneca on Catiline is seen in several quotations and borrowings, and in the conception of the characters of Catiline and Cethegus. There are similarities between Godfrey's The Prince of Parthia and Catiline.

646 MUSTARD, W. P. "Notes on Ben Jonson's Catiline." MLN 36 (1921):154-57.
Sources for Catiline include Horace, Cicero, Ovid, Juvenal, Sallust, and Livy.

647 STINCHOMB, JAMES. "Catiline on the Stage." Classical Weekly, 19 November 1934, pp. 49-52.
Offers summaries and criticism of plays on Catiline by Jonson, Crébillon, Voltaire, Dumas, and Ibsen.

648 WARREN, MICHAEL J. "Ben Jonson's Catiline: The Problem of Cicero." YES 3 (1973):55-73.
Discusses Cicero as a complex, personally motivated, and over-esteemed political figure. Critics should pay more attention to the Chorus in this satiric comedy.

649 _____. "The Location of Jonson's Catiline III. 490-754." PQ 48 (1969):561-65.
The meeting referred to in III.490-754 actually occurred at Porcius Laeca's, where Jonson places it. The play disposes the audience to assume that the conspirators met at Catiline's home, but sufficient evidence is absent.

650 _____. "A Note on Jonson's Catiline, IV.229-231: Sources and Meaning." N&Q 221 (1976):213-14.
Jonson's Latin texts give an insight into the meaning of "opprest" (constrained) and his eclectic translation methods. He either used Sallust (1564) and Cicero (1584) simultaneously or Cicero only.

651 WILLIAMS, WELDON. "The Influence of Ben Jonson's Catiline upon John Oldham's Satyrs upon the Jesuits." ELH 11 (1944):38-62.

Oldham drew heavily on Catiline in his first, third, and fourth satires, for design, style, atmosphere, and content. The first satire very directly imitates the play's prologue.

Sejanus His Fall: Editions

652 William Dinsmore Briggs, ed. Boston and London: D. C. Heath and Company, 1911. 358 pp.

Although Sejanus emphasizes characters more than action, its figures are easily classified and lack subtle emotional gradations. The play differs from Jonson's comedies mainly in its scale and does not offer a clear picture of his doctrine of tragedy. Defects, resulting often from extra-dramatic purposes, include: lack of unity in presenting the steps of the intrigue, more attention to the preparation than to the action of the conspiracy, the appearance of Silius's trial as a climax. Itself dependent on ancient doctrine and sources, the play is important in the development of historical English drama, with Jonson expressing many parallels between the classical and English worlds. The edition is based on the 1616 Folio.

Reviewed by C. R. Baskervill in JEGP 13 (1914):366-68.

653 Henry de Vocht, ed. Materials for the Study of the Old English Drama, Series 2, Vol. 11. Louvain: Uystpruyst, 1935. 264 pp. [Reprint. Vaduz: Kraus, 1963.]

Text based on 1605 Quarto. Comparison of the Quarto and Folio editions indicates that Jonson carefully supervised the former but not the latter. Includes detailed metrical analysis of the play.

654 Jonas A. Barish, ed. New Haven: Yale University Press, 1965. 219 pp.

Sejanus mediates between two extremes: academic, Senecan closet-drama and popular theatre; but it is a radical departure from both traditions in its "extraordinary fidelity to its sources." Jonson's moral evaluation of history is based on an accurate, though selective, transcription of history. As in the comedies, the characters are simplified as types to clarify the moral issues of the play, thus serving a corrective function. The contemporary applicability of Sejanus is clear from Jonson's having been cited for treason because of it, despite his putting a disclaimer in the mouth of Cordus in Act III. Jonson's

Sejanus His Fall

concern over strictly logical motivation and plot construction work against the tragic effect of the play.

Reviewed by B. Harris in YWES 46 (1965):163-64; G. R. Hibbard in MLR 61 (1966):672-73; D. Novarr in ELN 4 (1966):65-68; G. R. Proudfoot in N&Q 212 (1967):356-60; E. Robinson in SCN 24 (1966):10-11; in TLS, 9 December 1965, p. 1165.

655 W. F. Bolton, ed. London: Ernest Benn, 1966. 158 pp. [Reprint. New York: Hill and Wang, 1969.]

Suggests Chapman as "the second pen" of the original (1603) playscript and proposes that Jonson's decision to drop his collaborator's lines from the Quarto version (1605) meant taking full responsibility for the politically risky passages. Notes classical and Renaissance sources, and claims that Jonson "reassembled the facts of history to form his dramatic structure, and elaborated them to make his poetic fabric." Places the play in the de casibus tradition; praises Jonson's handling of verse and the power and effectiveness of the language, which does more than the plot to realize the characters.

Reviewed by G. Bas in EA 22 (1969):311-12; G. R. Proudfoot in N&Q 212 (1967):356-60; in TLS, 28 April 1966, p. 373.

656 Amsterdam: Theatrum Orbis Terrarum; New York: Da Capo Press, 1970. 110 pp.

A facsimile reprint of the 1605 Quarto.

Sejanus His Fall: Translations and Adaptations

657 MAUTHNER, MARGARETE. "Der Sturz des Sejanus." "Volpone; oder der Fuchs." "Der Bartholomäus-Markt." Berlin: Cassirer, 1912. (German translations.)

Sejanus His Fall: Criticism and Commentary

658 ASHE, GEOFFREY. "William Strachey." N&Q 195 (1950):508-11.

Proposes Strachey as the "second pen" whose share in the play Jonson rewrote either because he did not want to take credit for another man's work, or because Strachey wished to remain anonymous.

659 BAYFIELD, M. A. A Study of Shakespeare's Versification. Cambridge: The University Press, 1920, pp. 295-313. [Reprint. Norwood, Pa.: Norwood Editions, 1976.]

Textual study of Sejanus in the 1616 Folio indicates that the book was not accurately printed. The printers' many elisions disturb the versification and can spoil the speaking of the lines.

660 BOUGHNER, DANIEL C. "Jonson's Use of Lipsius in Sejanus." MLN 73 (1958):247-55.
Lipsius's commentary on Tacitus plays a major role in the characterizations in Sejanus, particularly that of Tiberius Caesar.

661 _____. "Juvenal, Horace and Sejanus." MLN 75 (1960):545-50.
Juvenal is a "pervasive influence" but not a "predominant source." Reconciling Satire X to the play creates difficulties regarding Fortune and Sejanus's fall. Jonson fundamentally reinterprets Tacitus and rejects his own carefully documented sources in the interests of drama.

662 _____. "'Rhodig' and Sejanus." N&Q 203 (1958):287-89.
Sejanus IV.283-87, and Jonson's notes, indicate his compression of varied sources and knowledge of what would impress audiences.

663 _____. "Sejanus and Machiavelli." SEL 1 (Spring 1961):81-100.
Jonson drew heavily on both Machiavelli's The Discourses (III.6) and The Prince. A comedy of wits, the play analyzes the triumph of statecraft over power by successful application of "Tirannes Artes" (I.70).

664 BRIGGS, WILLIAM DINSMORE. "Studies in Ben Jonson. V." Anglia 39 (1914-16):303-18.
Shows that Samuel Sheppard was not involved in the writing of Sejanus, and that Robert Baron plagiarized Jonson's plays.

665 BRYANT, JOSEPH ALLEN, JR. "The Nature of the Conflict in Jonson's Sejanus." Vanderbilt Studies in Humanities 1 (1951):197-219.
The play sets its own ethical, moral framework, providing a study of how good characters learn both the meaning of evil and how to deal with it without denying their own virtue. The audience's suspense results from Sejanus's being both a would-be usurper and legitimate extension of Tiberius. Jonson emphasizes good's potential for survival.

666 CHANG, JOSEPH. "Of Mighty Opposites: Stoicism and Machiavellianism." RenD 9 (1966):37-57.
Stoic resolution becomes a counterforce to the tyranny of Sejanus (IV.294-98).

Sejanus His Fall

667 EVANS, K. W. "Sejanus and the Ideal Prince Tradition." SEL 11 (1971):249-64.
In contrast to Poetaster, Sejanus shows what happens when a court functions incorrectly. Jonson analyzes his own society but fails to recognize sufficiently its complexity.

668 GILBERT, ALLAN. "The Eavesdroppers in Jonson's Sejanus." MLN 69 (1954):164-66.
Herford and Simpson may err in having the spies (IV.95-218) mount a rope ladder into a hut rather than use reading holes confirmed in Tacitus and possible for The Globe.

669 GOLLANCZ, SIR ISRAEL. "Ben Jonson and Greneway's Annals." TLS, 10 May 1928, p. 355.
The unnamed English source Jonson refers to in the preface to Sejanus may be Greneway's Annals (1598), a translation of Tacitus's Annals. Jonson adopts Greneway in many difficult parts of Tacitus; Tiberius's speech to Sejanus when the latter requests marriage to Livia (III.ii) shows similarities to Greneway's translation. (See 670 and 691.)

670 _____. "Ben Jonson and Richard Greneway." TLS, 21 June 1928, p. 468.
Responds to Simpson (TLS, 14 June 1928, p. 450), defending an opinion that Jonson borrowed from Greneway's translation of Tacitus for portions of Sejanus. ". . . certain parallels . . . can hardly be explained as mere coincidences." (See 669 and 691.)

671 GUNBY, D. C. "Webster: Another Borrowing from Jonson's Sejanus?" N&Q 215 (1970):214.
Sejanus I.33-34 is probably the source for The Duchess of Malfi I.i.124-26.

672 HAMILTON, GARY D. "Irony and Fortune in Sejanus." SEL 11 (1971):265-81.
The play's dramatic impact comes from its irony and satire. Jonson emphasizes man's use and misuse of fortune. The play focuses more on what produces a tyrant than on what brings him down.

673 HONIG, EDWIN. "Sejanus and Coriolanus: A Study in Alienation." MLQ 12 (1951):407-21.
Comparison of the plays and their protagonists. Both dramatists use the Roman pattern to react against Puritans'

restraints and to fulfill the dictate that theatre should provide moral instruction. Sejanus presents an overt theory of power by which all becomes simultaneously possible and impossible.

674 KIEFER, FREDERICK. "Pretense in Ben Jonson's Sejanus." ELWIU 4 (1977):19-25.
Secrecy and pretense are endemic to the play. While the evil characters both conceal their dispositions and fabricate strategy, the good characters attempt to pierce through to reality. Sejanus goes down to defeat for the same reason which, in part, defeats the Germanicans: failure to perceive correctly.

675 KORNINGER, SIEGFRIED. "Zu Ben Jonsons Römerdrama Sejanus." Innsbrucker Beiträge zur Kulturwissenschaft 4 (1955-56): 99-109.
Sees Sejanus as Jonson's most original work, his masterpiece of organization, containing much wisdom and truth. But in view of its failure, attempts to determine first, why it was a failure, and second, why the King's Men performed it if they thought it might not suit public taste. Suggests that the players appreciated the play and wanted to try it, but that the audience felt it was too cold and rational, or that the performance did not do justice to the play's real qualities.

676 LAW, RICHARD A. "Sejanus in 'the wolves black jaw.'" The PCTE Bulletin (Pennsylvania Council of Teachers of English), No. 15 (August 1967), pp. 27-40.
Discusses aspects of the play "that militate against the dramatic articulation of the tragic view of man in the universe."

677 LEVER, J. W. "Roman Tragedy: Sejanus, Caesar and Pompey," in his The Tragedy of State. London: Methuen, 1971, pp. 59-77.
Unlike other contemporary writers of tragedy Jonson "was more concerned with the political forces at work in history" than with historical personalities. He offers a history "made by men as ruthless and amoral as they." Chapman's play is inferior to Jonson's because he does not focus his dramatic-historic concerns as Jonson does.

678 LEVIN, LAWRENCE L. "Justice and Society in Sejanus and Volpone." Discourse 13 (1970):319-24.
Sejanus contains elements directly influencing Jonson in the composition of Volpone. The two plays portray tragic and comic counterparts of ethical and juridical degeneracy.

Sejanus His Fall

679 LINDSAY, BARBARA N. "The Structure of Tragedy in Sejanus." ES (Anglo-American Supplement) 50 (1969):xliv-l.
Tragedy occurs on three levels simultaneously: personal, parochial, and universal. Jonson uses the characters allegorically.

680 McDANIEL, WALTON BROOKS. "An Anachronism Ascribed to Jonson." MLN 28 (1913):158-59.
William Gifford wronged the erudite Jonson by stating that there was an anachronism in a line in Sejanus, "Obserue him, as his watch obserues his clocke" (I.i.36), thinking that Jonson was referring to the checking of the accuracy of a pocket watch against a clock. The Romans had sundials and water-clocks, which were observed by slaves who would report the correct time to their masters. Thus the slave was a "watch" who observed a clock.

681 MAROTTI, ARTHUR F. "The Self-Reflexive Art of Ben Jonson's Sejanus." TSLL 12 (1970):197-220.
Jonson's self-conscious rhetoric and double theme (play acting and play making) give Sejanus an anti-tragic character and demonstrate his power of comedy.

682 MAXWELL, J. C. "The Poems of Herrick?" N&Q 200 (1955):500.
"The lines which Professor Howarth cites [N&Q 200 (1955):381] as possibly 'Herrick's salute to religion' are in fact, except for the first, the opening lines of Jonson's Sejanus, Act V, with a few errors and omissions."

683 MUIR, KENNETH. "William Strachey." N&Q 196 (1951):19-20.
Sufficient evidence for identifying William Strachey as the second pen involved in Sejanus has not yet been presented. Parallels between Timon of Athens and Sejanus exist, but are not striking.

684 OLIVE, W. J. "Sejanus and Hamlet," in A Tribute to George Coffin Taylor. Edited by Arnold Williams. Chapel Hill: University of North Carolina Press, 1952, pp. 178-84.
Shakespeare's acting the title role in Sejanus may have influenced his Hamlet. Both plays show a satiric tone, a depravity at court, seriousness about the critical purposes of drama, and contempt for popular drama.

685 ONO, KYOICHI. "A Turning Point of Ben Jonson." SELit 27 (1950):61-74. (In Japanese.)

686 PRIOR, MOODY E. The Language of Tragedy. New York: Columbia University Press, 1947, pp. 112-19. [Reprint. Gloucester, Mass.: Peter Smith, 1964.]

Sejanus recalls early English adaptations of Seneca, although it reflects Elizabethan enthusiasm for figurative language and creation of striking images. Jonson achieved the logical clarity and sharpness he admired, but the play fails because of its dullness, non-integral images, and speeches which merely state the obvious.

687 RICKS, CHRISTOPHER. "Sejanus and Dismemberment." MLN 76 (1961):301-08.

The many references to body parts simply but powerfully anticipate the fate of both Sejanus and the body politic.

688 ROBERTSON, J. M. The Shakespeare Canon. London: George Routledge & Sons; New York: E. P. Dutton, 1922 [Part I], pp. 51, 54, 69-140 passim.

Cites several plays, of which Sejanus is the most important, in support of the hypothesis that Jonson abridged Julius Caesar.

689 ROLLINS, HYDER E. "Samuel Sheppard and His Praise of Poets." SP 24 (1927):509-55.

Sheppard has been incorrectly identified as Jonson's secretary and as the "second pen" involved with the Sejanus acted on the public stage.

690 SIMPSON, EVELYN MARY. "The Folio Text of Ben Jonson's Sejanus." Anglia 61 (1937):398-415.

De Vocht's theory that Jonson did not supervise the 1616 Folio is incorrect. It rests on insufficient evidence, inability to recognize editorial changes, and failure to assume the mental attitude of an Elizabethan author, particularly Jonson. As they do in the Quarto of Sejanus, errors exist in the Folio because Jonson was unable to prevent them. (See 653.)

691 SIMPSON, PERCY. "Ben Jonson and Richard Greneway." TLS, 14 June 1928, p. 450.

Disagrees with the suggestion by Gollancz (TLS, 28 May 1928, p. 335) that portions of Jonson's English version of Tacitus in Sejanus are dependent on a prior translation by Richard Greneway. (See 669 and 670.)

Sejanus His Fall

692 VAWTER, MARVIN L. "The Seeds of Virtue: Political Imperatives in Jonson's Sejanus." SLitI 6 (April 1973):41-60. (See 40.)

Rome's sickness is the failure of her good characters to move beyond their Stoic acceptance of evil and to act. Jonson and others associated Stoicism with shortsightedness and imprudence based on a too-absolute value system.

693 WAGNER, BERNARD M. "A Jonson Allusion, and Others." PQ 7 (1928):306-08.

An anonymous play, written ca. 1654 (Brit. Mus. ms. Add. 25348), dealing with the Howard-Essex divorce and the Howard-Carr marriage, refers to the initial failure of Sejanus and its later success.

694 WOODWARD, PARKER. "Bacon as Playwright." Baconiana 9 (1911):107.

"Sejanus was issued in the name of Bacon's friend and assistant, Jonson, who collaborated in it."

Sejanus: Performance Review

695 BROWN, IVOR. "The Theatre: Platform Points." Saturday Review (London), 18 February 1928, pp. 190-91.

Holborn Empire Theatre production.

Catiline and Sejanus: Criticism and Commentary

696 ADAMS, ROBERT P. "Transformation in the Late Elizabethan Tragic Sense of Life: New Critical Approaches." MLQ 35 (1974):352-63.

At the turn of the 16th century the early humanist perception of tragedy as history ruled by divine Providence and of rulers as being either legitimate Christian princes or illegitimate Machiavellian tyrants was abandoned for the perception of tragedy as history ruled by raison d'état and of rulers as being both Christian princes and Machiavellian tyrants. Jonson was among the dramatists responsive to this change of outlook which grew out of the increasing signs of despotism in the reign of Elizabeth I and the corresponding decay of the Tudor myth.

697 ANDERSON, RUTH L. "The Mirror Concept in the Drama of the Renaissance." The Northwest Missouri State Teachers College Studies 3 (1939):47-74.

Briefly touches on conventional elements in the plays.

Catiline and *Sejanus*

698 BLISSETT, WILLIAM. "Lucan's Caesar and the Elizabethan Villain." *SP* 53 (1956):553-75.

Lucan's contribution to the Elizabethan literary imagination was his hero Caesar, "the restless, ruthless, impious and intelligent villain-hero, bent on imposing his will on all the world, at the risk of pulling the whole fabric down in ruins. Sometimes this figure bears the name of Caesar . . . more often he owns another name--Tamburlaine, the Guise, Mortimer, Catiline, Sejanus. . . ."

699 BOYER, CLARENCE V. *The Villain as Hero in Elizabethan Tragedy*. London: George Routledge, 1914, pp. 174-82. [Reprint. New York: Russell and Russell, 1964.]

Jonson's tragedies fail as dramas because of too many orations not associated with plot, situations where characters suffer in silence, and minor characters made more interesting than the protagonists. Although he has the heroic potential which Sejanus lacks, Catiline never reaches heroic stature.

700 BRYANT, JOSEPH ALLEN, JR. "The Significance of Ben Jonson's First Requirement for Tragedy: 'Truth of Argument.'" *SP* 3 (1952):195-213.

Jonson insisted that dramas' arguments come from history and be verifiable even in small details. Puritan attacks on the stage constituted a major reason for his stress on truth. His tragedies were unpopular because his audiences lacked sufficient familiarity with his sources.

701 BURTON, K. M. "The Political Tragedies of Chapman and Jonson." *EIC* 2 (1952):397-412.

The dramatists' works differ according to the view of evil's source and the dramatic implications as well as the enactments of it. The plays focus on flaws in the social order, not in individuals.

702 CHAMPION, LARRY S. *Tragic Patterns in Jacobean and Caroline Drama*. Knoxville: University of Tennessee Press, 1977, pp. 62-88.

Sejanus and *Catiline* are among the first late-Renaissance plays to present the tragedy of a society through the experience of one major figure. They present no positive figures to balance their evil. Sejanus assumes increasingly evil proportions, but Catiline evokes some sympathy as other characters reveal their shortcomings and selfishness.

703 No entry

Catiline and Sejanus

704 DUFFY, ELLEN M. T. "Ben Jonson's Debt to Renaissance Scholarship in Sejanus and Catiline." MLR 42 (1947):24-30.
Annotations in his primary sources indicate that Jonson drew heavily on Renaissance commentators on Roman historians.

705 GILBERT, A. H. "Seneca and the Criticism of Elizabethan Tragedy." PQ 13 (1934):370-81.
Although Jonson's classicism has sometimes been insisted on to the concealment of his romantic tendencies, his Senecan intention requires recognition before critical evaluation of his tragedies can be made.

706 HIBBARD, G. R. "Goodness and Greatness: An Essay on the Tragedies of Ben Jonson and George Chapman." RMS 11 (1967):5-54.
Jonsonian tragedy is committed to opposed ideals: presentation of morals and fidelity to historical events. Sejanus marks the beginning of Jonson's strong poetic verse, but fails as a tragedy, for Sejanus's execution achieves nothing, and Jonson himself counterbalances the evils portrayed. Catiline, although presented as a monster, becomes progressively emptier and hence less a part of tragedy. Jonson saw his conspiracy as prototypic, but had too much material for effective moralizing.

707 HILL, GEOFFREY. "The World's Proportion: Jonson's Dramatic Poetry in Sejanus and Catiline." Stratford-upon-Avon Studies, 1 (1960):113-31.
The Roman plays brilliantly satirize the political situation in the decades prior to the Civil War. Jonson indicates his vision of the moral and civic disorder by reversing sex roles and giving his protagonists hyperbolic rhetoric. Ambiguity gives the plays great subjectivity and cunning, and requires suspension of judgment. The dedication of Catiline is both a self-defense and a testimony to the importance of conserving legitimate order.

708 HUNTER, GEORGE K. "A Roman Thought: Renaissance Attitudes to History Exemplified in Shakespeare and Jonson," in An English Miscellany Presented to W. S. Mackie. Edited by Brian S. Lee. Cape Town: Oxford University Press, 1977, pp. 93-118.
Both Tudor historians and Elizabethan and Jacobean playwrights focused more on the myth than the facts of Rome. Searching for models of conduct, they romanticized the past and emphasized individual figures rather than the sweep of political process. Jonson's familiarity with the literature of the Silver Age allowed him to see the changes

between the republic and the empire and pointed up the appropriateness of plays about Sejanus and Catiline. Both Shakespeare and Jonson recognized the fatal conflict between real but outdated values and opportunism, but each envisioned and emphasized a different outcome. In Jonson's view, ethics inevitably lost in a true presentation of public life.

709 KYTZLER, BERNHARD. "Notae Jonsonianae." Archiv 213 (1976): 112-15.

Jonson drew on both Cicero's Brutus and Sallust's Catilina for many details of Catiline, including Cicero's ridicule of his colleagues' inherited glory. Portions of Sejanus come from Statius's Thebaid; the scepticism linking fear and the gods, however, is a commonplace.

710 NASH, RALPH. "Ben Jonson's Tragic Poems." SP 55 (1958): 164-86.

Sejanus and Catiline, experiments in an unsuccessful kind of tragic poem, place truth of history and principles of political theory above the personal appeal of central characters or creation of psychologically complex characters. Both plays emphasize manipulation and maneuvering as good characters question how to cope with established, but evil, authority. Parallels between Sejanus and The Prince indicate the currency of Jonson's topics. The tragedies show artistic competency.

711 ORNSTEIN, ROBERT. "Ben Jonson," in his The Moral Vision of Jacobean Tragedy. Madison: University of Wisconsin Press, 1960, pp. 84-104. [Reprinted as "The Moral Vision of Ben Jonson's Tragedy," in Elizabethan Drama: Modern Essays in Criticism. Edited by Ralph J. Kaufmann. New York: Oxford University Press, 1961, pp. 187-207.]

Jonson failed in tragedy because he could neither come to terms with his own view of politics nor present his political insights powerfully. Both tragedies lack ethical meaning, despite their moral commentaries.

712 SCHLÖSSER, ANSELM. "Ben Jonson's Roman Plays." KN 8 (1961): 123-59.

The plays consitute a brave statement about 17th-century England. Catiline shows no dramatic growth from Sejanus but again reinterprets historical tradition with satiric twists.

Catiline and Sejanus

713 _____. Shakespeare und der Tragödienstil seiner Zeit. Bern: A. Francke, 1947, pp. 7, 8, 18-19, 34, 53-55, 65, 99-109, 167-68, 170.

Jonson differs from his contemporaries in his didactic, Palladianist approach to tragedy, and his general effort to avoid pandering to public taste for sensationalism and low comedy. He presents the events of Sejanus more like an historian than a poet. Less capable than Shakespeare in the creation of a tragic hero, he is weak in developing and revealing complexity of character. In Catiline the characterization is better, but tends towards exaggeration. In comparing Catiline with Lady Macbeth, both in part derived from the Senecan tradition, one sees that the latter is more fully realized as a human being.

714 SCHÜCKING, LEVIN LUDWIG. The Baroque Character of the Elizabethan Tragic Hero. Annual Shakespeare Lecture. Read 27 April 1938. London: British Academy, 1938. 27 pp. [Reprint. Folcroft, Pa.: Folcroft Library Editions, 1969.]

Jonson's tragic heroes exhibit "extraordinary intensification" of emotion, a predilection for the bizarre, and "a certain self-exalting attitude." This follows an Elizabethan tendency which is related to the Jonsonian concept of humours in comedy.

715 STAGG, LOUIS CHARLES. Index to the Figurative Language of Ben Jonson's Tragedies. Charlottesville: Bibliographical Society of the University of Virginia, 1967. 47 pp.

A general concordance to the tragedies is followed by seven indices which cross-list the plays' figurative language.

716 STODDER, JOSEPH HENRY. Satire in Jacobean Tragedy. JDS 35, 1974, 186 pp.

Neither Jonsonian tragedy succeeds as such, for want of a tragic hero who excites sympathy. Jonson played a major role in the Renaissance experiment to link satire and tragedy. Sejanus meets his requirements for tragedy; Catiline includes tragic elements as a background for comic and satiric elements.

716a VILLIERS, JACOB I. DE. "Ben Jonson's Tragedies." ES 45 (1964):433-42.

Critics must focus on differences in dramatic verse in the tragedies. Jonson created pathetic dilemmas by not exploring characters, situations, and reactions.

717 WELLS, HENRY W. "Senecan Influence on Elizabethan Tragedy: A Re-Examination." Shakespeare Association Bulletin 19 (1944):71-84.

Seneca's heroes "materially assisted in forming the intellectual doctrine of the super-man typical of Elizabethan thought," for example, Jonson's Sejanus, Catiline, and Cicero. His aphoristic powers are evidenced by frequent English paraphrases by Jonson and others. His influence on the playwrights of the early Jacobean period, including Jonson, "is noble and almost entirely salutary."

Pastoral

The Sad Shepherd: Editions

718 Introduction by L. J. Potts. Cambridge: Cambridge University Press, 1929. 50 pp.

The play ranks high in the pastoral genre owing to Jonson's extensive learning and knowledge of the world. It invites comparison with The Tempest. Text for the edition is the 1641 (i.e., 1640) Folio.

719 The Unfinished Pastoral Comedy of Ben Jonson, Now Completed by Alan Porter. New York: John Day Co., 1944. 94 pp.

Porter finished the third act and added acts four and five. The completed play was first performed at Vassar College 1935. A rather anti-Elizabethan effort at an ending had been made by Francis Godolphin Waldron (1744-1818). The textual basis of the edition is that of Percy Simpson (1941).

The Sad Shepherd: Criticism and Commentary

720 HARRISON, T. P., JR. "Jonson's The Sad Shepherd and Spenser." MLN 58 (1943):257-62.

Jonson's play, his last attack on the Puritans, contains many echoes of The Faerie Queene and The Shepheardes Calendar.

721 HERRICK, MARVIN T. "Ben Jonson's Sad Shepherd: Or a Tale of Robin Hood," in his Tragicomedy: Its Origin and Development in Italy, France and England. ISLL 39, 1955, pp. 164-65.

Jonson's intention was to write a pastoral tragicomedy in the English tradition by using native setting, characters, humor, and elements of the morality play.

The Sad Shepherd

722 SPENCE, LEWIS. "Ben Jonson's Scottish Witches." Scots Magazine, August 1926, pp. 372-76.
The language of the witches in The Sad Shepherd is Scots. Jonson's familiarity with the dialect derived from his Scottish origins as well as his sojourn in Scotland. His use of it in the play may be connected with James VI's propaganda against witchcraft, which seems to have created, in people's minds, an association between Scotland and witches.

723 URBAN, RAYMOND. "The Somerset Affair, the Belvoir Witches, and Jonson's Pastoral Comedies." HLB 23 (1975):295-323.
When referred to in the masque, The May Lord, the Somerset affair and the bewitching of the Earl of Rutland's household at Belvoir Castle were disturbing events. By the time Jonson adapted the masque for The Sad Shepherd, the topics had lost their implications and developed humorous association.

SPECIAL TOPICS

Humours Theory

724 CAZAMIAN, LOUIS. "Humors and Humor," in The Development of English Humor. Durham: Duke University Press, pp. 308-30. [Reprint. New York, AMS Press, 1965.]
Jonson did more than any other English writer to relate "humors" to "humor," first taking the traditional concept of "humors," which was rooted in classical medicine, and giving it its physiological meaning, then relating the idea to decorum in two ways: a character had to remain consistent to his humour; the deviant humour character sharpened the perception of what right conduct should be. Jonson is not precise in his attitude toward his "humors." Apparently he is deriding and exaggerating imbalance of character rooted in organic and mental origin. At times the imbalance is presented only as a whim, so that at one time Jonson seems to be attacking an excessive whim, at others a serious central feature of character. In Every Man out of his Humour, the point of view remains ambiguous to the end. Yet "through his strong relish for the raciness of full-blooded eccentricities and his abundant vein of comic invention . . . he destroyed whatever impression might still linger that the physical bondage implied in the medical sense of 'humor' was a tragic element. . . . He made the atmosphere of the word and the notion definitely comic." Jonson's use of "humor" was "passive" because it denoted a mode of being unconscious of itself but recognized

by others. The meaning of the word shifted from "passive" to "active" during the 17th and first half of the 18th centuries.

725 CLANCY, JAMES H. "Ben Jonson and the 'Humours.'" TA 11 (1953):15-23.
Jonson produced four general types of humour figures: the man with an inborn bent who is incapable of self-correction (Morose, Volpone, Epicure Mammon); the man with an ingrained but not inborn bent (Macilente, Sordido, Kitely); the person who assumes a humour (Sir Politic Would-be, Zeal-of-the-Land Busy); the man who seeks prestige through a humour (Sogliardo, Stephen).

726 FINDEISEN, HELMUT. "'Humour' und Satire bei Ben Jonson." SJW 109 (1973):47-50.
Jonson adapted the ancient concept of humours to the end of reflecting reality critically--of society as well as individuals. The satiric use of the humour character developed into a second tradition besides that of Shakespeare, influencing 18th- and 19th-century novelists.

727 FRASER, RUSSELL. "Elizabethan Drama and the Art of Abstraction." CompD 2 (1968):73-82.
Jonson is the chief representative of the rationalistic Renaissance tendency to conceive of dramatic characters as abstractions. The "humorous" characters are often like Morality figures, voluntarily if blindly forfeiting their autonomy, and thereafter undergoing no change.

728 FURLONG, NORMAN. "Ben Jonson," in his English Satire: An Anthology. London: George G. Harrap, 1946, pp. 72-81.
Comedy of humours asserted the realistic and satirical side of comedy, freeing it from "romantic extravagance." Jonson gives "the liveliest satirical pictures of the fools and rascals of his age."

729 GOTTWALD, MARIA. "Koncepja 'Humorów' u Beniamina Johnsona" [Benjamin Jonson's Conception of Humours]. GW 12 (1968): 3-14. (In Polish.)
Sees a relationship between the modification in the meaning of the term "humour" as described in the Quarto edition of Every Man in his Humour and the evolution of Jonson's theory of comedy. The original meaning included vice and folly; after 1606, when vice was sharply castigated in Volpone, Jonson turned his attention to less harmful vanities. This shows an evolution in his comic theory from vigorous moralizing toward an acknowledgement of the pleasure-giving qualities of comedy.

Humours Theory

730 HARRISON, G. B. "Ben Jonson," in his The Story of Elizabethan Drama. Cambridge: Cambridge University Press, 1924, pp. 79-97. [Reprint. Philadelphia: R. West, 1978.]
An analysis of Jonson's humour theory through a brief discussion of an extract from Every Man in his Humour.

731 HAYDN, HIRAM. The Counter-Renaissance. New York: Charles Scribner's Sons, 1950, pp. 382-87. [Reprint. Gloucester, Mass.: Peter Smith, 1966.]
Jonson's original presentations of "humour," including its expression in Volpone, relate it to singularity, one aspect of the strong philosophy of individualism. Rather than embracing this philosophy, however, Jonson uses it for satirical purposes.

732 REDWINE, JAMES D., JR. "Beyond Psychology: The Moral Basis of Jonson's Theory of Humour Characterization." ELH 28 (1961):316-34.
Jonson's definition of "humour" rests on the moral as well as the psychological. Proclamations of Asper (Every Man out of his Humour) and Crites (Cynthia's Revels) emphasize both disciplines. Commentators have too often forgotten that "in the Renaissance 'psychology' and 'decorum' were elements of moral philosophy."

733 SCHÄFER, JÜRGEN. Wort und Begriff "Humour" in der Elisabethanischen Komödie. Neue Beiträge zur englischen Philologie, 6. Münster: Aschendorff, 1966. 241 pp., passim.
Explores the meanings and associations of the word "humour," already well developed by the time Jonson wrote Every Man in his Humour, which was the culmination of the theory of humours. Jonson employed the word and concept in all their possible applications. The ideas included in the term have connections with modern psychological theory.

734 SMITH, WILLARD. "The Evolution of the Comic Form on the English Stage," in his The Nature of Comedy. Boston: Richard G. Badger, 1930, pp. 138-40.
Sees Jonson's use of the humours theory as "an oversimplification of character" and a lack of understanding of complex characters, but states that Jonson's comedy of humours did make two contributions to the evolution of English comedy: emphasis upon character in the comedy of manners, and elevation of the comic form as an ethical artform.

735 SNUGGS, HENRY L. "The Comic Humours: A New Interpretation." PMLA 62 (1947):114-22. [Reprinted in Shakespeare's Contemporaries. Edited by Max Bluestone and Norman Rabkin. Englewood Cliffs, N.J.: Prentice-Hall, 1961, pp. 172-77.]

Critics failing to derive Jonson's definition of "humour" from the entire Induction to Every Man out of his Humour have been embarrassed because the psychological definition alone does not account for Jonson's practice of portraying affected and eccentric humours. A close reading of the Induction discloses Jonson's full meaning: through Asper he says that he intends to scourge not only the psychological humours, but also "an apish, or phantastic straine," the affected humour. Passages in other comedies support this view. In practice, Jonson created few true humoural characters such as Macilente and Morose, but the pseudo-humours such as Stephen, Matthew, Bobadill, Sir John Daw, Philautia, and Carlo Buffone abound.

736 SYMONS, JULIAN. "Ben Jonson as a Social Realist: Bartholomew Fair." SoR 6 (1940-41):375-86.

Jonson's success as a realist had nothing to do with the humours, which are primarily satiric in their effect. In fact, Jonson failed when he tried to be a realist and a satirist at the same time. The Alchemist successfully uses the humours for moral and satiric effect. In Bartholomew Fair, which succeeds as realistic drama, the characters are what Congreve called "Habits," which he distinguishes from humours in that, rather than showing us as we are, they show us as we appear.

See also: 27, 29, 299, 305, 312, 714, 741, 761, 762, 841, 1029, 1056, 1102, 1109, 1169, 1197, 1200, 1206, 1236.

Influence and Allusions

737 ALLEN, DON CAMERON. "A Jonson Allusion." TLS, 18 April 1936, p. 336.

Suggests that the word "Alchymistas" in a passage in "De Providentia Dei" (1623), by the "puritan zealot and controversialist" Richard Crakanthorp, is a thrust at Jonson.

738 ALLEN, HERBERT F. A Study of the Comedies of Richard Brome Especially as Representative of Dramatic Decadence. Stanford, Calif.: Stanford University Press, 1912, pp. 21-22, 35-38, 43-47, 52-55.

Jonson's was the single strongest influence on comedy in the period following his own. Brome was typical of his age in his frequent use of the realistic comedy of humours. In his use of out-of-the-way learning he was probably following Jonson, but he was more concerned with, and successful at, pleasing his public, and did not make Jonson's mistake of loading his plays with didactic material. Brome often kept a character's identity a secret from his audience, an idea borrowed from Epicoene; echoes of Bartholomew Fair appear in his Spargus Garden. In general, Jonson's followers fell below him in the creation of characters.

739 ALLEN, NED BLISS. The Sources of John Dryden's Comedies. University of Michigan Publications. Language and Literature, 16. Ann Arbor: University of Michigan Press, 1935, pp. 10-21, passim. [Reprint. Folcroft, Pa.: Folcroft Library Editions, 1973.]

In his first play, The Wild Gallant, Dryden imitated one type of Jonsonian humour, the type--such as Morose, Justice Clement, Puntarvolo, and Carlo Buffone--who personifies a caprice or whim. He also imitated Jonson's great fault of characterization: description rather than presentation of character.

740 ANDREWS, CLARENCE EDWARD. Richard Brome: A Study of his Life and Work. Yale Studies in English, 46. New York: Holt, 1913, pp. 1-76 passim, 81-98, 128-34. [Reprint. Hamden, Conn.: The Shoe String Press, Archon Books, 1972.]

Explores the influence of Jonson on Brome; the latter's Antipodes shows considerable use of Jonson's satirical principles and techniques.

741 AUDUBERT, MICHÈLE. "Thomas Shadwell: The Miser (1672)," in Dramaturgie et Société: Rapports entre l'oeuvre théâtrale, son interprétation et son public aux XVIe et XVIIe siècles. Vol. 1. Edited by Jean Jacquot et al. Paris: Editions du Centre National de la Recherche Scientifique, 1968, 343-52.

In Shadwell's adaptation of Molière's Miser, Harpagan's name is changed to Goldingham, which places him among those humour characters defined by their names. Shadwell, a great admirer of Jonson, is perhaps following the theory of humours and centering the whole play around a personality type.

742 AUFFRET, JEAN. "Etherege a l'école de Molière," in Dramaturgie et Société: Rapports entre l'oeuvre théâtrale, son interprétation et son public aux XVIe et XVIIe siècles. Vol. 1. Edited by Jean Jacquot et al. Paris: Editions du Centre National de la Recherche Scientifique, 1968, 395-407.

Indicates Etherege's indebtedness to Jonsonian themes and language. Love in a Tub borrows from The Devil is an Ass and Bartholomew Fair; Man of Mode from Every Man in his Humour.

743 BAMBOROUGH, J. B. "Joyce and Jonson." Review of English Literature (Leeds) 2 (October 1961):45-50.

Proposes some general similarities between the two authors, in use of language, "hidden structure," and allegory, and in method of working, desire for self-sufficiency. Bartholomew Fair is a "kind of sketch for Ulysses."

744 BECKER, CAROL. "Johnson's 'The Vanity of Human Wishes' Lines 285-90." N&Q 222 (1977):250-52.

Volpone, particularly I.iv and V.xiii, may have been a major influence on Samuel Johnson's lines. The play appeared twenty-one times on the London stage between Johnson's coming to London (1737) and the publication of "The Vanity of Human Wishes." Johnson most likely saw it; he could not have been unaware of it.

745 BENSLY, EDWARD. "Jonson Allusion in Jeremy Taylor." N&Q 149 (11 July 1925):31.

Objects to Clark's reference to a Volpone allusion (see 757). Claims that the passage from Taylor's Holy Living is a close translation from Seneca.

746 BENTLEY, G. E. "Seventeenth-Century Allusions to Ben Jonson." HLQ 5 (1941):65-113.

Presents a chronological list of 152 allusions not included in Jonson Allusion Book (see 751). All but two passages mention Jonson's name, a work, or a character, or contain a quotation from a work. Differences exist between 17th-century allusions to Jonson and to Shakespeare, but are outside the scope of the article.

747 BOAS, F. S. "Edward Howard's Lyrics and Essays." ContempR 174 (1948):107-11.

Notes poems by Edward Howard praising Jonson omitted by previous collectors of Jonson allusions. Cites a passage from Howard's "Criticism and Censure," which he considers "the high water mark of Restoration worship of Jonson's dramatic art," and "weighty support" for G. E. Bentley's conclusion that Jonson was more popular than Shakespeare in England throughout the 17th century.

Influence and Allusions

748 BOORMAN, S. C. "Some Elizabethan Notes (2)." Trivium (St. David's College, Lampeter, Wales) 2 (1967):149-50.
Two notes on Jonson: 1) A favorable reference to "the Comoedy that treateth of the Humors of men" is made in a moral tract published in 1602 by Robert Mason of Lincoln's Inn. It is likely that either Every Man in his Humour or Every Man out of his Humour is alluded to. 2) John Boys, in a 1617 edition of a book on the Psalms, refers ironically to a playwright printing his "Works," possibly the earliest example of the expression of this attitude toward the 1616 Folio.

749 BOWERS, FREDSON THAYER. "Problems in Thomas Randolph's Drinking Academy and its Manuscript." HLQ 1 (1938):189-98.
In attempting to date The Drinking Academy, calls attention to borrowings from The Alchemist and The Staple of News, and possible references, in the latter, to an earlier play of Randolph's, The Ffary Knight.

750 BRADLEY, JESSE FRANKLIN. "Robert Baron's Tragedy of Mirza." MLN 34 (1919):402-08.
Shows, by means of parallel columns, that several speeches in Baron's Mirza are plagiarized from Jonson's Catiline, though not often word for word. The choruses in Mirza borrow some of the phraseology, and imitate the placement and the meter of those in Catiline. The themes of the third chorus in each play are strikingly similar.

751 BRADLEY, JESSE FRANKLIN, and ADAMS, JOSEPH QUINCY. The Jonson Allusion Book: A Collection of Allusions to Ben Jonson from 1597 to 1700. Cornell Studies in English, 6. New Haven: Yale University Press, 1922. 472 pp. [Reprint. New York: Russell and Russell, 1971.]
Traces the course of 17th-century critical opinion of Jonson. In the first critical references cited, Jonson is usually mentioned only with several other contemporary writers; then he is singled out for praise together with Shakespeare, Greene, and Fletcher. Eventually, Shakespeare and Jonson stand out from the others.
Reviewed by A. Nicholl in YWES 3 (1922):94-95; C. G. Moore Smith in MLR 19 (1924):111-13.

752 BRIGGS, WILLIAM DINSMORE. "The Influence of Jonson's Tragedy in the Seventeenth Century." Anglia 35 (1912):277-337.
Study of parallel passages from the works of other 17th-century authors indicates extensive borrowing from Jonson's tragedies. The Machiavellian cast Jonson gave to politics was particularly influential. Sejanus offers the best presentation of Machiavelli's political philosophy in English until the 1640 translation of The Prince.

753 _____. "Studies in Ben Jonson. III." Anglia 39 (1914-16): 16-44.
Several of Henry Tubbe's epigrams (Harl. ms. 4126) are directly imitative of character portraits in Epicoene, Every Man out of his Humour, and The Alchemist.

754 BRINKLEY, ROBERTA FLORENCE. Nathan Field, the Actor-Playwright. Yale Studies in English, 77. New Haven: Yale University Press, 1928, pp. 72-77. [Reprint. Hamden, Conn.: The Shoe String Press, Archon Books, 1973.]
A Jonsonian actor, Field participated in the "tribe of Ben" and was strongly influenced by Jonson in many aspects of his own drama: type of plot, adherence to the unities, expository soliloquies, use of humours for designating characters, subjects for satire. Unlike Jonson, Field often maintained several stories of similar interest in his plays. Many of his works directly parallel those of Jonson.

755 BROOKS, HAROLD F. "Oldham and Phineas Fletcher: An Unrecognized Source for Satyrs Upon the Jesuits." RES 22 (1971): 410-22.
Oldham's satires have parallels with both Fletcher's The Locusts and Jonson's Catiline.

756 CHATTERJI, RUBY. "Unity and Disparity in Michaelmas Term." SEL 8 (1968):349-63.
Middleton definitely knew Volpone and imitated many of its features: the theme of cupidity; ethics based on draft and wit; association of money with family and children. He failed, however, to assimilate his borrowing into his own work.

757 CLARK, A. M. "Jonson Allusion in Jeremy Taylor." N&Q 148 (27 June 1925):459.
Finds an unrecorded allusion to Volpone in Jeremy Taylor's Holy Living. (See 745.)

758 CLAUSEN, WENDELL. "The Beginnings of English Character-Writing in the Early Seventeenth Century." PQ 25 (1946): 32-45.
Jonson, through his literary prestige and personal friendship, exerted a strong influence on Sir Thomas Overbury and his development of the character. Overbury took his form from Theophrastus, but much of his content and style from Jonson. His characters, consequently, have strong satiric wit and focus on the fancies of the times.

Influence and Allusions

759 COOK, ELIZABETH. "The Plays of Richard Brome." More Books: The Bulletin of the Boston Public Library 22 (October 1947):285-301.

Brome was strongly influenced by Jonson--and more by his practice than his principles--but altered Jonsonian elements to suit the tastes of his age. For example, "he deflected Jonson's comedy of humors into a more 'refined' comedy of manners."

760 CORBALLIS, R. P. "Keats and Ben Jonson." N&Q 222 (1977):330.

Keats may have drawn the opening of "Ode to a Nightingale" from Sejanus III.595-98. His letters indicate that he was reading and thinking about Jonson at the time of writing the poem.

761 DAVIS, JOE LEE. The Sons of Ben: Jonsonian Comedy in Caroline England. Detroit: Wayne State University Press, 1967, pp. 7-8, 15-18, 29-31, 81-91, 154-64, passim.

Identifies eleven minor dramatists of the Caroline period who attempted to imitate the comic practices of Jonson "more diligently than they did other masters." Discusses three reasons they imitated Jonson: his primacy "in recreating for his age the image of man and making this image live in contemporary terms," his humour theory and practice, and the principles of the craft he stressed.

Reviewed by J. A. Barish in MLQ 29 (1968):356-58; R. Harrier in ELN 5 (December 1967):141-42; R. A. Harris in QJS 54 (1968):88; L. Tennenhouse in SCN 28 (1970):28-29; C. G. Thayer in MQR 7 (1968):222-24.

762 DRAPER, JOHN W. "The Theory of the Comic in Eighteenth-Century England." JEGP 37 (1938):207-23.

Although Jonson was widely accepted as "the classic of English comedy," 18th-century literary criticism generally had only a vague understanding of Jonson's theory of humours, "having lost the underlying medical concept." It eventually freed itself from Jonson's authority in comic theory, as it did from that of Aristotle and Hobbes.

763 DUNCAN, DOUGLAS. "Synge and Jonson (with a parenthesis on Ronsard)," in A Centenary Tribute to John Millington Synge, 1871-1909: Sunshine and the Moon's Delight. Edited by Suheil B. Bushrui. New York: Barnes and Noble; London: Colin Smyth, 1972, pp. 205-18.

Jonson's rich dramatic speech, blending of art and nature, and imaginative presentation of serious issues appealed to Synge. Differences between the playwrights include amount of concern for aesthetic appeal, scope of dramatic ends, and components first considered in dramatic composition. Bartholomew Fair invites comparison with The Playboy of the Western World and The Tinker's Wedding.

764 EASSON, ANGUS. "Marina's Maidenhead." SQ 24 (1973):328-29.
Shakespeare may have taken Boult's threat to Marina (Pericles IV.vi.127-28) from the end of Sejanus, where the hangman violates Sejanus's young daughter just before her death.

764a ECKHARDT, EDUARD. "Deutsche Bearbeitungen älterer englischer Dramen." Englische Studien 68 (1933):195-208.
Discusses Ludwig Tieck's 1793 adaptation of Volpone (Herr von Fuchs) as well as Stefan Zweig's, the conclusion of which he finds less satisfactory than Jonson's. Hugo F. Koenigsgarten's comic opera version of Epicoene, Lord Spleen (see 264), eliminates the subplot, provides a contemporary setting, and heightens the comedy of the original.

765 EDWARDS, PHILIP, and GIBSON, COLIN, eds. The Plays and Poems of Philip Massinger. 5 vols. Oxford: Clarendon Press, 1976, 2:184-85; 3:3-4; 4:3-5.
Ideas for many parts of Massinger's The City Madam came from Jonson's plays: The Alchemist, Volpone, and Epicoene. Massinger's The Roman Actor and The Unnatural Combat have correspondences with Sejanus and Catiline respectively.

766 ELLEHAUGE, MARTIN. English Restoration Drama, Its Relation to Past English and Past and Contemporary French Drama, from Jonson via Molière to Congreve. Folcroft, Pa.: Folcroft Library Editions, 1970. 322 pp., passim. [Originally published Copenhagen: Levin and Munksgaard, 1933.]
Although the majority of Restoration dramatists rejected Jonson's idea that drama should instruct by its appeal to reason, they were significantly influenced by his works. Following him, they focused on deficiencies in the times, class distinction in morals, and satire on particular groups (especially lawyers and clergymen). Restoration drama brought together elements of Jacobean and French drama, with Jonsonian humours very popular in a comedy of manners setting. Plays were judged according to a desired effect more than rules. Jonson provided a model for a simultaneous movement toward formal regularity and greater liberty.

767 ELLISON, LEE MONROE. "Elizabethan Drama and the Works of Smollett." PMLA 44 (1929):842-62.
Despite his debt to Shakespeare's realistic comedies, Smollett is even more closely akin to Jonson in satiric attitude and method.

Influence and Allusions

768 EVANS, G. BLAKEMORE. "Dryden's *Mac Flecknoe* and Dekker's *Satiromastix*." *MLN* 76 (1961):598-600.
Mac Flecknoe (11.87-89) refers more to *Satiromastix* than to *Poetaster*.

769 _____, ed. *The Plays and Poems of William Cartwright*. Madison: University of Wisconsin Press, 1951, pp. 262-68; 610-60, passim; 664, 684, 695, 728, 736.
Enumerates Cartwright's borrowings from Jonson, showing especially the dependence of *The Ordinary* on *The Alchemist*.

770 FLEISSNER, ROBERT F. "The Three Base Indians in *Othello*." *SQ* 22 (1971):80-82.
Othello V.ii.346 should read "base Indian," not "base Judean." *Volpone* may have been one of Shakespeare's sources.

771 FOAKES, R. A. *Shakespeare: The Dark Comedies to the Last Plays: From Satire to Celebration*. Charlottesville: The University Press of Virginia, 1971, pp. 34-38, 78-81, 84-85.
Shakespeare's last plays should be thought of as dramatic structures; starting with the dark comedies, Shakespeare was influenced by the new experiments in satirical drama of Jonson and Marston. Among the Jonsonian satiric techniques that Foakes analyzes are the uses of the satirists' voices in *Every Man out of his Humour*, *Cynthia's Revels*, and *Poetaster*, and the methods of bridging satire and tragedy in *Sejanus*.

772 FOX, ROBERT C. "A Source for Milton's Comus." *N&Q* 207 (1962):52-53.
The Comus mentioned in *Poetaster* may have been the source of Milton's Comus. Both figures are associated with drunkenness and lechery.

773 GIBSON, C. A. "Massinger's Use of his Sources for *The Roman Actor*." *AUMLA* No. 15 (May 1961): pp. 60-72.
The Roman Actor contains over forty verbal borrowings from *Sejanus*, "ranging in length from two or three words to considerable speeches." Many situations are borrowed as well.

774 GRAHAM, C. B. "Jonson Allusions in Restoration Comedy." *RES* 15 (1939):200-04.
Points out sixteen allusions not previously recorded. Taken from the texts of the plays, these include five references to Jonson by name, three to his plays, and eight to his characters. They would be easily recognized and are evidence of Jonson's popularity.

775 _____. "The Jonsonian Tradition in the Comedies of John Dennis." MLN 56 (1941):370-72.
In two of his three plays, Dennis employs comedy of humours, intriguers directing action, and reform proposed by the presentation of folly. He directly approved of Jonson's dramatic theories.

776 _____. "The Jonsonian Tradition in the Comedies of Thomas D'Urfey." MLQ 8 (1947):47-52.
Besides making specific allusions to Jonson, his plays, and his characters, D'Urfey's comedies contain Jonsonian humour-characters, employ Jonson's device of "episodic humour-study," and exhibit gulling in the Jonsonian manner.

777 HEWETT-THAYER, HARVEY W. "Tieck and the Elizabethan Drama: His Marginalia." JEGP 34 (1935):377-407.
Notes the marginal remarks made about Jonson and others by Ludwig Tieck in his copies of Collier's History of English Dramatic Poetry, Hazlitt's Lectures on the Dramatic Poetry of the Age of Elizabeth, the 1692 Folio of Jonson's Works, and the 1816 Gifford edition of Jonson.

778 HOLDSWORTH, R. V. "Early References to Plays by Jonson, Shirley, and Others." N&Q 222 (1977):208-09.
The Marriage of Armes and Arts (1651) alludes quite directly to Epicoene, Catiline, and The Alchemist.

779 HOWARTH, HERBERT. "The Joycean Comedy: Wilde, Jonson, and Others," in A James Joyce Miscellany. 2nd series. Edited by Marvin Magalaner. Carbondale: Southern Illinois University Press, 1959, pp. 179-94.
Although Joyce mastered the art of Jonsonian comedy, thus concerning himself with distinguishing between the acceptable and unacceptable, he moved beyond Jonson and treated everything as simultaneously ridiculous and beautiful.

780 _____. "Twelfth Night with a Touch of Jonson," in his The Tiger's Heart: Eight Essays on Shakespeare. New York: Oxford University Press, 1970, pp. 94-119.
Traces the influence of Jonson in Twelfth Night, concluding that Malvolio, Sir Andrew Ague-Cheek, and the raucous subplot are Jonsonian.

781 JOHNSTON, GEORGE BURKE. "Scott and Jonson." N&Q 195 (1950): 521-22.
John Gibson Lockhart, in his Memoirs of the Life of Sir Walter Scott, attests to Scott's familiarity with Jonson's plays. Johnston adds to these three allusions to Jonson not labeled by Scott or Lockhart.

Influence and Allusions

782 JOST, FRANÇOIS. "Ludwig Tieck: English and French Sources of His William Lovell (1795/6)," in Studies in Eighteenth-Century Culture: Proceedings of the American Society for Eighteenth-Century Studies. Vol. 2. Edited by Harold E. Pagliaro. Cleveland: The Press of Case Western Reserve University, 1972, 181-93.

Tieck drew on The New Inn for the name and character traits of his protagonist. Both Jonson's and Tieck's heroes represent specific concepts of love.

783 KAUFMANN, RALPH JAMES. "Under the Seal of Ben," in his Richard Brome: Caroline Playwright. New York and London: Columbia University Press, 1961, pp. 35-46.

Brome adhered to the same value system as Jonson--"a belief in the public good." He came under the influence of Jonson when the latter was experiencing the failures of his last plays, but was critical enough of his master not to imitate his mistakes. Instead, Brome aimed at pleasing the restless contemporary audience with "the creation of laughter."

784 KEAST, W. R. "Some Seventeenth-Century Allusions to Shakespeare and Jonson." N&Q 194 (1949):468-69.

In IV.i of Part 2 of Thomas Killigrew's Thomaso: or, The Wanderer (1664), Thomaso says, "I would not have a tearing, ranting Whore, no Doll Common, no Tear-sheet."

784a KERR, MINA. Influence of Ben Jonson on English Comedy. [Philadelphia:] University of Pennsylvania, 1912. 132 pp. [Reprint. New York: Phaeton Press, 1967.]

Jonson's main influence on his contemporaries included the theory of humours, tight construction, and the use of satire. Later followers either simply imitated his spirit or copied him closely--and unwisely. His works encouraged incorporation of or allusions to the classics.

785 KIRSCH, ARTHUR C. "Guarini and Jonson," in his Jacobean Dramatic Perspectives. Charlottesville: The University Press of Virginia, 1972, pp. 7-24.

Shows how the tragicomedy of Guarini and the satiric comedy of Jonson influenced Beaumont and Fletcher in developing their plays, which combined romance and satire, stressed complex plot and style, and "conscious theatricalism."

786 LaFRANCE, MARSTON. "Fielding's Use of the 'Humor' Tradition." BuR 17 (December 1969):53-63.

Fielding combined the epic form and humour characters--from Jonson and Congreve--to serve "the traditional satiric purpose of teaching by horrible example."

787 LA REGINA, GABRIELLA. "Ben Jonson e la sua fortuna nel seicento." EM 16 (1965):37-86.
Traces Jonson's life and literary career. Explores his popularity and influence, especially in the latter half of the 17th century.

788 LeBOIS, ANDRÉ. "Elémir Bourges et les élizabéthains." RLC 22 (1949):237-54.
Gives evidence of Bourges' interest in Jonson, and of the influence of Volpone on his novel, Les Oiseaux s'envolent et les feuilles tombent (1893).

789 LÜDEKE, HENRY. Ludwig Tieck und das alte englische Theater: Ein Beitrag zur Geschichte der Romantik. Frankfort am Main: Moritz Diesterweg, 1922, pp. v-vii, 1-10, 19-38 passim, 53, 67, 92, 122, 146-56, 186-201 passim, 264-74. [Reprint. Hildesheim: H. A. Gerstenberg, 1975.]
Traces the influence of Jonson and other Elizabethan dramatists on German theatre, playwrights, and critics through the early 19th century. Summarizes Tieck's critical evaluation of Ben Jonson--not a genius, like Shakespeare, but a "powerful talent"--and shows its similarities to that of Coleridge. Discusses Tieck's translations of Volpone and Epicoene and the influence of Jonson on Tieck's own works.

790 McALINDON, T. "Yeats and the English Renaissance." PMLA 82 (1967):157-69.
Yeats's commitment to "an aristocratically oriented poetry" at the beginning of this century was strengthened by his reading of Spenser, Shakespeare, and Jonson. Cynthia's Revels and Poetaster "offered to Yeats the precedent of a famous poet making heroic satire out of his grievances and quarrels as a writer and basing all his criticisms of his opponents on aristocratic values and snobberies." Between 1905 and 1915 he developed "a personal bitterness akin to Jonson's." He also associated Synge with Jonson, which was natural in view of Synge's having drawn inspiration from Jonson's comedy.

791 McDONALD, CHARLES O. "Restoration Comedy as Drama of Satire: An Investigation into Seventeenth-Century Aesthetics." SP 55 (1958):164-86.
Discriminating between varied meanings of "wit," McDonald examines the influence of Jonson on Restoration comedy. Most plays use Jonson's division of comic characters into knaves and fools. Restoration dramatists' claims to being subtle moralists are well founded.

Influence and Allusions

792 MACKIN, COOPER R. "The Relation of Macbeth to Sophonisba." N&Q 200 (1955):373-74.
Volpone influenced Sophonisba, which influenced Macbeth.

793 _____. "The Satiric Technique of John Oldham's Satyrs upon the Jesuits." SP 62 (1965):78-90.
Oldham modelled his work on Catiline, but many stylistic differences exist between the two pieces. Oldham created a more expansive villain.

794 MERCHANT, PAUL. "A Jonson Source for Herrick's 'Upon Julia's Clothes.'" N&Q 219 (1974):93.
The poem closely resembles Epicoene I.i.97-102.

795 MITCHELL, JOHN ARTHUR, ed. "The Warde" by Thomas Neale. Philadelphia: University of Pennsylvania, 1937, pp. 26-30.
Neale may have known Jonson personally. The Warde (1637) shows the direct influence of Jonson's play in its humour-type characters, dialogue, classical allusions, lack of romance, and certain specific echoes of Volpone and The Alchemist. The Warde includes a character borrowed directly from Eastward Ho--Sir Petronel Flash.

796 MUESCHKE, PAUL, and FLEISHER, JEANNETTE. "Jonsonian Elements in the Comic Underplot of Twelfth Night." PMLA 48 (1933): 722-40.
In writing his comic underplot in Twelfth Night, Shakespeare was indebted to the Jonsonian comic method first developed in Every Man in his Humour and Every Man out of his Humour. The similarities are evident in the relationship between Sir Toby and Sir Andrew and the Jonsonian victimizer and gull, and in Shakespeare's adaptation of the Jonsonian method in exposing Malvolio's "humour" of self-love. Shakespeare, however, is able to achieve comic effects superior to those of Jonson.

797 NASH, RALPH. "Milton, Jonson and Tiberius." Classical Philology 41 (1946):164.
Sejanus could have been the source of the Greek proverb assigned to Tiberius in The Reason of Church Government.

798 NELSON, CATHRYN ANNE. A Critical Edition of "Wit's Triumverate, or The Philosopher." JDS 57, 1975, pp. 1-14, 21-26.
Compares Wit's Triumvirate (ca. 1635, B.M. Add. ms. 45865) with The Alchemist and concludes that the author "is greatly indebted to Jonson for his dramatic technique and for incidents and relationships in his play."

799 _____. "Two Notes on Pope's 'Epistle to Bathurst.'" N&Q 219 (1974):251-52.
Cites a portion of the opening scene of Volpone as a source for several lines in Pope's "Epistle to Bathurst," which was composed during the time of the play's greatest popularity on the 18th-century stage, 1730-1732.

800 NORMAN, ARTHUR M. Z. "Source Material in Antony and Cleopatra." N&Q 201 (1956):59-61.
The rope of pearls presented to Volpone may have been Shakespeare's inspiration for having Alexas bring Cleopatra a pearl from Antony.

801 O'DONNELL, NORBERT F. "The Authorship of The Careless Shepherdess." PQ 33 (1954):43-47.
John Gough, rather than Thomas Goffe, probably wrote this pastoral and drew on Jonson's The Sad Shepherd.

802 PARTRIDGE, A. C. "Shakespeare's Orthography in Venus and Adonis and Some Early Quartos." ShS 7 (1954):35-47.
Jonson's influence on Shakespeare's orthography is evident about the turn of the century.

803 PERRY, WILLIAM. "The Influence of Ben Jonson on Nathan Field." SP 43 (1946):482-97.
Disputes the assertions of many critics, based on external evidence, that Nathan Field, the actor-playwright, was greatly influenced by Jonson. Drawing on internal evidence, Peery claims "that the influence of Jonson on Field has been exaggerated" and that further study will probably prove that he was really as much indebted to Chapman and Middleton.

804 PERKINSON, RICHARD H. "Topographical Comedy in the Seventeenth Century." ELH 3 (1936):270-90.
Restoration dramatists frequently make use of "a popular locale as the background for comedy of manners and intrigue." This practice can be traced to Jonson's Bartholomew Fair, although Jonson's play cannot be called a comedy of manners. Dramatists such as Shirley, Nabbes, and Brome imitated Jonson's use of London topography to achieve their purpose, not merely to be "realistic."

805 SCHOENBAUM, S. "Peut-on parler d'une 'décadence' du théâtre au temps des premiers Stuart?" in Dramaturgie et Société: Rapports entre l'oeuvre théâtrale, son interprétation et son public aux XVIe et XVIIe siècles. Vol. 2. Edited by Jean Jacquot et al. Paris: Editions du Centre National de la Recherche Scientifique, 1968, 829-45.

Influence and Allusions

Massinger's City Madam has characters and situations similar to those found in Eastward Ho and directly imitates Volpone in Luke Frugal's invocation of his gold (III.iii. 18-25).

806 SIMPSON, EVELYN M. "Jonson and Dickens: A Study in the Comic Genius of London." E&S 29 (1944):82-92.
Both authors loved the people and places of their city and could present them with vibrancy. Jonson had a direct influence on Dickens.

807 SORELIUS, GUNNAR. 'The Giant Race Before the Flood': Pre-Restoration Drama on the Stage and in the Criticism of the Restoration. Uppsala: Almqvist & Wiksells, 1966. 227 pp., passim.
Restoration admiration for Jonson was probably due more to his prestige as a critic than to the plays themselves, which for the most part did not exhibit the refinement suitable to Restoration tastes. Discusses performances, popularity, influence of, and critical response to eleven of Jonson's plays.

808 STOKES, E. E., JR. "Jonson's 'Humour' Plays and Some Later Plays of Bernard Shaw." Shavian 2 (1964):13-18.
Shaw, in the writing of his later plays, used many of the techniques used by Jonson: transparent names for characters, the character sketch, and commentator-characters.

809 TEN HOOR, GEORGE JOHN. "Ben Jonson's Reception in Germany." PQ 14 (1935):327-43.
Jonson's satiric, detailed presentation of London and Germany's lack of a society centered in a capital have long combined to minimize Jonson's influence on German drama. Except for performances of Sejanus (1663, 1671), Germany knew almost nothing of Jonson until Lessing's work on Dryden and Tieck's studies on earlier English drama. German critics have consistently compared Jonson and Shakespeare rather than studied Jonson as an author in his own right.

810 TIEDJE, EGON. Die Tradition Ben Jonsons in der Restaurationskomödie. Britannica et Americana, 11. Hamburg: Cram, de Gruyter, 1963. 168 pp.
Lists Restoration performances of Jonson's plays, and references to him and his work. Explores the influence of Jonson on Restoration comic practice in terms of realism of place and language; comic and satiric techniques; individual scenes, motifs, and effects; character types; themes. In

comparison with Restoration comedy, Jonson's was more pedagogical and satirical, more inclusive in portrayal of social strata, less concerned with erotic intrigue and elegant repartee, more dependent on monologue than dialogue.

811 URE, PETER. "A Simile in Samson Agonistes." N&Q 195 (1950): 298.
Milton may have taken his woman-ship comparison from The Devil is an Ass and/or The Staple of News.

812 VINCENT, HOWARD P. "Ben Jonson Allusions." N&Q 177 (8 July 1939):26.
Notes two allusions not included in The Jonson Allusion Book. (See 751.)

813 WARREN, AUSTIN. "Pope and Ben Jonson." MLN 45 (1930):86-88.
Pope's library contained the 1692 Folio of Jonson's Works, with Pope's autograph on the title page and a number of annotations. The few marginal notes and the presence of incomplete indexes of "admired passages" on the front and back fly-leafs suggest that Pope might have intended at one time to bring out an edition of Jonson. Pope approvingly marks passages in several plays, makes an editorial emendation to a line in Poetaster, and notes in several places Jonson's indebtedness to several classical authors.

814 WILEY, AUTREY NESS. Rare Prologues and Epilogues, 1642-1700. London: George Allen and Unwin, 1940, pp. 13-17, 233, 260. [Reprint. Port Washington, N.Y.: Kennikat Press, 1970.]
A 1660 "Prologue to the Reviv'd Alchemist" helps to show how early in the Restoration the Jonson vogue began. Some Restoration prologues and epilogues scourged and anatomized frailties "in the style perfected by Ben Jonson."

815 WILLIAMS, WELDON. "The Genesis of John Oldham's Satyrs upon the Jesuits." PMLA 58 (1943):958-70.
After significant exploration for a model for his satires, Oldham focused on the vision model as used in the opening of Catiline. Oldham openly acknowledged his debt to Jonson, whom he greatly admired, and found Jonson's modification of the Senecan ghost highly effective.

816 WILLSON, ROBERT F., JR. "Beaumont and Jonson Once More." NM 78 (1977):264-67.
Jonson's influence on Beaumont appears in the latter's The Woman Hater and The Knight of the Burning Pestle. The younger dramatist particularly liked Jonson's neoclassical method and his ability to portray public and private vice in one character. Both dramatists believed that playwrights should work for coterie audiences.

Influence and Allusions

817 WITHINGTON, ROBERT. Excursions in English Drama. New York: Appleton-Century, 1937, pp. 102-13.

Jonson and Shaw resemble each other in their disparagement of the public, lack of stage action, and emphasis on theories. Shaw may become as infrequently staged as Jonson, but the plays in which either dramatist satirizes universal failings will probably last.

See also 29, 37, 97, 108, 219, 233, 253, 271, 319, 321, 333, 335, 337, 349, 532, 545, 547, 554, 603, 638, 640, 651, 671, 684, 693, 726, 734, 822, 830, 831, 838, 852, 854, 864, 898, 906, 907, 927, 946, 958, 959, 1006, 1007, 1013, 1016, 1033, 1122, 1152.

Jonson and Shakespeare

818 ALLEN, PERCY. "Every Man Out of His Humour," "Cynthia's Revels," and "The Poetaster," in The Oxford-Shakespeare Case Corroborated. London: Cecil Palmer, 1931, pp. 43-92, 93-150, 151-164.

This sequel to the author's earlier book, The Case for Edward de Vere 17th Earl of Oxford as "Shakespeare," examines from the "Oxfordian view point" Ben Jonson's plays, especially Every Man out of his Humour and Cynthia's Revels, and finds them "daring burlesques" of the "Shakespearean plays generally, and particularly of Twelfth Night, and Romeo and Juliet." Allen's topical analysis of Jonson's comical satires reinforces his claim that Oxford is the author of the plays claimed to have been written by William Shakespeare.

819 _____. "Every Man out of his Humour and Twelfth Night" and "Twelfth Night and Epicoene," in his Shakespeare, Jonson, and Wilkins as Borrowers: A Study in Elizabethan Dramatic Origins and Imitations. London: Cecil Palmer, 1928, pp. 43-97, 136-84.

Jonson borrowed from or satirized Shakespeare, especially in Every Man out of his Humour, Sejanus, and Epicoene. The two comedies remold the plot of Twelfth Night, satirizing Shakespearean romantic comedy and showing how life should be presented on the stage. There are numerous parallel passages and situations between Every Man out of his Humour and Twelfth Night, and Epicoene appropriates nearly 500 lines from the latter. Sejanus is largely drawn from Julius Caesar but, though it criticizes Shakespeare's views, it treats him well in the character of Cremutius Cordus.

820 _____. The Life Story of Edward De Vere as "William Shakespeare." London: Cecil Palmer, 1932. 401 pp.
Claims to have made "a thousand contacts with the plays and poems" in his study of the life of Edward de Vere, 17th Earl of Oxford, and concludes that Oxford is "Shakespeare." Attacks the credibility of Jonson and other Folio witnesses in their claims regarding Mr. William Shakespeare; points out references to Shakespeare (Oxford) in Jonson's plays.

821 BAYLEY, JOHN. "The Shakespearian Freedom in Literature." EDH 37 (1972):1-16.
Jonson's calculated dramatic planning and his sense of importance are contrasted with Shakespeare's methods and aims. In plays based on history, Jonson was more concerned than Shakespeare with historical accuracy and in general with creating more outwardly consistent characters.

822 BENTLEY, GERALD EADES. Shakespeare & Jonson: Their Reputations in the Seventeenth Century Compared. 2 vols. Chicago: University of Chicago Press, 1945. 468 pp. [Reprinted, 2 vols. in 1, 1965. 469 pp.]
Adds new discoveries to already recorded allusions to Shakespeare and Jonson. First volume defines "allusion," surveys existing allusion books, criticizes collectors' failure to test allusions against a "well-defined standard," and challenges the prevalent opinion that Shakespeare was more popular than Jonson among 17th-century writers. Discusses the procedure for determining literary reputation, shows the distribution of allusion by decades and types, and supplies lists showing the comparative popularity of individual plays and characters. The second volume provides 59 new allusions to Shakespeare and 1,079 to Jonson, as well as several pages of relevant allusions to other Jacobean and Caroline playwrights.
Reviewed by T. W. Baldwin in JEGP 45 (1946):232-34; A. Harbage in MLN 60 (1945):414-17; B. Maxwell in PQ 24 (1945):91-93; P. Simpson in RES 21 (1945):334-36; C. J. Sisson in MLR 41 (1946):73-74; in N&Q 188 (2 June 1945): 241-42; in TLS, 28 April 1945, p. 200.

823 _____. The Swan of Avon and the Bricklayer of Westminster. Princeton: Princeton University Press, 1948. 18 pp.
Shakespeare and Jonson differ "in their position in the theatre as professional and as amateur playwrights . . . in the type of theatre for which they normally wrote. They differ finally in their reputations." Jonson was preferred to Shakespeare in the 17th century because of the neoclassicism of the age and the type of audience viewing the plays.

Jonson and Shakespeare

824 BEVINGTON, DAVID. "Shakespeare vs Jonson on Satire," in Shakespeare 1971: Proceedings of the World Shakespeare Congress, Vancouver, August 1971. Edited by Clifford Leech and J. M. R. Margeson. Toronto and Buffalo: University of Toronto Press, 1972, pp. 107-22.

The difference between Jonson and Shakespeare did not exist on the personal, acrid level of the Poetomachia, but on a professional level only. The two dramatists held opposing positions on the use of satire in drama. While Jonson let it be known that the dramatist had an obligation to expose the follies of the time and "was recognizably the chief spokesman of satire's defense against a charge of libelling," Shakespeare's attitude was more subtle. Examines As You Like It and Twelfth Night and concludes "that Shakespeare maintained a characteristic distance from the Jonsonian norm but still experimented in a spirit of genuine interest and commitment."

825 BOUGHNER, DANIEL C. "Jonsonian Structure in The Tempest." SQ 21 (1970):3-10.

In writing The Tempest, Shakespeare used the four-part structure invented by Terence and introduced to the English stage by Jonson in Every Man in his Humour. Jonson experimented with the structure in his later comedies, and frequently commented on it in his discussions of playwriting.

826 BROWN, IVOR. "Not so Big Ben." Drama 99 (1970):44-46.

Explains why Shakespeare is preferred to Jonson.

827 CHAMBERS, E. K. William Shakespeare: A Study of Facts and Problems. Oxford: Clarendon Press, 1930, 1:69-72; 2:202-11, passim.

In connection with biographical data on Shakespeare, briefly touches upon the War of the Theatres. Discusses the possible allusions to Shakespeare in Every Man in his Humour, Every Man out of his Humour, Poetaster, Sejanus.

828 CRANE, MILTON. "Twelfth Night and Shakespearian Comedy." SQ 6 (1955):1-8.

Nevill Coghill is incorrect in his distinction between Shakespearean and Jonsonian comedy. "The individual playwright may at will stress either the pleasurable or the didactic, but both elements will be present in his work, and the most successful comic artist . . . will be the one who best contrives to combine both elements in his play."

829 CURREY, R. N. "Jonson and The Tempest." N&Q 192 (1947):468.
Although it uses a magician and spirits, Shakespeare's play is not less realistic than Jonson's works. Face is more of a deus ex machina than is Prospero.

830 FROST, DAVID L. "G. E. Bentley and Shakespeare," in his The School of Shakespeare: The Influence of Shakespeare on English Drama 1600-1642. Cambridge: Cambridge University Press, 1968, pp. 19-22.
Objects to Bentley's method of judging allusions and to his conclusion, in Shakespeare and Jonson (see 822), that Jonson's reputation was greater than Shakespeare's in the 17th century.

831 _____. "Shakespeare in the Seventeenth Century." SQ 16 (1965):81-89.
Challenges G. E. Bentley's conclusion in Shakespeare and Jonson (see 822), that "Jonson's reputation stood higher in the seventeenth century than Shakespeare's." Questions Bentley's method of arriving at conclusions, his assessments of allusions, and his ignoring of the Shakespeare apocrypha.

832 FRYE, NORTHROP. "Comic Myth in Shakespeare." PTRSC 3rd Series, 46 (1952):47-58.
Jonson's comedies are comedies of manners employing realistic illusion. Their emphasis falls on character rather than the Shakespearean "final discovery," and with their ironic qualities come close to the notion of speculum consuetudinis, appropriate to Renaissance perceptions of classical New Comedy. The important writers of English comedy have followed Jonson's example rather than Shakespearean "romanticism," even though the latter is part of a more genuinely "primitive" and "popular," if less well-defined, tradition.

833 _____. "Mouldy Tales," in his A Natural Perspective: The Development of Shakespearean Comedy and Romance. New York and London: Columbia University Press; New York: Harcourt, Brace and World, 1965. pp. 1-33.
Compares The New Inn to Shakespeare's romances. Feels that the different conceptions of drama held by the two playwrights must be understood if the Jonsonian and Shakespearean traditions are to be valued properly.

Jonson and Shakespeare

834 GOLDSWORTHY, WILLIAM LANSDOWN. Ben Jonson and The First Folio. London: Cecil Palmer, 1931. 64 pp. [Reprint. New York: Haskell House, 1972.]

Jonson developed the masque Neptune's Triumph for the Return of Albion into The Staple of News. The play's Court prologue, as well as much about Lickfinger, identify Francis Bacon, not Shakespeare, as the author of the First Folio.

835 GRAY, HENRY DAVID. "The Date of Hamlet." JEGP 31 (1932): 51-61.

A 1601 date for the composition and first production of Hamlet is supported by allusions to the Chamberlain's men in Poetaster and is based partly on the supposition that Hamlet alludes to Poetaster and that Return from Parnassus refers to that allusion.

836 GREEN, WILLIAM. "Humours Characters and Attributive Names in Shakespeare's Plays." Names 20 (1972):157-65.

Shakespeare's familiarity with Jonson's work--co-producing Every Man in his Humour and Every Man out of his Humour--accounts for his linking of humours characterizations and attributive names in late romantic comedies. Although Shakespeare wrote humours comedies before Jonson, Jonson developed the schema and theory of humours characterization.

837 GREENWOOD, SIR GEORGE. Ben Jonson and Shakespeare. Hartford, Conn.: Edwin Valentine Mitchell; London: Cecil Palmer, 1921. 60 pp.

Jonson's contributions to the First Folio (the tributary poem acknowledged as his as well as the Epistle Dedicatory) are part of a 17th-century attempt to conceal the true authorship of Shakespeare's plays. Jonson signals the cover-up in Poetaster and Every Man out of his Humour and there gives his true (negative) opinion of Shakespeare.

838 GREG, W. W. "Shakespeare and Jonson." RES 22 (1946):58.

The reputations of the two playwrights must be seen in association with printing. Prior to the Restoration, Shakespeare was printed twice as much as Jonson; this accounts, in part, for the greater number of allusions to Shakespeare than to Jonson.

839 HAYASHI, TETSUMARO. "Ben Jonson and William Shakespeare: Their Relationship and Mutual Criticism." East-West Review 3 (Winter 1966-67):23-47.

The themes and attitudes in the playwrights' works are quite different; the conflict created a challenge for

Jonson's skills. Negative references to Shakespeare occur in Every Man in his Humour, Every Man out of his Humour, Poetaster, and Cynthia's Revels.

840 HOLLANDER, JOHN. "Twelfth Night and the Morality of Indulgence." SR 67 (1959):220-38.
Demonstrates that Shakespeare's Twelfth Night is as moral a comedy as Jonson's Every Man in his Humour, but claims that Shakespeare "was representing human experience in terms of fully dramatized metaphor rather than as a static emblematic correspondence [humour]; and, finally, that the drama operated to refute the moral validity of comedy of humours in its insistence on the active metaphor of surfeiting the appetite, upon which the whole plot is constructed."

841 KELLER, WOLFGANG. "Ben Jonson und Shakespeare." Shakespeare-Jahrbuch 73 (1937):31-52.
Contrasts the characters and artistic temperaments of the two playwrights. Suggests relationships and influences between Henry IV and The Case is Altered; Twelfth Night and Epicoene; Merry Wives of Windsor and the theory of humours. Deems Shakespeare the superior dramatist; he ruled in practice while Jonson ruled in theory.

842 LASCELLES, MARY. "Shakespeare's Comic Insight." PBA 48 (1962, pub. 1963):171-86.
Jonson is less tolerant of his own unsympathetic characters than Shakespeare of his, more likely to allow them to suffer the consequences of their folly or knavery. He is less likely to bring his characters to a realization that they are men with immortal souls and mortal bodies.

*843 LEVITCHI, LEON. "Three Linguistic Analogies between William Shakespeare and Ben Jonson." AUB-LG 21 (1972):25-36.

*844 LEVÝ, JIŘÍ. "Ben Jonson a William Shakespeare, dva typy dramatu," in Alchymista (1956), pp. 33-51. (In Czech.) (See 63a.)

*844a _____. "Divadelní prostor a čas v dramatech Williama Shakespeara a Bena Jonsona" [Dramatic space and time in the plays of William Shakespeare and Ben Jonson], in F. Wollmanovi k sedmdesátinam [Festschrift in honor of Frank Wollman]. Prague: Státní pedagogické nakladatelství, 1958, pp. 648-56. (In Czech.)

Jonson and Shakespeare

845 MUSGROVE, S. Shakespeare and Jonson: The Macmillan Brown Lectures, 1957. Bulletin No. 51, English Series No. 9. Auckland: Auckland University College, 1957. 55 pp. [Reprint. Folcroft, Pa.: Folcroft, 1975.]

The two playwrights were close friends who stimulated, criticized, and influenced each other's work directly. The first lecture considers the sort of relationship that existed between them and how it affected their work. The second analyzes King Lear and Volpone, showing similarities between them. The third proposes that Jonson is "Shakespearean" in his imaginative qualities and his wide range of sympathy.

Reviewed by J. B. Bamborough in RES 10 (1959):308; G. E. Bentley in SQ 9 (1958):575; in TLS, 14 February 1958, p. 91.

846 NELSON, RAYMOND S. "Measure for Measure as Satiric Comedy." Iowa State Journal of Research 47 (1973):253-63.

Identifies Measure for Measure as Jonsonian satiric comedy. Angelo is the fraud who, like Volpone, Subtle, and the long list of other knaves, must be unmasked.

847 O'DONOVAN, MICHAEL [Frank O'Connor]. The Road to Stratford. London: Methuen, 1948, p. 135.

Shakespeare sought a poetic and humorous realism, Jonson "a satiric Renaissance realism such as he achieved in his own gigantic 'constructions' which were the 'Ulysses' of his own day."

848 OGBURN, DOROTHY, and OGBURN, CHARLTON. This Star of England. "William Shakes-speare" Man of the Renaissance. New York: Coward-McCann, 1952. 1320 pp., passim. [Reprint. Westport, Conn.: Greenwood Press, 1972.]

Jonson drew from and consciously imitated Edward de Vere, 17th Earl of Oxford, the true Shakespeare. He presented William Shaksper, the imposter, in four of his own tedious, overrated plays.

849 ORNSTEIN, ROBERT. "Shakespearian and Jonsonian Comedy." ShS 22 (1969):43-46.

Jonson denied part of his own genius by rejecting the romantic mode of comedy--used only in Every Man in his Humour. On the whole, his comedies, in their sordid realism and emphasis on appetite, hypocrisy, and folly, reflect the facts of life; but Shakespearian comedy comes closer to the value of life because it "admits the possibility of tragic experience."

850 PAGE, FREDERICK. "Jonson and Shakespeare." N&Q 184 (1943):79.
Baconians err in identifying the Poet-Ape of Jonson's epigram and Sogliardo (Every Man in his Humour) as Shakespeare.

851 PHIALAS, PETER G. "Comic Truth in Shakespeare and Jonson." SAQ 62 (1963):78-91.
The playwrights differ in their vision, the comic truths they offer, their presentation of love, and their attitudes toward the fall of man.

852 PROUTY, CHARLES TYLER. "Some Observations on Shakespeare's Sources." Shakespeare-Jahrbuch 96 (1960):64-77.
The language of the Countess and Lafeu in All's Well That Ends Well is similar to that in Jonson's comical satires. Shakespeare may have been influenced by Jonson through having acted in several of his plays.

853 RANSOM, JOHN CROWE. The New Criticism. Norfolk, Conn.: New Directions, 1941, pp. 158-75. [Reprint. Folcroft, Pa.: Folcroft Library Editions, 1971.]
Jonson's works have a weaker texture than Shakespeare's but effectively unite situation and idiom. His dramas possess the third dimension--discourse differentiating poetry from science or prose. The characters in Volpone both support the play's structure and increase its density.

854 SCHLÖSSER, ANSELM. "Ben Jonson und Shakespeare." SJW 109 (1973):22-39.
A significant difference between the two playwrights resides in Jonson's historical pessimism, his sharper, narrower, and more sceptical views about the economic and political world, which contribute to his being an unorthodox moralist comparable to Swift. Jonson's humours characters are paralleled in Shakespeare and have predecessors in Sebastian Brant, Erasmus, and Rabelais. Sordido and Macilente of Every Man out of his Humour perhaps influenced the creation of Coriolanus and Thersites respectively. Jonson is the specialist of his time in treating the economic motives behind human action.

855 SIMPSON, PERCY. "A Modern Fable of Aesop." MLR 43 (1948): 403-05.
In his article, "The Chamberlain's Men and the Poetaster" (see 392), H. D. Gray errs in concluding that Jonson satirized Shakespeare in the character of Aesop in Poetaster. The 1602 Quarto refers to "Father Aesope," suggesting that the character was an elderly man, probably, as

T. W. Baldwin suggests, Heminge. "Politician" refers to the business manager of an acting company. Jonson's description of Shakespeare in *Discoveries* cannot be reconciled with the description of Aesop as a "sycophant-like slave." (*See* 393.)

856 STOLL, ELMER EDGAR. "Shakespeare and Jonson," in his *Shakespeare and Other Masters*. Cambridge, Mass.: Harvard University Press, 1940, pp. 85-120. [Reprint. New York: Russell and Russell, 1962.]

Compared to his contemporaries, Jonson is more classical, more concerned with the veracity and exactitude of motivation in his dramas, and employs a "truer and more consistent 'psychology.'" Like them, however, he is traditional in his dependence on the form and quality of speech for characterization, as evident particularly in *Every Man in his Humour*. In *Volpone*, *Epicoene*, and *The Alchemist* the characters are less fully presented through speech, more through contrast and conduct, and the victimizers are more complex and more completely developed than the victims. Jonson reacted against his predecessors' romantic tendencies; Shakespeare absorbed them.

857 _____. *Shakespeare Studies: Historical and Comparative in Method*. New York: G. E. Stechert, 1942, pp. 153-57, 164-69, 178-79.

In discussing Jonson's method of creating comic characters, finds that a comic method of Jonson's not found in Shakespeare is that of "repeated *motif* and rhythmical movement, but above all . . . abstract method of characterization, the ruling passion shown in every light and from every side." This method is exemplified in *Every Man in his Humour*, where the jealous Kitely fears to leave his home, and in *Volpone*, where Mosca makes up his inventory.

858 SUDDARD, MARY. "Ben Jonson and Shakespeare." *ContempR* 99 (1911):316-28.

Analyzes the character and work of the two playwrights. Finds that throughout his career, Jonson "uses his lucid intelligence to apply rules already established, whose wording he understands, but whose true signification he does not grasp."

859 _____. "A Parallel Between Ben Jonson and Shakespeare," in her *Keats, Shelley and Shakespeare: Studies & Essays in English Literature*. Cambridge: Cambridge University Press, 1912, pp. 182-204. [Reprint. Folcroft, Pa.: Folcroft Library Editions, 1976.]

Between them, Shakespeare and Jonson "invented" dramatic art. Jonson supplies the rules from antiquity, Shakespeare his knowledge of the human soul. Both observe and use real life, but Jonson's "snap-shot" realism, without psychological depth, is subservient to plot construction. *Epicoene* "is a positively faultless masterpiece of construction, but it rests on nothing."

860 TAVE, STUART M. "Corbyn Morris: Falstaff, Humor, and Comic Theory in the Eighteenth Century." *MP* 50 (1952):102-15.

Believes that Morris's *An Essay towards Fixing the True Standards of Wit, Humour, Raillery, Satire, and Ridicule. To Which Is Added an Analysis of the Characters of an Humourist, Sir John Falstaff, Sir Roger de Coverly, and Don Quixote* (1774) was important in effecting a change in taste in the early 18th century. This change, which eventually effected the preference of Shakespeare over Jonson, was the result "of the general development of comic theory, practice, and criticism . . . from a theory that assumed human nature to be naturally evil to one that assumed it to be naturally good."

861 URE, PETER. "Shakespeare and the Drama of his Time," in *A New Companion to Shakespeare Studies*. Edited by Kenneth Muir and S. Schoenbaum. Cambridge: Cambridge University Press, 1971, pp. 211-21.

In a section of the chapter, "Jonson and the Satirists" (pp. 216-18), states that, in the humours comedy of Jonson and others, satire came close to being allegory. Although Shakespeare used elements associated with this type of comedy, satire never took control. "Even his early humour-characters, Pistol and Nym in *Henry V*, have got an extra un-Jonsonian dimension."

862 WILSON, J. DOVER. "Ben Jonson and *Julius Caesar*." *ShS* 2 (1949):36-43.

Discusses Jonson's four instances, extended over a period of twenty-five years, of criticizing Shakespeare's *Julius Caesar*. In *Every Man out of his Humour*, III.iv., Clove and Orange make fun of what Jonson sees as Antony's faulty "philosophical" (scientific) knowledge, which actually was correct. In I.vi., Carlo Buffone's "Et tu Brute!" calls attention to Shakespeare's ignorance of history, for Jonson knew these were not the Roman's dying words. While Jonson could make fun of Shakespeare's knowledge of philosophy and history, he was not above picking up some Galenic physiology from Shakespeare in his description of Crites in *Cynthia's Revels*, II.iii.123 ff., which borrows from Antony's praise of Brutus. Wilson claims that

Jonson's allusion to Julius Caesar in the Induction of The Staple of News was used to raise a laugh, implying that Jonson found the original words ("Know, Caesar doth not wrong, nor without cause") in their context absurd.

See also: 186, 250, 252, 333, 337, 342, 345, 347, 349, 351, 353, 354, 356, 359, 363, 390, 393, 401, 430, 684, 708, 747, 764, 770, 771, 796, 800, 802, 881, 883, 884, 885, 995, 1022, 1024, 1026, 1029, 1035, 1041, 1042, 1046.

Language and Usage

863 BARISH, JONAS A. "Baroque Prose in the Theater: Ben Jonson." PMLA 73 (1958):184-95. [A revised version appears in Chapter 2 of his Ben Jonson and the Language of Prose Comedy (1960)(see 864).]

Jonson uses the baroque (or anti-Ciceronian) style in several ways. The first subdivision of the baroque style, the "curt" style, "lends itself to the expression of quick shifts in feeling, afterthoughts, self-corrections, unexpected interpolations or dislocations of attention; and since in so doing it simulates so convincingly the processes of live thought, it becomes an ideal instrument for certain kinds of theatrical prose." Jonson uses it as a vehicle for wit and a device of characterization. He also uses "asymmetry," defined as "bending the logical axis of syntax a few degrees one way or another in order to interrupt symmetrical pattern." The second subdivision of the baroque style, "the loose style," a multiplying of connectives, is used by Jonson straightforwardly (Crites's censure of perfume), with exaggeration (Truewit's tirade against matrimony), or as affected eloquence (fops like Amorphus and Fastidious Brisk). Jonson's other techniques include disturbance of logical word order, the separation of two related words, the suppression of some grammatical elements to avert symmetry, and the coupling of incongruent elements. Barish evaluates Jonson's deliberate use of these techniques: "There is music in Jonson's prose, but it is a music of brusque dissonances and irregular rhythms. . . ."

864 _____. Ben Jonson and the Language of Prose Comedy. Cambridge, Mass.: Harvard University Press; London: Oxford University Press, 1960. 343 pp. [Reprint. New York: W. W. Norton; Toronto: George J. McLeod, 1970.]

Shows that Jonson's prose adheres to the "non-logical maneuvers" and asymmetrical devices of the "curt" and "loose" anti-Ciceronian styles rather than to the logicality and elaborate balance of the Ciceronian, Euphuistic, and other rhetorical styles. Surveys prose comedy before

Jonson, and the characteristics of Jonson's "baroque prose"; and illustrates his growth in subtlety and control. Analyzes Epicoene and Bartholomew Fair in depth; traces Jonson's influence on subsequent French, Italian, and English comic dramatists.

Reviewed by W. Blissett in UTQ 30 (1960-61):251-54; J. A. Bryant, Jr. in MLQ 21 (1960):372-73; M. Crane in SQ 12 (1961):336-38; R. Davril in EA 14 (1961):243-44; E. G. Fogel in Renaissance News 15 (1962):42-45; H. C. Heffner in QJS 47 (1961):75-81; G. K. Hunter in RES 13 (1962): 193-96; E. Partridge in JEGP 61 (1962):339-402; S. Schoenbaum in MP 60 (1962-63):61-64; C. G. Thayer in Books Abroad 36 (1962):72; P. Ure in N&Q 206 (1961):196-98.

865 _____. "Jonson's Dramatic Prose," in Literary English Since Shakespeare. Edited by George Watson. London: Oxford University Press, 1970, pp. 111-55.

Reprints pp. 41-89 of Ben Jonson and the Language of Prose Comedy (1960). (See 864.)

866 CAMDEN, CARROLL. "Spenser's 'Little Fish that Men Call Remora.'" Rice Institute Pamphlet 44 (April 1958):1-12.

Discusses the various uses to which the story of the little fish called the remora from "unnatural natural history" is put by Elizabethan writers. The glosses on the word provided by two editors of Eastward Ho, John W. Cunliffe and Felix Schelling, reflect the "jumbled muddle of 16th-century thought." Jonson uses the word figuratively in Eastward Ho, IV.ii.6-20, Poetaster, III.ii.1-5, The Magnetic Lady, II.i.25-29.

867 CEJP, LADISLAV. "Some Allegorical Terms in Jonson's Plays." Sborník Vysoké školy pedagogické v Olomouci. Jazyk a literatura 5 (1959):123-29.

Cites Jonson's frequent use of "application" and other terms that show the richness of his allegorical vocabulary.

868 CLOUGH, WILSON O. "The Broken English of Foreign Characters of the Elizabethan Stage." PQ 12 (1933):255-68.

Of foreigners speaking broken English on the Elizabethan stage, the French are the most common, but Jonson is represented by only one, the servant Pacue in The Case is Altered, whose dialect is conventional. Other foreign dialects found in his plays are Spanish, in The Alchemist and The Devil is an Ass; Irish, in The New Inn; and Scottish, in Eastward Ho and The Sad Shepherd.

Language and Usage

869 COPLEY, J. Two Shakespearian Puns." *ES* 46 (1965):250-52.
The "fool/fowl" pun in *Bartholomew Fair* (III.iv and IV.iii) is probably based on a colloquial variant of pronunciation.

870 CRANE, MILTON. *Shakespeare's Prose*. Chicago: The University of Chicago Press, 1951, pp. 33-41.
Examines each of Jonson's plays, with the exception of *A Tale of a Tub*, *Eastward Ho*, and *The Devil is an Ass*, to determine his purpose for using either prose or verse. Discerns "no single universal principle governing the use of prose and verse."

871 DREW-BEAR, ANNETTE. *Rhetoric in Ben Jonson's Middle Plays: A Study of Ethos, Character Portrayal and Persuasion*. JDS 24, 1973, 311 pp.
The middle plays' themes relate to and are affected by rhetoric; their protagonists cultivate feigned ethos and demonstrate mastery of the deceptive uses of various rhetorical methods.
Reviewed by C. A. Asp in *SCN* 32 (1974):14, 16; R. B. Parker in *MLR* 70 (1975):145-48.

872 HOEPNER, ARTHUR. *Über den Gebrauch des Artikels in Ben Jonsons Dramen*. Printed summary of doctoral dissertation. Flensburg: Schmidt, 1921. 8 pp.
Analyzes Jonson's use of the definite and indefinite articles.

873 JUNGNELL, TORE. "Notes on the Language of Ben Jonson." *SMS* NS 1 (1960):86-110.
Presents "a few grammatical, mainly syntactical phenomena" found in the 1616 Folio.

874 LEVIN, RICHARD. "'The Ass in Compound': A Lost Pun in Middleton, Ford, and Jonson." *ELN* 4 (1966):12-15.
A playwright's orthography often indicates his punning on "ass." The pun occurs in *The Case Is Altered* (I.ii.52), *The Magnetic Lady* (I.vii.50-51), *The Devil Is An Ass* (II.i.30-31).

875 _____. "'Nuns' and 'Nunnery' in Elizabethan Drama." *N&Q* 213 (1968):248-49.
The last scene of *The Alchemist* uses "nun" to mean "courtesan." This predates the first usage given in the *OED* (1770).

876 _____. "Quomodo's Name in Michaelmas Term." N&Q 218 (1973): 460-61.

Unusual typographical treatment of the word "how" in Epicoene II.v.124 and The Staple of News I.v.32 suggests that Jonson was in each case probably alluding to a person's name.

877 McINTOSH, CAREY. "A Matter of Style: Stative and Dynamic Predicates." PMLA 92 (1977):110-21.

Comparison of the number of stative and dynamic verbs used in the description of Sir Amorous La Foole (Epicoene I.iii) and that of Sir Wilful (The Way of the World I.v) indicates that Jonson's description is more energetic than Congreve's although it has less intellectual energy. Congreve drew on Jonson's play for his own.

878 MEIER, T. "The Naming of Characters in Jonson's Comedies." ESA 7 (1964):88-95.

Jonson names his characters to define their roles in the plays. In Volpone, The Alchemist, Every Man in his Humour, Every Man out of his Humour, and Bartholomew Fair the characters may be divided into four groups. One group is ascribed names to indicate physical characteristics or deformities. A second group is named by profession or position; a third, by actions or manner; and a fourth, metaphorically.

879 NEUMANN, J. H. "Notes on Ben Jonson's English." PMLA 54 (1939):736-63.

Dryden erred in criticizing Jonson's "antiquated" expressions and false grammar, his bypassing of some rhetorical principles. Jonson was deeply concerned with major linguistic movements of the Renaissance and led in the movement toward standardization and modernity. His works are significant in terms of dialect, attention to phonetics, system of classifying verbs, dislike of artificial language, concern for development of English vocabulary, and criticism of excessive borrowing from foreign languages.

880 ORAS, ANTS. "Shakespeare, Ben Jonson, and Donne," in his Pause Patterns in Elizabethan and Jacobean Drama: An Experiment in Prosody. UFMH 3, 1960, pp. 13-19.

In a brief discussion of Jonson's pause distribution, finds him unusually even.

Language and Usage

881 PARTRIDGE, A. C. The Accidence of Ben Jonson's Plays, Masques and Entertainments, with an Appendix of Comparable Uses in Shakespeare. Cambridge: Bowes & Bowes, 1953. 333 pp.

Provides a study of grammatical inflections. Includes two appendixes, one on dialect forms, the other comparing Jonson's accidence with Shakespeare's. Jonson's plays offer the opportunity to study Elizabethan and Jacobean English as it was spoken.

882 _____. "The Periphrastic Auxiliary Verb 'Do' and Its Use in the Plays of Ben Jonson." MLR 43 (1948):26-43.

Jonson gains different effects by alternating forms of the verb.

883 _____. "The Punctuation of Shakespeare and Ben Jonson," in his Orthography in Shakespeare and Elizabethan Drama: A Study of Colloquial Contractions, Elision, Prosody and Punctuation. Lincoln: University of Nebraska Press; London: Edwin Arnold, 1964, pp. 130-40.

Jonson favored a logical method of punctuation while "Shakespeare preferred a partly rhythmical system." Jonson alone among his contemporaries took punctuation seriously; "the only author-punctuation of the time that can be studied with any degree of certainty is Jonson's."

884 _____. Studies in the Syntax of Ben Jonson's Plays. Cambridge: Bowes & Bowes, 1953. 104 pp.

Analyzes Jonson's use of "the periphrastic auxiliary verb do, the nouns, pronouns (excluding . . . thou and you), and the definite article." Jonson's dramatic language comes closer to actual speech than that of other playwrights. Despite similarities in grammatical usage between Jonson and Shakespeare, "Jonson is probably more conservative, from the syntactical point of view."

885 PENNANEN, ESKO V. Chapters on the Language in Ben Jonson's Dramatic Works. Annales Universitatis Turkuensis, Ser. B, Tom. 39. Turku, Finland: Turun Yliopiston Julkaisuja, 1951. 350 pp.

Examines Jonson's contributions to the English language found in his plays and masques, especially those words and phrases that appeared first in his work, or were given new meaning there. These include foreign borrowings, and words made up by compounding, conversion, and the use of affixes. Jonson's contributions were less extensive and less bold than Shakespeare's, confirming his linguistic conservatism. Many of the words introduced into literature by Jonson were already in colloquial use. His neologisms are mostly matter-of-fact. ". . . the absurdities and peculiarities of idiom one comes across in Jonson are in the great majority of cases a consequence of his desire to single them out for ridicule."

Reviewed by E. G. Stanley in MLR 49 (1953):368-69.

886 _____. Notes on the Grammar in Ben Jonson's Dramatic Works. Acta Academiae Socialis, Ser. A, Vol. 3. Tampere, Finland: Yhteiskunnallinen Korkeakoulu, 1966. 100 pp.

Detailed analysis of Jonson's use of the genitive; the possessive "its"; forms of comparison; the third person singular present; and the "new" participles (i.e., the active perfect and passive present). Concludes that on the whole Jonson did not deviate from general Elizabethan grammatical practice.

887 PRAZ, MARIO. "Fortuna della lingua e della cultura italiana in Inghilterra." Romana (Florence) 3 (August 1939):465-82. [Reprinted in his Machiavelli in Inghilterra ed altri saggi sui rapporti letterari anglo-italiani. Second edition. Florence: G. C. Sansoni, 1962, pp. 365-95.]

The word "buffoon" appeared originally in English in its Italian spelling, buffone. The name of Carlo Buffone, in Every Man out of his Humour, is an example.

888 RANKIN, DAVE. "Ben Jonson: Semanticist." ETC 19 (1962): 289-97.

Even though Jonson would not have known the 20th-century terminology of general semantics, he was "a remarkably acute semanticist." Citations from The Alchemist, Volpone, and Every Man in his Humour prove that Jonson understood the following principles of general semantics: (1) the word is not the thing, (2) words may be used to deceive oneself, (3) idealization is dangerous, and (4) the map is not the territory.

889 SACKTON, ALEXANDER HART. Rhetoric as a Dramatic Language in Ben Jonson. New York: Columbia University Press, 1948. 190 pp. [Reprint. New York: Octagon Books, 1967.]

Jonson's rhetoric--specifically his use of jargon and hyperbole--is examined to determine its use in the dramatic context.

Reviewed by M. L. Anderson in SAQ 48 (1949):156; D. C. Bryant in QJS 35 (1949):94-95; R. G. Cox in Scrutiny 16 (1949):71-74; J. Gerritsen in ES 31 (1950):223-24; C. T. Harrison in SR 57 (1949):709-14; A. K. McIlwraith in RES 1 (1950):166-68; Sister M. J. Rauh in JEGP 48 (1949):409-11; E. W. Talbert in MLQ 12 (1951):110-11.

Language and Usage

890 _____. "The Rhymed Couplet in Ben Jonson's Plays." Texas Studies in English 30 (1951):86-106.

Jonson's use of rhyme was not widespread, but he used it with distinct purposes in some plays. The couplet is his predominant form of rhyme; in only three plays, Poetaster, Sejanus, and The Sad Shepherd, is rhyme prominent. The rhymed couplet is used in the early plays such as A Tale of a Tub for satiric purposes or informal set speeches. Most rhymes in Poetaster are in passages directly translated from Ovid, Horace, or Virgil; in the moral sentences of Caesar, Virgil, and Horace; and in the author's prologue. Not until writing Sejanus did Jonson use the form with sure dramatic purpose. The three great comedies and the later plays show very little use of rhyme except in the nondramatic prologues and epilogues. The quality of the fifty lines of rhymed couplets in The New Inn and The Magnetic Lady evidence Jonson's deterioration in the use of language.

891 TAYLOR, WALT. "Arabic Words in Ben Jonson." LeedsSE No. 3 (1934):pp. 44-50.

Lists over 100 words of Arabic origin occurring in the works of Jonson, indicating the number of times each occurs and whether or not its initial appearance in English was in Jonson. Notes that "the technical vocabulary of The Alchemist is taken largely from Chaucer's Canon's Yeoman's Tale," but mentions other sources as well.

892 WELLS, HENRY W. "Ben Jonson, Patriarch of Speech Study." SAB 13 (1938):54-62.

Jonson's plays demonstrate his love for and sensitivity to language. Characters of different classes, jobs, and personalities all speak distinctively.

See also: 7, 27, 34, 49, 52, 79, 153, 162, 163, 177, 207, 211, 235, 292, 294, 350, 396, 421, 438, 489, 635, 655, 715, 722, 852, 907, 908, 924, 926, 941, 1027, 1030, 1045, 1050, 1152, 1158, 1188, 1222, 1226.

Literary Relations and Sources

893 ANGELL, C. F. "A Note on Jonson's Use of Sir Edward Dyer's 'My mynde to me a kyngdome is.'" PLL 10 (1974):417-21.

Jonson uses Dyer's line twice in his early comedies but does not accept it uncritically. In The Case Is Altered, he holds that the mind left to its own devices builds a kingdom of appetite and willfulness; in Every Man out of his Humour, that such a stance builds up and destroys fools.

894 ATKINS, J. W. H. English Literary Criticism: The Renascence. London: Methuen, 1947, pp. 256-59, 329-31. [Reprint. New York: Barnes and Noble, 1968.]

Jonson, the first dramatist to give criticism a significant place in his creative work, was inspired by Sidney in several points, among them the belief in the lofty nature of poetry and concern over the general neglect by dramatists of unity of time and place. Unlike his contemporaries, Jonson advocated and offered realistic comedy "which sports with human follies, not with crimes." His characters were more than English copies of Roman types; they exemplified a desire for realism.

895 BASKERVILL, CHARLES READ. English Elements in Jonson's Early Comedy. Bulletin of The University of Texas, 178. Austin: The University of Texas, 1911. 338 pp. [Reprint. New York: Johnson Reprint Company, 1972.]

Reveals the influence of native English literature on Jonson's comedy during the formative period of his career, 1597-1601. Acknowledges Jonson's debt to classical literature and his genius in converting material from his observation of contemporary life to comedy, but points out the English medieval and Renaissance influences and conventions evident in Jonson's early humour plays. Points out the general dependence on conventions in the literature of England at the end of the 16th century.

Reviewed by W. S. Johnson in JEGP 12 (1913):337-40.

896 BECK, ERVIN. "Terence Improved: The Paradigm of the Prodigal Son in English Renaissance Comedy." RenD NS 6 (1973): 107-22.

Keeping in mind the parable and the influence of Roman comedy, Beck concludes that prodigal-son comedy is best described in contrast to Roman comedy. "It presents a certain narrative sequence and contains a certain insight into human experience. The insight into human experience derives from Christian theology; the narrative sequence imitates--often imperfectly--the parable in Luke." The prodigal-son elements of Jonson's The Staple of News are discussed briefly.

897 BOUGHNER, DANIEL C. The Devil's Disciple: Ben Jonson's Debt to Machiavelli. New York: Philosophical Library, 1968. 264 pp. [Reprint. Westport, Conn.: Greenwood Press, 1975.]

Points out Jonson's indebtedness to Machiavelli's theory and practice for the structure of his comedy and for political ideals in his plays. Notes further that Machiavelli, in turn, derived his four-part structure from Terence's comedy. Analyzes in detail three distinct attitudes in England toward Il Principe during the century after its appearance and suggests where in Jonson's plays these various attitudes are reflected.

Reviewed by W. A. Armstrong in RenQ 23 (1970):333-34; K. J. Atchity in Italica 47 (1970):216-18; I. Donaldson in N&Q 214 (1969):310-13; B. Harris in YWES 49 (1968):172; G. R. Hibbard in MLR 65 (1970):872-73; V. R. Mollenkott in SCN 27 (1969):47-48; K. S. Rothwell in Comparative Literature Studies 7 (1970):113-14; C. G. Thayer in MQR 8 (1969): 66-67; M. Valency in Romanic Review 61 (1970):56-57.

898 BOWERS, FREDSON T. "Ben Jonson, Thomas Randolph, and The Drinking Academy." N&Q 173 (4 September 1937):167.

Points out borrowings from The Alchemist in Randolph's play, The Ffary Knight (1622-24), and subsequent references, in The Staple of News, to the performance of The Ffary Knight at Westminster School.

899 BREDVOLD, LOUIS I. "The Rise of English Classicism: Study in Methodology." CL 2 (1950):253-68.

Classicism originated in England in the same manner as it did in France: by the adoption of ancient literary ideals, the school training in humanistic rhetoric, and the assumption of the Italian formulation of a stricter literary doctrine. Jonson's procedure in Every Man in his Humour exemplifies this practice of adapting classical materials, for in his play he merely applied classical literary modes to indigenous material. His classicism and that of his age were imperfect and immature.

900 BRIGGS, WILLIAM DINSMORE. "Source Materials for Jonson's Plays." MLN 31 (1916):193-205, 321-33.

Specific sources are demonstrated or proposed for passages in eleven plays. Most are from classical, several from Renaissance authors.

901 _____. "Studies in Ben Jonson. IV." Anglia 39 (1914-16): 209-52.

Cites manuscripts attributing songs in Cynthia's Revels and Poetaster to poets other than Jonson. Proposes that "A Speech out of Lucane" (Harl. ms. 4064) is "a preliminary study for a portion of Sejanus."

902 BROICH, ULRICH. "Machiavelli und das Drama der Shakespearezeit." Anglia 89 (1971):326-48.

The views of Machiavelli, usually distorted on the English stage, are genuinely examined in Tamburlaine and Sejanus. Tiberius's monologue in Sejanus (III.639-45) depends on The Discourses, Book III, Chapter 6, a pronounced example both of Jonson's deviation from classical sources and of his familiarity with the actual writings of Machiavelli, whose concepts of virtù, fortuna and necessità are visible in the play. Although Jonson pays lip service to anti-Machiavellian sentiments, perhaps to protect himself from the accusation of treason, the triumph of Tiberius suggests Jonson's appreciation of the Machiavellian truth that victory goes to the powerful and wise, not necessarily to the virtuous.

903 BROWN, HUNTINGTON. "Ben Jonson and Rabelais." MLN 44 (1929): 6-13.
Suggests that Juniper in The Case is Altered is a reference to Jacques, the miser of Rabelais. Sees borrowings from Rabelais also in Every Man in his Humour, Every Man out of his Humour, Volpone, The Alchemist, The Devil is an Ass, The Staple of News, The New Inn, and The Magnetic Lady.

904 _____. Rabelais in English Literature. Cambridge, Mass.: Harvard University Press, 1933, pp. 81-94. [Reprint. New York: Octagon Books, 1967.]
Jonson knew Rabelais well and had an affinity for him, particularly in the presentation of grotesques. The Devil Is an Ass, The Staple of News, The New Inn, The Magnetic Lady, Every Man in his Humour, and Epicoene all show parallels with Rabelais in context or tone.

905 No entry

906 BULMAN, JAMES C., JR. "The Date and Production of Timon Reconsidered." ShS 27 (1974):111-27.
Jonson's borrowing from "Old Timon" was minimal at most. The anonymous author of that play probably borrowed from Jonson and also drew on Poetaster and Cynthia's Revels.

907 CAPUTI, ANTHONY. John Marston, Satirist. Ithaca: Cornell University Press, 1961, pp. 144-46. [Reprint. New York: Octagon Books, 1976.]
Refers to Jonson's association with Marston, the difference in their approach to comedy, and the quarrel between the playwrights. Briefly analyzes the structure of Eastward Ho, attributing it to Jonson and citing its influence on Marston's Dutch Courtezan. Points out techniques common to both authors, and suggests that, as Jonson ridicules the type of language characteristic of Marston, he also ridiculed Marston's philosophical pretensions. Finds thrusts

against Marston's thought in Act III of Every Man out of his Humour and Act IV of Poetaster. Provides a brief survey of the War of the Theatres.

908 CROSS, K. GUSTAV. "The Authorship of Lust's Dominion." SP 55 (1958):39-61.

Jonson's satirical treatment, in Every Man out of his Humour, Cynthia's Revels, and Poetaster, of the style and vocabulary that appear in both Marston and Lust's Dominion, supports the theory that Marston had a share in writing that play.

909 DESSEN, ALAN C. Jonson's Moral Comedy. Evanston, Ill.: Northwestern University Press, 1971. 265 pp.

Shows that Jonsonian comedy evolved in part from the late Elizabethan "estates" morality play, in which the protagonist is society corrupted by a public Vice. Traces the development of the estates morality after 1560 and illustrates how its characteristics are evident in Jonson's comedies. In his earlier comedy, Jonson experiments with some of the possibilities of the late morality, but in Volpone his extensive use of the morality formula results in "the birth of Jonson's moral comedy." In structure The Alchemist is directly related to the late morality, but its tone is not in the didactic tradition associated with the morality play. Dessen's extended analysis of the morality structure and techniques of Bartholomew Fair leads him to conclude that in it Jonson "sets forth a panoramic treatment of contemporary society by adapting a dramatic pattern from the late morality."

Reviewed by J. A. Barish in MP 71 (1973):80-84; R. Battenhouse in SEL 12 (1972):419-21; B. Gibbons and B. Harris in YWES 53 (1972):201-02; W. D. Kay in JEGP 71 (1972):125-28; S. F. Slaton in RenQ 26 (1973):373-75.

910 DORAN, MADELEINE. Endeavors of Art: A Study of Form in Elizabethan Drama. Madison: University of Wisconsin Press, 1954. 497 pp., passim.

Applies the historical method, with an aesthetic aim, in an attempt to study the "frame of reference within which the practicing dramatists of the Elizabethan and Jacobean periods worked." In frequent references to Jonson, considers how he assimilated various elements from the morality play, Latin and Italian comedy, Aristophanes, New Comedy, contemporary life, and rhetoric.

911 DRAPER, JOHN W. "A Reference to Huon in Ben Jonson." MLN 35 (1920):439-40.

A speech by "A Boy of the House" in The Magnetic Lady, satirizing romances, refers to the need for a knight to "beget him a reputation" (Chorus I.21-22). This could be an echo of Huon of Bordeaux's "early exploits on the way to Babylon." Huon of Bordeaux was probably accessible to Jonson, Lord Berners's translation having been printed early in the 16th century. Jonson's satirical treatment of romances reflects the same critical tendencies as those seen in The Knight of the Burning Pestle and Don Quixote.

912 DUNCAN, DOUGLAS. "Ben Jonson's Lucianic Irony." ArielE 1 (1970):42-53.

Lucian invented a satiric mode, "coolly farcical, learnedly evasive, ironically sharp," which influenced Jonson as early as Every Man in his Humour and is especially evident in Sejanus, Volpone, The Alchemist, Bartholomew Fair, and Epicoene. It is Jonson's "impatience with irony" that marks his decline in The Devil is an Ass.

913 EDWARDS, ANTHONY S. G. "Libertine Literature." TLS, 18 February 1972, p. 189.

The earliest reference to erotic literature in England occurs in Volpone. Two references in the play mention Aretino's Sonetti Lussuriosi with engravings by Giulio Romano.

914 FELDMAN, SYLVIA D. The Morality-Patterned Comedy of the Renaissance. The Hague: Mouton, 1970, pp. 16-17, 30-33, 99-101, 120-22, 129-35.

The morality play tradition remained popular into Elizabethan England and offered Jonson an effective vehicle. It appears in Volpone, The Staple of News, and Eastward Ho. The latter is unique in the genre because of its parodies of the very elements it employs.

915 FRAJND, MARTA. "Teorijski Stavovi Bena Džonsona" [Theoretical Viewpoints of Ben Jonson]. FP 1 & 2 (1964):231-45. (In Serbo-Croatian.)

Jonson's literary criticism, mostly borrowed from ancient and Renaissance authors, has great unity, even though scattered through his works. His importance as a critic lies in his attempts to present his ideas on literary criticism in the texts of his plays, thus making them widely known to the Elizabethan audience.

Literary Relations and Sources

916 FRYE, NORTHROP. "Old and New Comedy." *ShS* 22 (1969):1-5.
New Comedy and Old Comedy differ in being "teleological" and "anti-teleological" respectively. Jonson's "humour" character is appropriate to a New Comedy plot "because in the humour comic structure and comic mood are unified." Although *Every Man out of his Humour* is within the conventions of New Comedy, Jonson spoke of it as closer to Old Comedy, perhaps because of its "more deeply sardonic tone."

917 GOLDMARK, RUTH INGERSOLL. "The Influence of the Classics on Ben Jonson," in her *Studies in the Influence of the Classics on English Literature*. Columbia University Studies in English and Comparative Literature. New York: Columbia University Press, 1918, pp. 1-40. [Reprint. Port Washington, N.Y.: Kennikat Press, 1965.]
Groups Jonson's dramas into four categories according to their classical associations. *Every Man in his Humour*, *Volpone*, *Epicoene*, *The Alchemist*, *Bartholomew Fair*, and *The Magnetic Lady* are indebted to New Comedy. The second group, the comedies of allegory and satire, evince the dominant influence of Aristophanes. These include *The Staple of News*, *The Devil is an Ass*, *Cynthia's Revels*, *Poetaster*, *Every Man out of his Humour*, and *The Tale of a Tub*. The tragedies imitate Seneca, and the fourth group includes those plays in which contemporary influence is evident: romantic comedy in *The Case is Altered* and *The New Inn*; romantic tragedy in the additions to *The Spanish Tragedy*; and pastoral drama in *The Sad Shepherd*.

918 GUM, COBURN. *The Aristophanic Comedies of Ben Jonson: A Comparative Study of Jonson and Aristophanes*. The Hague: Mouton, 1969. 207 pp.
Jonson set himself to adapt Old Comedy to the English stage and clearly imitated Aristophanes in plot construction (simple, episodic, farcical), characters (typal and allegorical) and the creation of an inverted world. He is less polished than the Greek in indecent, obscene material, and did not make the effort to conceal his didacticism, as did Aristophanes. The two differ most in use of personal satire, with Jonson doing very little. Many parallel passages can be presented, but they offer little evidence of imitation, owing to Jonson's eclectic methods in the assimilation of classical material. Jonson failed to meet his goal because he adapted too freely and did not enjoy the same stage or state that Aristophanes did.
Reviewed by P. Davison in *MLR* 65 (1970):382-83.

919 HERRICK, MARVIN T. Comic Theory in the Sixteenth Century. ISLL 34, nos. 1 and 2, 1950, 256 pp., passim.

Terence and Terentian commentators were the main force in establishing the comic theory of the 16th century, even after Aristotle's Poetics had become the most important critical text. In plotting his early comedies, Jonson followed the simple classical intrigue established by Plautus and Terence, but from Every Man in his Humour to Bartholomew Fair his structure became progressively more complex. Types of Terentian characters found in Jonson's comedies are the senex, the clever manservant or slave, the parasite, and the braggart-soldier. Jonson admired Terentian dialogue as a standard of comic diction.

920 _____. The Fusion of Horatian and Aristotelian Literary Criticism, 1531-1555. ISLL 32, no. 1, 1946, pp. 104-05.

One of the more learned poets and critics of his time, Jonson knew the dramatic "rules" and also that they were not delivered ab initio, but "merely evolved in practice." Cordatus, in the Induction to Every Man out of his Humour, claims that modern writers should be free to "develop their own inventions," and not be tied to strict conventions.

921 _____. The Poetics of Aristotle in England. Cornell Studies in English, 17. New Haven: Yale University Press, 1930, pp. 36-43, 45, 48. [Reprint. New York: Phaeton Press, 1976.]

The dedications and prologues to the plays help define Jonson's critical theories, which were influenced by Aristotle through the Heinsius Latin translation. He adopted the principle of the primary importance of plot and, although he stressed unity of action, did not reject the "unities" of time and place. However, in both theory and practice he often showed "either a serious misunderstanding of the Poetics, or a neglect of it that was contradictory to his preferred classical standards," the latter perhaps resulting from his concern for public success. Jonson seems to have arrived at his own concept of "comic catharsis."

922 HILBERRY, CLARENCE BEVERLY. Ben Jonson's Ethics in Relation to Stoic and Humanistic Ethical Thought. Chicago: University of Chicago Libraries, 1933. 31 pp. [Reprint. Norwood, Pa.: Norwood Editions, 1978.]

Jonson's satire was grounded in a firm and extensive system of ethics for which he was indebted to classical and Renaissance ethical thought. The primary influence upon him was Stoic, and particularly Senecan, but many of these

Stoic ideas came to Jonson through the medium of early humanists such as Vives, Erasmus, Elyot, More, and Lupset.

923 HOGAN, FLORIANA T. "Elizabethan and Jacobean Dramas and Their Spanish Sources." RORD 19 (1976):37-47.
Jonson was influenced by Don Quixote in both Epicoene and The Alchemist.

924 HOSKINS, JOHN. Directions for Speech and Style. Edited by Hoyt H. Hudson. Princeton Studies in English, 12. Princeton: Princeton University Press, 1935, pp. 60, 70. [Reprint. Ann Arbor, Mich.: University Microfilms, 1975.]
Possibly Jonson was following Hoskins in his use of "accommodate" in Every Man in his Humour (1616) I.v.126 and Poetaster III.iv.287, and of "agnomination" in Poetaster III.i.91.

925 HOWELL, A. C. "A Note on Ben Jonson's Literary Methods." SP 28 (1931):710-19.
Examines Jonson's method of adopting classical sources. Lists verse passages in The New Inn and The Staple of News that parallel prose passages in Discoveries which, in turn, have classical origins.

926 HOY, CYRUS. "The Shares of Fletcher and his Collaborators in the Beaumont and Fletcher Canon (VI)." SB 14 (1961):45-67.
Presents "pitifully slight" linguistic evidence for Jonson's contribution to Act IV, Scenes i and ii of Rollo, Duke of Normandy (Q2 1640), based primarily on the presence of certain contracted forms typical of Jonson's usage between 1614 and 1632 and not found as regularly in other playwrights. Agrees with Herford and Simpson that certain similarities between passages in The Staple of News (and Neptune's Triumph) and Rollo are not strong evidence for common authorship.

927 JACKSON, JAMES L. "Sources of the Subplot of Marston's The Dutch Courtezan." PQ 31 (1952):223-24.
The third episode in Marston's subplot--the apprehension of Mulligrub in the lost cloak--is taken from Every Man in his Humour. Plautus's Menaechmi is probably Jonson's source.

928 JANICKA, IRENA. The Popular Tradition and Ben Jonson. Lodz: Uniwersytet Lodzki, 1972. 273 pp.
Shows the influence of the morality and other popular genres on Jonson's plays, in motives, themes and devices, characters, comic climate. Specific sources are proposed for Volpone, Bartholomew Fair, The Staple of News, and The

New Inn. Examines the relationship between the structure of Jonson's plays and that of the moralities, and the resemblance of Jonson's technique to that of the baroque painters.

929 JOHNSON, STANLEY. "Donne's 'Autumnall Elegy.'" TLS, 30 April 1931, p. 347.
Lines in Epicoene, The Staple of News, and The New Inn were possibly borrowed from Donne's poetry.

930 JOHNSTON, MARY. "Ben Jonson and Martial." Classical Weekly, 8 October 1934, p. 13.
Jonson's play on the name Earinus (The Sad Shepherd) recalls Martial's epigrams 9, 11-13, 16.

931 JONES, THORA BURNLEY, and NICOL, BERNARD DE BEAR. Neo-Classical Dramatic Criticism, 1560-1770. Cambridge: Cambridge University Press, 1976, pp. 43-48.
Jonson adhered to classical rules for drama less than one might expect, considering the labels he has received. The characters in The Alchemist and Bartholomew Fair are closer to the comic figures of Henry IV or Measure for Measure than to creations of either Plautus or Terence. In his prefaces to Sejanus and Volpone, Jonson admitted he had to come to terms with the English theatre and its lack of understanding of Greek theatre.

932 KERMODE, J. F. "The Banquet of Sense." BJRL 44 (1961):68-99. Reprinted in his Shakespeare, Spenser, Donne: Renaissance Essays. London: Routledge and Kegan Paul, 1971, pp. 84-115.
Traces the banquet motif from its pagan and Christian sources through its appearances in Netherlands art, Poetaster, The New Inn, Chapman's poem, and other Renaissance literature. The theme rests on a tension between good and evil. Poetaster, IV, equates the banquet with the sensual, making Ovid a counter-Plato. Association of Ovid with the theme probably arose from misreading the Ars Amatoria and Amores. Lovel and Lord Beaufort exemplify tension between the Platonic and Ovidian views in The New Inn, III.

933 KIRSCHBAUM, LEO. "Jonson, Seneca, and Mortimer," in Studies in Honor of John Wilcox. Edited by A. Dayle Wallace and Woodburn O. Ross. Detroit: Wayne State University Press, 1958, pp. 9-22. [Reprint. Freeport, N.Y.: Books for Libraries Press, 1972.]
Mortimer, if completed, would have been very Senecan and probably not have included the comic, popular elements

present in Sejanus and Catiline. Many critical statements about Renaissance tragedy indicate the need for a re-examination of Seneca.

934 KNIGHTS, L. C. "Ben Jonson, Dramatist," in The Age of Shakespeare. Edited by Boris Ford. The Pelican Guide to Literature, Vol. 2. Baltimore: Pelican Books, 1956, pp. 302-17. [Reprint. Baltimore: Penguin Books, 1970.]

Jonson's statements of literary theory, which are classical or neoclassical, do not completely exemplify his dramatic practice; his genius lay in his ability to combine his classicism and his English literary inheritance to develop important contemporary themes.

935 _____. "Tradition & Ben Jonson." Scrutiny 4 (1935):140-57. [Reprinted in his Drama and Society in the Age of Jonson (1937), pp. 179-99 (see 30). Elizabethan Drama: Modern Essays in Criticism. Edited by Ralph J. Kaufmann. New York: Oxford University Press, 1961, pp. 153-69. Ben Jonson: A Collection of Critical Essays (1963), pp. 24-39 (see 3).]

Critics err in proposing that Jonson had little or no native spring of vitality but simply drew upon Latin and Greek sources. Sejanus illustrates his use of farce and juxtaposition of contrasts. It presupposes the playwright's active relationship with his particular audience and an ability to consider their native delight in splendor. Jonson's plays demand disciplined viewers who can both bring and enter into a rich English tradition.

936 McCAULLEY, MARTHA GAUSE. "Function and Content of the Prologue, Chorus, and other Non-Organic Elements in English Drama, from the Beginnings to 1642," in Studies in English Drama. First Series. Edited by Allison Gaw. Philadelphia: The University of Pennsylvania, 1917, pp. 161-258, passim.

Though he imitated the classical chorus in Catiline, Jonson more often suited the chorus's form and function to his own purposes, as in Every Man out of his Humour and Cynthia's Revels. His uses of induction, prologue, epilogue, and other non-organic elements show a variety of functions, such as literary criticism, topical satire, and comments on his audience, as well as on his own work.

937 McEUEN, KATHRYN A. "Jonson and Juvenal." RES 21 (1945): 92-104.

Points out the similarity of attitude and method between Juvenal and Jonson in the comical satires, exemplified particularly in Every Man out of his Humour. Like Juvenal, Jonson declares that he will expose the follies of his contemporaries by castigating many different types. He uses Asper and Macilente as spokesmen just as Juvenal adopts a satiric persona. In Poetaster, Horace and Ovid take turns speaking for Jonson. In Cynthia's Revels, Jonson speaks chiefly through Crites, occasionally through Mercury and Arete. In addition to illustrating that Jonson's method was similar to Juvenal's, McEuen points out several passages in the plays which echo Juvenal's Satires.

938 McGALLIARD, JOHN C. "Chaucerian Comedy: The Merchant's Tale, Jonson, and Molière." PQ 15 (1946):343-70.

Though the structure, design, and scope of Chaucer's The Merchant's Tale are similar to some of Jonsons humour plays, Jonson differs from Chaucer in his satiric method.

939 McPHERSON, DAVID. "Some Renaissance Sources for Jonson's Early Comic Theory." ELN 8 (1971):180-82.

A passage in the dedicatory epistle of Volpone (115-21), defending the punishments at the play's conclusion, is partially drawn from Scaliger's Poetices Libri Septem (1561). This is one of a number of pieces of evidence showing that Jonson was guided in his thinking by Renaissance critics and scholars as well as by the Ancients. A significant reference to Scaliger appears in Every Man out of his Humour, III.iv.14-18. The influence of Minturno's De Poeta (1559) on Jonson's comic theory has been shown by Maurice Castelain (Discoveries, Paris, 1907, pp. 155-56) and Henry Snuggs (MLN 65 (1950):543-44. See 362.)

940 PFEFFER, KARL. Das Elisabethanische Sprichwort in seiner Verwendung bei Ben Jonson. Giessen: R. Glasgow, 1935. 194 pp.

Lists alphabetically 457 proverbs found in Jonson, mostly in the plays, with parallel examples from other writers. Most are traditional English proverbs, but some are translated from Latin and several appear in Latin. The use of proverbs adds to a sense of realism in the comedies; they are, however, least used in the best comedies, that is, Volpone, Epicoene, The Alchemist. Proverbs are avoided in the tragedies because their use would detract from the tragic atmosphere.

941 PRAZ, MARIO. "Ben Jonson's Italy," in his The Flaming Heart: Essays on Crashaw, Machiavelli, and Other Studies in the Relations between Italian and English Literature from Chaucer to T. S. Eliot. Garden City, N.Y.: Doubleday, 1958, pp. 168-85. [Reprint. Gloucester, Mass.: Peter Smith, 1966; New York: W. W. Norton, 1973.]

English version of his "L'Italia di Ben Jonson" (see 944).

Jonson's knowledge of Italian literature "seems neither wide nor exceptional." The authenticity of the Italian elements in Volpone is owing to his personal acquaintance with John Florio, whose Italian-English dictionary, A Worlde of Wordes (1598), contains many Italian terms found in the play, and who probably familiarized Jonson with the works of Aretino. "Volpone . . . is the best of Aretino's plays, the play Aretino should have written. . . . what is this Volpone but the faithful image of Aretino himself?"

942 _____. "Introduction: Literary Relations between Italy and England from Chaucer to the Present," in his The Flaming Heart: Essays on Crashaw, Machiavelli, and Other Studies in the Relations between Italian and English Literature from Chaucer to T. S. Eliot. New York: Doubleday, 1958, pp. 3-28. [Reprint. Gloucester, Mass.: Peter Smith, 1966; New York: W. W. Norton, 1973.]

A shortened English version of his "Rapporti tra la letteratura italiana e la letteratura inglese" (see 943, 950). Actual Italian influence is doubtful in most Elizabethan drama; "only in Ben Jonson's Volpone do we find the Venetian local colour rendered with such exactness that a search for his source of information appears rewarding."

943 _____. "Introduzione: Rapporti tra la letteratura italiana e la letteratura inglese dall'epoca di Chaucer alla presente," in his Machiavelli in Inghilterra ed altri saggi sui rapporti letterari anglo-italiani. Second edition. Florence: G. C. Sansoni, 1962, pp. 1-27.

Slightly expanded Italian version of the "Introduction" to his The Flaming Heart (see 942). The latter is based on his "Rapporti tra la letteratura italiana e la letteratura inglese" (see 950).

944 _____. "L'Italia di Ben Jonson." Rivista italiana del dramma 2 (15 November 1937):257-71. [Reprinted in his Machiavelli in Inghilterra ed altri saggi. Rome: Tumminelli, 1942, pp. 173-92; second edition, Florence: G. C. Sansoni, 1962, pp. 195-210.] (See 941.)

945 _____. "L'Italia di Shakespeare," in his Machiavelli in Inghilterra ed altri saggi sui rapporti letterari anglo-italiani. Second edition. Florence: G. C. Sansoni, 1962, pp. 173-94.

Italian version of his "Shakespeare's Italy" (see 951).

946 _____. Machiavelli and the Elizabethans. Annual Italian Lecture, British Academy, March 21, 1928. London: H. Milford, 1928, pp. 9, 19, 25-26, 30-31, 47. [Reprint. Philadelphia: R. West, 1978.]

It is not possible to determine the stages of development of the Machiavellian figure in Elizabethan drama, nor when such a figure turned from an object of horror to one of derision. Jonson, who had indulged public taste for things Italian in the first version of Every Man in his Humour, and had borrowed several lines in Catiline from Cinthio, made Politick Would-be (Volpone) a "Machiavellian fop," and again ridiculed the Machiavellian statesman in the character of Bias in The Magnetic Lady. What appears to be taken from Machiavelli in Sejanus, however, is almost literally borrowed from Seneca. In Restoration comedy, "to call a subtle woman 'a Machiavel' became quite a fad, after the example of Ben Jonson (The Case is Altered, IV.iv)." (See 947, 948, 949.)

947 _____. "Machiavelli e gl'inglese dell'epoca elisabettiana," in his Machiavelli in Inghilterra ed altri saggi. Rome: Tumminelli, 1942, pp. 96, 111, 119-20, 126, 145; second edition, Florence: G. C. Sansoni, 1962, pp. 105, 119, 126-27, 132, 148.

Expanded version, in Italian, of Machiavelli and the Elizabethans (see 946. See also 948, 949).

*948 _____. "Machiavelli in Inghilterra." Civiltà moderna anno I, n. 4, (1929); anno II, n. 1, (1930). (See 946, 947, 949.)

949 _____. "The Politic Brain: Machiavelli and the Elizabethans," in his The Flaming Heart: Essays on Crashaw, Machiavelli, and Other Studies in the Relations between Italian and English Literature from Chaucer to T. S. Eliot. Garden City, N.Y.: Doubleday, 1958, pp. 99, 113, 120-21, 126, 143. [Reprint. Gloucester, Mass.: Peter Smith, 1966; New York: W. W. Norton, 1973.]

Expanded version of Machiavelli and the Elizabethans (see 946. See also 947, 948).

950 _____. "Rapporti tra la letteratura italiana e la letteratura inglese," in Letteratura Comparate. Problemi ed orientamenti critici di lingua e di letteratura italiana, Vol. 4. Edited by Attilio Momigliano. Milan: Marzorati, 1948, pp. 145-196.

Briefly restates some of the commentary contained in "L'Italia di Ben Jonson" (see 942, 944).

Literary Relations and Sources

951 _____. "Shakespeare's Italy." ShS 7 (1954):95-106. [Reprinted in slightly expanded form in his The Flaming Heart. Garden City, N.Y.: Doubleday, 1958, pp. 146-67. Reprint. Gloucester, Mass.: Peter Smith, 1966; New York: W. W. Norton, 1973.]

Shakespeare used the names of Italian cities as mere labels; it is London he is representing. "Something approaching a careful study of an historical [Italian] background can be found only in Ben Jonson. . . . Florio supplied Ben Jonson with whatever information that dramatist shows about Venice in Volpone." (See 945.)

952 RÉBORA, PIERO. Civiltà italiana e civiltà inglese: studie e ricerche. Florence: Felice le Monnier, 1936, pp. 14-16, 37, 215.

Claims that the egotistic, atheistic, "politic" character of Caesar in Catiline is a distortion based on the Machiavellian myth (influenced by The Jew of Malta) and a misinterpretation of Roman history, created to suit the tastes of the Elizabethan public, and that Jonson had already shown his anti-Caesar bias in Sejanus. Some passages in Shakespeare's Julius Caesar recall Jonson's oratorical style; Coryat's impressions of Milan are reflected in allusions in Jonson's late comedies.

953 _____. L'Italia nel dramma inglese (1558-1642). Milan: Modernissima, 1925, pp. 52, 66, 83, 116-49 passim, 180, 232.

Proposes that Jonson's great familiarity with commedia dell'arte, as reflected in Volpone, was based partly on his having seen performances and (possibly) scenarios, and partly on his knowledge of the writings of William Thomas, Tomaso Garzoni, and John Florio, the last of whom was a personal friend. Suggests influence of Italian erudite comedy on The Case is Altered and The Devil is an Ass, and specific borrowing, in The Alchemist, from Giordano Bruno's Il Candelaio. Disagrees with J. D. Rea's conclusion, in his 1919 edition of Volpone (see 444), that Jonson disliked "all things Italian."

954 REES, JOAN. Samuel Daniel: A Critical and Biographical Study. Liverpool: Liverpool University Press, 1964, pp. 38, 91-93, 96, 112, 119.

Cites Jonson's parody of Daniel's extravagant poetry in Every Man out of his Humour, the jibe at Daniel and his Italianate pastoral in Volpone, and Daniel's insulting references to Jonson.

955 RIDDELL, JAMES A. "Seventeenth-Century Identifications of Jonson's Sources in the Classics." RenQ 28 (1975):204-18.

Finds in a privately owned copy of the 1616 Folio of Jonson's works that marginalia in at least three different hands identify Jonson's classical sources. Of the 250 passages identified, Riddell transcribes 60 ignored by Herford and Simpson and 9 which "augment or disagree with identifications that Herford and Simpson give." Wherever possible, Riddell also indicates agreement between the Folio ascriptions and sources acknowledged by editors working either before or after Herford and Simpson.

956 ROBINSON, FORREST C. The Shape of Things Known: Sidney's Apology in Its Philosophical Traditions. Cambridge, Mass.: Harvard University Press, 1972, pp. 214-25.

Jonson's discussions of poetry reveal his stress on the visual. His plays relate quite directly to the emblem book tradition and carry his emphasis on clarity in moral portraits as well as his desire to present images of ideas in order to influence the viewers.

957 SACKTON, ALEXANDER H. "The Paradoxical Encomium in Elizabethan Drama." Texas Studies in English 28 (1949):83-104.

The classical and Renaissance rhetorical device of the paradoxical encomium--"the praise of what is obviously unworthy of praise, the disparagement of what is generally considered praiseworthy, or the formal treatment of a trivial subject"--is used with increasing dramatic skill in Eastward Ho (in a passage probably by Marston), Cynthia's Revels, Every Man out of his Humour, Volpone, and Bartholomew Fair. "The plays of Jonson offer richer examples . . . than those of any other Elizabethan dramatist."

958 SALINGAR, L. G. "The Revenger's Tragedy and the Morality Tradition." Scrutiny 6 (1938):402-22.

Tourneur's most effective contact with the tradition was through Jonson. The two playwrights were among the last to apply the techniques of the moralities.

959 SCHELLING, FELIX E. "Jonson and the Classics," in his Foreign Influences in Elizabethan Plays. New York: Harper and Row, 1923, pp. 1-37. [Reprint. New York: AMS Press, 1971.]

Traces the chief foreign influences affecting the drama in England from the reign of Henry VIII to the restoration of King Charles II. In an age predominantly romantic, Jonson marked the height of classical influence; however, he was saved from slavish imitation by his practical English nature. Schelling studies in detail the classical contributions in theory and practice that Jonson made to English drama.

Literary Relations and Sources

960 _____. Shakespeare and "Demi-Science": Papers on Elizabethan Topics. Philadelphia: University of Pennsylvania Press; London: Oxford University Press, 1927, pp. 69, 73-74, 165-66, 170-71, 179. [Reprint. New York: AMS Press, 1972.]

Almost everything present in Elizabethan drama can be found in Jonson, with the addition of the comedy of humours. Jonson's classicism is liberal in theory and practice. The Devil is an Ass probably owes its general design to Machiavelli's The Marriage of Belphegor; its savage irony exemplifies the fact that "the general absorption of the supernatural as a motive in Elizabethan drama is satirical."

961 SCOTT, MARY AUGUSTA. Elizabethan Translations from the Italian. Boston and New York: Houghton Mifflin, 1916, pp. 37, 45, 94, 99, 338, 447.

Shows direct and indirect use of Italian sources in Every Man out of his Humour, Sejanus, and The Devil is an Ass.

962 SECRETAN, DOMINIQUE. Classicism (The Critical Idiom, No. 27). London: Methuen, 1973, pp. 22-23, 48.

Jonson, level-headed and self-disciplined, was a "liberal classicist" who tried to synthesize native English genius and the rules of antiquity. His reputation as a classicist depends on "his Latinity, his grasp of Roman power-politics, his Horatian irony," rather than on his offering of a closed world picture of closed form. "His example of a half-way classicism did not suffice to lead to a real rapprochement" with French Neoclassicism.

963 SIMONINI, R. C., JR. "Ben Jonson and John Florio." N&Q 195 (1950):512-13.

Touchstone's speech to Security on cuckoldry (Eastward Ho, V.v.187-96) is "strikingly parallel" to a passage in Florio's Second Frutes, giving evidence of the literary relationship between Jonson and Florio, and supporting the belief that Jonson wrote most of Act V of Eastward Ho.

964 _____. Italian Scholarship in Renaissance England. The University of North Carolina Studies in Comparative Literature, 3. New York: Johnson Reprint Corporation, 1969, pp. 103-09. [Originally published Chapel Hill: The University of North Carolina Press, 1952.]

Much of Jonson's Italian dimension comes through John Florio and Italian language books. Allusions to and parallels with Florio's Second Frutes appear in Volpone, Cynthia's Revels, and Eastward Ho. Worlde of Wordes provided many Italian names found in Volpone and Every Man out of his Humour. Florio may have acquainted Jonson with Giordano Bruno's Il Candelaio, which has many parallels with The Alchemist.

965 SIMPSON, PERCY. "'Jonson's Sanguine Rival.'" RES 15 (1939): 464-65.
Jonson's contempt for Samuel Daniel's verse is seen in the Every Man plays and in The Staple of News.

966 SMITH, WINIFRED. The Commedia dell'arte. Columbia University Studies in English and Comparative Literature, 43. New York: Columbia University, 1912, pp. 178-79, 187-95, 247-48. [Reprinted with additional illustrations, New York: Benjamin Blom, 1964.]
The Zany is referred to in Every Man in his Humour and Cynthia's Revels. The mountebank scene in Volpone is probably based on an actual Italian source, but the nature of the source remains unknown. The Alchemist was "largely influenced" by Giordano Bruno's Il Candelaio; Epicoene shows parallels with Aretino's Il Marescalco.

967 SPIVACK, BERNARD. Shakespeare and the Allegory of Evil: The History of a Metaphor in Relation to His Major Villains. New York: Columbia University Press, 1958. 517 pp.
Traces the late medieval dramatic traditions which explain the character of Iago and many others like him in Elizabethan drama. Iago's antecedents are in the homiletic tradition and in the Vice of the medieval morality drama. Jonson uses the comic Vice figure in The Devil is an Ass and in The Staple of News.

968 STARNES, DeWITT T., and TALBERT, ERNEST WILLIAM. "Ben Jonson and the Dictionaries," in their Classical Myth and Legend in Renaissance Dictionaries: A Study of Renaissance Dictionaries in Their Relation to the Classical Learning of Contemporary English Writers. Chapel Hill: The University of North Carolina Press, 1955, pp. 135-212. [Reprint. Westport, Conn.: Greenwood Press, 1973.]
Discusses the popularity of the reference dictionaries and compendiums of classical learning during the Renaissance to prove that often the dictionaries influenced the phrasing and content of the great poetry and drama of the period. Points out the similarities in Jonson's use of mythic material and Renaissance dictionaries in The Case is Altered, Cynthia's Revels, and Poetaster. The extended discussion of the second play draws on material published earlier by Talbert: "The Classical Mythology and the Structure of Cynthia's Revels" (see 220).

Literary Relations and Sources

969 SYME, RONALD. "Roman Historians and Renaissance Politics," in *Society and History in the Renaissance: A Report of a Conference Held at the Folger Library on April 23 and 24, 1960*. Washington: Folger Shakespeare Library, 1960, pp. 3-12.

Though not successful, *Sejanus* shows Jonson's unusual achievement in the use of the Roman historians, both in direct translation, as of Tacitus, and in the pulling together of a variety of sources for particular events. *Sejanus* is "a venture on a 'Machiavellian' theme," combining Tacitus and Jonson's own imagination. *Volpone* is a "Machiavellian comedy." "With Jonson, imperial Rome and contemporary Italy converge and blend: political diagnosis and social satire."

970 THOMSON, J. A. K. *Classical Influences on English Poetry*. London: George Allen & Unwin, 1951, pp. 135-36, 152, 198, 223. [Reprint. New York: Macmillan Co., Collier Books, 1962.]

Refers to Jonson incidentally, considering briefly the influence of Plautus and Terence on his humour comedies and Horace on his satire and his lyrics.

971 THORNDIKE, ASHLEY H. "Ben Jonson," in his *English Comedy*. New York: Cooper Square Publishers, 1965, pp. 167-91. [Originally published New York: Macmillan, 1929.]

Provides a general introduction to Jonson's comedies; identifies classical influences on them.

972 URE, PETER. "On Some Differences Between Senecan and Elizabethan Tragedy." *DUJ* 10 (1948):17-23.

To the extent that he adopts the Roman satirical mode, Jonson uses it to attack forces of disintegration within his own society, as seen in *Poetaster*. His concern with cultural unity differentiates him from Seneca; along with Chapman he modifies Senecan heroic figures and forms to fit political and social circumstances of his age.

973 WATSON, THOMAS L. "The Detractor-Backbiter: Iago and the Tradition." *TSLL* 5 (1964):546-54.

Iago is related to the tradition of the detractor-backbiter but even more to Carlo Buffone (*Every Man out of his Humour*). The association of the hypocrite, detractor, buffoon, and low jester can be traced to Aristotle's *Ethics* and appears in many morality plays. Buffone is the best developed character in the tradition; Jonson uses the type in a more interesting way than his predecessors did.

974 WHEELER, CHARLES FRANCIS. Classical Mythology in the Plays, Masques, and Poems of Ben Jonson. Princeton: Princeton University Press, 1938. 218 pp. [Reprint. Port Washington, N.Y.: Kennikat Press, 1970.]

Considers Jonson a rather pure classicist in his use of ancient myth. After his experiment in Cynthia's Revels, Jonson learned "that myth lacks the vitality essential for even the shallowest of plots." Thereafter he resumed his practice of using allusions only in his dramas; his usual practice was to use these allusions to soften his satire, to characterize, to emphasize his themes, and to strengthen his observations on contemporary life by applying mythological parallels. The book includes a dictionary of Jonson's mythological allusions and a discussion of their sources.

Reviewed by D. Bush in JEGP 38 (1939):315; A. H. Gilbert in PQ 19 (1940):92-96; C. W. Lemmi in MLN 55 (1940):310-12; P. Simpson in MLR 34 (1939):435-36.

See also: 11, 23, 31, 68, 77, 80, 81, 90, 104, 107, 118, 156, 166, 170a, 171, 178, 179, 181, 186, 195, 197, 198, 201, 204, 215, 220, 224, 235, 247, 248, 250, 261, 270, 272, 275, 277, 279, 309, 312, 314, 325, 348, 356, 357, 362, 363, 365, 370, 371, 379, 386, 397, 413, 415, 416, 417, 428, 430, 431, 444, 447, 449, 451, 456, 457, 461, 466, 494, 495, 497a, 509, 510, 514, 515, 522, 533, 548, 556, 578, 583, 587, 589, 593, 594, 596, 634, 639, 643, 644, 645, 646, 650, 652, 660, 661, 662, 663, 669, 670, 691, 698, 704, 709, 710, 717, 720, 752, 819, 845, 890, 891, 1006, 1046, 1100, 1188, 1189, 1233.

Textual Studies

975 ASHLEY LIBRARY, THE. A Catalogue of Printed Books, Manuscripts and Autograph Letters Collected by Thomas James Wise. Introduction by Edmund Gosse. London: n.p., 1923. III, viii-ix, 1-8.

Describes various first and other early editions of individual plays. Includes photographic facsimile reproductions of title pages.

976 BENNETT, JOSEPHINE WATERS. "Benson's Alleged Piracy of Shakespeares Sonnets and of Some of Jonson's Works." SB 21 (1968):235-48.

Apparently Richard Meighen's second volume of Jonson's Works (1640) was made up of some sheets printed by Thomas Walkley and some from an unfinished 1631 edition, printed by John Benson for Robert Allot and later owned by Andrew Crooke.

Textual Studies

977 CARL H. PFORZHEIMER LIBRARY, THE. Ben Jonson 1573?-1637. New York: n.p., 1940. 38 pp. ["A Reprint from the Catalogue of English Books and Manuscripts 1475-1700 in The Carl H. Pforzheimer Library."]
Several early editions of Jonson's plays, held by the library, are described in detail.

978 FEATHER, JOHN. "Some Notes on the Setting of Quarto Plays." Library 5th series 27 (1972):237-44.
The Bodleian copy of The Alchemist contains, on B4, a possibly unique example of a line being set outside the measure. An omission may have been discovered and corrected at an earlier stage in the proofreading than extant variants record.

979 FORD, HERBERT L. Collation of the Ben Jonson Folios, 1616-31-1640. Oxford: Oxford University Press, 1932. 30 pp. [Reprint. Philadelphia: R. West, 1977.]
Ford describes each volume, working with a variety of copies.

980 GERRITSEN, JOHAN. "Stansby and Jonson Produce a Folio: a Preliminary Account." ES 40 (1959):52-55.
Printing records of the 1616 Folio are incomplete, but internal evidence and knowledge about William Stansby's shop suggest some conclusions.

981 GREG, W. W. A Bibliography of the English Printed Drama to the Restoration. 4 vols. London: Oxford University Press, 1939-1959. 1992 pp.
Volume One arranges the earliest surviving editions listed in the Stationers' Records and their location in British and American libraries. Volume Two continues the list and adds Latin plays and lost plays. Volume Three contains collections, an appendix, and reference lists. Volume Four includes an introduction, additions, corrections, and an index of titles.

982 _____. "The First Edition of Ben Jonson's Every Man Out of His Humour." Library 4th series 1 (1920):153-60.
The British Museum purchased (1908) a copy of "presumably the first edition, and unquestionably an earlier edition than any hitherto described." Although in poor condition, it is well printed; parallel passages are printed at the bottom of pages. Signatures are A-R. Reprinting of the Holmes Quarto was carefully done by two compositors.

983 _____. "Notes on Old Books. Jonson: Every Man Out of His Humour." Library 4th series 2 (1921):49.
Both American copies of the first edition of the play contain the alternative ending and four leaves in R, thus confirming the defectiveness of the British Museum copy.

984 _____. "Notes on Old Books. Jonson's Every Man Out of His Humour." Library 4th series 3 (1922):57.
The headpiece appearing twice in the first edition was used about that time by Adam Islip, thus linking the play to his press.

985 _____. "The Rationale of Copy-Text." SB 3 (1950-51):19-36. [Reprinted in his Collected Papers. Edited by J. C. Maxwell. Oxford: Clarendon Press, 1966, pp. 374-91.]
Since the Quarto and Folio versions of Sejanus differ so little, it would be appropriate to take the Quarto as the copy-text and make alterations based on the Folio. However, since the Folio version of Every Man in his Humour reflects numerous changes from the Quarto, and probably was seen through the press by Jonson, "an editor of the revised version has no choice but to take the Folio as his copy-text."

986 _____. "Thomas Walkley and the Ben Jonson Works of 1640." Library 4th series 11 (1931):461-65.
Identifies the "works" of Jonson referred to by Marcham (see 994) and provides details about the printing of them to support Walkley's case.

987 HENNING, STANDISH. "The Printer of Romeo and Juliet, Q1." PBSA 60 (Third quarter, 1966):363-64.
Study of repeated appearances of battered type confirms W. W. Greg's hypothesis that Nicholas Okes printed The Case is Altered.

988 HOOPER, EDITH S. "The Text of Ben Jonson." MLR 12 (1917): 350-52.
Van Dam's work with Every Man out of his Humour justifies his opposition to considering the 1616 Folio as the highest authority for the text of Jonson prior to 1617.

989 HOWARD-HILL, T. H. "Towards a Jonson Concordance: A Discussion of Texts and Problems." RORD 15-16 (1972-73):17-32.
An effective Jonson concordance would separate the dramatic and non-dramatic works. Early texts which supply an editor with necessary materials will prove more functional than edited texts.

Textual Studies

990 JEWKES, WILFRED T. Act Division in Elizabethan and Jacobean Plays, 1583-1616. Hamden, Conn.: The Shoe String Press, 1958, pp. 64-66, 86, 245-52, 320-21. [Reprint. New York: AMS Press, 1972.]

Solid evidence indicates that Jonson divided his plays carefully and took great pains to preserve their form when they were printed.

991 KEMPLING, W. B. "Dedicatory Copies." TLS, 5 December 1936, p. 1016.

A copy of the Quarto of Cynthia's Revels contains a dedicatory page to Camden, the historian. The ordinary Quarto edition is undedicated; in the 1616 Folio, the play is dedicated "To the Court."

992 LAVIN, J. A. "Printers for Seven Jonson Quartos." Library 5th Series 15 (1970):331-38.

By studying printers' ornaments, Lavin names the printers of the following Jonson Quartos: Every Man out of his Humour (Adam Islip), Every Man in his Humour (Simon Safford), Cynthia's Revels (Richard Read), Volpone (George Eld), The Masque of Blackness (George Eld), Entertainment through the City of London (George Eld), and Poetaster (Richard Braddock).

993 McKENZIE, D. F. "The Printer of the Third Volume of Jonson's Workes." SB 25 (1972):177-78.

Comparison with other books printed in 1639-40 proves that John Dawson, Jr., was the printer.

994 MARCHAM, FRANK. "Thomas Walkley and the Ben Jonson Works of 1640." Library 4th Series 11 (1930):225-29.

Prints the Chancery Bill in which Thomas Walkley, a stationer, sets forth the claim that he and not John Benson, Andrew Crooke, and John Parker had the right to print "the writings and works" of Jonson presented by the dramatist to Sir Kenelm Digby. (See 986.)

995 MÜLLERTZ, MOGENS. "De Fire Shakespeare Folioer" [The Four Shakespeare Folios]. Bogvennen (Copenhagen) New Vol., Part 4 (1949):9-59. (In Danish.)

The reason for the "merry meeting" of Shakespeare, Drayton, and Jonson in 1616 may have been the publishing of Jonson's Folio, which became the prototype of the first Shakespeare Folio. There are resemblances between the two publications.

996 NEWDIGATE, B. H. "Was Lady Bedford the Phoenix?" TLS, 28 November 1936, p. 996.

A holograph poem written by Jonson in the Countess of Bedford's copy of the Quarto of Cynthia's Revels confirms the view that she was the "Phoenix" referred to by several poets.

997 NICOLL, ALLARDYCE. "'Rohmaterial.'" Shakespeare-Jahrbuch 99 (1963):7-29.

Jonson, more than any other playwright of his time, took an active part in the publication of his works. There are discrepancies in the titles of plays between the Stationers' Register and printed copies. Cynthia's Revels was originally entered as "Narcissus, the Fountain of Self Love," but there is no Narcissus in the play. Poetaster had several titles.

998 SNELL, FLORENCE M. "A Note on Volume Two of the 1640 Folio of Ben Jonson's Plays." MLN 30 (1915):158.

Attempts to solve a problem of pagination in this volume: Bartholomew Fair, pp. 1-88; The Staple of News, pp. 1-75; The Devil is an Ass, pp. 93-170. A study of separate Folio copies of Bartholomew Fair and The Devil is an Ass shows that "the numbering of the pages of these two plays is, allowing for one blank leaf between them, consecutive," which "points to these two plays having appeared in one volume, and Staple of News in a separate volume, before the folio was made up."

999 WHITING, GEORGE W. "The Hoe-Huntington Folio of Jonson." MLN 48 (1933):537-38.

Replies to H. L. Ford's claim (see 979) that the Greenville (G) copy of the 1616 Folio in the British Museum presents certain unique readings for Epicoene. One of the four Huntington Library copies of the 1616 Folio, the Hoe-Huntington Volume I (H.62101), has all the distinctive readings of Epicoene claimed for G, with two minor spelling variations. These are corrected readings. "H.62101 in all cases, except on page 415 of Sejanus, includes Jonson's corrections."

1000 WILLIAMS, WILLIAM P. "Chetwin, Crooke, and the Jonson Folios." SB 30 (1977):75-95.

The history of the publication and ownership of Jonson's works illustrates the power of the Stationers' Company and reinforces the view that the greatest textual authority is the first Folio edition of each volume of works. Many questions about placing some plays, particularly The Devil is an Ass result from the legal confusions involving Philip Chetwin, Andrew Crooke, and John Legatt.

See also: 21, 50, 58, 76, 187, 222, 242, 281, 300, 301, 307, 364, 385, 408, 432, 445, 653, 659, 690, 1006, 1252.

Theatrical History

1001 ARMSTRONG, WILLIAM A. The Elizabethan Private Theatres: Facts and Problems. The Society for Theatre Research. Pamphlet Series, 6, 1957-58. London: Harper and Sons, 1958. 17 pp. [Reprint. Norwood, Pa.: Norwood Editions, 1977.]
Jonson's plays acted at Blackfriars are examined in connection with a discussion of the Blackfriars audience and stage, and the performance time of plays written for private theatres.

1002 AVERY, EMMETT L. "Ben Jonson in the Provinces." N&Q 173 (2 October 1937):238.
Points out that Noyes, in Ben Jonson on the English Stage, 1660-1776 (see 1017), does not include any performances in what might be called provincial theatres. Lists several such performances of Every Man in his Humour and Epicoene from the mid-18th century, including casts in some instances.

1003 _____. "A Tentative Calendar of Daily Theatrical Performances, 1660-1700." Research Studies of the State College of Washington 13 (1945):225-83.
Lists dates of performances of The Alchemist (7), Bartholomew Fair (9), Catiline's Conspiracy (5), The Silent Woman (12), and Volpone (5).

1004 _____. "Two Early London Playbills." N&Q 195 (1950):99.
A performance of Volpone intended for 19 May 1703, at Drury Lane, was postponed to 21 May "by reason of the extream hot weather."

1005 BARRETT, W. P. Chart of Plays 1584 to 1623. Cambridge: Cambridge University Press, 1934. 39 pp., passim.
Chronologically lists historical and literary events and the presumed dates of composition of plays, including Jonson's.

1006 BENTLEY, GERALD EADES. "Benjamin Jonson," in his The Jacobean and Caroline Stage. Vol. 4. Oxford: Clarendon Press, 1956, 603-77.

Provides a selected bibliography (primarily from 1935 to 1950), a pertinent biography, a list of manuscripts and editions, the sources of the plays, all 17th-century records bearing on performances, publications, and the reputation of the plays, and discussion of the plays in their theatrical context.

1007 _____. "The Diary of a Caroline Theatergoer." MP 35 (1937): 61-72.

Reproduces details relating to contemporary theatre from the diary and account book of Sir Humphrey Mildmay, covering the period between 26 or 27 January 1631-32 to 16 November 1643. Sir Humphrey mentions three of Jonson's plays by name: Catiline, Volpone, and The Alchemist.

1008 BROWN, IVOR. "Too Rare Ben Jonson." Observer (London), 8 August 1937, p. 11.

During the 18th century Jonson's comedies were still popular, but the 19th century, as it began to idolize Shakespeare, "dropped Ben with a thud." In 20th-century England, "Apart from the occasional salaams of the specialists, Jonson's theatre is without honour and without a home." The reasons for this are the difficulties of his language and allusions, and the plays' lack of romantic lyricism.

1009 COOKMAN, A. V. "Shakespeare's Contemporaries on the Modern English Stage." Shakespeare-Jahrbuch 94 (1958):29-41.

Reviews English productions of Sejanus, Volpone, The Alchemist, Every Man in his Humour, Epicoene, and Bartholomew Fair. Suggests that the general neglect of Jonson is owing to "The ruthlessness of his classical preference for types" over more human characters. Jonson is not strong on "story," and "falls readily into prolixity and pedantry." But his vitality and wit compensate for his weaknesses.

1010 HARBAGE, ALFRED. Annals of English Drama, 975-1700: An Analytical Record of All Plays, Extant or Lost, Chronologically Arranged and Indexed by Authors, Titles, Dramatic Companies, &c. Philadelphia: University of Pennsylvania Press, 1940. 264 pp.

Lists plays, masques, and other dramatic presentations in England or written by Englishmen abroad in the time designated in the title. The tabulation provides: author, title, date, genre, auspices of first production, dates of first editions and of most recent modern editions. Other lists include editions, dissertations, and names and locations of theatres. Included also are indexes of the following: English playwrights, English plays, foreign plays translated or adapted, dramatic companies, and the extant play manuscripts for the period together with their locations and catalogue numbers. (See 1011.)

1011 _____. Revised by S. Schoenbaum. Second edition. Philadelphia: University of Pennsylvania Press, 1964. 338 pp.
Includes a preface to the revised edition, additions and corrections. (See 1010; see also 1020 and 1021.)

1012 HILLEBRAND, HAROLD NEWCOMB. The Child Actors: A Chapter in Elizabethan Stage History. ISLL, 11, nos. 1 and 2, 1926, 355 pp., passim. [Reprint. New York: Russell and Russell, 1964.]
Traces the history of the performances, by the Children of the Chapel at Blackfriars, of The Case is Altered, Cynthia's Revels, Eastward Ho, Epicoene, and Poetaster.

1013 JACKSON, ALFRED. "Play Notices from the Burney Newspapers, 1700-1703." PMLA 48 (1933):815-49.
Gives all the references to the plays (acted and printed) from 1700-1703 in the Burney Collection at the British Museum. The Alchemist, Bartholomew Fair, Epicoene, and Volpone are included.

1014 KENNEDY-SKIPTON, A. L. D. "John Ward and Restoration Drama." SQ 11 (1960):493-94.
Ward's diary indicates that The Alchemist was performed in 1662 some time prior to September, and acted well.

1015 _____. "A Footnote to 'John Ward and Restoration Drama.'" SQ 12 (1961):353.
Ward's notebooks indicate that he attended a performance of The Alchemist between 1 September and 25 September 1662.

1016 NICHOLLS, GRAHAM. "Jeremy Collier and the Jonson revivals of 1700." Trivium (St. David's College, Lampeter, Wales) 10 (1975):51-61.
Jonson's plays were infrequently performed during the Restoration, the predominant taste being for witty comedy lacking didactic purpose. However, some writers (e.g., Thomas Shadwell), favored Jonsonian classicism. At the end of the century, the arguments of the neoclassical critics were adopted by moralists looking for weapons with which to attack contemporary comedy. Jeremy Collier, in his Short View of the Immorality and Profaneness of the English

Stage (1698), in praising Jonson, "at times goes to great lengths to exonerate him from any suggestion of bawdry or profanity." Such praise was partly responsible for the 1700 revivals of Volpone, The Alchemist, and Epicoene

1017 NOYES, ROBERT GALE. Ben Jonson on the English Stage, 1660-1776. Harvard Studies in English, 17. Cambridge, Mass.: Harvard University Press, 1935. 359 pp. [Reprint. New York: Benjamin Blom, 1966.]

Traces, with thorough documentation, the stage history of Jonson's plays from the Restoration until the retirement of Garrick. Shows the main currents of Jonson criticism during the period, and documents the specific appeal of certain plays to the theatrical taste of the time. Volpone, The Alchemist, and Epicoene held the stage successfully during the entire Restoration period. Bartholomew Fair was popular only early in the Restoration period, and the popularity of Every Man in his Humour was confined to the last quarter of Garrick's management. Despite attempts to revive Every Man out of his Humour and Catiline, these plays were not popular. Noyes points out an anomaly in this stage history: "the more obsolete they became, the more frequently they were played. . . . The anomaly is merely heightened when it is observed that upon Garrick's retirement in 1776, Jonson's plays fell immediately into a decline from which they have never recovered." Includes information on actors, acting companies, theatres, and changes made in the plays.

Reviewed by F. E. Budd in MLR 32 (1937):297-98; H. P. Grundy in MP 34 (1937):99-100; A. Nicoll in JEGP 35 (1936): 434-35; H. Spencer in MLN 52 (1937):437-42; in TLS, 14 March 1936, p. 219.

1018 RIDDELL, JAMES A. "Some Actors in Ben Jonson's Plays." ShakS 5 (1969):285-98.

Notations in a privately owned copy of the 1616 Folio of Ben Jonson, assigning the parts to actors, provide evidence to reassign the parts previously conjectured for early 17th-century actors.

1019 RULFS, DONALD J. "Reception of the Elizabethan Playwrights on the London Stage 1776-1833." SP 46 (1949):54-69.

Examines the critical reception (excluding the criticism of literary critics such as Coleridge, Hazlitt, Hunt, and Lamb) of the acted plays during the years between June 1776 (Garrick's retirement) and March 1833 (Kean's retirement). Jonson ranked after Beaumont and Fletcher and Massinger in popularity. The critical reception of Every Man in his Humour was the most diverse.

Theatrical History

1020 SCHOENBAUM, S. _Annals of English Drama, 975-1700_. A Supplement to the Revised Edition. Evanston, Ill.: Department of English, Northwestern University, 1966. 23 pp.
Includes lists of editions and dissertations too recent to have been included in the revised _Annals_ (1964), and corrections and additions. (_See_ 1010; _see also_ 1011 and 1021.)

1021 ______. A Second Supplement to the Revised Edition. Evanston, Ill.: Department of English, Northwestern University, 1970. 19 pp.
Includes corrections and additions. (_See_ 1010; _see also_ 1011 and 1020.)

See also: 21, 73, 78, 115, 116, 119, 120, 185, 300, 308, 313, 327, 341, 493, 565, 807, 810, 1145.

The War of the Theatres

1022 ACHESON, ARTHUR. _Shakespeare's Sonnet Story 1592-1598: Restoring the Sonnets written to the Earl of Southampton to their original books and correlating them with personal phases of the Plays of the Sonnet period; with documentary evidence identifying Mistress Davenant as the Dark Lady_. London: Bernard Quaritch, 1922, pp. 445-578, passim. [Reprint. New York: Haskell House, 1971.]
Conjectures that Ben Jonson alludes, in "On Poet-Ape," to Thorpe's dedication of Shakespeare's sonnets and that Jonson was allied, except in the early stages, with Chapman and Marston against Shakespeare in the "War of the Theatres." Attempts to identify several characters and allusions in the plays implicated in the War. Accounts for Jonson's praise of Shakespeare as evidence of Jonson's mature judgment and his "worldly wisdom."

1023 ALLEN, MORSE S. "Marston's Part in the Stage-Quarrel," "Dramatic Satire: _Eastward Ho_," and Appendix F: "The Authorship of _Eastward Ho_," in his _The Satire of John Marston_. Columbus, Ohio: F. J. Heer, 1920, pp. 20-83, 154-56, 173-77. [Reprint. New York: Haskell House, 1956.]
Reviews the so-called "War of the Theatres" and disposes "of a large mass of conjecture which further investigation proves to be idle." Reviews theories of authorship of _Eastward Ho_ and attributes to Jonson the Prologue, parts of IV.i., IV.ii., and V.i., and almost all of the remainder of the play.

1024 BERGMAN, JOSEPH A. "Shakespeare's 'Purge' of Jonson Once Again." ESRS 15 (1966):27-33.

The War of the Theatres, principally between Marston and Jonson, involved Shakespeare in some puzzling manner. Shakespeare's "purge" of Jonson, referred to in the Second Part of the Return from Parnassus, IV.iii, is contained in Hamlet.

1025 BEVINGTON, DAVID. "Satire and State," in his Tudor Drama and Politics: A Critical Approach to Topical Meaning. Cambridge, Mass.: Harvard University Press, 1968, pp. 260-88.

Examines the political framework of the War of the Theatres. The private theatre developed a critical view toward established law and order, which Jonson reflects in the creation of the merry judge in A Tale of a Tub and Every Man in his Humour and, in his later comedies, in ridiculing the justice figure, leaving satirical exposure to gentleman wits or manipulators outside the law. Jonson's satirical attitudes toward law were crucial in the misunderstanding between dramatists speaking for the public and private theatres. The issues are explored in Marston and Dekker's Satiromastix and Jonson's Poetaster. Jonson believed that the responsible moral critic, the poet, could save the state; his opponents, the public moralists, attacked him for inveighing against "Court, city, country."

1026 CHAMBERS, E. K. William Shakespeare: A Study of Facts and Problems. Oxford: Clarendon Press, 1930, 1:69-72, passim; 2:202-11, passim.

Looks briefly at the Poetomachia in analyzing biographical data about Shakespeare. Discusses possible allusions to Shakespeare in Every Man out of his Humour, Poetaster, Every Man in his Humour, Sejanus, and several non-dramatic works.

1027 CLARK, ELEANOR GRACE. "The War of the Poets," in her Ralegh and Marlowe: A Study in Elizabethan Fustian. New York: Fordham University Press, 1941, pp. 199-219. [Reprint. New York: Russell and Russell, 1965.]

Explaining that fustian was a device used to avoid the blue pencil of the censors, explicates some of the allusions in the plays involved in the War of the Theatres.

1028 DAVENPORT, ARNOLD. "The Quarrel of the Satirists." MLR 37 (1942):123-30.

Includes Hall, Marston, Guilpin, Weever, Jonson, and Breton in the War of the Theatres. Jonson is identified as the "humorist" attacked by Weever in The Whipping of the Satyre.

The War of the Theatres

1029 ENCK, JOHN J. "The Peace of the Poetomachia." PMLA 77 (1962):386-96.

Evidence in Every Man out of his Humour and Troilus and Cressida proves that Jonson and Shakespeare knew each other professionally about 1600. Shakespeare benefited from Jonson's experimentation with uses of the Elizabethan stage. Every Man out of his Humour shows a method of sound dramatic characterization through humours theory and character sketches, discontinuity in plot structure, decorum in language and satire. These experiments appear in Troilus and Cressida and other contemporary plays, offering proof that authors were "engaged by humours, standards, satire, and the personal Poetomachia." Discounts the idea that the War was based on personal differences.

1030 GAIR, W. G. "La compagnie des enfants de St. Paul Londres (1599-1606)." Dramaturgie et Société: Rapports entre l'oeuvre théâtrale, son interprétation et son public aux XVIe et XVIIe siècles. Vol. 2. Edited by Jean Jacquot et al. Paris: Editions du Centre National de la Recherche Scientifique, 1968, 655-74.

Briefly recounts the history of the War of the Theatres. Stresses the importance, to his role in this conflict, of Jonson's conservative attitudes towards the use and abuse of language.

1031 HALSTEAD, W. L. "What War of the Theatres?" CE 9 (1948): 424-26.

Dismisses the so-called War of the Theatres as less serious than critics have made it and offers as an explanation the possibility that Jonson, Marston, and Dekker feigned the War hoping to attract an audience. (See 1040.)

1032 HARRISON, G. B. Elizabethan Plays and Players. London: George Routledge and Sons, 1940, pp. 165-66, 168-90, 198-247 passim, 248-81. [Reprint. Ann Arbor: The University of Michigan Press, 1956; Folcroft, Pa.: Folcroft Library Editions, 1978.]

Reproduces primary material referring to Jonson. Traces the origins and development of the stage war in great detail.

1033 LEISHMAN, J. B., ed. The Three Parnassus Plays (1598-1601). London: Nicholson & Watson, 1949, pp. 50, 52, 53, 59-60, 83-88, 369-71.

Every Man in his Humour, Every Man out of his Humour, Cynthia's Revels, and Poetaster are discussed in connection with the War of the Theatres and the development of satirical comedy. The notes to the Parnassus plays point out numerous examples of Jonson being imitated or borrowed from.

1034 McDIARMID, MATTHEW P. "The Stage Quarrel in Wily Beguiled." N&Q 201 (1956):380-83.
Several allusions suggest the play's relationship to the War of the Theatres.

1035 MORSBACH, LORENZ. Der Weg zu Shakespeare und das Hamletdrama. Halle: Max Niemeyer, 1922, pp. 21-38, passim.
Discusses the role of Jonson in the War of the Theatres and the connection between that conflict and the artistic differences between Jonson and Shakespeare.

1036 REYBURN, MARJORIE L. "New Facts and Theories About the Parnassus Plays." PMLA 74 (1959):325-35.
Jonson's part in the War of the Theatres is touched upon in a discussion of the authorship and intentions of the Parnassus Plays.

1037 SALINGAR, L. G.; HARRISON, GERALD; and COCHRANE, BRUCE. "Les comédiens et leur public en Angleterre de 1520 à 1640." Dramaturgie et Société: Rapports entre l'oeuvre théâtrale, son interprétation et son public aux XVIe et XVIIe siècles. Vol. 2. Edited by Jean Jacquot et al. Paris: Editions du Centre National de la Recherche Scientifique, 1968, 525-76.
The War of the Theatres provided the stimulus for the writing of critical manifestos and prefaces, such as are found in Every Man out of his Humour, Sejanus, and Volpone; this practice led the theatre to an increased self-awareness. Every Man in his Humour set the style for realistic city comedies. Jonson's production of comedies, along with that of several of his contemporaries, fell off sharply after 1605; Jonson's career appeared over with the publication of The Works in 1616.

1038 SHARPE, ROBERT BOIES. The Real War of the Theaters: Shakespeare's Fellows in Rivalry with the Admiral's Men, 1594-1603. The Modern Language Association of America Monograph Series, 5. Boston: D. C. Heath; London: Oxford University Press, 1935. 268 pp., passim.
Summarizes the chronology and the satirical intention of each of the plays of the Poetomachia (pp. 192-93). Considers the "real" War of the Theatres to have been the long-standing rivalry between the Admiral's and the Chamberlain's men, which Elizabeth encouraged for political purposes.

The War of the Theatres

1039 _____. "Title-Page Mottoes in the Poetomachia." SP 32 (1935):210-20.

Translates, interprets, and gives the sources for the Latin mottoes attached to the printed versions of Jonson's comedies. Several employed after 1602 continue to allude to the Poetomachia.

1040 WITHINGTON, ROBERT. "What War of the Theatres?" CE 10 (1948):163-64.

Replies to Halstead (see 1031), arguing that Jonson's audience could have enjoyed the critical quarrels in the plays more than Halstead is willing to grant. More important than identifying the characters in the War is the recognition that Jonson shifted during this time from classical to realistic satire. When Jonson "put definite individuals on the stage, even if he caricatured them, he left the type; perhaps he found that realistic satire was more effective than the more general classical satire."

1041 WYNDHAM, G. Essays in Romantic Literature. London: Macmillan, 1919, pp. 290-309.

Although he attacked Dekker and Marston during the War of the Theatres, Jonson was much more allied with them than he was with Shakespeare and the romantics. Shakespeare probably wrote the Prologue to Troilus and Cressida while the Prologue to Poetaster was still an object of ridicule.

1042 ZBIERZKI, HENRYK. Shakespeare and the "War of the Theatres" (A Reinterpretation). Poznan Society of the Friends of Science. Works of the Philological Commission, Vol. 16, Part 5. Poznan: Panstwowe Wydawnictwo Naukowe, 1957, pp. 44-81, passim.

The War of the Theatres was basically a conflict between the private and popular theatres. Jonson, in the Prologue to Every Man in his Humour and in portions of Cynthia's Revels and Poetaster, attacks the popular theatre and the "common players," including Shakespeare. In his social, political, aesthetic, and moral condemnations, Jonson is revealed as a "renegade" and a "reactionary," as "the great informer against the popular theatre." His championing of the private theatre seems connected with his desire to be a court playwright.

See also: 201, 349, 363, 384, 392, 401, 406, 824, 907, 1075, 1123, 1125.

GENERAL TOPICS

*1043 ABERCROMBIE, LASCELLES. "Ben Jonson." *The British Institute of Paris* [*Journal*?], January 1938, pp. 7-13.

1044 ALDINGTON, RICHARD, comp. and trans. *A Book of "Characters" from Theophrastus; Joseph Hall, Sir Thomas Overbury, Nicolas Breton, John Earle, Thomas Fuller, and other English Authors; Jean de La Bruyère, Vauvenargues, and other French Authors*. London: George Routledge and Sons; New York: E. P. Dutton, 1924, pp. 335-42. [Reprint. Folcroft, Pa.: Folcroft Library Editions, 1978.]

The "characters" of Ben Jonson are drawn from *Cynthia's Revels* and *Every Man out of his Humour*.

1045 ALLEN, D. F., and DUNSTAN, W. R. "Crosses and Crowns: A Study of Coinage in the Elizabethan Dramatists." *British Numismatic Journal* 23 (1940):287-99.

Quotes passages in the plays where coins are mentioned; in most cases these passages involve word play or puns. Jonson's plays cited are *The Case is Altered* and *Every Man in his Humour*.

1046 ALLEN, PERCY. *The Plays of Shakespeare and Chapman in Relation to French History*. London: Archer, 1933, pp. 51-201, passim.

Jonson, along with Chapman, knew that "Shakespeare" was the Earl of Oxford. He imitates, burlesques, derides, and eulogizes some of his works in *Every Man out of his Humour*, *Cynthia's Revels*, *Epicoene*, and *Poetaster*. "Shaksper" of Stratford is caricatured in these plays.

1047 ALVOR, PETER. *Die Shakespeare-Frage und das Ben Jonson-Problem*. Wurzburg: C. J. Becker, 1930, pp. 69-97.

Francis Bacon, with Jonson's help, was the main author of the works attributed to Jonson. The poet-playwright of "On Poet-Ape" (*Epigrams*, LVI) is Jonson himself.

1048 ANDERSON, DONALD K. "The Banquet of Love in English Drama." *JEGP* 63 (1964):422-32.

Students of the drama have failed to pay attention to "the love banquet" employed by many dramatists of the period, including Chapman, Jonson, Marston, Fletcher, Middleton, Massinger, and Ford. Defines "the love banquet" as "sometimes . . . a scene, in which an assignation takes place or a seduction is attempted; at other times (or at the same time) as metaphor, becoming the language of love." Traces possible origins in Christian, Renaissance, and classical sources and points to related uses of the motif in poetry and painting.

General Topics

1049 ARDEN, JOHN. "An Embarrassment to the Tidy Mind." Gambit 6 (1973):30-38.

Jonson's experience with bricklaying contributed to his concern with form: fitting all into a preconceived design, controlling characters by humours, and curbing each speech by the bounds of its scene. He resembles Dickens in his interests and insights about human beings and offers young authors rich learning experiences.

1050 ARMSTRONG, WILLIAM A. "Ben Jonson and Jacobean Stagecraft," in Jacobean Theatre. Edited by John Russell Brown and Bernard Harris. Stratford-upon-Avon Studies, 1. New York: St. Martin's Press, 1960, pp. 43-61.

The strongest element in Jonson's stagecraft is his use of words. Spectacle and stage business are used only to reinforce meaning visually as, for example, when the Prologue in Poetaster sets his foot on Envy's head as he comes into sight through a trapdoor. Jonson uses the platform structure and stage doors with resourcefulness in plays in which his choric figures remain on the stage to observe the action and then stimulate and guide the attention of his audience by observations made between the acts. Also, jargon supersedes disguise in revealing the vanity of appearance in a number of characters.

1051 ARONSTEIN, PHILIPP. "Des nationale Erlebnis im englischen Renaissancedrama." Shakespeare-Jahrbuch 55 (1919):86-128.

Jonson is included in a broad discussion of the English Renaissance drama as both reflecting and participating in historical developments. He was especially important as a representative of a conservative world view in the losing struggle against Puritanism. In Sejanus he expressed the general national sentiment against tyranny.

1052 ASHTON, ROBERT. "Usury and High Finance in the Age of Shakespeare and Jonson." RMS 4 (1960):14-43.

Examines Tudor and Stuart attitudes towards moneylending and investing. Though not a usurer, Volpone is the "dramatic archetype" of the blasphemer who makes money his God, as seen in his opening lines. In The Staple of News, a moneylender's typical attitude toward impoverished clients is seen in Penniboy Senior's speech, II.iv.183-87.

*1053 ASTHANA, R. K. "The Dynamics of Jonson's Comedies," in Criticism and Research. Banaras: Hindu University, 1964, pp. 46-55.

1054 BABB, LAWRENCE. The Elizabethan Malady: A Study of Melancholia in English Literature from 1580 to 1642. East Lansing: Michigan State College Press, 1951, pp. 73-78.

Describes four discernible malcontent types found in English drama after the second half of Elizabeth's reign. Both the malcontent with a sense of neglected superiority and the melancholy scholar appear in Jonson (Carlo Buffone and Macilente in Every Man out of his Humour). The melancholy criminal intriguer and the cynic do not appear in the plays. The social critic possessing a balanced temperament must not be confused with the malcontent. Jonson's unhappy female lovers (The Case is Altered and The New Inn) often express themselves in language associated with melancholy.

1055 _____. "Melancholy and the Elizabethan Man of Letters." HLQ 4 (1941):247-61.

Explains the melancholy scholar, a recurrent type in Elizabethan drama, in terms of Renaissance medical theory and presents examples of intellectual melancholy from the drama of the time. Macilente (Every Man out of his Humour) embodies the main traits of the type.

1056 _____. "The Physiological Conception of Love in the Elizabethan and Early Stuart Drama." PMLA 56 (1941):1020-35.

Many passages in the drama of this period can only be fully understood when one realizes that emotion was thought to be a physiological as well as psychological phenomenon and that passion was thought to be provoked by movements of the humours to or from the heart; erotic love, since it implies desire, is a hot passion. Quotes several passages from contemporary health treatises and provides illustrations from dramatists showing how they employed this physiological conception of love. His example from Jonson is the young lady in The New Inn who, due to love, suffers excruciating pains in liver, heart, and blood.

1057 _____. "Scientific Theories of Grief in Some Elizabethan Plays." SP 40 (1943):502-19.

Jonson participated in the Renaissance practice of drawing more on scientific lore than on actual observation or experience in detailing emotions.

1058 BACON, WALLACE A. "The Magnetic Field: The Structure of Jonson's Comedies." HLQ 19 (1956):121-53.

Townsend (in Apologie for Bartholomew Fayre; see 41) presents "an inadequate representation of Herford and Simpson's notion of structure," since they do recognize Jonson's method of achieving unity in his great plays.

Townsend's own theory, that Jonson's unity is similar to the interweaving in a tapestry or painting, may account for spatial unity, but not necessarily unity in variety. Townsend seems so involved with criticizing the critics who argue for Jonson's singleness of plot that she seems to be pleading for variety rather than pointing out the unity of the plays. Bacon proposes a theory of structure.

1059 BAMBOROUGH, J. B. Ben Jonson. Bibliographical Series of Supplements to British Book News on Writers and their Works, 112. London: Longmans, Green, 1959. 43 pp.

Offers a short biography of Jonson, discusses his theory of drama--the "laws of drama" affirmed by Jonson and the moral purpose of drama--and surveys his works: the comedies, masques, tragedies, lyrics, and criticism.

1060 BARBER, C. L. The Idea of Honour in the English Drama, 1591-1700. Gothenburg Studies in English, 6. Göteborg: University of Göteborg, 1957. 362 pp., passim. [Reprint. Folcroft, Pa.: Folcroft Library Editions, 1977.]

Divides the uses of the noun "honour" into eighteen head-meanings and traces the changes in the head-meanings decade by decade. Jonson's comedies from Poetaster to The Magnetic Lady are often significant. Barber uses Lovel's definition of true valor in The New Inn, IV.iv, to illustrate Jonson's protest against the decline of the public elements in honour (glory, military achievement, and Christian morality) and the rise of private ones (reputation, the duello, etc.).

1061 BARISH, JONAS A. "Feasting and Judging in Jonsonian Comedy." RenD NS 5 (1972):3-35.

Feasting plays a significant role in all the major comedies, with Jonson setting himself up as host and presenting different views on who has the right to administer justice. A reverse correlation exists between the amount of feasting and the severity of judgment: festive moods produce lenient judgments. By Bartholomew Fair, comic permissiveness replaces justice.

1062 _____. "Jonson and the Loathèd Stage," in A Celebration of Ben Jonson (1973), pp. 27-53. (See 5.)

Jonson exhibited fundamental contradictions: antitheatricalism and a desire for illusion; unstable relations with audiences and a caustic attitude toward contemporary stage practices; specific, critical dramatic theories and large, ethical philosophical assumptions. His printing of the plays as "works" indicates his view of them as pieces destined for reading, not performance. The inherently impermanent form of drama made him distrust the genre.

1063 BARNES, PETER; BLAKELY, COLIN; HANDS, TERRY; WARDLE, IRVING; and HAMMOND, JONATHAN. "Ben Jonson and the Modern Stage." Gambit 6 (1973):5-30.
Jonson's unpopularity with modern audiences and reviewers stems from qualities in both him and them. Although highly didactic and clear-cut, he offers varied viewpoints and styles. A high level of professionalism makes the plays difficult to present, but many modern playwrights actually use their techniques. Bartholomew Fair ranks as his masterpiece, with each character's style of behavior being totally different from all the others'.

1064 BASTIAENEN, JOHANNES ADAM. The Moral Tone of Jacobean and Caroline Drama. Amsterdam: H. J. Paris, 1930, pp. 11-13, 49-61. [Reprint. New York: Haskell House, 1966.]
Compared to Shakespeare, finds Jonson one-sided; "he sees only the seamy side of life and neglects its counterpart, and would almost make us believe that this earth of ours is inhabited only by fools, cowards, rogues and imposters." Thus Jonson defeats his own purpose, which is to improve men's morals.

1065 BEAURLINE, L. A. "Ben Jonson and the Illusion of Completeness." PMLA 84 (1969):51-59.
Jonson, practicing in his drama what Bacon and Hoskins expressed in their rhetorical theory, designed his major comedies not by a comic inclusion, but by giving an illusion of completeness. This is achieved by presenting a simple situation, then by multiplying characters, incidents, and speeches to accelerate all into an intricate, complicated design. Jonson experimented with the technique in Volpone; it is more clearly evident in The Alchemist. Bartholomew Fair "offers the most complex and challenging example of Jonson's art of exhaustion." (See 1146.)

1066 BENTLEY, GERALD EADES. The Profession of Dramatist in Shakespeare's Time, 1590-1642. Princeton: Princeton University Press, 1971. 338 pp.
To focus his study on "the normal professional life of a writer of plays," Bentley chooses eight writers who fit his criteria. Jonson is not numbered among the eight because "from no later than 1602 he was not primarily dependent upon the commercial theatres for his livelihood." Bentley admits that Jonson's elimination may be questioned.

General Topics

1067 ______. Shakespeare and His Theatre. Lincoln: University of Nebraska Press, 1964, pp. 79-84.

Discusses Shakespeare's dramatic company and traces the history of public and private theatres, principally the Globe and Blackfriars, from the Elizabethan to the Caroline stages. Jonson was a clear choice as a new playwright for the King's men at the Blackfriars Theatre, Bentley suggests, for three reasons: Jonson's growing following among the courtly audience due to the popularity of his masques, his reputation among the intellectuals and critics, and his experience in writing plays for this theatre and in directing some rehearsals of the boy players.

1068 BERLIN, NORMAND. "Ben Jonson," in his The Base String: The Underworld in Elizabethan Drama. Rutherford, N.J.: Fairleigh Dickinson University Press, 1968, pp. 130-71.

Analysis of Jonson's use of rogues, thieves, whores, bawds, vagabonds, and other members of the underground leads to the conclusion that in the earlier plays Jonson's use of underground characters is minimal but that in Volpone, The Alchemist, Bartholomew Fair, and The Devil is an Ass the use of underground characters becomes a central structural device and an instrument of satire. Jonson's purpose in his middle period is not to punish underground characters as Dekker does, nor to conform to his audience's moral standards, but to "provide a valid satiric commentary on man's folly."

1069 BLACK, MATTHEW. "Enter Citizens," in Studies in the English Renaissance Drama in Memory of Karl Julius Holzknecht. Edited by Josephine W. Bennett, Oscar Cargill, and Vernon Hall, Jr. New York: New York University Press, 1959, pp. 16-27. [Reprint. London: P. Owen and Vision Press, 1961.]

Numbered background figures, common to pre-Elizabethan and Elizabethan plays, are few in Jonson. Only Eastward Ho is cited as using them.

1070 BOAS, FREDERICK S. "Ben Jonson," in his An Introduction to Stuart Drama. London: Oxford University Press, 1946, pp. 42-72, 106-31.

Surveys Jonson's entire canon and presents a critical discussion of his drama that includes fundamental background information. Admits the imperfections of the last plays, but argues with Dryden's condemnation of them as "dotages" by pointing out the evidence in these dramas of Jonson's remaining "massive genius."

1071 _____. "Charles Lamb and the Elizabethan Dramatists." E&S 29 (1943):62-81.

Analyzes the rationale for Lamb's selections and critical commentary in Specimens of English Dramatic Writers who lived about the Time of Shakespeare and his Extracts. Lamb selected passages from The Case is Altered, Poetaster, Sejanus, Catiline, and The New Inn and argued against the critics who would call Jonson a pedant. For examples of Jonson in his comic vein Lamb chose The Alchemist and Volpone.

1072 BOWDEN, WILLIAM R. The English Dramatic Lyric, 1603-42: A Study in Stuart Dramatic Technique. Yale Studies in English, 118. New Haven: Yale University Press, 1951, pp. 8, 72-92 passim, 116-17, 127. [Reprint. Hamden, Conn.: The Shoe String Press, Archon Books, 1969.]

Jonson frequently uses song for comic purposes (Poetaster, Eastward Ho, Bartholomew Fair) as well as for communication of ideas (Cynthia's Revels, Poetaster, Volpone). Possession by a god seldom causes song in Jonson, and few blank songs exist in the plays. There is little variation in the amount or quality of songs.

1073 BOYCE, BENJAMIN. The Theophrastan Character in England to 1642. Cambridge: Harvard University Press, 1947, pp. 99-107. [Reprint. London: Cass, 1967.]

The Characters of Theophrastus enjoyed a revival in Jacobean times partially because they employed many of the rhetorical figures taught in grammar schools. Jonson employed Characters or near-Characters in Every Man out of his Humour, Cynthia's Revels, The Magnetic Lady. He moved beyond the Character in Epicoene's Morose.

1074 BOYD, JOHN DOUGLAS. "T. S. Eliot as Critic and Rhetorician: The Essay on Jonson." Criticism 11 (1969):167-82.

Focuses "on the covert and therefore treacherous features" of Eliot's rhetoric while assuming the excellencies of the essay.

1075 BRADBROOK, M. C. "Character as Plot. II: The Definition of Comedy: Jonsonian Form" and "The Anatomy of Knavery: Jonson, Marston, Middleton," in her The Growth and Structure of Elizabethan Comedy. London: Chatto and Windus, 1955, pp. 94-116, 138-164. [Reprint. Baltimore: Penguin Books, 1963, pp. 103-25, 148-74.]

Traces the chronological development of Elizabethan comedy, exploring its characteristic forms and its influence (primarily Shakespearean) on Jacobean (Jonsonian) comedy. Reviews the Poets' War, Jonsonian comedy as Jonson understood it, and the influence of Jonson on the city comedy of the early 17th century.

1076 _____. The Growth and Structure of Elizabethan Comedy. New Edition. London: Chatto and Windus, 1973, pp. 94-116, 138-164, 207-222.

Reprints 1955 edition (see 1075), with additional chapter, "Elizabethan Comedy in the Theatre of Today," which notes that Jonson does not appeal much to modern theatrical tastes, but that his literary popularity has grown. "It may be that Jonson really is at his greatest in the study." L. C. Knights, like T. S. Eliot, "approaches Jonson as a reader."

1077 BREWER, WILMON. Shakespeare's Influence on Sir Walter Scott. Boston: Cornhill, 1925, pp. 73-78, 335, 477. [Reprint. New York: AMS Press, 1974.]

Scott believed that Jonson was both inspired by Shakespeare and on the whole inferior to him. However, he credited Jonson with "greater art" and in general overrated him; except for Volpone and The Sad Shepherd, Jonson's plays are "dull, clumsy, and unpleasant." Captain Colepepper, in The Fortunes of Nigel, seems based primarily on Bobadill. Scott discusses Jonson in The Life of Dryden, Essay on Drama, and the Introduction to The Monastery.

1078 BRIDGES-ADAMS, W. "Ben Jonson," in his The Irresistible Theatre: From the Conquest to the Commonwealth. London: Secker and Warburg, 1957, pp. 235-48.

Offers a "brief judgement" of Jonson as personality and dramatist to motivate the reader to become, as the author calls himself, "mad about the theatre," especially the theatre of Jonson.

1079 BROWN, ARTHUR. "Citizen Comedy and Domestic Drama," in Jacobean Theatre. Edited by John Russell Brown and Bernard Harris. Stratford-upon-Avon Studies, 1. New York: St. Martin's Press, 1960, pp. 63-83.

Discusses Dekker, Heywood, and Jonson, who were among the most consistent users of the materials of citizen comedy and domestic drama in the period. Jonson differed from the other two in his "anti-romantic attitude towards material and audience alike," as evidenced in the Hero and Leander burlesque in Bartholomew Fair and his satirical treatment of family relationships in Volpone, Epicoene, and Bartholomew Fair.

1080 _____. "Studies in Elizabethan and Jacobean Drama Since 1900." RORD 5 (1962):45-58.
Notes approximately fifty works on Ben Jonson as well as general studies on the drama of the period.

1081 BROWN, J. L. "Bodin et Ben Jonson." RLC 20 (1946):66-81.
Through Sir Politic Would-be (Volpone IV.i), Jonson says, in effect, that Bodin and Machiavelli, who held that the state is supreme, were atheists. But Jonson was wrong; for although his faith was not orthodox, Bodin remained a Catholic all his life, and his faith was profound. Both Bodin and Machiavelli looked upon religion as an indispensable social brake, which acts as an instrument of solidarity and a means of assuring the life of the republic. For Bodin, the deistic idea is the foundation of the state system. But when Jonson labeled Bodin "brother" to Machiavelli, the English who had earlier condemned what they thought to be the doctrines of Machiavelli formed the same opinion of Bodin. Jonson often refers to what he mistakenly understood as Bodin's view of the state, especially in Volpone and in The Magnetic Lady.

1082 BRULÉ, ANDRÉ. "Sur Ben Jonson." Revue Anglo-Américaine 13 (October 1935):3-17.
Discusses Jonson as classicist, moralist, satirist, and bourgeois. Points out similarities between some characters in Jonson and Molière. Criticizes the Zweig-Romains Volpone for its serious deviations from Jonson's intentions, and its lack of poetic qualities, suggesting that both the public and Jonson are the losers.

1083 BRYANT, J. A., JR. "Jonson's Satirist out of His Humor." Ball State Teachers College Forum 3 (1962):31-36.
Asserts that the three plays, Every Man out of his Humour, Cynthia's Revels, and Poetaster, "are, at least in part, parables designed to show that the satirist is a healthy member of society only when he enjoys the public support of an enlightened and morally responsible prince."

1084 BULAND, MABLE. The Presentation of Time in the Elizabethan Drama. New York: H. Holt, 1912, pp. 146-50, 295-98. [Reprint. New York: Haskell House, 1966.]
Jonson's practice in the observance of the unity of time in his comedies complied with his theory. However, because of his adherence to his historical sources, the time represented in his tragedies extends beyond one day.

General Topics

1085 CAMPBELL, OSCAR JAMES. Comicall Satyre and Shakespeare's "Troilus and Cressida." San Marino, Calif.: The Henry E. Huntington Library and Art Gallery, 1938. 255 pp., passim.
Devises a structural formula, Jonson's "synthesis of the practice of the ancients in old comedy and the theories of the Renaissance based on classical precept and example," and thus elucidates Every Man out of his Humour, Cynthia's Revels, and Poetaster.

1086 CHAMBERS, E. K. "Benjamin Jonson," in his The Elizabethan Stage. Vol. 3. Oxford: Clarendon Press, 1923, 352-94.
Includes a brief discussion of the plays in their dramatic, not literary, aspects. The four volumes of the work provide detailed accounts of various aspects of Elizabethan drama to 1616.

1087 COISCAULT-CAVALCA, M. "Les Romantiques français et les Elisabéthains." LR 20 (1966):334-55.
Reviews criticism of Jonson in 19th-century France, indicating that he was neither well known nor much appreciated.

1088 COLBY, ELBRIDGE [Francis Paul]. "Two Elizabethans. II." The American Catholic Quarterly Review 42 (1917):157-64. [Reprinted as "Ben Jonson," in his English Catholic Poets: Chaucer to Dryden. Milwaukee: n.p., 1936, pp. 84-96. Reprint. Freeport, N.Y.: Books for Libraries, 1967.]
Attempts "to record the noteworthy Catholic elements found in a reading of those early authors." Points out the condemnation of Presbyterianism in A Tale of a Tub, the attack on Puritanism in Bartholomew Fair and The Alchemist, the praise of a rigid Roman Catholic in Every Man in his Humour, and "a decent reference to a good Catholic" in Volpone.

1089 COLLEY, JOHN SCOTT. "Music in the Elizabethan Private Theatres." YES 4 (1974):62-69.
Aims at disproving two commonly held assumptions: that the style of vocal music was more sophisticated in the private than in the public theatres, and that the primary reason for the frequent use of songs in plays by Jonson, Chapman, Marston, and other "coterie" playwrights was the fact that the boys' companies were especially talented at singing. Claims instead that the two kinds of theatres used similar kinds of music, and that the frequent use of song was simply a matter of the playwrights' individual artistic preferences.

1090 CRUICKSHANK, ALFRED HAMILTON. Ben Jonson: A Paper Read Before the Durham Branch of the English Association, May 9, 1912. Durham, Eng.: Printed at the "Durham County Advertiser" Office, 1912. 20 pp. [Reprint. Philadelphia: R. West, 1978.]

For the reader who does not have time to read much of Jonson, recommends Every Man in his Humour, Volpone, Epicoene, and The Alchemist. Discusses the merits and faults of the author, whom he considers, as an artist, "very unequal."

1091 CULMSEE, CARLTON. "The Classicism of Ben Jonson." PUASAL 14 (1937):67-70.

Classical influence on Jonson is seen in his clarity, dignity, decorum, and seriousness of purpose. But his adherence to unities is inconsistent, and he is unclassical in his prolixity and his tendency towards the homiletic and allegorical. The tragedies are less classical than the comedies. "Jonson rarely reveals that he has recognized the true soul of the classics. . . . generally he lacks soundness of basic conception and the unity of moral impression which dominates all at the end." Nevertheless he was beneficially influenced by classicism and labored in the cause of learning and aesthetic control.

1092 DALE, LEONA. "Jonson's Sick Society." BRMMLA 24 (1970): 66-74.

Shows the contribution of the imagery of disease and cure to the development of character, plot, and theme in Every Man in his Humour, Every Man out of his Humour, and Volpone.

1093 DESSEN, ALAN C. Elizabethan Drama and the Viewer's Eye. Chapel Hill: University of North Carolina Press, 1977, pp. 11-12, 15-16, 47-48, 77-80, 113-16, 141-44, 154.

Jonson resembles his dramatic contemporaries in his strong use of non-verbal elements on the stage. Psychomachia, visual analogues, and elaborate fictions appear in many of his major plays. These non-realistic devices often curtail the modern reader's enjoyment of older works.

1094 DONALDSON, IAN. "Ben Jonson," in History of Literature in the English Language. Vol. 3: English Drama to 1710. Edited by Christopher Ricks. London: Sphere Books, 1971, 278-305.

Reasons frequently presented for the unpopularity of Jonson's play's include topicality, obscurity, non-introspective characters, unappealing females, and lack of theatricality. Study of the canon, however, proves these reasons to be unfounded. Jonson chose to present comedy of punishment and social revenge rather than of happy discovery. The plays are not realistic, for they repeat details and images until they become symbols.

1095 _____. "Damned by Analogies: Or, How to Get Rid of Ben Jonson." Gambit 6 (1973):38-46.

Critics' analogies during the past four centuries reveal much about the way they perceive Jonson. Donaldson studies the implications of the analogies of Coleridge ("a Skeleton . . . massive"), Hippolyte Taine ("literary Leviathan"), J. A. Symonds ("elephantine sprightliness"), Carlyle ("rhinocerous"), Thomas Fuller ("a Spanish great Gallion"), and William Archer ("a huge and cumbrous engine"). Donaldson finds the analogies which relate Jonson's work to the visual arts "most puzzling."

1096 _____. "Jonson and the Moralists," in Two Renaissance Mythmakers: Christopher Marlowe and Ben Jonson (1977), pp. 146-64. (See 28.)

Jonson enjoyed returning, throughout the canon, to certain themes and formulas and developing them in varied ways. His use of Cicero's "O tempora! O mores!" (Catiline, Bartholomew Fair, Every Man in his Humour) illustrates his experimenting with moral tone and his ability to parody. Jonson scholars need to balance their search for moral judgment in and about the plays with a recognition and acceptance of humanity.

1097 _____. The World Upside Down: Comedy from Jonson to Fielding. London: Oxford University Press, 1970. 211 pp. [Reprint. Oxford: Clarendon Press, 1974.]

Employing the traditional comic principles of inversion and levelling, Jonsonian drama often parallels periodic festivals, with their licensed social disorder. Epicoene and Bartholomew Fair stress the serious through inversion, and thus force questions onto spectators. Plot and symbol relate intimately in Epicoene; the metaphor of life and the theatre as game controls Bartholomew Fair. Jonson influenced Wycherly, Congreve, Gay, and Fielding.

1098 DREW, ELIZABETH. Discovering Drama. New York: W. W. Norton, 1937, pp. 148-52. [Reprint. Port Washington, N.Y.: Kennikat Press, 1968.]

Jonson and Shaw differ greatly in their satires, although neither had any illusions about life.

1099 DUDRAP, CLAUDE. "La 'Tragédie Espagnole' face à la critique élisabéthaine et jacobéene," in *Dramaturgie et Société: Rapports entre l'oeuvre théâtrale, son interprétation et son public aux XVIe et XVIIe siècles*. Vol. 2. Edited by Jean Jacquot et al. Paris: Editions du Centre National de la Recherche Scientifique, 1968, 607-31, passim.

In a discussion of contemporary critical attacks on *The Spanish Tragedy*, cites specific references and allusions to Kyd's play in nine of Jonson's comedies. The "new esthetic" of the private theatres, which exercised an almost absolute critical monopoly and defined itself chiefly by its condemnation of the popular stage, was a reformation movement orchestrated by Jonson.

1100 DUNCAN, DOUGLAS. "Ben Jonson's Lucianic Irony." *ArielE* 1 (April 1970):42-53.

Jonson's approach to dramatic art, especially after 1602, was "decisively influenced, or at least authoritatively supported" by the satiric standpoint of Lucian, and its development by the humanists, notably More and Erasmus. Jonson was not a sceptic, like Lucian, but in his best comedies made use of Lucianic irony as a means of challenging his audience's ability to make proper moral judgments of the characters' actions.

1101 DUNLAP, RHODES. "The Allegorical Interpretation of Renaissance Literature." *PMLA* 82 (1967):39-43.

Allegory, though used extensively in the Renaissance, was not always clear or precise. Jonson, in his Dedicatory Epistle to *Volpone*, warns against those who "profess to have a key for the decyphering of every thing."

1102 ELIOT, T. S. "Ben Jonson," in his *The Sacred Wood: Essays on Poetry and Criticism*. London: Methuen, 1920, pp. 95-111.

[Essentially, this essay synthesizes two articles by Eliot that appeared in *TLS*, 13 November 1919, pp. 637-38, and *The Athenaeum*, 14 November 1919, pp. 1180-81, each of which reviewed Gregory Smith's *Ben Jonson* and Percy Simpson's *Ben Jonson's "Every Man in his Humour*." It has ben reprinted frequently in variously dated collections of Eliot's essays issued in numerous English and American editions. These include *Elizabethan Dramatists*, *Elizabethan Essays*, *Essays on Elizabethan Drama*, and *Selected Essays*. It appears in *Ben Jonson: A Collection of Critical Essays* pp. 14-23 (*see* 3.)]

Although they have been neglected, Jonson's works reward study. Parts of *Catiline* are praiseworthy, although on the whole it is a failure. The importance of humours theory to

Jonson's comedy has been exaggerated; more important is his "immense dramatic constructive skill." What holds his plays together is a "unity of inspiration that radiates into plot and personages alike." Although his work is "of the surface," it is not superficial, and despite the lack of a third dimension there is a power animating his characters "which comes from below the intellect." His is an art of great caricature and great humor. "The 'world' of Jonson is sufficiently large; it is a world of poetic imagination; it is sombre. He did not get the third dimension, but he was not trying to get it."

1103 ELLIS-FERMOR, UNA. The Jacobean Drama: An Interpretation. 4th ed., rev. New York: Random House, Vintage Books, 1964, pp. 44-49, 98-117, 313-15. [Originally published London: Methuen, 1936.]

Minor changes from edition to edition are noted in the prefaces. In contrast to his contemporaries, Jonson was first a moralist, then an artist and theatreman. His ethical principles not only dictated the subject matter of his plays (the morals and manners of society) but also controlled their form, the latter tendency showing especially in the use of non-dramatic materials between 1597 and 1602. In the great comedies of the middle period, however, the material is shaped by his "strong imagination . . . [and] conscious and persistent art," resulting in the nearly perfect fusion of material and form in The Alchemist.

1104 ENRIGHT, D. J. "Crime and Punishment in Ben Jonson." Scrutiny 9 (1940):231-48.

All of Jonson's major plays are satires, focus on a kind of crime and punishment, and have spiritual modesty as a major theme.

1105 FARNHAM, WILLARD. "The Medieval Comic Spirit in the English Renaissance," in Joseph Quincy Adams Memorial Studies. Edited by James G. McManaway, Giles E. Dawson, and Edwin E. Willoughby. Washington: The Folger Shakespeare Library, 1948, pp. 429-38.

Writers and characters of the medieval period enjoyed the things and desires of the flesh, but kept them subservient to those of the mind and spirit. The figures of folly which Jonson helped to introduce assist in the death of this comic spirit. The later works consider folly as a disease or an object for the entertainment of superior persons.

1106 FISHER, W. "Tieck als Ben Jonson-Philologe." Shakespeare-Jahrbuch 62 (1926):117-31.
Annotates Ludwig Tieck's notes on the 1816 Gifford edition of Jonson's works. Considers Tieck to have been one of the best Jonson interpreters of his time (late 18th-early 19th centuries), or at any rate the best Jonson scholar in Germany then.

1107 FOAKES, R. A. "The Player's Passion: Some Notes on Elizabethan Psychology and Acting." E&S NS 7 (1954):62-77.
Examines behavior, "personality," convention, and character development and provides discussions of acting by contemporary writers. Jonson's condemnation of those who "over-act prodigiously" is cited from The Staple of News.

1108 FORSYTHE, ROBERT S. "Comic Effects in Elizabethan Drama." NDQ 17 (1927):266-92, passim.
Includes several of Jonson's comedies in a general survey of comic uses of situation, character, dialogue, and a miscellaneous group of devices, including topical satire.

1109 FRASER, RUSSELL. "Elizabethan Drama and the Art of Abstraction." CompD 2 (1968):73-82.
The rationalizing tendency of the English Renaissance is best seen in Jonson, in whom "the abstracting impulse governs to present the Naked Truth. It is in response to that impulse that he formulates his Theory of Humours." The two-dimensional, unvarying, mechanical behavior of his humours characters is not psychologically determined "in the grain." Rather, it results from their misuse of reason and free will. Shadwell was especially influenced by Jonson's practice of conceiving of characters as abstractions.

1110 FREEBURG, VICTOR OSCAR. Disguise Plots in Elizabethan Drama: A Study in Stage Tradition. New York: Benjamin Blom, 1965. 250 pp., passim. [Originally published New York: Columbia University Press, 1915.]
Jonson employed the rich dramatic technique of disguise in a variety of plays, most notably The Alchemist, The New Inn, The Staple of News, and Epicoene. The latter may be the first instance of an unforeseen resolution of plot by revelation of disguise.

1111 FRENCH, JOHN THATCHER. "Ben Jonson: His Aesthetic of Relief." TSLL 10 (1968):161-75.
In his effort to help cure the world's sicknesses by means of his plays, Jonson appropriates "the ancient Greek

concept of physical purgation as a form of relief (literal and figurative). . . ."

1112 FRIEDLAND, LOUIS SIGMUND. "The Dramatic Unities in England." JEGP 10 (1911):56-89.

The two "minor unities" (time and place) achieved major importance in the Italian Renaissance. Under the influence of Scaliger and Castelvetro, rigid adherence to them became standard critical dogma. Aristotle's "major unity" (action) was virtually neglected. Sidney's Apology was the link between Italian critical theory and Jonson's. In England, before 1650, only Jonson's work shows more than tentative and casual treatment of the unities. "Jonson argued for the rules so often and at such length, that the sum of his criticism on the question is the most considerable prior to Dryden." "Jonson is a classicist as far as the minor unities are concerned," but in his dramatic practice the unity of action is usurped by the "unity of persons." This is a version of "decorum," a doctrine universally promulgated, whereas the unities were largely neglected by playwrights. Jonson, a "reactionary spirit," managed to influence only a few of his contemporaries, but in the later 17th century his importance as a model for employing the unities was recognized.

1113 FRYE, NORTHROP. Anatomy of Criticism: Four Essays. Princeton: Princeton University Press, 1957, pp. 45, 48, 58, 84, 164-80 passim, 228.

Classifying fiction by the hero's power of action, Frye establishes modes of drama: high mimetic, low mimetic, and ironic. Jonson exhibits arrogance in his ironic comedy. Every Man in his Humour, The Alchemist, and Volpone provide good illustrations both of major types of comic figures (alazons or imposters, eirons or self-deprecators, and buffoons) and of specific phases of comedy. The dramatic function of the humours character is "to express a state of what might be called ritual bondage."

1114 _____. "The Argument of Comedy." EIE, 1948, pp. 58-73. [Reprinted in Comedy: Plays, Theory, and Criticism. Edited by Marvin Felheim. New York: Harcourt Brace and World, 1962, pp. 236-41.]

The resolutions of Volpone and The Alchemist follow the laws of comic form, regardless of the moral quality of the society presented. However, whereas The Alchemist is "more concentrated comedy [,] Volpone is starting to move toward tragedy, toward the vision of a greatness which develops hybris and catastrophe." Jonson is the only Elizabethan who wrote what might be called New Comedy.

1115 GARDINER, JUDITH K., and EPP, SUSANNA S. "Ben Jonson's Social Attitudes: A Statistical Analysis." *CompD* 9 (1975):68-86.

On the basis of a computer-assisted statistical study of 223 characters in Jonson's comedies, concludes that, in these plays, Jonson is persistently and vehemently negative toward about 90% of the "common" class, favorable to about 50% of the gentry, and negative toward titled figures by a ratio of about two to one. These attitudes do not vary significantly for the two sexes.

1116 GIANAKARIS, CONSTANTINE J. "The Humanism of Ben Jonson." *CLAJ* 14 (1970):115-26.

Trained in the humanist tradition, Jonson tended to overinterpret classical pronouncements on the function of poetry and rhetoric, and thus allowed an insistent didacticism to color much of his work, a practice strengthened by his stoical and moralistic views. Overt didacticism harms *Every Man out of his Humour*, *Cynthia's Revels*, *Poetaster*, and most of the last comedies. The closer he came to Horace's original intention, which is to provide audiences with ethical criteria from which they can form judgments, the more successful Jonson's comedies were, as for example *Epicoene*, *The Alchemist*, *Bartholomew Fair*, and, to a great degree, *Volpone*.

1117 GOTTWALD, MARIA. "Ben Jonson's Theory of Comedy." *GW* 10 (1966):31-53.

Throughout his dramas Jonson maintained his definition of comedy: an imitation of life, a mirror of manners, an image of truth meant to profit and delight. He frequently defined terms so as to link comedy and satire. Early plays emphasize profit/instruction more than later works. Although not an original thinker, Jonson developed a fairly comprehensive theory of comedy which is polemic, critical, apologetic, and prescriptive.

1118 GREENE, THOMAS M. "Ben Jonson and the Centered Self." *SEL* 10 (1970):325-48.

English version of his "Ben Jonson e l'io accentrato." (*See* 1119.)

Presents the images of circle and center as "an organizing principle of all Ben Jonson's work. The circle (suggesting perfection, harmony, equilibrium in cosmos, society, household, soul) is doubled by the center (suggesting governor, king, house, inner self)." The masques, which assume the existence of an order, evince the images as achieved ideals, but in his other works the circle is broken.

General Topics

1119 _____. "Ben Jonson e l'io accentrato." SCr 3 (1969):236-62. (See 1118.)

1120 GREENFIELD, THELMA N. The Induction in Elizabethan Drama. Eugene: University of Oregon Books, 1969. 189 pp.
Examines plays with inductions and divides these into four categories. Jonson's The Devil is an Ass falls under the heading "Occasional Induction." Other comedies are discussed under "Critical Induction": Every Man out of his Humour, Cynthia's Revels, Poetaster, Bartholomew Fair, The Staple of News, and The Magnetic Lady.

1121 GREG, W. W. "The Riddle of Jonson's Chronology." Library 4th Series 6 (1926):340-47.
Before 1620 Jonson generally used "Calendar dating" (beginning the year with January 1); after 1620 he generally used "Legal dating" (beginning the year with March 25).

1122 GRIERSON, H. J. C. "Criticism and Creation: Their Interactions." E&S 29 (1944):7-29.
Unlike other Renaissance dramatists, Jonson cared for rules but did not bind himself to observe the unities. He differs from Shakespeare mainly by the sustained dignity of his tragic scenes. His plays have had minimal effects on English drama.

1123 HARBAGE, ALFRED. Shakespeare and the Rival Traditions. New York: Macmillan, 1952. 411 pp., passim. [Reprint. Bloomington: Indiana University Press, 1970.]
Distinguishes between the popular and coterie theatre of Shakespeare's time by pointing out that the former represented the taste and outlook of the public and produced plays characterized by optimism, good feeling, and delight in concord, while the private and higher-priced theatres attracted a more sophisticated audience and produced the less representative kind of drama, characterized by cynicism, lewdness, and sensationalism. The War of the Theatres was a conflict between rival traditions. A mark of the playwrights of the coterie theatre is their lack of religious sentiment and inspirational use of Christianity. The alternate view of life which was recognized and respected in the Renaissance, the Stoic, is exemplified by Jonson's Crites (Cynthia's Revels) and Horace (Poetaster); but Stoicism, too, held only superficial sway in the coterie drama. Harbage finds Jonson's comedies "soulless, and of only the slightest ethical interest." The philosophical stance of coterie drama "denied man the dignity

for the truly tragic and the complexity for the truly humorous." An appendix presents a list of the plays in the public and private theatres from 1560 to 1613.

1124 HARRISON, G. B. "Ben Jonson," in his Elizabethan Plays and Players. London: George Routledge and Sons, 1940, pp. 168-90. [Reprint. Ann Arbor, University of Michigan Press, 1956; Folcroft, Pa.: Folcroft Library Editions, 1978.]

Reproduces primary material referring to Jonson from Henslowe's Diary, Fuller's Worthies of England, Aubrey's Brief Lives, Drummond's Conversations, and Henslowe's letter to Edward Alleyn, and refers to other contemporary works such as Dekker's Satiromastix and Nashe's writings. Occasionally points out factual errors in the sources. Interjects a brief critical appraisal of Every Man in his Humour.

1125 _____. Shakespeare's Fellows: Being a Brief Chronicle of the Shakespearean Age. London: John Lane, 1923, pp. 94-103, 136-40, 153-57. [Reprint. Folcroft, Pa.: Folcroft Library Editions, 1978.]

Provides "a background for the study of the early dramatists," and information about Jonson's personal and professional life. The events of the Poetomachia are judiciously deduced from the plays involved in the War.

1126 HART, ALFRED. "Acting Versions of Elizabethan Plays." RES 10 (1934):1-28.

Argues that the longer plays of Shakespeare and Jonson were not presented in full on the Elizabethan stage.

1127 _____. "The Length of Elizabethan and Jacobean Plays," RES 8 (1932):139-54.

Disproves the belief generally held by scholars that the average length of Elizabethan plays was 3,000 lines. A study of all extant plays written or acted 1594-1616 leads to the following conclusions: plays of 3,000 lines and more were rarely written except by Jonson or Shakespeare. Jonson's plays average nearly 3,580 lines. The average for all plays except Jonson's is 2,490 lines.

1128 _____. "The Time Allotted for Representation of Elizabethan and Jacobean Plays." RES 8 (1932):395-413.

Quotes from Shakespeare, Jonson, Fletcher, Beaumont, and others, who speak of "two hours" as the time needed for the representation of a play. Judging from the length of time needed to utter words of blank verse and other tests, concludes that the average length of the plays acted in two hours was about 2,300 lines.

Bibliography

General Topics

1129 HAYS, H. R. "Satire and Identification: An Introduction to Ben Jonson." *Kenyon Review* 19 (1957):267-83.

Explains prejudices which can prevent audiences from understanding and appreciating Jonson's comedies. Unlike Shakespeare, Jonson employs caricature in his character development and avoids suspense in his plots. Many of the moral issues presented remain today. *The Alchemist* and *Bartholomew Fair* should appeal to modern audiences. The Stanislavski school of acting works against Jonsonian comedy, which must be projected.

1130 HEDRICK, DON K. "Cooking for the Anthropophagi: Jonson and His Audience." *SEL* 17 (1977):233-47.

A fairly popular topic in Jonson's day, cannibalism appears often in his plays through puns and offhand remarks, stage devices and direct reference. The subject provides a complex of ideas related to Jonson's associations with his audience. He moves from the metaphor of "poetry is food" to "poetry making is cooking"; the poet must know what will delight the taste of his audience. Distinguishing between "taste" and "delight," Jonson employs different approaches and serves, at different times, as cook rather than as critic.

1131 HEFFNER, RAY L., JR. "Unifying Symbols in the Comedy of Ben Jonson," in *English Stage Comedy*. Edited by W. K. Wimsatt. EIE, 1954. New York: Columbia University Press, 1955, pp. 74-97. [Reprinted in *Elizabethan Drama: Modern Essays in Criticism*. Edited by Ralph J. Kaufmann. New York: Oxford University Press, 1961, pp. 170-86; *Shakespeare's Contemporaries*. Edited by Max Bluestone and Norman Rabkin. Englewood Cliffs, N.J.: Prentice-Hall, 1961, pp. 196-202; Ben Jonson: *A Collection of Critical Essays*, pp. 133-46 (*see* 3.)]

Defines the "unity of inspiration" which T. S. Eliot and other critics have found in Jonson's comedy. Despite the differences in structure, a thematic unity, which is expressed in similar symbolic devices, is evident in the plays, even those as divergent as *Epicoene* and *Bartholomew Fair*. In each of his major plays Jonson explores an idea or a cluster of related ideas through action and characters that exaggerate human folly. The result is not a fully developed plot but an exaggerated comic conceit.

1132 HENINGER, S. K., JR. "Ben Jonson," in his *A Handbook of Renaissance Meteorology, With Particular Reference to Elizabethan and Jacobean Literature*. Durham, N.C.: Duke University Press, 1960, pp. 179-82. [Reprint. New York: Greenwood Press, 1968.]

Meteorology, the study of sublunary occurrences, found a place in Jonson's plays in reference to and in parodies of pseudosciences and in the uses of poetical conventions.

1133 HERRINGTON, H. W. "Witchcraft and Magic in the Elizabethan Drama." JAF 32 (1919):447-85.

Witchcraft appears as an important dramatic motif only late in the Elizabethan period, and is evidenced through the use of witches, fairies, magicians, devils, and similar figures. Jonson's burlesque treatment of the "Queen of Fairy" in The Alchemist may be regarded as the most important use of the fairy theme in the later period. Devils appear in The Devil is an Ass. The Alchemist, with its vulgar practitioners of the supernatural, follows the realistic trend in its treatment of rogues. Realism also appears in the imposture in the scene of possession in Volpone, V.viii, and the counterfeit attack of Fitzdottrel in The Devil is an Ass, V.viii. A Tale of a Tub, IV.v, employs the haunted house theme.

1134 HETZEL, VIRGIL B. "The Dedication of Tudor and Stuart Plays," in Studies in English Language and Literature Presented to Professor Dr. Karl Brunner on the Occasion of His Seventieth Birthday. Edited by Siegfried Korninger. Wiener Beiträge zur Englischen Philologie, 65. Vienna, Stuttgart: Wilhelm Braumüller, 1957, pp. 74-86.

Attempting to increase the respectability of ordinary stage plays, Jonson used private inscriptions long before he openly sought patronage for his dramas and was very influential in developing the practice of dedicating plays. Catiline contains his first public appeal to a patron.

1135 HIBBARD, G. R. "Ben Jonson and Human Nature," in A Celebration of Ben Jonson (1973), pp. 55-181. (See 5.)

The motivation of the characters in Jonson's plays is not merely "inordinate desire" (the view of Professor Knights), but "'idées fixes' in the form of that 'great thought' which keeps back the information, brought by the senses, from reaching the reason to which those senses are no longer subject, and as a consequence, the invasion of the mind by the passions, leading to a blinding of the mental faculties."

1136 HOLDEN, WILLIAM P. Anti-Puritan Satire, 1572-1642. Yale Studies in English, 126. New Haven: Yale University Press, 1954. 177 pp., passim.

Jonson ranks among the playwrights bringing anti-Puritan stage satire to its climax. The Alchemist manipulates characters in designed settings and plays on the theme of human vanity. Bartholomew Fair offers his most complex, sharply delineated presentation, with Busy as an enduring symbol of the Puritan. Unlike those who focused on the sexuality of stage Puritans, Jonson emphasized their self-righteousness and hypocrisy. Moderation is proposed as a cure.

1137 HONIG, EDWIN. "Notes on Satire in Swift and Jonson." New Mexico Quarterly 18 (1948):156-63.

Creating literary works evidencing a right moral view of life, the writers seem closest in their almost psychopathic obsession with the moral abnormalities which separate men from their fellows. This type of distancing is most evident in their genius for distortion in characterization. In Swift, these distortions are elaborate exaggerations of real defects present in all men, but Jonson "depends upon a social elaboration of the practical joke, a caustic form of burlesque intrigue, wherein the observed normal sympathies for the dupe are transferred to the deceiver, who, it turns out, is himself the greater dupe."

1138 HOY, CYRUS H. The Hyacinth Room; An Investigation into the Nature of Comedy, Tragedy, & Tragicomedy. New York: Alfred A. Knopf, 1964, pp. 127-41, 172-74.

Both The Alchemist and Volpone depend upon and illustrate the theme of transvaluation. Surly and Sir Epicure Mammon, conversing about the need for holiness in relation to the philosopher's stone, illustrate the distance between alchemy as a symbol of the spiritual quest and alchemy as a tool for crime. The highly ironic scene emphasizes that nothing is exempt from the vulgar touch. Volpone's language points to transvaluations and to the strong contrast between the inheritance of the faithful (Christ) and that of the gulls. The play rests on I.ii.66-67, as all scramble for a self-designed paradise. Study of Volpone and Tartuffe indicates the association of pleasure with disguise, and opulent language with depraved intentions.

1139 HUSSEY, MAURICE. The World of Shakespeare and His Contemporaries: A Visual Approach. London: Heinemann; New York: Viking Press, 1971, pp. 108-21.

Jonson designed the title page of Works (1616) as a schema of his dramatic writing and a re-statement of his doctrine of dramatic decorum. The Alchemist and Bartholomew Fair have many parallels with the visual arts, particularly with Brueghel and the Mannerist tradition.

1140 HUXLEY, ALDOUS. "Ben Jonson," in his On the Margin. New York: George H. Doran, 1923, pp. 177-93. [Reprint. London: Chatto and Windus, 1971.]
Develops the thesis: "we find ourself unable to give any very glowing account of Ben or his greatness."

1141 INGLIS, FRED. "Classicism and Poetic Drama." EIC 16 (1966): 154-69.
Jonson is a chief example of the classically trained writer whose ratiocinative habit of mind limits his poetic achievement, preventing him from exploring the "deeper springs in life" even though possessing a clarity of moral vision. Jonson's failure to write "a great and entire tragedy" is related to a "Racinian" dominance of the critical over the creative power.

1142 IRMSCHER, JOHANNES. "Die Klassische Bildung zur Zeit Ben Jonsons." SJW 109 (1973):51-55.
Discusses the development of the humanist tradition in England and its influence on Jonson.

1143 JACKSON, GABRIELE BERNHARD. "Structural Interplay in Ben Jonson's Drama," in Two Renaissance Mythmakers: Christopher Marlowe and Ben Jonson (1977), pp. 113-45. (See 28.)
Comedy and tragedy offer opposed perspectives of an action, not different types of actions. Each perspective deals with fantasy. In comedy, the central character acts out his fantasy in the real world; in tragedy, the fantasy becomes realized and the character collapses. Study of Volpone, The Alchemist, and Bartholomew Fair illustrates the dialectical relationship of fantasy and counterfantasy in an attempt to define the space of reality in each play. The sexual angle of vision proves particularly useful in determining the basic fantasies.

1144 JACQUOT, JEAN. "Le repertoire des compagnies d'enfants à Londres (1600-1610). Essai d'interprétation socio-dramaturgique." Dramaturgie et Société: Rapports entre l'oeuvre théâtrale, son interprétation et son public aux XVIe et XVIIe siècles. Vol. 2. Edited by Jean Jacquot et al. Paris: Editions du Centre National de la Recherche Scientifique, 1968, 729-82.
Discusses Jonson's connections with the children's companies; his relationships with other playwrights and his attitudes towards them and the public; the characteristics of his comedies; his use of music; and the question of the accuracy with which his and other plays written for the children's companies reflect their society. Jonson was

highly independent and capable of some degree of ironic detachment from self.

1145 JAMIESON, MICHAEL. "Introduction," in his Three Comedies: "Volpone," "The Alchemist," "Bartholomew Fair." Harmondsworth: Penguin Books, 1966, pp. 7-34.
The plays are Jonson's best, with strong theatrical possibilities. Jonson's chief virtues are construction, presentation of obsessed characters, and language.
The book provides an introduction to each play, giving stage history and a summary of the location and time scheme. "A Note on Alchemy" is included.

1146 JENSEN, EJNER J., and BEAURLINE, L. A. "L. A. Beaurline and the Illusion of Completeness." PMLA 86 (1971):121-27.
Jensen claims that Beaurline's "Ben Jonson and the Illusion of Completeness" (see 1065) is "speculation disguised as scholarship, critical fancy dressed in the latest learned fashion." Jensen objects on two main points: he argues that Beaurline does not prove that the intellectual concept of "setting . . . limits to a composition" was well established nor does he "document its existence." Beaurline in his reply offers supporting evidence for his interpretation of "the Baconian idea." Jensen finds fault with the methodology and several of the conclusions of Beaurline's reply. Beaurline concludes that he and Jensen disagree on their general assumptions about literary history; he discusses these assumptions.

1147 JOHANSSON, BERTIL. Law and Lawyers in Elizabethan England as Evidenced in the Plays of Ben Jonson and Thomas Middleton. Stockholm Studies in English, 18. Stockholm: Almqvist and Wiksell, 1967. 65 pp.
A compilation of documents concerning law, examples of legal practice in Elizabethan England, and evidence in the plays regarding such practice.

1148 JOHNSON, EDGAR. "Ben Jonson's Terrifying Caricatures of Reality," in his A Treasury of Satire. New York: Simon and Schuster, 1945, pp. 181-83.
In contrast to Shakespeare, Jonson focuses almost totally on highly limited aspects of his characters, and emphasizes the venality and baseness of the age. He exhibits Rabelais's toughness without his geniality.

1149 JONAS, LEAH. The Divine Science: The Aesthetic of Some Representative Seventeenth-Century English Poets. Columbia University Studies in English and Comparative Literature, 151. New York: Columbia University Press, 1940, pp. 16-46. [Reprint. New York: Octagon Books, 1973.]

Jonson's plays effectively reveal his theory of poetry, particularly his scorn for poetasters and those seeking rewards, his use of translation, the importance of the classics for dramatic formulae, and the functions of comedy.

1150 KAY, W. DAVID. "The Shaping of Ben Jonson's Career: A Reexamination of Facts and Problems." MP 67 (1970):224-37.

Disputes the common view of literary historians who have "depicted Ben Jonson's career as . . . a sequence of events marked both by meteoric success and by resounding failure, by plays which met with public indifference or hostility and by those which decisively altered the mode of comedy dominant in his age." Concludes that The Case Is Altered, not Every Man in his Humour, was Jonson's first popular play. There is no evidence to support the assumptions of modern literary historians regarding the sudden success of Every Man in his Humour; it merely established further Jonson's identity as a serious playwright. Every Man out of his Humour was intended for discriminating spectators or readers, not for those who considered comedy merely an amusing pastime. Jonson knew he would find this audience not in the popular but in the private theatre, so he wrote Cynthia's Revels for the Blackfriars Theatre.

1151 KERNAN, ALVIN B. "Alchemy and Acting: The Major Plays of Ben Jonson." SLitI 6 (April 1973):1-22. (See 40.)

The folly of the major plays' characters is alchemy, with each fool trying to overleap nature and change his nothingness to gold. Beginning with Sejanus, Jonson became increasingly respectful of folly's power and less certain of society's ability to control it.

1152 _____. The Cankered Muse: Satire of the English Renaissance. Yale Studies in English, 142. New Haven: Yale University Press, 1959. 261 pp., passim. [Reprint. Hamden, Conn.: The Shoe String Press, Archon Books, 1976.]

Jonson participated in carrying the conventions of English satire from the printed page into the theatre. In many plays, the employment of a variety of satiric types accompanies an inquiry into the nature of satire itself. Moving beyond formal satire, Jonson came to stress the scene rather than the satirist, in the Menippean manner. The comedies are all "a process of alchemy" in which characters attempt to transform themselves into higher beings.

Jonson exposes each fool through his use or misuse of language and, by indirectly showing these characters as perverted, establishes the moral norms of Nature and society. His practice after 1604 became the pattern for comical satire for a generation.

1153 _____. The Plot of Satire. New Haven: Yale University Press, 1965, pp. 4, 14, 24, 38, 52, 73, 83, 103, 121-42, 172, 221, 223.

Applies a theory of satire to specific works, including Volpone. Names art and morality as "the two poles of satire." In analyzing the rhetoric of satire, concludes that the satirist's practice is to take "a figure which would be a stylistic fault if used unselfconsciously and . . . to [employ] it to dramatize rhetorically some aspect of dullness." Agrees with Pope who, in Peri Bathous, identifies three classes of such figures as satiric rhetoric: "the confusing, the magnifying, and the diminishing." These figures constitute in part the major actions of dullness which generate the plot of satire, "plot" being defined, not in Aristotelian terms, but as "any action in which there is a shift of position or scene." In a chapter on Volpone (an abridgement of the introduction to his edition of the play, see 452), Kernan sees the action of the plot as "rising and falling."

*1154 KIM, SEYONG. "Ben Jonson the Playwright." English Language and Literature (English Literary Society of Korea, Seoul) No. 5 (1958):28-50.

1155 KIRSCH, ARTHUR C. "A Caroline Commentary on the Drama." MP 66 (1969):256-61.

Transcribes a commonplace book compiled by Abraham Wright, an Anglican divine, in approximately 1640, containing critical comments on twenty-eight plays, among them The Staple of News and Bartholomew Fair. Comments on the importance of Wright's reflections: "He mirrors perfectly the critical assumptions and judgments of his contemporaries, and his comments thus provide exceptionally clear revelations of Caroline dramatic taste. . . ."

1156 KLEIN, DAVID. The Elizabethan Dramatists as Critics. New York: Philosophical Library, 1963. 420 pp., passim. [Reprint. New York: Greenwood Press, 1968.]

Excerpts from a cross-section of Jonson's plays present his critical views on literature and its demands on both writers and readers.

1157 KNIGHT, W. NICHOLAS. "Equity and Mercy in English Law and Drama (1405-1641)." CompD 6 (1971):51-67.

The development of the justice-figure in Jonson's plays reveals the decadence of the judicial concepts of equity and mercy. During the reign of Elizabeth, such figures (e.g., Justice Clement) are morally powerful. After her death, representatives of the law "become tainted by moral corruption" (Sejanus, Volpone). "The judicial representative, or figure functioning in a similar capacity, is faked in Epicene . . . bribed in The Alchemist . . . and foiled in Bartholomew Fair." In later plays, they are fools and crooks (The Devil is an Ass, The Staple of News).

1158 _____. Shakespeare's Hidden Life: Shakespeare at the Law 1585-1595. New York: Mason & Lipscomb, 1973, pp. 159, 175, 183.

"Synderisis," one of the inkhorn terms ridiculed in Every Man out of his Humour (III.iv), is taken from William West's treatise, Symboleography (1594). In 1594 Twelfth Night was selected over Cynthia's Revels for performance at the Inns of Court. A warrant issued against Shakespeare in 1596 is glanced at in Every Man in his Humour.

1159 KNIGHTS, L. C. "Education and the Drama in the Age of Shakespeare." Criterion 11 (1932):599-625.

Describes the type of audience for whom Jonson was writing, most of whom would have had a good grammar school or private school education, and thus would have read Latin and Greek classics and been trained in rhetoric and oration. This would have equipped them for intelligent understanding of the language of the drama.

1160 KNOWLTON, EDGAR C. "The Plots of Ben Jonson." MLN 44 (1929): 77-86.

Jonson built a formula for a dramatic plot which he employed with variation from the writing of his first humour play to the writing of The Magnetic Lady (1632). Several features of his plots reflect the influence of the Elizabethan stage. Because of the division of the plot into five acts, Elizabethan dramatists often found difficulty with the fourth act: since the turning point came in the third act, the catastrophe had to be delayed until the fifth act. Jonson met the problem and also brought about the assemblage of the characters by means of the following formula: in the first and second acts he developed thoroughly the exposition of characters and situation; the third act was devoted to action and the fourth to a solution of the intrigue of the characters and to reform or exposure.

General Topics

1161 KOSSICK, SHIRLEY. "Ben Jonson: Some Aspects of his Life and Work." UES 11 (March 1973):4-11.
Discusses Jonson's work in relation to certain of his attributes and interests: his quick temper, his knowledge of the classics and of contemporary life, his moral purposes. Jonson is not a cynic, but rather cares about humanity.

1162 KREIDER, PAUL V. Elizabethan Comic Character Conventions as Revealed in the Comedies of George Chapman. University of Michigan Publications. Language and Literature, 17. Ann Arbor: University of Michigan Press, 1935, pp. 10, 17-18, 46, 145-46, 150, 168-76, passim. [Reprint. New York: Octagon Books, 1975.]
A typical Elizabethan dramatist, Chapman used conventional techniques for character identification and exposition. Many appear in Jonson's comedies: direct self-identification, direct self-characterization, preliminary direct characterization, direct characterization immediately preceding first appearance, direct characterization during or subsequent to first appearance, narrative for purposes of characterization, epithetic direct characterization, and identification of disguised figures.

1163 KRISHNAMURTHI, M. G. "The Ethical Basis of Ben Jonson's Plays." JMSUB 11 (1962):139-57.
Traces Jonson's basic attitudes in five of the comedies and concludes that he presents a highly ethical view of life, labeled "classical." Studies Jonson's view of greed in Volpone, greed and lust in The Alchemist, the lack of self-knowledge as the source of follies in Bartholomew Fair, and greed in Poetaster and The Staple of News.

1164 LANGSAM, G. GEOFFREY. Martial Books and Tudor Verse. New York: King's Crown Press (Columbia University), 1951, pp. 105-12.
A rich supply of military books enabled the 16th-century theatre-goer and reader to notice and enjoy military allusions popular in the drama. Jonson presented the miles gloriosus in Bobadill and Brainworm.

1165 LAWRENCE, W. J. "The Dedication of Early English Plays." Life and Letters 3 (July 1929):30-44.
Dedicating "common" plays was highly unfashionable and of the utmost rarity until Jonson, whose prestige was very great in his middle period, created a precedent in 1607 by dedicating Volpone to the Universities, and then, in his first public dedication to a single individual, Catiline to the Earl of Pembroke in 1611. Jonson was "the first

dramatist permitted to inscribe an ordinary theatre piece to a reigning English monarch," Bartholomew Fair in 1614. In the dedication to Camden of Every Man in his Humour (Works, 1616), Jonson acknowledged that the practice was not universally deemed appropriate.

1166 _____. "Double Titles in Early English Drama." Criterion 8 (1928):35-46.

Although it is possible that some double-titled Elizabethan plays acquired their second titles upon revival, there can be little doubt that Cynthia's Revels, or The Fountain of Self-Love, and Poetaster, or The Arraignment, both had double titles when first performed. Volpone and Epicoene, like several other plays of the period, eventually became known primarily by their second titles: The Fox and The Silent Woman.

1167 _____. Those Nut-Cracking Elizabethans: Studies of the Early Theatre and Drama. London: Argonaut Press, 1935, pp. 3, 12, 13, 14, 47, 119, 144-47, 182-83, 185, 192. [Reprint. Ann Arbor, Mich.: University Microfilms, 1975.]

Cites examples from Jonson's plays of several minor Elizabethan theatrical conventions.

1168 LECOCQ, LOUIS. "Le théâtre de Blackfriars de 1596 à 1606." Dramaturgie et Société: Rapports entre l'oeuvre théâtrale, son interprétation et son public aux XVIe et XVIIe siècles. Vol. 2. Edited by Jean Jacquot et al. Paris: Editions du Centre National de la Recherche Scientifique, 1968, 675-704.

The fact that Cynthia's Revels was one of the first plays performed at the reopened Blackfriars in 1601 possibly means that the Queen herself authorized the reopening. Eastward Ho was among the satirical plays contributing to the closing of Blackfriars in 1608. Jonson's condemnation of The Spanish Tragedy in Cynthia's Revels suggests that the private theatres constituted an intellectual coterie, a "theatre of authors."

1169 LEECH, CLIFFORD. "The Incredibility of Jonsonian Comedy," in A Celebration of Ben Jonson (1973), pp. 3-25. (See 5.)

Jonson's dramas present familiar scenes, but in breathtaking ways which customarily defy belief and create shock. In true comic tradition they are usually self-contained and depend on varied restrictions. Jonson worked himself free from the constraints of the humours theory in Every Man out of his Humour but returned to the technique in The Magnetic Lady.

General Topics

1170 _____. "Pacifism in Caroline Drama." DUJ 1 (1939):126-36.
Jonson is witness to the "deteriorating status of military honour" in the Caroline period. Lovel's idealistic discourse on valor in The New Inn (1629) is ludicrously parodied by Sir Diaphanous Silkworm in The Magnetic Lady (1632). "This may be Jonson's way of showing that the quality of valour depends on the man who uses it, but it is tempting to believe that the change is more than that, that Jonson has come to share the growing temper of his age, to question the goodness of a gentleman's proudest property."

1171 LEGGATT, ALEXANDER. Citizen Comedy in the Age of Shakespeare. Toronto and Buffalo: University of Toronto Press, 1973, pp. 27-28, 37-39, 44-45, 74-77, 87-90, 143-46.
Studies comedies dated between 1585 and 1625 dealing with a middle-class milieu and set in London. Examines Jonson's comedies under the following topics: The Staple of News (money as "an idol and a slave" and the prodigal), Bartholomew Fair and The Alchemist (the comedy of intrigue), Every Man out of his Humour and Epicoene (disruption of husband-wife relations), and The Alchemist and The Devil is an Ass (adultery).

1172 LENNAM, T. N. S. "Sir Edward Dering's Collection of Playbooks, 1619-1624." SQ 16 (1965):145-53.
The record shows Sir Edward Dering's expenses incurred in attending the theatre, in purchasing play books (at least 221), and in binding some of them. Only two playwrights are mentioned: Shakespeare and Jonson.

1173 LEVIN, HARRY. "Introduction," in his Ben Jonson: Selected Works. New York: Random House, 1938, pp. 1-36. [Reprinted in his Grounds for Comparison. Cambridge, Mass.: Harvard University Press, 1972, pp. 183-206, and in Ben Jonson: A Collection of Critical Essays, pp. 40-59 (see 3). Both reprints omit the first four paragraphs.]
Jonson's reputation, in decline in the last two centuries, has benefited from recent scholarship. Jonson did not write comedies simply because he had a theory of comedy; nor was he more scholar than dramatist. He was a careful craftsman who adapted both classical and native literary traditions while remaining fully aware of contemporary life. He is understood better in light of the Reformation than of the Renaissance. "For it is Jonson's career which most strongly marks the transition in English literature from sonnet to satire, from comedy of the court to comedy of the city, from poets who celebrated imaginary mistresses to poets who dedicated themselves to detraction,

from the virtuous conduct of Castiglione's Courtier to the gross etiquette of Dedekind's Grobian."

1174 _____. The Myth of the Golden Age in the Renaissance. Bloomington: University of Indiana Press, 1970, pp. 129-36. [Reprint. New York: Oxford University Press, 1972.]

By cramping people into cities in his satires, Jonson brings out the monstrous aspects of human nature. Gold, a standard means of social corruption, provides the main motivation for action in the comedies. Jonson participates in the distinction between the Golden Age and the Age of Gold.

1175 LEVIN, LAWRENCE L. "Replication as Dramatic Strategy in the Comedies of Ben Jonson." RenD NS 5 (1972):37-75.

Multiple plots interacting with the main line of action provide a major source of unity. Jonson developed the unsatisfactory fourth-act solution, with characters having renewed activity in the fifth act, and a central analogue occurring primarily in Act IV.

1176 LEVIN, RICHARD. The Multiple Plot in English Renaissance Drama. Chicago and London: The University of Chicago Press, 1971, pp. 88-90, 184-91, 202-14.

Studies "the structures and functions of the multiple plot in English Renaissance drama." Although most of Jonson's comedies are discussed, special stress is given to Eastward Ho under "three-level hierarchies" (a main plot, a subplot, and a third set of characters independent of these), The Staple of News under "equivalence plots" (multiple-plot dramas in which experiences are not obviously parallel but equivalent), and Bartholomew Fair under "the limits of multiplicity." Levin finds the structure of the latter in the division of the characters between those associated with the fair and the outsiders who visit it, and notes three parties among the visitors and the pairing off of eight visitors.

1177 _____. "Some Second Thoughts on Central Themes." MLR 67 (1972):1-10.

Cites twelve unidentified studies of Volpone to exemplify the tendency of much modern criticism to claim a single central theme for a work, and the great differences of opinion about what constitutes the central theme of a given work. The positing of increasingly inclusive abstractions (e.g., "appearance vs. reality") as central themes "draws us further and further away from the unique centre of each play," and escalates the "profundity" of the works examined. Searching for "the illusory profundity of abstract truism" prevents us from appreciating the real profundity, in the best plays, deriving from the experiences of characters who are not abstractions but "unique personalities sharing and calling out to our common humanity."

1178 _____. "Thematic Unity and the Homogenization of Character." *MLQ* 33 (1972):23-29.
Questions the usefulness of the trend, evident in criticism since the 1930s, which he calls "homogenization of character," with critics directing their analysis "to proving the essential similarity of all . . . of the major characters in a play by reducing them to a single category exemplifying the central theme." Plays should be viewed "as the dramatization of a particular moving human experience. . . ."

1179 LINDSEY, EDWIN S. "The Music in Ben Jonson's Plays." *MLN* 44 (1929):86-92.
Twenty-six songs are scattered throughout *Cynthia's Revels*, *Poetaster*, *Epicoene*, *Bartholomew Fair*, *The Devil is an Ass*, *Volpone*; main types are ballads, airs, and madrigals. Since Jonson set most of his lyrics to classical music, a genre varying more from age to age than does popular music, his songs today sound more antiquated than Shakespeare's. He used songs only for specific dramatic purposes.

1180 LITTLEWOOD, S. R. *Dramatic Criticism*. London: Sir Isaac Pitman & Sons, 1939, pp. 85, 176-77, 231.
Jonson's wealth of knowledge and choice of models make many of his plays dull. Unlike Shakespeare, he never gets near the inner heart and "had not enough of the woman in him for creation." The Prologue to *Every Man in his Humour* provides "an invaluable sidelight" on the drawbacks of his stage. *Bartholomew Fair*, valuable for its Hogarthian qualities, is one evidence that Jonson needed something concrete he could evaluate and criticize.

1181 McCLENNEN, JOSHUA. *On the Meaning and Function of Allegory in the English Renaissance*. UMCMP 6, 1947, pp. 11-12, 15-16.
In *Cynthia's Revels* the world "allegory" (V.vii.42) is used to mean "symbol." Among the many associations the word had among English Renaissance writers, "Jonson's is both mythological and astronomical." In *The Alchemist* Subtle's reference to allegory (II.iii.207) shows Jonson's familiarity with the belief that "the ancient poets concealed their wisdom from the eyes of the vulgar by means of allegories."

1182 McCOLLEY, GRANT. "The Theory of a Plurality of Worlds as a Factor in Milton's Attitude Toward the Copernican Hypothesis." MLN 47 (1932):319-25.
In the 17th century, some men, like Donne in the Anatomie, linked the Copernican hypothesis with a doctrine of plurality of worlds or systems. "In his Staple of News and News From the New World, Jonson satirizes the invention [the telescope] which had given the Copernican hypothesis such prestige as to bring upon it the official disapproval of the Roman Church."

1183 MacKENZIE, AGNES MURE. The Playgoer's Handbook to the English Renaissance Drama. London: Jonathan Cape, 1927, pp. 21, 25, 50, 67, 95, 161. [Reprint. New York: Cooper Square Publishers, 1971.]
Jonson's classicism and the impetus to follow what seemed natural to him place him, spiritually, in the 18th century. His power for abstract thought is not a virtue in his plays, which lack the humanity of Dekker's, Heywood's, and Shakespeare's. He ranks as the strongest critic-dramatist of his time.

1184 MAIN, WILLIAM W. "Dramaturgical Norms in the Elizabethan Repertory," SP 54 (1957):128-48.
Systematizes a method of analysis of plays dating 1598-1602 according to treatment, themes, and dramatic roles. Every Man out of his Humour falls under domestic plot, satiric treatment of wooing, with a gay wife who deceives her husband without viciousness. Other Jonson plays in the study include Every Man in his Humour, Cynthia's Revels, and Poetaster.

1185 MANIFOLD, J. S. The Music in English Drama from Shakespeare to Purcell. London: Rockliff, 1956, 208 pp., passim.
Surveys the use of songs, instrumental music, and references to music, in Jonson's plays.

1186 ______. "Theatre Music in the Sixteenth and Seventeenth Centuries." M&L 19 (1948):366-97.
Lists plays employing instrumental music or songs: The Alchemist, Bartholomew Fair, Cynthia's Revels, Eastward Ho, Epicoene, Every Man out of his Humour, Volpone.

1187 MARSHALL, GEOFFREY. "Comic Worlds Within Worlds." CE 32 (1971):418-27.
Argues that "comic characters are typically complete characters, psychological wholes, who inhabit complete worlds . . . usually distorted and grotesque when compared to ours, but worlds which are nevertheless whole within

themselves." Comments on Jonson's "world of heightened aural sensitivity" (Epicoene) and world of "fatal illness" (Volpone).

1188 MASON, H. A. "The Humanistic Heritage," in his Humanism and Poetry in the Early Tudor Period. New York: Barnes and Noble, 1959, pp. 255-89.
Jonson developed what existed only potentially in the works of More and Wyatt. He was indebted to Vives for his leading humanistic principles: the importance of good literature to formation of a good life, the moral purposes of literature, and the study of literature as essential for conducting life. Jonson differed from Vives on the importance and language of poetry. Mason considers Jonson a Christian humanist.

1189 MAXWELL, BALDWIN. Studies in Beaumont, Fletcher, and Massinger. Chapel Hill: University of North Carolina Press, 1939, pp. 2, 17-19, 31, 36-37, 49, 112-15. [Reprint. New York: Octagon Books, 1966.]
Although new titles were often given to old plays in order to fool the public, Jonson's use of double titles had valid purposes, usually explanatory. Notes echoes of Epicoene and The Alchemist in several plays by Beaumont and Fletcher, but suggests that Jonson borrowed lines in The New Inn from Fletcher's Love's Pilgrimage.

1190 MÉLÈSE, PIERRE. "O rare Ben Jonson!" Cahiers du Sud 10 (June 1933):183-85. (In French.)
Proud of the supremacy of his intellect, Jonson only occasionally attempted to please the general public, preferring an erudite audience. In general, his plays were not theatrical successes. He wanted to give the drama a new direction, but the Elizabethans did not care about the unities or psychological subtleties. His sharply realistic focus on the individual meant a neglect of a larger view. His characters are types, his eloquence lacks warmth, his jokes depend on sarcasm. These faults are overcome in Volpone, a great comedy sustained by a philosophy of good sense and a love of truth. He is worth consideration because he attacked disorder, hypocrisy, and ignorance.

1191 MOORE, JOHN B. The Comic and the Realistic in English Drama. Chicago: University of Chicago Press, 1925, pp. 204-09. [Reprint. New York: Russell & Russell, 1965.]
A brief treatment of Jonson's view of comedy, imitation of Latin comedy, and method of characterization.

1192 MOORE, JOHN ROBERT. "The Songs of the Public Theaters in the Time of Shakespeare." JEGP 28 (1929):166-202.

Discusses question of what actors might have played roles in Jonson's comedies that required singing, specifically The Devil is an Ass and Volpone. Notes that Eastward Ho contains parodies and echoes of popular songs, and states that Carlo Buffone's song and dance in Every Man out of his Humour were of a type that became very popular in plays later in the century. Considers unlikely the possibility that the fourth song in Volpone is meant to be sung off-stage, and the fifth spoken by Volpone rather than sung.

1193 MYERS, AARON MICHAEL. Representation and Misrepresentation of the Puritan in Elizabethan Drama. Philadelphia: University of Pennsylvania, 1931. 151 pp., passim. [Reprint. Philadelphia: R. West, 1978.]

Includes examples from Jonson in a discussion of the stage treatment of Puritan beliefs, attitudes, and behavior. The Puritan characters of The Alchemist and Bartholomew Fair are given brief individual treatment; other plays mentioned are Epicoene, The Staple of News, The Magnetic Lady, and The Sad Shepherd. Claims that "no playwright more persistently and cleverly unmasks the Puritan as a rascal" than Jonson, and that Elizabethan satire of the Puritan was generally justified, though sometimes unfair.

1194 NAKANO, YOSHIO. "Ben Jonson's Comedies." SELit 9 (1929): 256-75. (In Japanese.)

1195 NASH, RALPH. "Shylock's Wolfish Spirit." SQ 10 (1959): 125-28.

Trial and execution of both domestic and wild animals had been customary for over 1000 years, in Europe, in Jonson's times. Using traditional symbolic references, Jonson associates animals with evils in Every Man out of his Humour (I.iii.163) and Poetaster (V.iii.46-104).

1196 NAZARETH, PETER. "Aldous Huxley and his Critics." ESA 7 (1964):65-81.

Huxley is like Jonson in that he creates "two-dimensional" people, "isolates some impulses, vices, and perversions from real life and creates 'caricatures' embodying them," and "creates the positives in the reader by means of negatives."

General Topics

1197 NICOLL, ALLARDYCE. "Comedy," in his The Theory of Drama. 2d ed. [i.e., a revised and enlarged edition of An Introduction to Dramatic Theory (see 1200).] New York: Benjamin Blom, 1966, pp. 218-24. [Originally published London: G.G. Harrap, 1931.]

Jonson's great contribution to English literature was the popularization of the ancient comedy of "humours," intensified by realism and treated in a satirical spirit. Critics who claim that Jonson was the founder of the comedy of manners err; he was concerned with the follies of men or a group of men, not with social affectation.

1198 _____. "The Comedy of Satire," in his The Theatre and Dramatic Theory. New York: Barnes and Noble, 1962, pp. 126-27, passim. [Reprint. Westport, Conn.: Greenwood Press, 1978.]

Looks briefly at Jonson's satires in relation to the thesis of his book, which investigates the relationship between comic theory and the tastes of modern audiences. Concludes that Jonson's satire "is not fitted for the stage" because it is cold and didactic and presents only caricatures of men. Grants, however, that The Alchemist, because of its lively plot, does keep the spectator's interest.

1199 _____. English Drama: A Modern Viewpoint. New York: Barnes and Noble, 1968, pp. 56-74. [Reprint. Cambridge: Cambridge University Press, 1973.]

Satirical comedy and the theatre of disgust were popular about 1600-1615. Jonson's descent to personal animosities in the first genre prevents him from being a major dramatist for all time. He offers little of a constructive viewpoint in plays that are better read than seen.

1200 _____. An Introduction to Dramatic Theory. London: George G. Harrap, 1923, pp. 182-86. [Reprint. New York: B. Blom, 1966.]

Jonson's comedy of humours is not original or different from romantic comedy in its use of humour characters but in its intense realism and its satirical spirit. His comedy cannot be considered a comedy of manners, for its stress is not on manners but on natural idiosyncrasies. (See 1197.)

1201 NORTHCOTE-BADE, KIRSTY. "The Play of Illusion in Ben Jonson's Comedies." Words: Wai-te-ata Studies in Literature (Victoria University, Wellington, New Zealand), No. 2 (December 1966), pp. 82-91.

Discusses the "embodied ethic" in three comedies and its relation to the theme of deception and the development of Jonson's manipulation of his audiences' illusions.

". . . the traditional ethic of Volpone leads us to experience an unsatisfactory smugness; the semi-approval of an untraditional ethic in The Alchemist allows us some feeling of guilty pleasure; the subjective world where we are stranded at the end of Bartholomew Fair lets us either participate with a totality of engagement or reject in disenchantment."

1202 OLIPHANT, E. H. C. "Problems of Authorship in Elizabethan Dramatic Literature." MP 8 (1911):411-59.
Describes various problems inherent in determining authorship. Jonson is mentioned in various contexts. Every Woman in her Humour is ascribed to Jonson because of similarity of title to Every Man in his Humour. The problem of The Case is Altered is discussed, and Jonson's possible authorship of other plays now generally acknowledged not to be his.

1203 OUTRAM, A. E. "Time and Some Elizabethan Plays." New Oxford Outlook 2 (1934):58-80.
The use of time as an integrative element in Elizabethan drama was based upon an understanding of the theory of the psychological duration of time. Quotes briefly from The New Inn.

1204 PARFENOV, A. T. "Marlo, Šekspir, Džonson kak sovremenniki" [Marlowe, Shakespeare, Jonson as Contemporaries]. FN 17, no. 3 (1975):88-96. (In Russian.)

1205 PARKER, R. B. "The Problem of Tone in Jonson's 'Comicall Satyrs.'" HAB 28 (1977):43-64.
Every Man out of his Humour, Cynthia's Revels, and Poetaster exhibit an arrogant, autocratic, yet humorous tone owing, among other things, to their literary form, the foci of satire, and the satiric voice used. Jonson was adapting social, theatrical, and theoretical influences, including his own low social status, his mistrust of seeming, and the actors of Blackfriars. Somewhat anticipating Cavalier poetry in tone, the satire of the three plays deliberately provoked the aggressiveness of very assertive audiences, putting comedy at the service of satire and promoting comic catharsis.

1206 PARROTT, THOMAS MARC, and BALL, ROBERT HAMILTON. "Ben Jonson," in their A Short View of Elizabethan Drama. New York: Charles Scribner's Sons, 1943, pp. 126-51.
A handbook which does not pretend to present original research or criticism, its special merit is its manner of treating the dramatists and their work against the

General Topics

historical, social, and theatrical background of the time. The survey of Jonson's dramas evaluates his poetic ideal, subject matter, plot construction, characters, dialogue, and theory of humours from the viewpoint of live theatre.

1207 PARTRIDGE, EDWARD B. "Ben Jonson: The Makings of the Dramatist (1596-1602)," in Elizabethan Theatre. Stratford-upon-Avon Studies, 9. London: Edward Arnold, 1966; New York: St. Martin's Press, 1967, pp. 221-44.

Provides a close study of The Case is Altered, Every Man in his Humour, Every Man out of his Humour, Cynthia's Revels, and Poetaster. Jonson conceived the function of comedy "as derisive, not comforting, and as bracing, not relaxing"; he assumed the role of educator and enlightener of the world, but failed to develop an audience for his type of play. Early in his career he recognized as the subject matter and governing principle of his special comic world an ironic caricature of the real world. His skills in dramatic structure and in the uses of dramatic speech were already developed in the early plays.

1208 _____. "Jonson's Large and Unique View of Life," in The Elizabethan Theatre IV (1974), pp. 143-67. (See 22.)

The quality and quantity of his competition, which he recognized, perhaps shaped Jonson's genius and caused him to create "Ben Jonson, Man of Letters." Many Jonsons exist: celebrator of heroes as well as castigator of fools and rascals.

1209 _____. "The Symbolism of Clothes in Jonson's Last Plays." JEGP 56 (1957):396-409.

Jonson was sensitive to the symbolism of clothes in his early plays, but became increasingly concerned with, and changed his use of, the sartorial motif in the plays written after his return to the public theatre in 1626. Prefatory material in these later plays indicates that Jonson considers the audiences divided into scholars and groundlings, those who recognize reality and those who merely see appearances. His plays of this period also deal with characters who can and those who cannot make this distinction. The symbolism of clothes is used to make these points.

1210 PASTER, GAIL KERN. "Ben Jonson's Comedy of Limitation." SP 72 (1975):51-71.

In Jonson's four great comedies the classical unities of time and place express his vision by defining the distance between his characters' illusions and the actuality of the dramatic world in which they live. The limitations are evident also in the absence of nature imagery in the characters' language and in many characters' lack of family or existence before the immediate action of the play.

1211 PERRY, HENRY TEN EYCK. "The Revival of Classical Comedy," in his Masters of Dramatic Comedy and Their Social Themes. Cambridge, Mass.: Harvard University Press, 1939, pp. 79-116. [Reprint. Port Washington, N.Y.: Kennikat Press, 1968.]
Analyzes "social themes" in the dramas of Ben Jonson. States that "Jonson saw in the love of money one of humanity's basic weaknesses."

1212 PFISTERER, MIKLÓS. Realitás és Irrealitás Viszonya Ben Jonson Klasszikus Naturalizmusában. Budapest: Királyi Magyar Egyetemi Nyomda, 1931. 74 pp. (In Hungarian.)

1213 POTGIETER, J. T. "Ben Jonson en die leser." TvL 6 (1956): 14-23.
Jonson's attitude towards his reader has both an emotional and an intellectual basis which can be described as "tone." (In Afrikaans.)

1214 POTTS, L. J. "Ben Jonson and the Seventeenth Century." E&S NS 2 (1949):7-24.
With his grasp of the notion of eccentricity and his ability to link this with comedy, Jonson was able "to raise comedy to the level of a serious criticism of life, different in aim and character from tragedy, but not inferior."

1215 _____. "Character and Plot," in his Comedy. New York: Capricorn Books, 1966, pp. 115-24. [Originally published London and New York: Hutchinson's University Library, 1949.]
Sees as integral to comedy man's desire to measure himself against the norms set by other men and by nature and to resist the forces of destruction within himself. Disagrees with Jonson's assumption that comic situations arise only among flawed characters, and claims that the playwright, largely through the example of his own "vigorous, meaty, and often very amusing" prose and his advocacy of realism, was greatly responsible for banishing poetry from the English stage. Comedy of manners differs from comedy of humours in dealing more with behavior than with the character underlying it.

General Topics

1216 PRAZ, MARIO. Studies in Seventeenth-Century Imagery. 2d ed. Rome: Edizione di Storia e Letteratura, 1964, pp. 222-23. [Originally published London: Warburg Institute, 1939.]
English version of his Studi sul concettismo (see 1217.) Cites references to emblems and devices in Jonson's comedies.

1217 _____. Studi sul concettismo. Florence: G. C. Sansoni, 1946, pp. 295-96. [Originally published Milan: "La Cvltvra," 1934 (see 1216).]

1218 PUTNEY, RUFUS. "Jonson's Poetic Comedy." PQ 41 (1962): 188-204.
Dryden was the last critic to appreciate fully the greatness of Jonson's poetic comedy. To enjoy Jonson's poetry one must put aside the "lyrical heresy," the belief that poetry must be lyrical, and accept the dictum that "the chief business of dramatic poetry must be to express imaginatively and delightfully the thoughts and feelings of the characters. If the follies, meanness, affectations, and lesser vices of mankind provide the subject matter for comedy, then the comic poet is he who can transmute these ingredients into poetry." Jonson achieves greatness with this type of poetry in Volpone and in The Alchemist.

1219 PUTT, S. GORLEY. "The Relevance of Jacobean Drama." E&S NS 23 (1970):18-33.
Attention to the theoretical basis of Jonson's comedies tends to blind us to the liveliness of their world and its similarity to our own. Every Man in his Humour reflects a familiar conflict of old against young, and Jonson's own sympathies with "senior citizens." Epicoene creates more sympathy in the modern audience for the eccentric, "humorous" characters than for the hollow young men who set the plot in motion. Further, we share Jonson's intolerance for the Puritans, who want to put limits on society, knowing that, then as now, the "innocent silliness of temperamental and self-indulgent eccentrics" makes the world more interesting.

1220 REDDAWAY, T. F. "London and the Court." ShS 17 (1964):3-21.
Describes the rapidly growing London of Elizabethan times. Shakespeare, whose subjects were national in scope, ignored the rich life of London; Jonson, the native Londoner, drew from it copiously.

1221 REED, ROBERT R., JR. Bedlam on the Jacobean Stage. Cambridge, Mass.: Harvard University Press, 1952. 196 pp., passim. [Reprint. New York: Octagon Books, 1970.]

In examining the use of insanity as a Jacobean theatrical device, explores the influences leading to the portrayal of madness found in the drama and interprets the mad characters in the light of Elizabethan psychopathic theory. Refers to characters in Jonson's Every Man in his Humour, Every Man out of his Humour, Epicoene, Bartholomew Fair, and The Devil is an Ass.

1222 REYNOLDS, G. F. "Aims of a Popular Elizabethan Dramatist," in Renaissance Studies in Honor of Hardin Craig. Edited by Baldwin Maxwell, W. D. Briggs, Francis R. Johnson, and E. N. S. Thompson. Stanford: Stanford University Press; London: Oxford University Press, 1941, pp. 148-53. [Reprint. Norwood, Pa.: Norwood Editions, 1977.]

Jonson's "To the Readers" and prologues make clear what Elizabethan pseudo-classical dramatists were looking for. Only Dekker comes close to Jonson in offering this material; the importance of language constitutes their common concern.

1223 RIDING, LAURA. "Crime." Epilogue 2 (1936):8-56.

Notes briefly that Jonson used crime for satirical purposes only.

1224 ROBIN, P. ANSELL. Animal Lore in English Literature. London: John Murrary, 1932. 205 pp., passim. [Reprint. Philadelphia: R. West, 1976.]

Records "the many allusions in English literature to old beliefs and fancies about the animal creation" and traces the origin of these ideas. Cites use of animal lore in the following plays: The Alchemist, Volpone, Cynthia's Revels, Every Man out of his Humour, Poetaster, and The Magnetic Lady.

1225 SALESKI, R. E. "Supernatural Agents in Christian Imagery: Word Studies in Elizabethan Dramatists." JEGP 38 (1939): 431-39.

Has gathered a group of words which refer to supernatural agents in Christian imagery from the plays of Shakespeare, Greene, Jonson, Kyd, and Marlowe in order to answer the question: How much was each dramatist concerned in his plays with supernatural Christian beings? Jonson's method of using the supernatural would indicate that no actual belief in them is implied and that Jonson was consciously determined to keep religious questions off the stage.

General Topics

1226 SALOMON, BROWNELL. "Visual and Aural Signs in the Performed English Renaissance Drama." RenD NS 5 (1972):143-69.

Use of major regional dialects in the vaporous characters of Bartholomew Fair reinforces Jonson's theme of the fair as a microcosm of English appetite and quarrelsomeness. Use of commedia dell'arte in the mountebank scene of Volpone creates a unique kind of satire in English drama.

*1227 SASAYAMA, TAKASHI. "Kiritsu to Honno no aida" [Jonson's Imagination]. EigoS 116 (1970):632-34. (In Japanese.)

1228 SAVAGE, JAMES E. "Ben Jonson in Ben Jonson's Plays." UMSE 3 (1962):1-17. [Reprinted in his Ben Jonson's Comic Characters and Other Essays, pp. 126-44 (see 36).]

Jonson, who considered himself a scholar, soldier, poet, critic, and censor of morals, portrayed himself in characters reflecting his personality in the Every Man plays, Cynthia's Revels, and Poetaster. Savage calls the character speaking for and exemplifying Jonson the "Horace-character" and illustrates how each manifests qualities Jonson admired; in the Every Man plays he controls the fates of almost all other characters. Jonson abandoned the Horace-characters after Poetaster, distributing their functions in the combined actions of characters.

1229 _____. "The Formal Choruses in the Comedies of Ben Jonson." UMSE 11 (1971):11-21. [Reprinted, in expanded form, in his Ben Jonson's Basic Comic Characters (see 36).]

Formal choric groups, outside of the main action, appear in Every Man out of his Humour, The Staple of News, and The Magnetic Lady. They function chiefly, first, to interpret character, action, and even the laws of comedy to the audience and, second, to represent segments of the audience itself--both intelligent understanders and, more often, ordinary fools and those who "cannot understand a play, but would censure it."

1230 SCHELLING, FELIX E. "Jonson and the Classical and Satirical Reaction," in his English Drama. London: E. P. Dutton, 1914, pp. 148-73. [Reprint. New York: AMS Press, 1975.]

Appreciatively examines the plays as "a satirical picture of contemporary life presented vividly and amusingly," following the best classical models.

1231 SCHOENBAUM, S. "The Humorous Jonson," in The Elizabethan Theatre IV (1974), pp. 1-21. (See 22.)

Too much Jonson scholarship has been solemn pedantry. The plays encourage laughter as well as learning and have excellent comic devices.

1232 SEVERS, KENNETH. "Imagery and Drama." DUJ 41 (December 1949):24-33.

Quotes brief passages from Volpone and The Alchemist as examples of the use of iterative imagery in the "impassioned" (rather than "reflective") mode.

1233 SHAPIRO, MICHAEL. Children of the Revels; the Boy Companies of Shakespeare's Time and Their Plays. New York: Columbia University Press, 1977. 328 pp., passim.

Cynthia's Revels and Poetaster, written for the Chapel Children, began the shift of the balance between praising and abusing royal authority figures. Jonson introduced comical satire by making monarchs remote and encouraging spectators to condemn pretenders to courtliness. Returning to the public theatre with Epicoene, he continued his technique of subtly flattering the audience through the Prologue in order to prevent disruptive behaviour. This play contains his most ambitious attempts at audience control and presents the antithesis of aristocratic conduct. Unlike other dramatists writing for children, Jonson incorporated elements of neoclassical comedies and Christian Terence (The Case Is Altered).

1234 SHARPE, ROBERT BOIES. "Jonson's 'Execration' and Chapman's 'Invective': Their Place in Their Authors' Rivalry." SP 42 (1945):555-63. [Appeared concurrently in Studies in Language and Literature. University of North Carolina Sesquicentennial Publications. Chapel Hill: University of North Carolina Press, 1945, pp. 177-85.]

The "Invective" suggests a long-lasting rivalry between Jonson and Chapman as playwrights that might have begun around or before 1598.

1235 SIMPSON, EVELYN M. "Jonson and Dickens: A Study in the Comic Genius of London." E&S 39 (1943):82-92.

The plays of Jonson and the novels of Dickens evince a fascination with London. In Every Man in his Humour, The Alchemist, Epicoene, and especially Bartholomew Fair, Jonson presents with great gusto a satirist's view of London. Neither author could create attractive heroines; however, both could create outstanding female minor comic characters.

1236 SIMPSON, PERCY. "The Art of Ben Jonson." E&S 30 (1944):35-49. [Reprinted in his Studies in Elizabethan Drama. Oxford: Clarendon Press, 1955, pp. 112-30. Reprint. Philadelphia: R. West, 1978.]

Study of Jonson's dramatic canon against his own prescriptions shows that he followed much of his own advice.

General Topics

Limitations exist in his humours theory and his presentation of high-level women. Imposition of his theories probably would have stifled, even while helping, the contemporary stage.

1237 SISSON, CHARLES J. The Elizabethan Dramatists Except Shakespeare. London: Ernest Benn, 1928, pp. 49-52.
Even the cultured portion of the Renaissance audience probably did not theorize about drama until Jonson addressed questions to it. His humours comedy neither created a new school of comedy nor defeated romantic comedy but rather merged with the latter to produce realistic comedy.

1238 _____. Le goût public et le théâtre élisabéthain jusqu'à la mort de Shakespeare. Dijon: Darantière, 1922. 196 pp., passim.
Jonson's experience proves the impossiblity of imposing a literary taste on the public. Despite his frequent conflict with public taste, he is more willing to accommodate it than is generally acknowledged, and comes close to it in his best plays, Epicoene, Volpone, and The Alchemist, where the "instinctive" playwright wins out over the "theoretical" moralist and satirist. He fails when he subordinates action to analysis and psychology to satire. Ultimately, the dominance in him of the critical spirit is the index of a certain ineptitude for the dramatic genre.

1239 SLIGHTS, WILLIAM W. E. "The Trickster-Hero and Middleton's A Mad World, My Masters." CompD 3 (1969):87-98.
Identifies varieties of trickster-heroes serving satirical ends in Jonson's comedies. Discusses Truewit in Epicoene; Mosca in Volpone; and, in The Alchemist, Subtle, Face, Dol, and Lovewit, "who represents a new, cynical, efficient breed of London trickster."

1240 SMET, ROBERT DE [Romain Sanvic]. Le théâtre élisabéthain. Brussels: Office de Publicité, 1955, pp. 80-86.
Compared to Molière, Jonson's creative power flowed less easily and his classicism was less instinctive. For creation of humour characters, the French writer to whom Jonson comes closest is Desmaret de Saint-Sorlin, in his Visionnaires (1637). The 1928 adaptation of Volpone is strongly affected by the personalities of Zweig and Romains. They omitted the Politic Would-Be subplot, but the success of Jonson's original at the Malvern festival (1935) showed that English audiences still found the subplot funny. Jonson's tragedies attempt to achieve a classical style, but they are cold, contrived, and self-conscious.

1241 SPEAIGHT, GEORGE. The History of the English Puppet Theatre. London: George G. Harrap, 1955, pp. 57-67.

Jonson's plays offer important evidence in the history of English puppetry. The show in Bartholomew Fair, perhaps written fifteen years before the play and specifically for puppets, helps identify the London locales of such performances and demonstrates, through Leatherhead, the role of the puppets' interpreter or translator. Poetaster contains clear references to "motions" or glove puppets, while A Tale of a Tub includes a shadow show, a type of popular entertainment.

1242 SPENCER, T. J. B. "Shakespeare v. the Rest: the Old Controversy." ShS 14 (1967):76-89.

Literary men's opinions about Jonson have changed greatly; a revival of approval began in the Romantic period in both England and Germany.

1243 SPURGEON, CAROLINE. Shakespeare's Imagery and What It Tells Us. Cambridge: Cambridge University Press; New York: Macmillan, 1935, pp. 30-42 passim, 49-50, 94-95, 373. [Reprint. Boston: Beacon Press, 1958.]

A collection, classification, and cross-referencing of images from Shakespeare's plays and those of eleven of his contemporaries. Jonson uses many images from sports, but seems to have had little firsthand knowledge of any sport except fencing. Other Jonson images evince his interest in the fairly well-to-do town types, trades, and the body. In connection with a detailed chart of images dealing with "daily life" in six dramatists, notes that Jonson has the greatest number of "topical" images, that is, references to local or contemporary events, places, customs, or persons.

*1244 STAPLETON, R. "Ben Jonson as a Comic Artist." Sequence (Smith College) 39 (March 1931):43-52.

1245 STOLL, ELMER EDGAR. "The Old Drama and the New: Ben Jonson," in his Poets and Playwrights: Shakespeare, Jonson, Spenser, Milton. Minneapolis: The University of Minnesota Press, 1930, pp. 139-51. [Reprint. New York: Russell and Russell, 1965.]

Answers William Archer's book of the same title in which Archer denies that Jonson is a gifted dramatist. Defends Jonson's ability to plot, to motivate characters, and to satirize. Warns that the comedies must be judged by the standards of comedy and satire.

General Topics

1246 STROUP, THOMAS B. *Microcosmos: The Shape of the Elizabethan Play*. Lexington: University of Kentucky Press, 1965, pp. 67-70, 102-04, 138-39, 161-65, 196-97.

Applies Jaques's metaphor, "All the world's a stage/And all the men and women merely players," in the light not only of the medieval stage heritage but also of the thought of the Fathers of the Church, the Neoplatonists, and Renaissance humanists to explain the structure of the Elizabethan play. Stroup discovers that in Elizabethan drama "the vertical metaphor of the Great Chain of Being was not destroyed or twisted or greatly blurred by the horizontal metaphor of a series of corresponding planes." Examines Jonson's plays briefly and finds the moral order reasserted in the conclusions and often in inductions, prologues, and choruses.

1247 SUGDEN, EDWARD HOLDSWORTH. *A Topographical Dictionary to the Works of Shakespeare and His Fellow Dramatists*. Manchester: University of Manchester Press; New York: Longmans, Green, 1925. 599 pp., passim. [Reprint. Hildesheim, Germany, and New York: Georg Olms, 1969.]

Provides accounts of the places mentioned in the plays and illustrative quotations.

1248 VENEZKY, ALICE V. *Pageantry on the Shakespearean Stage*. New Haven, Conn.: College and University Press, 1951, pp. 93, 145, 147-48, 152.

Jonson insisted that the popular pageant should maintain artistic standards. He occasionally used the form himself as a vehicle for satire (*The Case is Altered* and *Cynthia's Revels*). The original dénouement of *Every Man out of his Humour* incorporates elements of the pageant, including belief in the power of the sovereign to change people.

1249 WAITH, EUGENE M. "Things as They Are and the World of Absolutes in Jonson's Plays and Masques," in *The Elizabethan Theatre IV*, pp. 106-26. (*See* 22.)

The staging in *The Devil is an Ass* and *The Staple of News* reflects Jonson's combination of two mimetic modes and his need to present the ideal world on the stage.

1250 WELLS, HENRY W. *Elizabethan and Jacobean Playwrights*. New York: Columbia University Press, 1939, pp. 52-57, 190-209, 258-63, 270-72.

Jonson's tragedies preclude a tragic effect because they present unqualified villains who deserve their suffering. He shows his excellence in his satiric comedies, through his ability to harmonize "a mad mass of subject matter." Like Shakespeare, he is partly medieval, partly modern.

"The father of English Neoclassicism. . . . [Jonson] prepares the way for the light comedy of wit without actually inventing it."

1251 _____. Elizabethan and Jacobean Playwrights. 2d ed. New York: Columbia University Press, 1940, pp. 52-57, 190-209, 258-63, 270-72. [Reprint. Port Washington, N.Y.: Kennikat Press, 1964.]
Same as first edition, with a supplement: "A Chronological List of Extant Plays Produced in or about London 1581-1642." (See 1250.)

1252 WELLS, STANLEY. Literature and Drama, with Special Reference to Shakespeare and His Contemporaries. London: Routledge and Kegan Paul, 1970, pp. 41-49.
Jonson's dissatisfaction with many aspects of the popular theatre led him to a careful printing of his plays, which conferred respectability on popular drama. Significant innovations include character sketches rather than simply lists of dramatis personae, comments on theatrical changes made during production, and printing of commendatory verses. The layout of plays in the 1616 Folio indicates Jonson's association with the printing of that volume and his desire to emphasize perceived links between his own plays and classical drama.

1253 WILD, FRIEDRICH. "Zum Problem des Barocks in der englischen Dichtung." Anglia 59 (1935):414-22.
Briefly touches upon Jonson in a discussion of the baroque style in English Renaissance literature.

1254 WILSON, EDMUND. "A Definitive Edition of Ben Jonson." NY, 6 November 1948, pp. 116-17.
Reviews various editions of Jonson's plays on the occasion of the appearance of Volume VIII of the Oxford edition. Criticizes T. S. Eliot's essay (see 1102) for minimizing Jonson's "glaring defects," which Wilson enumerates.

1255 _____. "Morose Ben Jonson," in his The Triple Thinkers: Twelve Essays on Literary Subjects. New York: Oxford University Press, 1948, pp. 213-32. [Originally published New York: Charles Scribner's Sons, 1938. Reprinted in Ben Jonson: A Collection of Critical Essays, pp. 60-74 (see 3).]
Jonson is an example of the "anal erotic," evincing the characteristics of the type: orderliness, parsimony, and obstinacy. His pedantry is "an over-accentuated" orderliness; his "compulsive" citing of precedents and his defiance of his audience and critics, a cover for his anxiety

about the adequacy of his powers. His learning and collecting of words is a form of hoarding and "he depends on the exhibition of stored-away knowledge to compel admiration." His warped characters and bizarre themes reflect his neuroses.

1256 WILSON, HAROLD S. "Some Meanings of 'Nature' in Renaissance Literary Theory." JHI 2 (1941):430-48.

Supplements the tabulation of the meaning of the word "nature" in aesthetic theory published by Arthur O. Lovejoy (MLN 42 [1927]:444-50). Jonson, in the Discoveries, like other Renaissance critics, sees nature as maintaining "an approximately uniform excellence in literary achievement from one cycle of literary development to another." Assuming this posture, these critics defend the moderns against the ancients. In the dedication to Volpone, "nature" is "a moral-aesthetic principle which does not permit a bad man to be a good poet." Although Jonson, in Discoveries and the induction to Every Man out of his Humour, states that the author must not be haunted by ancient tradition but must be free to work and enlarge its limits, he does value "the norm of judgment and traditional order."

1257 WINSLOW, OLA ELIZABETH. Low Comedy as a Structural Element in English Drama from the Beginning to 1642. Chicago: University of Chicago Press, 1926, pp. 133-38, 150-54. [Reprint. Philadelphia: R. West, 1977.]

After the beginning of the 17th century, "the center of interest [in English drama] became the exaggeration of humours, the exposure of folly, and the humiliation of rogues by means of trivial intrigues." Therefore, the need for such contrasting elements as comic underplot, burlesque, and clownage lessened. In such comedies of manners as The Alchemist, Epicoene, and Bartholomew Fair, the exaggerated realism of the comedy episodes is embodied in the central rather than the subsidiary action. In Every Man in his Humour the secondary action (Cob and his wife) furnishes comedy by the echo device. Peter Onion and Juniper in The Case is Altered and Pug in The Devil is an Ass illustrate the use of lower characters in the underplot to add more comedy. Often, undue elaboration of comic underplots can be explained as the result of collaboration, as in Eastward Ho. Sometimes the dramatist admits that he is satisfying popular demand by his use of lower levels of humour, as Jonson does in The Staple of News and A Tale of a Tub.

Reviewed by T. W. Baldwin in JEGP 27 (1928):139-40; L. W. Wright in MLN 43 (1928):66-67.

1258 WOLFF, MAX J. "Die soziale Stellung der englischen Renaissancedramatiker." Englische Studien 71 (1936):171-90.
The seriousness with which Jonson took his dramas--evidenced by his didacticism, his publication of his Works, and his claims to legitimacy seen in inductions and dedications--helped improve the social status of English Renaissance dramatists. Plays began to be looked upon as literature.

1259 WOOLF, LEONARD. "The World of Books: Ben Jonson." Nation and Athenaeum, 23 June 1923, p. 396. Reprinted as "Rare Ben Jonson" (see 1260).
Eliot and Huxley "seem to praise Jonson apologetically," but Volpone, Epicoene, and The Alchemist "will stand with any play written in English outside Shakespeare."

1260 _____. "Rare Ben Jonson." The Living Age, 11 August 1923, pp. 281-82. Reprint of 1259.

1261 YATES, FRANCES A. "Ben Jonson and the Last Plays," in her Shakespeare's Last Plays: A New Approach. London: Routledge and Kegan Paul, 1975, pp. 109-26.
Approaches Shakespeare's last plays historically and politically and sees them as advocating for England the role of universal reformer or supporter of European Protestantism. Because John Dee was associated with the Elizabethan type of British imperialism and because his "science" was labeled "black magic," interprets Shakespeare's sympathetic portrayal of Prospero as a Dee-like magus as an indication of Shakespeare's political expression. Sees The Alchemist, with its negative presentation of science, as Jonson's "political-religious satire" antagonistic to the German Rosicrucian movement which was informed by the philosophy of John Dee. Explains other details of Jonson's career in the light of her historical-political theory.

1262 YOUNG, STEVEN C. "A Check List of Tudor and Stuart Induction Plays." PQ 48 (1969):131-34.
"The list contains fifty-six plays, arranged in chronological order, spanning the period from the earliest beginnings of the secular drama in England to the closing of the theaters." Only Jonson and Randolph used the induction device more than twice: Jonson, six times; Randolph, three.

General Topics

1263 ____. The Frame Structure in Tudor and Stuart Drama. ElizS 6, 1974, pp. 125-47.

Jonson exerted great influence in the use of "extra-dramatic" passages which express the dramatist's consciousness of the audience. The Induction in Every Man out of his Humour sets the tone for his later uses of the device: satiric, spontaneous, colloquial. The extra-dramatic passage serves to distance the play, educate the audience, and convey the dramatist's vision of life and art. Modified frames appear in The Staple of News and The Magnetic Lady.

1264 ZWAGER, NICOLAAS. Glimpses of Ben Jonson's London. Amsterdam: Swets & Zeitlinger, 1926. 219 pp., passim. [Reprint. Philadelphia: R. West, 1978.]

Provides information about various aspects of London life as reflected in Jonson's plays and other contemporary sources.

Reviewed by P. Aronstein in Anglia Beiblatt 38 (1927): 204-05; M. Byrne in RES 3 (1927):481-82.

Appendix I

PH.D. DISSERTATIONS

1265 ABADIE, ANN JULIAN. "The Dramatic Kinship of John Ford and Ben Jonson." University of Mississippi, 1973.

1266 ADKINS, MARY G. M. "Puritanism in Elizabethan Drama as Represented by Beaumont and Fletcher, Jonson, Dekker, and Shakespeare." University of Texas at Austin, 1938.

1267 ALLEN, RICHARD OTTAWAY. "Jacobean Drama and The Literature of Decay: A Study of Conservative Reaction in Literature." University of Michigan, 1969.

1268 ANDERSON, MARK ANDREW. "Jonson's Criticism of Society: Development in the Major Comedies." University of Wisconsin, 1968.

1269 ANGELL, CHARLES FRANCIS. "'The Center Attractive'. The Function of Women in Ben Jonson's Comedy." University of Massachusetts, 1974.

1270 ANKLESARIA, SHIRIN SAROSH. "Ben Jonson: The Biographical Tradition and Its Relation to Critical Appraisal." Cornell University, 1974.

1271 ANNAL, CHARLES WILLIAM. "Black Humor in Selected Works of Donne, Jonson, Shakespeare and Burton." University of Connecticut, 1976.

1272 ARMBRISTER, VICTOR S. "The Origins and Functions of Subplots in Elizabethan Drama." Vanderbilt University, 1938.

1273 ARMES, WILLIAM DAVID. "Ben Jonson's Comical Satires and _Vetus Comoedia_." University of Illinois at Urbana-Champaign, 1974.

Appendix I

Dissertations

1274 ARNOLD, HANS STEPHAN. "The Reception of Ben Jonson, Beaumont and Fletcher, and Massinger in Eighteenth Century Germany." University of Maryland, 1962.

1275 ARNOLD, JUDD BALDWIN. "Form and Meaning in the Comedies of Ben Jonson." University of Connecticut, 1965.

1276 BAKER, CHRISTOPHER PAUL. "Ben Jonson and the Inns of Court: The Literary Milieu of Every Man Out of His Humour." University of North Carolina at Chapel Hill, 1974.

1277 BALESTRI, CHARLES ANGELO. "English Neoclassicism and Shakespeare: A Study in Conflicting Ideas of Dramatic Form." Yale University, 1970.

1278 BARISH, JONAS A. "Ben Jonson's Dramtic Prose." Harvard University, 1953.

1279 BARKAN, LEONARD. "Elementated Man: Studies in the Metaphor of the Human Body." Yale University, 1972.

1280 BARKER, WALTER LAWTON. "Three English Pantalones: A Study in Relations Between the 'Commedia dell'arte' and Elizabethan Drama." University of Connecticut, 1966.

1281 BASKERVILL, CHARLES READ. "English Elements in Jonson's Early Comedy." University of Chicago, 1911.

1282 BAUER, ROBERT V. "The Use of Humors in Comedy by Ben Jonson and His Contemporaries." University of Illinois at Urbana-Champaign, 1948.

1283 BEECHER, D. A. "Ben Jonson's Sejanus." University of Birmingham, 1972-73.

1284 BERNHARD, GABRIELE JOHANNA. "Vision and Judgment in Ben Jonson's Dramas." Yale University, 1961.

1285 BLACKBURN, WILLIAM GEORGE. "Perilous Grace: The Poet as Protean Magician in the Works of Marlowe, Jonson, and Spenser." Yale University, 1977.

1286 BOCAN, AGNES. "Nature and Art Themes in the Middle Comedies of Ben Jonson." University of Notre Dame, 1970.

1287 BRADFORD, ALAN TAYLOR. "Ben Jonson and Roman Political Tragedy on the Jacobean Stage." Harvard University, 1966.

Appendix I

Dissertations

1288 BRADLEY, JESSE FRANKLIN. "The Jonson Allusion Book: A Collection of Allusions to Ben Jonson from 1597 to 1700." Cornell University, 1919.

1289 BRETTLE, R. E. "John Marston." University of Oxford, 1928.

1290 BROCK, DEWEY HEYWARD. "Poet and Society: A Critical Study of Ben Jonson's Concept of Society in the Light of Classical and Christian Ideals." University of Kansas, 1969.

1291 BROOKS, H. F. "The Complete Works of John Oldham." University of Oxford, 1940.

1292 BURNS, ROBERT LEE. "A Critical Study of Thomas Middleton's Early Realistic Comedies." University of Louisville, 1969.

1293 CAMPBELL, MARIAN SELMA JOHNSON. "The Beginnings of the English Comedy of Manners in the Renaissance." University of Colorado, 1971.

1294 CARR, JOAN CHRISTINE. "Poetry and the Nature of Satire in Jonsonian Comedy: A Study of the Comicall Satyres." University of Virginia, 1973.

1295 CARTER, HENRY HOLLAND. "*Every Man in His Humor*, by Ben Jonson, Edited with Introduction, Notes, and Glossary." Yale University, 1914.

1296 CHAIT, RACHAEL. "Satire of Ben Jonson." Cornell University, 1932.

1297 CHALFANT, FRAN CERNOCKY. "Ben Jonson's London: The Plays, The Masques, and The Poems." University of North Carolina at Chapel Hill, 1971.

1298 CHAMPION, LARRY STEPHEN. "The Comic Intent of Ben Jonson's Late Plays." University of North Carolina at Chapel Hill, 1961.

1299 CHAPMAN, MILDRED SHOWS. "Ben Jonson and the Court." Louisiana State University and Agricultural and Mechanical College, 1969.

1300 CHRISTOPHER, GEORGIA BELLE. "A Study of the Jonsonian, Pastoral and Apocalyptic Strains in 'Silex Scintillans.'" Yale University, 1967.

Appendix I

Dissertations

1301 CHUTE, EDWARD JOSEPH. "Comic Wrestling: A Comparative Analysis of the Comic Agon and Its Dramatic Idea and Form in Selected Comedies of Aristophanes, Shakespeare, Jonson, Shaw and Calderón." University of Minnesota, 1977.

1302 CLEARMAN, MARY REBECCA HOGELAND. "Aspects of Juvenal in Ben Jonson's Comical Satires." University of Missouri--Columbia, 1969.

1303 CLUBB, ROGER LANE. "The Relationship of Language to Character in Ben Jonson's Every Man Out of His Humor." Yale University, 1958.

1304 COCHRAN, CAROL MARIE. "Flyting in Pre-Elizabethan Drama, in Shakespeare and in Jonson." University of New Mexico, 1973.

1305 COHEN, GERALD. "A Comparative Evaluation of the Pastoral Tradition in English and French Literature in the Early Seventeenth Century." University of Washington, 1959.

1306 COHEN, RALPH ALAN. "London and the Techniques of Setting in Ben Jonson's Comedies." Duke University, 1973.

1307 CONE, MARY. "Fletcher Without Beaumont: A Study of the Independent Plays of John Fletcher." University of Mississippi, 1970.

1308 CONNOR, RODNEY VINCENT. "A Study of Ben Jonson's Comedies: The Comic Perspectives." University of Washington, 1962.

1309 CORNELIA, M. BONAVENTURE. "The Function of the Masque in Jacobean Tragedy and Tragicomedy." Fordham University, 1969.

1310 COUILLARD, THEOPHANE VENARD. "Anti-Puritan Satire in Ben Jonson's Dramatic Works." University of Colorado at Boulder, 1967.

1311 CRUPI, CHARLES WILLIAM. "Pastoral Elements in Plays from the Elizabethan Public Theatres of the 1590's." Princeton University, 1967.

1312 CULP, JAMES WILLIAM. "The Judgment Denouement of Renaissance Comedy." Vanderbilt University, 1956.

1313 CURRY, JOHN VINCENT. "Deception in Elizabethan Comedy: An Analytical Study." Columbia University, 1951.

Appendix I

Dissertations

1314 DALE, LEONA FORD. "Health Imagery and Rhetoric in the Major Comedies of Ben Jonson." Texas Tech University, 1969.

1315 DAVIS, J. L. "The 'Sons of Ben' in English Realistic Comedy, 1625-42." University of Michigan, 1934.

1316 DEARMIN, EVALYN MARIE CELINE TITUS. "Ben Jonson's Emblem Drama: Convention to Innovation in Masques and Satiric Comedies, 1605 to 1616." University of Nevada, Reno, 1974.

1317 DEAS, M. C. "A Study of the Life and Poetry of Edmund Waller." University of Cambridge, 1931.

1318 DE LUNA, BARBARA NIELSON. "Jonson's Romish Plot: A Study of Catiline and Its Historical Context." University of Iowa, 1963.

1319 DENNISTON, ELLIOTT AVERETT. "Jonson's Bartholomew Fair and the Jacobean Stage." University of Michigan, 1970.

1320 DESSEN, ALAN CHARLES. "Ben Jonson and the 'Estates' Morality Tradition." Johns Hopkins University, 1963.

1321 DREW-BEAR, ANNETTE. "Rhetoric in Ben Jonson's Middle Plays: A Study of Ethos, Character Portrayal, and Persuasion." University of Wisconsin, 1971.

1322 DUCKLES, VINCENT H. "John Gamble's Commonplace Book: A Critical Edition of New York Public Library MS Drexel 4257." University of California, Berkeley, 1953.

1323 DUDLEY, LEONA BARBOUR. "The Language of Comedy: An Introductory Analysis of the Verbal Forms of the Comic Spirit in Drama." Cornell University, 1944.

1324 DUNN, ESTHER CLOUDMAN. "Contemporary Life and Letters in Ben Jonson's Work." University of London, 1922.

1325 DUTTON, A. R. "Ben Jonson's Plays." Nottingham University, 1971-72.

1326 ELLIOTT, LYNN HUMPHREY. "Engagement and Detachment: The Function of the Induction in Ben Jonson's Plays." University of California, Santa Barbara, 1972.

1327 EMLEY, EDWARDS. "Dr. Johnson and the Writers of Tudor England." New York University, 1958.

Appendix I

Dissertations

1328 ENCK, JOHN J. "Ben Jonson's Imagery." Harvard University, 1951.

1329 EVANS, WILLA McCLUNG. "Ben Jonson and Elizabethan Music." Columbia University, 1929.

1330 FERRIS, DIANNE RUTH ANNE. "Ben Jonson: The Road to 1616." University of Washington, 1975.

1331 FIRESTINE, MARTHA WARN. "The Doctrine of Imitation in the English Renaissance: Roger Ascham, Sir Philip Sidney, and Ben Jonson." Indiana University, 1974.

1332 FLACHMANN, MICHAEL CHARLES. "Ben Jonson and the Alchemy of Satire." University of Chicago, 1973.

1333 FLANAGAN, JAMES DONALD. "The Satirist-Intriguer in Elizabethan and Jacobean Comedy." University of Minnesota, 1973.

1334 FLOWER, ANNETTE CHAPPELL. "The Disguised Prince in English Drama, 1590-1615." University of Maryland, 1970.

1335 FOAKES, R. A. "Imagery in Elizabethan and Jacobean Drama." University of Birmingham, 1951-52.

1336 FOWLER, A. MURRAY. "Comparative Study of Humours Characters in Ben Jonson and Henry Fielding." University of Oregon, 1939.

1337 FREDEMAN, PATSY DALE HINES. "Ben Jonson: Principles of Criticism and Creation." University of Oklahoma, 1972.

1338 FRIEDRICH, K. "Die englische Dramatisierung des Katalinastoffes." Erlangen, 1934.

1339 FUSSELL, BETTY HARPER. "Tragicomedy in Lyly, Shakespeare, and Jonson." Rutgers--The State University of New Jersey, 1975.

1340 GARDINER, JUDITH KEGAN. "Craftsmanship in Context: Ben Jonson's Poetry." Columbia University, 1968.

1341 GARLOCH, GAIL. "Role-Playing and the Idea of the Play in Ben Jonson's Comedies." University of Tennessee, 1975.

1342 GERTMENIAN, DONALD. "Folly, Virtue, and Social Order in Ben Jonson's Comedies From Every Man in his Humour to Bartholomew Fair." Harvard University, 1970.

Appendix I

Dissertations

1343 GIANAKARIS, CONSTANTINE. "Humanistic Thought and the Moment of Judgment in Ben Jonson's Comedies." University of Wisconsin, 1961.

1344 GIBBONS, B. C. "A Critical Examination of Jacobean City Comedy." University of Cambridge, 1966-67.

1345 GRAHAM, CARY B. "The Influence of Ben Jonson on Restoration Comedy." Ohio State University, 1937.

1346 GRAHAM, HUGH RICHARD. "Ben Jonson's Didactic Tragedies: Sejanus and Catiline." Temple University, 1966.

1347 GROW, GERALD OWEN. "Paradise Lost and the Renaissance Drama: Milton's Theme of Fall and Its Dramatic Counterpart in Marlowe, Shakespeare, Jonson, and Middleton." Yale University, 1968.

1348 GUM, COBURN. "The Aristophanic Comedies of Ben Jonson." Duke University, 1962.

1349 GUTMANN, J. "Die dramatischen Einheiten bei Ben Jonson." Munich, 1913.

1350 HAFER, CAROL BRAXTON. "Themes, Techniques, and Tone in Ben Jonson's Last Four Comedies." Northern Illinois University, 1975.

1351 HAMEL, GUY A. "Structure in Elizabethan Drama." University of Toronto, 1974.

1352 HAMMOOD, EMILY EVANS. "Directorial Analysis of Ben Jonson's Volpone." Case Western Reserve University, 1972.

1353 HARRIS, JULIA HAMLET. "Eastward Hoe, by Chapman, Jonson and Marston, Edited with Introduction, Notes and Glossary." Yale University, 1922.

1354 HARRIS, LYNN HAROLD. "Catiline His Conspiracy, by Ben Jonson, Edited with Introduction, Notes and Glossary." Yale University, 1914.

1355 HARTMEYER, KAETHE. "Die Sozial-und Kulturverhoeltnisse Englands in der Elisabethaneschen Zeit, gesehen mit der Dichtern Thomas Deloney, Thomas Dekker und Ben Jonson." Muenster, 1951.

Appendix I

Dissertations

1356 HAWKINS, HARRIETT BLOKER. "Five Poetic Worlds: A Study of the Relationship Between Thematic Content and Dramatic Construction in Representative Works of Ben Jonson." Washington University, 1964.

1357 HEDRICK, DONALD KEITH. "The Elizabethan Satiric-Heroic Mode: Jonson, Shakespeare, and Marston." Cornell University, 1974.

1358 HELBIG, RUDOLF. "Kulturhistorische Studien zu Ben Jonson's Komödien." Göttingen, 1944.

1359 HENKE, JAMES THOMAS. "Elizabethan-Jacobean Dramatic Bawdy: A Glossary and Critical Essay." University of Washington, 1970.

1360 HILBERRY, CLARENCE BEVERLY. "Jonson's Ethical Ideas in Their Relations to Classic and Renaissance Ethical Thought." University of Chicago, 1930.

1361 HIMMEL, ADOLF. "Strukturtypen der Kömodie Ben Jonsons." Bonn, 1953.

1362 HINZE, O. "Studien zu Ben Jonsons Namengebung in seinen Dramen." Leipzig, 1919.

1363 HOEPNER, A. "Über den Gebrauch des Artikels in Ben Jonsons Dramen." Keil, 1916 (1921).

1364 HOHL, EDWARD DAVID. "The Politics of Art: The Jonsonian Masque and Jacobean Drama." Stanford University, 1973.

1365 HOLDEN, WILLIAM P. "The Religious Controversy and Anti-Puritan Satire, 1572-1642." Harvard University, 1950.

1366 HOLT, ALBERT HAMILTON. "The Nature of the Dramatic Illusion and Its Violations in Jonson's Comedies--His Precedents in Theory and Practice." Vanderbilt University, 1958.

1367 HOUCK, JOSEPH KEMP. "Rhetorical Motifs in Ben Jonson's Early Comedy, with Special Reference to Epicoene. University of North Carolina at Chapel Hill, 1967.

1368 HOUSER, DAVID JOHN. "The Tradition of Honesty in Elizabethan and Jacobean Drama." University of Wisconsin, 1970.

1369 HUNT, EFFIE NEVA. "Ben Jonson's Five-Act Structure." University of Illinois at Urbana-Champaign, 1950.

1370 HUNTER, C. K. "A Comparison of the Use of the Sententia, Considered as a Typical Rhetorical Ornament, in the Tragedies of Seneca, and in Those of Cascoigne, Kyd, Jonson, Marston, and Greville." University of Oxford, 1950.

1371 JACOBS, HENRY EDWARD. "Theaters Within Theaters: Levels of Dramatic Illusion in Ben Jonson's Comedies." Indiana University, 1974.

1372 JAMES, KATHERINE H. "The Widow in Jacobean Drama." University of Tennessee, 1973.

1373 JAY, BRUCE LOUIS. "The Comic Art of Ben Jonson and Molière." University of Connecticut, 1974.

1374 JOHNSTON, GEORGE B. "Ben Jonson: Poet." Columbia University, 1946.

1375 JONES, ROBERT CHARLES. "Well-Made Men and Men-Making Poets: Ben Jonson and the Problem of the Poet as a Teacher of Men." Harvard University, 1964.

1376 JUDSON, ALEXANDER CORBIN. "Cynthia's Revels, or The Fountain of Self-Love, by Ben Jonson; Edited with Introduction, Notes, and Glossary." Yale University, 1911.

1377 JUNEJA, RENU. "The Ground of Art: Cosmological Structure in Ben Jonson's Comedies." Pennsylvania State University, 1974.

1378 KAY, W. DAVID. "Ben Jonson, Horace, and the Poetomachia: The Development of an Elizabethan Playwright's Public Image." Princeton University, 1968.

1379 KENNEDY, DENNIS EDWARD. "Character and Disguise in Ben Jonson's Major Plays." University of California, Santa Barbara, 1972.

1380 KINDLER, EKKEHARD. "Das Verhältnis von Handlung und Charakter in Ben Jonsons Römertragödien." Innsbruck, 1951.

1381 KIRK, ALISON LEA. "The Place of Knighthood in English City Comedy from Every Man Out of his Humour to The Magnetic Lady." University of Colorado at Boulder, 1973.

1382 KNIGHTS, L. C. "Aspects of the Economic and Social Background in the Early 17th Century." University of Cambridge, 1936.

Appendix I

Dissertations

1383 KOMAROVA, V. P. "Individual vs. State in the Historical Plays of Shakespeare and His Contemporaries." Leningrad University, 1973.

1384 KRISHNAPPA, JOSEPHINE BALAMANI. "The Development of Jonson's Major Comedies." Case Western Reserve University, 1969.

1385 LAFFITTE, SUSAN CAMERON MILLER. "The Literary Connections of Sir Thomas Egerton: A Study of the Influence of Thomas Egerton upon Major Writers of Renaissance Literature." Florida State University, 1971.

1386 LAFKIDOU, ALIKI. "The Aristophanic Spirit in the Comedies of Ben Jonson." University of Denver, 1971.

1387 LAPINER, ROBERT STANLEY. "'Seeds of Goodness Left': The Unified Vision of Ben Jonson's Last Major Period, 1616-1626." Harvard University, 1975.

1388 LAWSON, ANITA SAFFELS. "In Dispraise of Folly: Satiric Themes and Techniques in Selected Plays of Chapman, Jonson, and Marston, 1597-1606." Tulane University, 1971.

1389 LEARNED, G. "Ben Jonson's Debt to the Comedies of Plautus." Ohio State University, 1937.

1390 LEDFORD, TED ROLAND. "A Critical Study of Ben Jonson's Last Plays." Ohio University, 1974.

1391 LEMLY, JOHN WILLIAM. "Into Winter Quarters Gone: The Last Plays of Jonson and Dryden." Yale University, 1972.

1392 LEVIN, LAWRENCE LEE. "Justice and Justice Figures in Jonson." University of Wisconsin--Madison, 1969.

1393 LEWIS, MINEKO S. "Humor Characterization in Restoration Comedy, 1660-1700." University of Tennessee, 1973.

1394 LIEBEZEIT, HELENE. "Die Bildersprache in den Dramen Ben Jonsons." Vienna, 1962.

1395 LINDEN, STANTON JAY. "Alchemy and the English Literary Imagination: 1385-1633." University of Minnesota, 1971.

1396 LINN, JOHN G. "The Court Masque and Elizabethan Dramatic Structure, 1558-1604." Cornell University, 1951.

Appendix I

Dissertations

1397 LLOYD, JAMES BARLOW. "Humours Characterization and the Tradition of the Jonsonian Comedy of Manners in William Faulkner's Early Fiction: New Orleans Sketches, Soldier's Pay, and Mosquitoes." University of Mississippi, 1975.

1398 LONG, M. D. "Ben Jonson and Renaissance Sacralism." University of Cambridge, 1968-69.

1399 McCLURE, NANCY KYOKO. "Jonson's Artistic Practice and Obsessional Needs Revealed in the Comedies." Case Western Reserve University, 1977.

1400 MacDONALD, ANDREW FERGUS. "Rhetorical Strategy in Ben Jonson's Comedy." University of Texas at Austin, 1972.

1401 McDONALD, ELMER MILTON. "John Day's Coterie Comedy." University of Virginia, 1970.

1402 McDONALD, RUSS FRANK. "Ben Jonson and the Comedy of Intrigue." University of Pennsylvania, 1976.

1403 McEACHERN, BARBARA ELISABETH. "'The Abstract of the Kingdom': The Court as an Element of Design in English Renaissance Drama." University of Rochester, 1973.

1404 McGINNIS, PAUL JOHN. "Integrity in the Story: A Study of Ben Jonson's Tragedies." Indiana University, 1964.

1405 MANDELBAUM, GEORGE. "Skein of Silk: The Structure of Ben Johnson's Major Comedies." Columbia University, 1975.

1406 MEBANE, JOHN SPENCER. "Art and Magic in Marlowe, Jonson, and Shakespeare: The Occult Tradition in Dr. Faustus, The Alchemist, and The Tempest." Emory University, 1974.

1407 MERVIN, KATHLEEN McCONNELL. "The Development of Jonson's Dramatic Organization from The Case Is Altered through Volpone." Cornell University, 1965.

1408 MILLARD, BARBARA CASACCI. "Ben Jonson's Comedies and the Pastoral Tradition." University of Delaware, 1974.

1409 MILLS, LLOYD LESLIE. "Ben Jonson's Last Plays: A Critical Reconsideration." University of Washington, 1965.

1410 MOORE, NANCY ANN NEWELL. "Ben Jonson's Concept of Decorum: A Study of His Theory and Three Comedies." University of Illinois at Urbana-Champaign, 1968.

Appendix I

Dissertations

1411 MORAHAN, RICHARD EDWARD. "I. Samuel Johnson and William Lauder's Milton Forgeries. II. Poetry in Space: Disjunction in Language and Stage Action in Jonson's Sejanus. III. Jane Austen's Endings." Rutgers--The State University of New Jersey, 1971.

1412 MORAN, JOSEPHINE BANGS. "The 'Recent Humours Still' in Jonson's Last Four Comedies." Northwestern University, 1965.

1413 MUESCHKE, PAUL. "Prototypes of Restoration Wits and Would-Bees in Ben Jonson's Realistic Comedy." University of Michigan, 1929.

1414 MUNDHENK, ROBERT THOMAS. "The Jonsonian Comedy of Humours." University of California, Los Angeles, 1971.

1415 MUSIAL, THOMAS JAMES. "The Evolution of Ben Jonson's Dramatic Theory: A Study in the Development of a Moral Art." University of Notre Dame, 1970.

1416 NELSON, CATHRYN ANNE. "A Critical Edition of Wit's Triumvirate, or The Philosopher." University of Arizona, 1970.

1417 NICHOLS, MARIANE. "Dramatic Language in Shakespeare, Jonson and Middleton." New York University, 1971.

1418 NORLAND, HOWARD BERNETT. "The Development of Ben Jonson's Dramatic Technique." University of Wisconsin--Madison, 1962.

1419 NOYES, ROBERT G. "Ben Jonson on the English Stage, 1660-1776." Harvard University, 1929.

1420 O'DELL, JERRY CLINTON. "The Influence of Poetic Theory and Roman Comedy and Satire on Ben Jonson's Plays, 1596-1614." Stanford University, 1972.

1421 OMANS, STUART E. "The War of the Theaters: An Approach to its Origins, Development, and Meaning." Northwestern University, 1969.

1422 OSTROWSKI, CAROL ANNE CARR. "The Dynamics of Roguery: Studies of the Jacobean Rogue in Selected Plays of Jonson and Middleton." University of Connecticut, 1977.

Appendix I

Dissertations

1423 PAPENHAUSEN, RICHARD WILLIAM, JR. "Identity and Sexuality in Ben Jonson: A Psychoanalytic Reading of Three Comedies and a Masque." State University of New York at Buffalo, 1974.

1424 PARKER, RANDOLPH. "A Rite for Scholars: The Experience of Jonsonian Comedy." Cornell University, 1975.

1425 PARTRIDGE, EDWARD BELLAMY. "The Broken Compass: A Study of the Imagery in Ben Jonson's Comedies." Columbia University, 1950.

1426 PASTER, GAIL KERN. "The Idea of the City in the Plays, Masques, and Pageants of Ben Jonson and Thomas Middleton." Yale University, 1972.

1427 PAULEY, HARRY W. "A Study of Early Tudor Comedies." University of Missouri--Columbia, 1965.

1428 PECK, HARVEY WHITEFIELD. "The Magnetic Lady; or Humors Reconciled, by Ben Jonson, Edited with Introduction, Notes, and Glossary." Yale University, 1913.

1429 PERRY, DAVID S. "Hazlitt, Lamb, and the Drama." Princeton University, 1966.

1430 PERRY, GEORGE FRANCIS. "A Study of the Image of Man in Jacobean City Comedy." Fordham University, 1971.

1431 PFEFFER, KARL. "Das Elisabethanische Sprichwort in seiner Verwendung bei Ben Jonson." Giessen, 1934.

1432 POTTER, L. D. "The Fop and Related Figures in Drama from Jonson to Cibber." University of Cambridge, 1964-65.

1433 PREUSSNER, ARNOLD WALTER. "Ben Jonson and Comic Tradition: A Study of Five Jonsonian Comedies in the Light of Sixteenth-Century Comedy and Comic Theory." University of Colorado at Boulder, 1977.

1434 RANSOM, SHIRLEY FARLEY. "Myth and Ritual in Ben Jonson's Earlier Dramatic Satires." Purdue University, 1971.

1435 REA, JOHN DOUGAN. "Volpone, or, the Fox, by Ben Jonson, Edited with Introduction, Notes, and a Glossary." Yale University, 1918.

1436 READ, FORREST GODFREY. "Audience, Poet, and Structure in Ben Jonson's Plays." Cornell University, 1961.

Appendix I

Dissertations

1437 RHOME, FRANCES DODSON. "Variations of Festive Revel in Four English Comedies, 1595-1605." Indiana University, 1969.

1438 RICHARDSON, DAVID ANTHONY. "Decorum and Diction in the English Renaissance." University of North Carolina at Chapel Hill, 1973.

1439 RIDDELL, JAMES ALLEN. "The Evolution of the Humours Character in Seventeenth-Century English Comedy." University of Southern California, 1966.

1440 RILEY, MICHAEL HOWARD. "Ritual and the Hero in English Renaissance Tragedy." Boston University, 1970.

1441 ROBBINS, MARTIN LEWIS. "Shakespeare's Sweet Music: A Glossary of Musical Terms in the Work of Shakespeare (with Additional Examples from the Plays of Lyly, Marston, and Jonson)." Brandeis University, 1968.

1442 ROBINSON, JAMES EDWARD. "The Dramatic Unities in the Renaissance: A Study of the Principles, with Application to the Development of English Drama." University of Illinois, 1959.

1443 ROSENBLITHE, ANITA RUTH. "A Comparison of the Moral and Aesthetic Vision of Three Seventeenth-Century Dramatists: Corneille, Molière, and Ben Jonson." University of Illinois at Urbana-Champaign, 1969.

1444 RUSSELL, H. K. "Certain Doctrines of Natural and Moral Philosophy as an Approach to the Study of Elizabethan Drama, with an Appendix Containing Illustrative Material from the Plays of Ben Jonson." Cornell University, 1932.

1445 SAKOWITZ, ALEXANDRE HIRSCH. "Language as Drama: Uses of Rhetoric in Ben Jonson." Harvard University, 1941.

1446 SANTA LUCIA, GAETANO F. "Irony in Sejanus and Catiline." Case Western Reserve University, 1974.

1447 SARAFINSKI, DOLORES. "The Comedies of Ben Jonson: A Review of Research and Criticism, 1919-1968." Duquesne University, 1973.

1448 SARTORIUS, HEINRICH. "Die klassische Götter-und Heldensage in den Dramen Beaumonts und Fletchers, Chapmans, Ben Jonsons und Massingers." Strassburg, 1912.

Appendix I

Dissertations

1449 SCHULZ, GRETCHEN ELIZABETH. "The Satiric Strategy of Ben Jonson's Plays." The University of Wisconsin--Madison, 1975.

1450 SELIN, WILLIAM EDWARD. "The Case Is Altered by Ben Jonson, Edited with Introduction, Notes, and Glossary." Yale University, 1917.

1451 SHANKER, SIDNEY MORRIS. "Conservatism and Change: A Study of the Relationship Between the Elizabethan-Jacobean Milieu and the Works of Jonson and Chapman for the Decade 1605-1614." New York University, 1951.

1452 SHAW, CATHERINE MAUD. "The Dramatic Function of the Masque in English Drama: 1592-1642." University of Texas at Austin, 1967.

1453 SLATER, JOHN FREDERICK. "Edward Garnett: The Splendid Advocate, Volpone, and Antony and Cleopatra: The Play of Imagination, Self-Concealment and Self-Revelation in Shelley's 'Epipsychidion.'" Rutgers--The State University of New Jersey, 1971.

1454 SLIGHTS, WILLIAM WELLINGTON ENT. "Dramatic Form in Ben Jonson's Middle Comedies." University of Illinois at Urbana-Champaign, 1966.

1455 SLOCUM, KEITH DALE. "The Problem of Judgment in Ben Jonson's Plays, 1598-1614." University of Pennsylvania, 1973.

1456 SMITH, BRUCE R. "The Gods Impersonated: Classical Mythology on English Renaissance Stages." The University of Rochester, 1972.

1457 SOMERSET, J. A. B. "The Comic Turn in English Drama, 1470-1616." University of Birmingham, 1966-67.

1458 SOULE, DONALD ERNEST. "Irony in Early Critical Comedy." Stanford University, 1959.

1459 SOUTH, MALCOLM HUDSON. "Animal Imagery in Ben Jonson's Plays." University of Georgia, 1968.

1460 STAGG, LOUIS CHARLES. "An Analysis and Comparison of the Imagery in the Tragedies of Chapman, Heywood, Jonson, Marston, Webster, Tourneur, and Middleton." University of Arkansas, 1963.

Appendix I

Dissertations

1461 STALLINGS, WALTON D., JR. "The Decline of Debate: Changing Attitudes Towards Rhetoric in English Renaissance Drama." University of South Carolina, 1971.

1462 STERN, CHARLES HERMAN. "Jonson's Satiric Commentator and Molière's 'Raisonneur': A Study Arising out of Parallels in Molière and Jonson." Columbia University, 1961.

1463 STEVENSON, HAZEL A. "Herbal Lore as Reflected in the Works of the Major Elizabethans." University of North Carolina, 1931.

1464 STODDER, JOSEPH HENRY. "Satire in Jacobean Tragedy." University of Southern California, 1964.

1465 SULLIVAN, ELIZABETH QUAY. "1. Lawrence Among the Aztecs: Travels, Readings, and Poems. 2. Functions of Disguise in Ben Jonson's Comedies. 3. The Language of the Theater in Hawthorne's Tales and The Scarlet Letter." Rutgers--The State University of New Jersey, 1975.

1466 SUTHERLAND, M. V. "A Design Project for Bartholomew Fair." Yale University, 1935.

1467 SWEENEY, JAMES GERARD. "Ben Jonson's Modern Literary Reputation as a Dramatist (1925-1958)." Boston University, 1961.

1468 SWENSON, LARRY BARTON. "Awakening Antiquity: Some Notes on Ben Jonson's Literary Imitations." University of Chicago, 1974.

1469 TAIT, MICHAEL STRONG. "The Didactic Norm and the Dramatic Mode in the Principal Plays of Ben Jonson." University of Toronto, 1972.

1470 TARGAN, BARRY DONALD. "Two Comic Worlds: An Analysis of the Structure of Thirteen of Ben Jonson's Comedies." Brandeis University, 1962.

1471 TEAGUE, FRANCES NICOL. "Ben Jonson's Stagecraft in his Four Major Comedies." University of Texas at Austin, 1975.

1472 THIEL, LELAND MARSHAL. "Ben Jonson's Odyssey: The Search for Truth." Washington State University, 1973.

Appendix I

Dissertations

1473 THOMPSON, MARVIN ORVILLE. "Uses of Music and Reflections of Current Theories of the Psychology of Music in the Plays of Shakespeare, Jonson, and Beaumont and Fletcher." University of Minnesota, 1956.

1474 TIEDJE, EGON. "Die Tradition Ben Jonsons in der Restaurationskomödie." Hamburg, 1963.

1475 TOWNSEND, FREDA LIVERANT. "Jonson and His Critics: A Study in the Classifical Fallacy." Duke University, 1944.

1476 TRIENENS, ROGER J. "The Green-Eyed Monster: A Study of Sexual Jealousy in the Literature of the English Renaissance." Northwestern University, 1951.

1477 VALIAN, MAXINE KENT. "A Study of the Maturing of Ben Jonson's Methods of Characterization." University of Southern California, 1961.

1478 VAN KEUREN, ERNEST CANFIELD. "The Poetomachia Between Ben Jonson and the Poetasters, 1599-1601." Cornell University, 1931.

1479 VAWTER, MARVIN LEE. "Shakespeare and Jonson: Stoic Ethics and Political Crisis." University of Wisconsin--Madison, 1970.

1480 WAITH, EUGENE M. "The Influence of Ben Jonson on John Fletcher." Yale University, 1939.

1481 WALKER, ELLEN LOUISE. "The Varieties of Comedy: A Study of the Dramatic Comedies of Molière, Jonson and Shakespeare." University of Connecticut, 1971.

1482 WALTON, G. "The English Writings of Abraham Cowley." Cambridge University, 1941.

1483 WARREN, MICHAEL JOHN. "The Verse Style of Ben Jonson's Roman Plays." University of California, Berkeley, 1968.

1484 WATTS, HELENA BRAWLEY. "Jonson's Theory and Practice in Regard to the Didactic Theory of Poetry." Duke University, 1943.

1485 WAYNE, DON EDWARD. "Ben Jonson: The 'Anti-Acquisitive Attitude' and the Accumulated Discourse: Contribution to a Historico-Semiotics." University of California, San Diego, 1975.

Appendix I

Dissertations

1486 WEISSER, PAUL HERBERT. "To Suckle Fools and Chronicle Small Beer (A Study of Humor and Comic Theory)." University of California, Berkeley, 1971.

1487 WHEELER, CHARLES F. "Classical Mythology in the Plays, Masques, and Poems of Ben Jonson." University of Cincinnati, 1935.

1488 WHITE, GAIL LANA. "Pastoral Plays and Masques of Shakespeare, Jonson, Milton." University of California, Irvine, 1973.

1489 WILLIAMS, MARY CAMERON. "Unifying Methods in Jonson's Early Comedy." University of North Carolina at Chapel Hill, 1970.

1490 WILLIAMS, PATRICK REED. "Ben Jonson's Satiric Stagecraft." University of Michigan, 1976.

1491 WILLIAMS, ROBERT ILEROY. "Skepticism in the Jacobean Comedies of Thomas Middleton, Ben Jonson, and John Fletcher." University of California, Berkeley, 1966.

1492 WILSON, HAROLD S. "Concepts of 'Nature' in the Rhetorical Tradition: A Chapter in the History of Classical Humanism Before Ben Jonson." Harvard University, 1939.

1493 WILSON, JOHN DELANE. "Some Uses of Physiognomy in the Plays of Shakespeare, Jonson, Marlowe and Dekker." Michigan State University, 1965.

1494 WITT, ROBERT WAYNE. "Ben Jonson and the Play-Within." University of Mississippi, 1970.

1495 WOLF, WILLIAM DENNIS. "'Vigilance, Counsell, Action': Success in Five of Ben Jonson's Plays." University of Wisconsin--Madison, 1968.

1496 WOODARD, LAWRENCE E. "A Study of the Argumentation Used in Four Selected Elizabethan Plays: Julius Caesar, Volpone, Dr. Faustus, and The Spanish Tragedy." Brigham Young University, 1974.

1497 YOUNG, STEVEN CARTER. "The Induction Plays of the Tudor and Stuart Drama." University of California, Berkeley, 1970.

Appendix II

BIBLIOGRAPHY OF SOURCES

ABSTRACTS OF ENGLISH STUDIES. 1-20 (1958-1976/77). Boulder, Colo.: National Council of Teachers of English, 1958-1977.

ALTICK, RICHARD D., and WRIGHT, ANDREW, eds. _Selective Bibliography for the Study of English and American Literature_. 5th ed. New York: Macmillan, 1975.

BAKER, BLANCH MERRITT. _Theatre and Allied Arts: A Guide to Books Dealing with the History, Criticism, and Technic of the Drama and Theatre and Related Arts and Crafts_. New York: H. W. Wilson, 1952.

BALDENSPERGER, FERNAND, and FRIEDERICH, WERNER P. _Bibliography of Comparative Literature_. Chapel Hill: University of North Carolina Studies in Comparative Literature, 1950.

BAMBOROUGH, J. B. "Jonson and Chapman," in _English Drama (excluding Shakespeare): Select Bibliographical Guides_. Edited by Stanley W. Wells. London and New York: Oxford University Press, 1975, pp. 54-68.

BATESON, F. W. _A Guide to English Literature_. 2d ed. Chicago: Aldine, 1968, pp. 80-81.

BATESON, F. W., and WATSON, GEORGE, eds. _The Cambridge Bibliography of English Literature_. 5 vols. I-IV, Cambridge: Cambridge University Press, 1940. Vol. V, _Supplement: A.D. 600-1900_. Edited by George Watson. Cambridge: Cambridge University Press, 1957.

BELL, INGLIS F., and GALLUP, JENNIFER. _A Reference Guide to English, American, and Canadian Literature: An Annotated Checklist of Bibliographical and Other Reference Materials_. Vancouver: University of British Columbia Press, 1971, p. 99.

Appendix II

Bibliography

BESTERMAN, THEODORE. A World Bibliography of Bibliographies. 3d ed. Geneva: Societas Bibliographica, 1955-1956.

BIBLIO: Catalogue des ouvrages parus en langue français dans le monde entier (1934-70). Paris: Hachette, 1935-1971.

BIBLIOGRAPHIC INDEX: A Cumulative Bibliography of Bibliographies (1937-1976). New York: H. W. Wilson, 1938-1977.

BIBLIOGRAPHIE INTERNATIONALE DE L'HUMANISME ET DE LA RENAISSANCE. 1-8 (1965-1972). Geneva: Droz, 1966-1973.

BIBLIOTHEQUE D'HUMANISME ET RENAISSANCE. Paris and Geneva: Droz, 1941-1965.

BIOGRAPHY INDEX. A Cumulative Index to Biographical Material in Books and Magazines (1946-1976). New York: H. W. Wilson, 1949-1977.

BOOK REVIEW DIGEST (1911-1977). New York: H. W. Wilson, 1911-1978.

BOOK REVIEW INDEX (1965-1977). Detroit: Gale Research Company, 1966-1978.

BOOKS IN PRINT. New York: R. R. Bowker, 1948-1978.

BRITISH MUSEUM GENERAL CATALOGUE OF PRINTED BOOKS: Ten-Year Supplement, 1956-1965. 50 vols. London: Trustees of the British Museum, 1968.

BRITISH NATIONAL BIBLIOGRAPHY (1950-1976). London: Council of the British National Bibliography, 1951-1977.

BROCK, DEWEY HEYWARD, and WELSH, JAMES M. Ben Jonson: A Quadricentennial Bibliography, 1947-1972. Metuchen, N.J.: The Scarecrow Press, 1974.

CATALOGUE GÉNÉRAL DES LIVRES IMPRIMÉ DE LA BIBLIOTHÈQUE NATIONALE. AUTEURS. 224 vols. Paris: Imprimerie Nationale, 1897-1976.

COMPREHENSIVE DISSERTATION INDEX, 1861-1972. 37 vols. Ann Arbor, Mich.: Xerox University Microfilms, 1973. Five-Year Cumulation, 1973-1977. 19 vols. Ann Arbor, Mich.: University Microfilms, 1979.

CRAIG, HARDIN. "Recent Scholarship of the English Renaissance: A Brief Survey." SP 42 (1945):498-529.

Appendix II

Bibliography

CUMULATIVE BOOK INDEX (1928/32-1977). New York: H. W. Wilson, 1933-1977.
Permanent volumes covering the years 1928-1969.

ENGLISH ASSOCIATION. The Year's Work in English Studies. 1-55 (1919-1974). Oxford: University Press, 1921-1961; London: John Murray, 1962-1975.

ESSAY AND GENERAL LITERATURE INDEX. New York: H. W. Wilson, 1934-1978.

GASTON, PAUL L. "Commendation and Approbation: Recent Ben Jonson Scholarship." PLL 9 (1973):432-49.

GREG, W. W. A Bibliography of the English Printed Drama to the Restoration. 4 vols. London: Oxford University Press, 1939-1959.

GUFFEY, GEORGE ROBERT, comp. "Ben Jonson, 1947-1965." Elizabethan Bibliographies Supplements, III. London: The Nether Press, 1968, 19-44.

HUMANISME ET RENAISSANCE. Paris: Droz, 1934-1940.

HUMANITIES INDEX. 1-3 (1974/75-1977). New York: H. W. Wilson, 1974-1977.

INDEX TO BOOK REVIEWS IN THE HUMANITIES. 1-18 (1960-1977). Williamston, Mich.: Philip Thomson, 1960-1978.

INDEX TRANSLATIONEM. Nos. 1-31 (1932-1940). 7 vols. Nendeln, Liechtenstein: Kraus, 1974.

"LITERATURE OF THE RENAISSANCE." SP 14-66 (1917-1969). Title varies.

LOGAN, TERENCE P., and SMITH, DENZELL S., eds. The New Intellectuals: A Survey and Bibliography of Recent Studies in English Renaissance Drama. Lincoln: University of Nebraska, 1977.

McNAMEE, LAWRENCE F. Dissertations in English and American Literature: Theses Accepted by American, British, and German Universities, 1865-1964. Supplement I, 1964-1968. Supplement II, 1969-1973. New York: R. R. Bowker, 1968, 1969, 174.

MODERN HUMANITIES RESEARCH ASSOCIATION. Annual Bibliography of English Language and Literature. 1-50 (1920-1975). Cambridge: Cambridge University Press, 1921-1964; Cambridge: Modern Humanities Research Association, 1965-1978.

Appendix II

Bibliography

MODERN LANGUAGE ASSOCIATION OF AMERICA. MLA Abstracts of Articles in Scholarly Journals. 1-5 (1971-1975). New York: Modern Language Association of America, 1973-1977.

_____. MLA International Bibliography, 1921-1977.

NANIA, ANTHONY J. "Ben Jonson: A Checklist of Editions, Biography, and Criticism, 1947-1964." RORD 10 (1967):32.

NATIONAL UNION CATALOGUE. Pre-1956 Imprints. 664 vols. to date. Chicago: Mansell, 1968-1979.

_____. 1942-1962. 152 vols. Detroit: Gale Research Co., 1969-1971.

_____. 1963-1967. 67 vols. Ann Arbor, Mich.: J. W. Edwards, 1969.

_____. 1968-1972. 119 vols. Ann Arbor, Mich.: J. W. Edwards, 1973.

_____. 1973-1977. 135 vols. Totowa, N.J.: Rowman and Littlefield, 1978.

PALMER, HELEN, and DYSON, ANNE JANE. European Drama Criticism. Hamden, Conn.: The Shoe String Press, 1968. Supplement I, 1970; Supplement II, 1974.

PENNINGER, FRIEDA ELAINE. English Drama to 1660 (Excluding Shakespeare): A Guide to Information Sources. Detroit: Gale Research Co., 1976.

PINTO, V. DE SOLA. "Students' Guide to Reading," in English Renaissance, 1510-1688. 3d rev. ed. London: Cresset Press, 1966, pp. 133-394.

"RECENT STUDIES IN ELIZABETHAN AND JACOBEAN DRAMA." SEL 1-17 (1961-1977).

RIBNER, IRVING. Tudor and Stuart Drama. Goldentree Bibliographies. New York: Appleton-Century-Crofts, 1966.

SARAFINSKI, DOLORES. "Book-Length Studies of Ben Jonson Since 1919: A Review." RORD 17 (1974):67-83.

_____. The Comedies of Ben Jonson: A Review of Research and Criticism, 1919-1968. Ph.D. dissertation, Duquesne University, 1973.

"SHAKESPEARE: AN ANNOTATED BIBLIOGRAPHY." SQ 1-26 (1950-1975).

Appendix II

Bibliography

"SHAKESPEARE AND HIS CONTEMPORARIES." Shakespeare Association Bulletin 1-24 (1924-1949). Title of bibliography varies.

SOCIAL SCIENCES AND HUMANITIES INDEX. 1-27 (1907/15-1973/74). New York: H. W. Wilson, 1907-1974.

STEENSMA, ROBERT C. "Ben Jonson: A Checklist of Editions, Biography and Criticism," RORD 9 (1966):29-46.

TANNENBAUM, SAMUEL A., and TANNENBAUM, DOROTHY R. Elizabethan Biographies. Port Washington, N.Y.: Kennikat Press, 1967. Vol. IV, "Ben Jonson: A Concise Bibliography," pp. 1-151. Bound with 1947 Supplement, pp. 1-66.

THOMSON, S. HARRISON. Progress of Medieval and Renaissance Studies in the United States and Canada. Nos. 15-25 (1940-1960). Boulder: University of Colorado Press, 1940-1960.

TUCKER, MARTIN, ed. The Critical Temper: A Survey of Modern Criticism on English and American Literature from the Beginnings to the Twentieth Century. 3 vols. New York: Ungar, 1969.

TUVE, ROSEMOND. "A Critical Survey of Scholarship in the Field of English Literature of the Renaissance." SP 40 (1943):204-55.

WALCUTT, CHARLES CHILD, and WHITESELL, J. EDWIN, eds. The Explicator Cyclopedia. Vol. II, Traditional Poetry: Medieval to Late Victorian. From The Explicator, I-XX (1942-1962). Chicago: Quadrangle Books, 1968.

YEARBOOK OF COMPARATIVE AND GENERAL LITERATURE. 1-9 (1952-1960), Chapel Hill: University of North Carolina Press. 10-25 (1961-1975), Bloomington: Indiana University.

Author Index

Author Index

Author Index

Author Index

Author Index

Author Index

Author Index

Subject Index

Subject Index